Ideal Vocabulary for Reading and Writing

A Novel Approach

Peter Roger

Collegial Press, Inc • New York

Ideal Vocabulary for Reading and Writing: A Novel Approach
Peter Roger

Technical Director: Anand Sangtani
Cover Designer: Jenine Zimmers
Cover Photo: iStock © miki1991
Interior Layout Designer: Andrea Lau
Coordinating Editor: Juliet Emanuel
Copy Editor: Justin Golschneider
Assistant Copy Editor: Julia Falsetti
Assistant Editors: Gabriella Oldham, Angela Davis, Angela Bates, and Sri Roopnarain Persaud

Publisher: Collegial Press, Inc.
Contact Information: P.O. Box 190275, Richmond Hill, Queens, NY 11419
E-mail: collegeprepusa@aol.com
Website: www.howtoprepareforcollege.net

TABLE OF CONTENTS

ACKNOWLEDGMENTS

Ideal Vocabulary for Reading and Writing: A Novel Approach is the result of the hard work of a team of committed, dedicated, and passionate educators. They have drawn on their many years of classroom experience to offer invaluable suggestions, enabling me to improve the manuscript and better address the needs of our students.

I am grateful to Julia Falsetti, who revised the entire first draft, for her editorial skills. Her brainstorming sessions have led to several revisions of the story and the vocabulary exercises. Maria Alvarez's enormous contribution to developing the Context Clues exercises is also appreciated. Shane McConnell put his outstanding research skills to work to help me create the answers for those exercises, for which I am very thankful.

Amanda Hall, Angela Davis, and Sri Roopnarain Persaud made valuable contributions to the vocabulary tests. Roop's recommendations, derived from a wealth of experience working with students from diverse backgrounds, resulted in a story that more clearly reflects the issues facing immigrants in America. Jenny Gonzalez, Ana Daniels, Saima Sarsaraz, Nevin Pahlad, Rayan Singh, Sohan Seavcharran, Anand Sangtani, Parbattie Bernard, Bradley J. St. Martin, and Omesh Hiraman, also contributed to this project.

I am grateful for Gabriella Oldham's extremely helpful recommendations and her efforts in editing and proofreading the final draft. Words of thanks go to Juliet Emanuel for sharing her insight and knowledge throughout the preparation of the manuscript. Her superb editorial skills made a big difference. I thank Jilani Warsi at Queensborough Community College for sharing his guidance and experience as an author of college textbooks. Additional thanks go to this book's talented cover designer, Jenine Zimmers, for her conscientious work, and to Andrea Lau for lending her professional expertise in designing the layout.

I am indebted to Justin Golschneider, my copy editor, for working tirelessly on this project. His superb editing skills made this book come to life. Especially remarkable were his revisions to the novel, which dramatically improved it and left next to nothing for the proofreader to do. Copy editing credit also goes out to Angela Bates. Her lightning-fast work on tests and exercises helped bring this project to a timely conclusion.

Furthermore, I want to thank the following faculty members at Borough of Manhattan Community College, The City University of New York for their suggestions and ideas, which shaped the revisions:

Juliet Emanuel
Cheryl Comeau-Kirschner
Shane McConnell
Amanda Hall
Elisa Pigeron
Maria Alvarez
Kenneth Cotton
Cynthia Wiseman
Mabel Asante
James Michel
Annette Lachman
Sonia Omulepu
Eurita Butler
Oksana Vorobel
Laszlo Arvai
Caroline Johnson
Margaret Barrow

Finally, I appreciate the patient support that Stella Artiga has given me throughout this project.

TO THE INSTRUCTOR

The main feature of *Ideal Vocabulary for Reading and Writing: A Novel Approach* is a story, *Trial of Love*, that is used as one approach to teach vocabulary. Students can learn the meanings of highlighted words from the context of the story or from their dictionaries, which they should keep handy while working through the exercises. In addition to the highlighted vocabulary, each chapter of the text contains a variety of exercises pulling together important vocabulary words that students and future professional workers will find helpful on a daily basis. Both general and specialized vocabulary are featured in the "Matching Column" exercises. An array of exercises on synonyms and antonyms will help students find important connections between words that will increase the versatility of their writing and self-expression. Fill-in-the-blank types of exercises will challenge them not only to find the appropriate words to complete the sentences, but also to think "outside the box" by rephrasing sentences to make them grammatically correct.

Additionally, students are encouraged to keep their own practice notebooks to add new words they encounter as a result of this study. They should continue using these words actively and vividly in composition and speech at every opportunity. It is also a valuable exercise to "dissect" words for their roots, prefixes, and suffixes to understand how their meanings are derived from these parts. A vocabulary test in each chapter enables students to "test" themselves and each other regularly without the help of a dictionary so that the meanings of these new words can become ingrained in their thinking process and their use can become second nature. A model table that students can replicate or modify as needed to record their word discoveries and knowledge is presented as a sample at the end of each chapter. While the definitions provided in this book are the most commonly used, it is important to keep in mind that words have multiple meanings, multiple grammatical forms for the same word, and a wider selection of synonyms and antonyms than could fit within the scope of this book.

TO THE STUDENT

Does Vocabulary Really Matter?

You already know that widening your vocabulary can help you earn higher grades. Does that alone make it worth your time and effort, though? Of course, it does not. The main goal of education is to gain knowledge that will help you later in life. How will learning new words do that? Does vocabulary really matter?

You have probably memorized lists of words to do well on tests more than once. How many of those words have you forgotten? Perhaps half of them or even more? If so, it is probably because you did not see a point to remembering them after the semester ended. You decided that those words were not going to help you get a job or do anything else that interested you.

People remember what they care about and often forget the rest to make room for more important information. Why should you keep your brain packed full of words like “clandestine” and “belligerent” when you no longer have pop quizzes to worry about? Why should you learn more than the minimum you need to pass?

Vocabulary has an enormous impact on the learning experience beyond a single test. Having a wide selection of words at your command makes it easier to follow complicated lectures and read advanced works throughout college. Its uses are not limited to school, though.

After you finish college, a strong vocabulary will make you stand out from the crowds of graduates searching for jobs. Those who write well will secure more interviews, thanks to their strong résumés and cover letters. Those who speak eloquently will make better impressions during those interviews. Yet, these occasions are not the only times when your knowledge of a strong vocabulary will play a critical role.

Vocabulary is useful in other ways. It matters when performing an important presentation at the office and speaking to your boss and colleagues. It matters when writing a letter to request a grant, or when holding an elected position and explaining your views and actions to the press. It matters when describing ideas to friends, when expressing your feelings, and when answering children who look up with bright, expectant eyes and ask, “What does this word mean?”

Our understanding of language controls our ability to interact with the people around us. By improving our skills as listeners, readers, speakers, and writers, we open ourselves to deeper, more meaningful discussions and relationships. We become more effective communicators and listen attentively to what others have to say when our vocabulary is broad and rich. Strong words take us on a journey to greater success.

In short, vocabulary *really* matters.

How and Why You Should Use This Book

Have you ever spent hours reading a homework assignment, or listening to a long lecture only to have your teacher ask a question you could not answer? It feels terrible. You did all of the work, but the lesson just did not stick in your memory.

This happens to many students—even those who try hard to pay close attention in their classes. Several different factors can cause this problem. One of the most common and frustrating, though, is the presence of words that you do not know.

When you read or hear even one unknown word, the entire sentence can be meaningless to you. Thus, the whole paragraph can seem like nonsense. You might miss an important point and, as a result, the rest of the story or lesson may be challenging to understand.

If you can figure out what new words mean, you will understand nearly everything you hear and read. However, if you try looking up a word during a lecture, you will miss so much of what the speaker is saying that it may be a wasted effort. Searching for the definition of every new word can also make a four-hour reading assignment last eight hours instead.

Luckily, there are faster ways to figure out what new words mean. Identifying context clues and word parts is a very effective way to determine the meanings of unfamiliar words.

Solving Word Meanings with Context Clues

In *The Effective Reader*, author D. J. Henry recommends using *context clues* to find the meanings of difficult words. *Context* refers to the words before and after the ones you do not know. This surrounding text can provide clues for what the new words mean.

Henry listed four types of context clues: synonyms, antonyms, general context, and examples. I have defined these four types of context clues below, and illustrate how you can use them to figure out what the new words mean. The example vocabulary words are **boldfaced**, while the context clues are *italicized.*

1. **Synonyms:** Words with a meaning similar to that of another word
   "The American **bison**, or *buffalo*, nearly went extinct due to overhunting."
   - **Bison** and *buffalo* are different words for the same animal. I know what *buffalo* are, so now I know what **bison** are.

2. **Antonyms:** Words that have a meaning opposite to that of another word
   "René is very **cruel**, unlike her *kind* sister, Adelia."
   - Being **cruel** is the opposite of being *kind*. I know that someone who is *kind* is nice, so now I know that someone who is **cruel** is mean.

3. **General context:** The overall sense of the passage
   "The British **frigate** *had dozens of cannons and large, square sails, and it moved quickly through the water.*"
   - If it *has sails and cannons and moves quickly* through the water, then a **frigate** is probably a fast sailing ship that is built for war.

4. **Examples:** Words showing what another word refers to
   "Some of the world's most famous **capital** cities are *Moscow, London, Tokyo, Beijing,* and *Washington, DC.*"
   - I know the main Japanese government is in *Tokyo*, and the main Chinese government is in *Beijing*, so a **capital** is probably a city that serves as the seat of a government.

Henry writes that certain words tell you not only that a sentence has a context clue, but which type of context clue it is. These are "signal words." Look for the following when reading, and pay careful attention to them.

- Synonym signal words: Or, that is
- Antonym signal words: In contrast, on the other hand, unlike, instead, yet, however
- Example signal words: For instance, for example, such as, including, consists of

Figuring Out Definitions with Word Parts

In *Essential Academic Vocabulary*, Helen Huntley explains that many long words in English can be broken down into three parts: the prefix, the root, and the suffix.

- A **prefix** is a letter, or group of letters, that has a specific meaning and can be added to the beginning of a word. This addition creates a new word with a new meaning.
- A **root** is the basic or main part of a word. New words are created when prefixes and suffixes are added to roots.
- A **suffix** is a letter, or group of letters, that has a specific meaning and is added to the end of a word. This addition creates a new word with a new meaning.

If you learn what each of these parts means by itself, then many long, complicated words will become simple puzzles for you to solve. You can split each word into two or three parts, think of the meaning of each part, and then combine the meanings. This will often let you figure out what the word means even without context clues.

The tables below, reprinted by permission from Huntley's book, list common word parts and their meanings. They provide examples as well. Study them to learn useful prefixes, roots, and suffixes.

Roots	Meaning	Examples
agr	field	agriculture, agrarian
ann, enn	year	annual, biennial
anthrop	human	anthropology, anthropologist
aqua	water	aquarium, aquatic
astro, aster	star	astrology, asteroid
audi	hear	auditorium, audience
bibli	book	bibliography, bible
bio	life	biology, biography
capit	head	capital, capitalization
card, cord	heart	cardiac, cordial
cede, ceed	go	intercede, proceed
celer	fast	accelerate, decelerate
cent	one hundred	century, percent
chron	time	chronic, chronology
clud, clus	close, shut	include, exclusion
corp	body	corpse, corporation
cosm	world	cosmos, microcosm
cred	believe	credible, credentials
dec	ten	decade, decimal
demo	people	democracy, undemocratic
dent	tooth, teeth	dentist, dental
derm	skin	dermatitis, dermatology
dict	speak	dictator, dictation
domin	master	dominate, dominion
duc, duct	lead	conductor, deduct
fac, fic, fect	make, do	factory, fiction, defect
flect, flex	bend	reflection, flexible
frater	brother	fraternity, fraternization

Roots	Meaning	Examples
gen geo gloss, glot gram, graph gress, grad	race, birth earth tongue write step	gender, generation geography, geology glossary, polyglot telegram, graphic digress, grade
hydr	water	hydroelectric, dehydrate
ject jud	throw judge	reject, subject judicial, judgment
lect, leg ling, lang log loqu, loc luc	choose, gather language word speak light	collect, legion linguistics, bilingual logic, logistics loquacious, elocution lucid, lucidity
mania manu mar mater max med, mid mini mit, miss mono mort multi	crazy hand sea mother more middle less, little send one death many	manic, maniac manual, manufacture marine, submarine maternity, maternal maximum, maximize medium, midland minimum, mini transmit, mission monologue, monolingual mortuary, mortal multiplication, multinational
naut neo neuro nomin, nomen	sail new nerve name	nautical, astronaut neonatal, neophyte neuron, neurotic nominate, nomenclature
pater path ped, pod pend phil phob phon phot, phos phys plex, plic poly port pos, pon psych	father feelings, disease foot hang love fear sound light physical, body fold many carry place, put mind	paternity, paternal sympathy, pathology pedestrian, podiatrist pendant, pendulum philosophy, anglophile phobia, claustrophobic telephone, phonology photograph, phosphorus physique, physics complex, complicate polygon, polygamous portable, report deposit, postpone psychology, psychic

Roots	Meaning	Examples
quad	four	quadrangle, quadruple
reg, rect	rule, right	regulation, correct
rupt	break	rupture, interrupt
scop	look	microscope, scope
scrib, script	write	scribble, description
sect	cut	dissect, section
sens, sent	feel	sensation, sentimental
soph	wise	sophisticated, philosopher
soror	sister	sorority
spec, spic	look	spectator, despicable
tact, tang	touch	tactile, tangible
tend, tens, tent	strength	tendon, tension, tentacle
terr(a)	earth	terrestrial, territory
therm	heat	thermometer, thermostat
tri	three	triple, tripod
vac	empty	vacant, vacuum
ven	come	convention, adventure
vis, vid	see	vision, video
vita, viv	life	vitality, vivacious
voc, voke	call	vocalize, evoke
vor	eat	herbivore, voracious

Prefixes	Meaning	Examples
ab-	away from	absent, abolish
am-	love	amicable, amorous
a-, an-	not, without	atypical, anorexia
ante-	before, in front	antebellum, anteroom
anti-	against	antiwar, antisocial
arch-	first	archbishop, architect
auto-	self	automatic, autobiography
bene-	well	benefit, benevolent
bi-	two	binary, biannual
circum-	around	circumnavigate, circumference
co-, con-, col-, cor-	with	coauthor, convention, collection, correlate
contra-, counter-	against, opposite	contrary, counteract
de-	not, away, down	deduct, descent
dis-, di-, dif-	apart, away, not	disappear, divide, different
dys-	bad	dysfunctional, dyslexia
e-, ex-	out, away	egress, exhale
eu-	good	eulogy, euphoria
extra-	outside, beyond	extraordinary, extracurricular

Prefixes	Meaning	Examples
hetero- homo- hyper- hypo-	other, different same above under	heterogeneous, heterosexual homogeneous, homosexual hyperactive, hypertension hypothetical, hypocrite
il-, ir-, im-, in- inter- intra-	not among within	illegal, irrelevant, impolite, infertile interstate, interaction intrastate, intravenous
mal- mega- micro- mis-	bad, ill, wrong large, one million very small bad(ly)	malady, malfunction megacity, megabyte microscopic, microorganism mistake, misfortune
non-	not	nonstop, nonsense
out- over-	more more than normal	outdo, outrun oversleep, overestimate
peri- post- pre- pro-	around after before forward, before	perimeter, period postpone, postdate previous, prerequisite project, promote
re- retro-	back, again backward	return, reread retroactive, retrospect
semi- sub- super-	half under over	semicircle, semicolon submarine, subway superhuman, supervise
tele- trans-	distant across	television, telephone transmit, transaction
ultra- un- uni-	beyond, excessive not one	ultrasound, ultraviolet unhappy, unpleasant uniform, unique

Noun Suffixes	Meaning	Examples
-an, -ian	of, belonging to	American, Canadian
-ance, -ence	act, quality	importance, independence
-ancy, -ency	state of	vacancy, fluency
-ary, -arium	place where	library, solarium
-ary, -ess, -eer, -ant	person who	secretary, heiress, volunteer, assistant
-ation	action, institution	situation, foundation
-cide	kill	genocide, suicide
-ian, -er, -or, -ist	person who	mathematician, teacher, sailor, artist
-ion, -tion, -ity	state, quality, act	union, organization, minority
-ism	quality, doctrine	communism, pessimism
-logy, -ology	study	geology, astrology
-ment	act, state	statement, argument
-ness, -dom	state, quality	kindness, freedom
-ory, -orium	place where	laboratory, auditorium
-ship, -hood	state, quality	friendship, neighborhood

Adjective Suffixes	Meaning	Examples
-able, -ible	able to be	capable, illegible
-al, -ative, -ent, -ic	like, related to	dental, talkative, evident, atomic
-ful	having	useful, careful
-ish, -ive, -ous, -ious	like, related to	stylish, active, nervous, delicious
-less	without	useless, careless
-ly	having the quality of	womanly, friendly

Adverb Suffixes	Meaning	Examples
-ly	in the manner of	slowly, lightly
-ward	toward	forward, backward
-wise	in the manner of	clockwise, counterclockwise

Verb Suffixes	Meaning	Examples
-ate, -ify, -ize	make, act	eliminate, magnify, finalize
-en	make	flatten, soften

Features of the Book

Ideal Vocabulary for Reading and Writing: A Novel Approach was written to teach you more than 1,500 powerful words. These words will help you succeed at school, at work, and in life. After you finish this book, you will have an easier time understanding the words you read and hear, and you will be a more eloquent writer and speaker.

The Story

The main feature of this book is a novel, *Trial of Love*, which is described below. Reading this story will show you how and when real people use important vocabulary words. You will not simply memorize a list—you will see the words you are learning in action. This is one of the most effective ways to learn something new.

Kamla Kumar is a young Indian research scientist and college professor. Although she has a good life in India, she decides to move to America illegally because she hopes to advance her career and win a Nobel Prize. Her parents place great value on family and cross the border with her.

The move to America goes poorly. Dangerous people try to take advantage of the Kumars. The challenge of finding work forces them to rely on others for survival. Perhaps worst of all, Kamla's desire to live like Americans, especially by marrying an American man, puts her at odds with her parents, who cannot understand why she would abandon their Indian traditions. This tests their love for each other and threatens to destroy the family.

Still, this is not the greatest of Kamla's worries. The man she has fallen in love with has powerful enemies. These men will do anything to protect their secrets—and Kamla may well have learned too much.

The Exercises

In addition to the story, this book has exercises designed to help you master the meanings of new words. These include the following strategies:

- Identifying synonyms and antonyms
- Matching words with their definitions
- Using context clues to identify a missing word or to figure out a word's meaning
- Writing essays using the new words you have learned
- Reviewing hard-to-remember words

At the end of each chapter, you will take a vocabulary test and create a record to keep track of your learning progress. This will allow you to reflect on everything you have learned. After just a couple of chapters, you will acquire a powerful collection of new and useful words that you feel confident using in various situations.

The Vocabulary

The Word List, found on page xvi, includes more than 1,500 words that you will learn with the help of this book. It provides partial meanings for each word, as well as which part of speech (noun, verb, adjective, adverb, conjunction, or preposition) each one is. This Word List features many of the words most commonly used in college, including several identified in Averil Coxhead's "A New Academic Word List." Use it to get a quick idea of what new words mean.

Good luck, and have fun learning!

Word List

Study the partial meanings of the following words before you begin working on the exercises. Note that the meanings were selected based on the context in which the words are used in this book. Many of these words have alternative meanings. If you encounter one of these words in an unfamiliar context, or if you do not understand the listed meanings, please refer to a dictionary.

Word	Meaning
abandoned (adj.)	vacant; unoccupied
abbreviate (verb)	shorten; curtail
abduct (verb)	seize; taken by force
abhor (verb)	hate; despise; detest
abnormal (adj.)	strange; weird; unusual; odd
abominable (adj.)	unpleasant; bad
abolish (verb)	cancel; put an end to
abrupt (adj.)	sudden; unexpectedly
absent (adj.)	away; not there
absentminded (adj.)	forgetful
abstain (verb)	refrain; stay away from
abstract (adj.)	theoretical; nonconcrete
absurd (adj.)	foolish; ridiculous; senseless
abundant (adj.)	plentiful; copious
abuse (verb)	violate; hurt; injure
academy (noun)	school for special instruction
accelerate (verb)	speed up; go faster; hasten
accept (verb)	approve; agree; allow
access (noun)	entry; admittance
accident (noun)	misfortune; disaster
acclaim (verb)	praise; honor; applaud
accommodate (verb)	adjust to; make room for
accompany (verb)	go with; join
accumulate (verb)	build up; collect; gather
accurate (adj.)	exact; correct; precise
accuse (verb)	blame; find fault
achieve (verb)	accomplish; obtain; gain
acknowledge (verb)	admit; recognize
acquaint (verb)	familiarize; learn about
acquire (verb)	gain; obtain; procure
acrimonious (adj.)	bitter in speech and manner
acute (adj.)	sharp; severe; poignant
adamant (adj.)	inflexible; determined not to change
adapt (verb)	change; adjust to a different environment
adept (adj.)	skillful; dexterous
adequate (adj.)	enough; sufficient
adhere (verb)	cling; stick to; hold on
adjacent (adj.)	next to
adjudicate (verb)	make judgment or decision; mediate
adjust (verb)	change; alter; modify
admit (verb)	consent; allow to enter
admonish (verb)	warn; reprimand; scold
adopt (verb)	choose and follow something
adroit (adj.)	skilled; clever
adversary (noun)	enemy; someone competing with; opponent; foe
adverse (adj.)	unfavorable; detrimental
advocate (noun)	supporter; spokesperson for
aesthetic (noun)	appreciation of beauty
affection (noun)	strong feelings of love
affect (verb)	influence feelings
affiliate (verb)	associate; close connection
affirm (verb)	confirm; express agreement
affluence (noun)	wealth; opulence; affluence; riches
aggrandize (verb)	make greater or more powerful
aggravate (verb)	irritate; worsen; annoy
aggregate (verb)	put together; combine; total
aggressive (adj.)	pushy; forceful
agile (adj.)	fast; active
agitate (verb)	disturb; excite emotionally
aid (noun)	help; support; assistance
ailment (noun)	disease; illness; infirmity
alias (noun)	nickname; false name
alien (adj.)	foreign
allegiance (noun)	support; loyalty
alleviate (verb)	lessen; relieve; mitigate
allocate (verb)	distribute; divide among; allot
allude (verb)	refer to indirectly; insinuate; suggest
aloof (adj.)	distant; not friendly; detached
alter (verb)	change; modify; transform
alternative (noun)	option; another choice
altruistic (adj.)	generous; concern for others; benevolent
ambiguous (adj.)	vague; unclear; more than one meaning; uncertain
ambivalent (adj.)	doubtful; conflicted
amend (verb)	revise; improve; correct
ample (adj.)	plentiful; abundant
analogy (noun)	comparison; similarity
analyze (verb)	examine carefully; scrutinize
animosity (noun)	hatred; dislike; resentment
annihilate (verb)	wipe out or destroy completely
annual (adj.)	yearly; once a year
anonymous (adj.)	unidentified; unknown
antagonize (verb)	provoke; cause angry feelings
anticipate (verb)	expect; look forward to
apathy (noun)	lack of emotion or interest
apparent (adj.)	clear; obvious; noticeable
append (verb)	add to
appease (verb)	calm; satisfy; pacify
applaud (verb)	praise; cheer; clap hands
appoint (verb)	designate; assign; choose
appreciate (verb)	like; to be grateful or thankful
apprehensive (adj.)	fearful; afraid; timid

Word	Meaning
apprentice (noun)	learner or beginner; novice
approach (verb)	come nearer; advance
appropriate (adj.)	suitable; opportune
arbitrary (adj.)	left to one's judgment or choice
arbitrator (noun)	one who settles a dispute
area (noun)	section; area; part of
aristocrat (noun)	upper-class person
arrogant (adj.)	haughty; feeling superior
arsonist (noun)	someone who intentionally sets fires
articulate (adj.)	well-spoken; eloquent
ascertain (verb)	to make sure; learn
askew (adj.)	to one side; sideways
aspect (noun)	part
aspire (verb)	strong desire to achieve; yearn; wish
assemble (verb)	put or come together; congregate
assertive (adj.)	bossy
assess (verb)	evaluate; determine
assiduous (adj.)	showing care and effort
assign (verb)	give to do; designate
assist (verb)	help; facilitate
assume (verb)	accept; take responsibility
assurance (noun)	guarantee; certainly true
astonish (verb)	amaze; surprise
astute (adj.)	smart; clever
attach (verb)	join; connect; fasten; affix
attain (verb)	obtain; accomplish; gain; achieve
attest (verb)	verify; prove true
attitude (noun)	way of thinking and feeling
attribute (noun)	quality; characteristic; feature; trait
attrition (noun)	decrease
audible (adj.)	clear; can hear easily
audit (noun)	examination of financial records for correctness
auspicious (adj.)	favorable; propitious
austere (adj.)	harsh; strict; severe
authenticate (verb)	establish as genuine; verify; confirm
author (noun)	writer; person who writes
authority (noun)	power; control
automate (verb)	perform without human input
available (adj.)	ready; obtain readily
aware (adj.)	know about; cognizant
awkward (adj.)	clumsy; lack grace; inept
bad (adj.)	evil; harmful; detrimental
baffle (verb)	puzzle; perplex; cannot understand
balance (noun)	stability; steadiness
ban (verb)	disallow; must not be done
bankrupt (adj.)	deplete; financially ruined
barren (adj.)	infertile; cannot support growth
barrier (noun)	obstacle; prevents movement; impediment
behalf (noun)	for someone else
belated (adj.)	late; after expected time
belief (noun)	trust; feel certain about something
belligerent (adj.)	ready to fight or quarrel
benefactor (noun)	supporter; donor
beneficial (adj.)	helpful; valuable; useful
beneficiary (noun)	inheritor; someone who gains
benefit (noun)	help; advantage
benevolent (adj.)	kind; magnanimous; altruistic
benign (adj.)	harmless; not cancerous
bereft (adj.)	deprived of; lacking of
betray (verb)	trick; disloyal; unfaithful
better (adj.)	superior ; surpassing; prominent
bewilder (adj.)	confused; appalled; astonished
bias (noun)	prejudice; favoritism; one-sidedness
bigot (noun)	intolerant of a race that is not one's own
bilingual (adj.)	capable of speaking two languages
bitter (adj.)	unpleasant; acrimonious; resentful; nasty
blame (verb)	fault; hold responsible; accuse
blatant (adj.)	conspicuous; obvious; clear
blemish (noun)	spot; stain; defect; flaw
boast (verb)	show off; speak proudly of
boisterous (adj.)	noisy; rambunctious; vociferous
bond (noun)	relationship; strong feeling
boredom (noun)	lack of interest; ennui
borrow (verb)	for temporary use
boss (noun)	person in charge
bother (verb)	disturb; give trouble; annoy; harass; pester
boundary (noun)	border
bourgeois (adj.)	middle-class
boycott (verb)	ban; refuse to be involved in something
brave (adj.)	courageous; not afraid; audacious
brawl (noun)	rough fight; scuffle; altercation
brevity (noun)	conciseness; shortness
brief (adj.)	short time; succinct
bright (adj.)	shining; illuminated; luminous
brilliant (adj.)	very intelligent; extremely clever
brisk (adj.)	vigorous; quick
browse (verb)	skim; look around
brutal (adj.)	cruel; callous; heartless
budget (noun)	amount of money needed for something
bulk (noun)	large amount
bundle (noun)	package; quantity of something bound together
buoyant (adj.)	floating; light in weight
burden (noun)	hardship; stress; sorrow
bursar (noun)	office where one can pay fees in college
burst (verb)	explode; breaks open; blow up
buy (verb)	purchase
cab (noun)	taxi
calamity (noun)	disaster; great damage; catastrophe
calculate (verb)	figure; determine
callous (adj.)	insensitive; cruel
calm (noun)	quietness; peacefulness; tranquil
camouflage (noun)	disguise; false appearance
cancel (verb)	terminate; will not happen
candid (adj.)	frank; outspoken; honest
candidate (noun)	applicant
cantankerous (adj.)	quarrelsome; bad-tempered; contentious

Word	Meaning
capable (adj.)	having ability to perform; proficient
capacitate (verb)	give an ability; enable; empower
capacity (noun)	capability; ability to perform
capitulate (verb)	give in; surrender; succumb; submit
capricious (adj.)	changeable; change one's mind unexpectedly; temperamental
capsize (verb)	overturn; upside down
capture (verb)	arrest; seize
care (noun)	protection; personal interest
career (noun)	profession or occupation
caress (verb)	fondle; touch lovingly
casual (adj.)	not planned; spontaneous
catalyst (noun)	something speeding up reaction
catastrophe (noun)	tragedy; great suffering; calamity
categorize (verb)	arrange; put in order
category (noun)	group
cause (noun)	reason
caution (noun)	care; advice; prudence; vigilance
cease (verb)	stop doing; terminate; halt
celebrate (verb)	observe; honor; commemorate
censure (verb)	criticize severely
chagrin (noun)	displeasure; disappointment; dismay
challenge (verb)	confront; question
chance (noun)	opportunity
change (verb)	convert; make it different
channel (noun)	waterway
chaos (noun)	confusion; disorder; turmoil; pandemonium
charisma (noun)	personal charm; attraction; appeal
charismatic (adj.)	appealing by personal qualities
chastise (verb)	punish; scold; castigate
cheap (adj.)	inexpensive; low-priced; bargain
cheat (verb)	rob; obtain by dishonesty
check (verb)	verify; make sure; inspect
cherish (verb)	treasure; keep in mind for a long time
chief (adj.)	primary; most important; essential
chilly (adj.)	very cold
chore (noun)	task; everyday work
chubby (adj.)	stocky; a little fat
circumstance (noun)	condition; situation
circumvent (verb)	avoid; stay away; evade
cite (verb)	mention; quote; point out
civil (adj.)	kind; courteous; cordial
clandestine (adj.)	done secretly; surreptitious; covert
clarify (verb)	explain; make clear
classic (adj.)	traditional
clause (noun)	individual section
claustrophobia (noun)	abnormal fear of being in an enclosed space
clean (adj.)	pure; not dirty; immaculate
coach (verb)	instruct; teach

Word	Meaning
code (noun)	set of standards
coerce (verb)	force to do something; compel; intimidate
cognizant (adj.)	fully aware; knowledgeable
coherent (adj.)	consistent; organized; clear
cohesive (adj.)	connected; fit together; unified
coincide (verb)	correspond; happen at the same time
cold (adj.)	frigid; extremely low temperature
collaborate (verb)	cooperate; work together; collude
collapse (verb)	fall; break down; crumble
colleague (noun)	associate; people you work with; co-worker
collide (verb)	crash; violent contact; clash
combine (verb)	mix; join together; unify
comedian (noun)	joker; jester; makes people laugh
comfort (verb)	support; console; soothe
commence (verb)	start; initiate
comment (noun)	spoken statement; remark
commission (noun)	share of a profit
commitment (noun)	promise to do; pledge
commodity (noun)	product sold for money
commotion (noun)	disturbance; very noisy; turmoil
communicate (verb)	exchange information
community (noun)	group of people
compare (verb)	examine for similarities and differences
comparison (noun)	likeness; similarity
compassion (noun)	feeling of sympathy
compatible (adj.)	going together; agreeable
compel (verb)	force to do
compensate (verb)	pay for service; remunerate; reward
competent (adj.)	efficient; skilled; proficient
compile (verb)	put together; gather
complacent (adj.)	self-satisfied; unconcerned
complain (verb)	protest ; whine; disapprove
complement (noun)	something added to complete a whole
complex (adj.)	complicated; difficult to understand
compliment (verb)	praise; make kind remark; applaud
comply (verb)	follow instruction; obey
component (noun)	part of
compose (verb)	create; make up
comprehend (verb)	understand; grasp
comprehensive (adj.)	extensive; thorough; wide
comprise (verb)	include; be made of
compulsory (adj.)	required; must be completed
compute (verb)	determine; figure out
concede (verb)	admit; acknowledge; accept
conceited (adj.)	self-important; egotistical; too proud
concept (noun)	idea; thought
conceive (verb)	imagine; think of an idea
concentrate (verb)	focus attention
conciliate (verb)	placate; win over; satisfy

Word	Meaning	Word	Meaning
concise (verb)	brief; short; succinct	contribute (verb)	give; provide; donate
conclude (verb)	end; finish; terminate	controversy (noun)	dispute; disagreement; quarrel
concoct (verb)	create; think up; devise	convene (verb)	meet; come together
concur (verb)	agree; acquiesce	convenient (adj.)	suitable; appropriate; acceptable
concurrent (adj.)	at the same time	conventional (adj.)	customary; normal; in use for long time
condemn (verb)	strongly disapprove of	converse (verb)	chat; talk with; discourse
condescending (adj.)	snobby; talk down to	convert (verb)	change; transport
condone (verb)	overlook; disregard	convey (verb)	transmit; carry; communicate
conduct (verb)	manage; handle	convince (verb)	persuade; encourage
confer (verb)	discuss; deliberate	cooperate (verb)	work together; collaborate; assist
confess (verb)	admit; acknowledge	coordinate (verb)	put in order; organize; pull together
confide (verb)	tell trustingly	cop (noun)	police officer
confidence (noun)	certainty; belief in something	copious (adj.)	plentiful; abundant; profuse
confine (verb)	restrict; prevent from leaving	core (noun)	central part; most important
confirm (verb)	verify; make certain	corroborate (verb)	give support; back up; endorse
confiscate (verb)	seize; steal; take away	correspond (verb)	communicate with
conflict (noun)	fight; argument; disagreement	counterfeit (adj.)	fake; not real; fraudulent
conform (verb)	agree; fit in	couple (noun)	pair; two; duo
confront (verb)	challenge; meet face-to-face	courteous (adj.)	polite; mannerly; gentle
congenial (adj.)	pleasant; friendly	covert (adj.)	secret; concealed; clandestine
conscious (adj.)	awake; aware; vigilant; alert	create (verb)	make; bring about; concoct
consecutive (adj.)	continuous; one after another	credible (adj.)	believable; trustworthy
consensus (noun)	general agreement	credit (noun)	recognition; praise; tribute
consent (noun)	approval	cripple (verb)	paralyze; disable; incapacitate
consequence (noun)	result	crisis (noun)	emergency; serious or critical situation
conservative (adj.)	traditional; not willing to accept new ideas	criteria (noun)	standard to judge
considerable (adj.)	sizable; large	crucial (adj.)	important; vital; urgent; essential
consistent (adj.)	steady; constant	cry (verb)	sob; weep; lament
consist (verb)	made up of	cultural (adj.)	relating to a group of people
conspicuous (adj.)	easily seen or noticed	cumbersome (adj.)	difficult to handle; huge; heavy
conspire (verb)	act together secretly	curtail (verb)	reduce; diminish
consternation (noun)	fear that makes one feel helpless; trepidation	debilitate (verb)	weaken; enervate
constituent (noun)	component; part of	decagon (noun)	ten-sided figure
constitute (verb)	comprise; form; make up	decade (noun)	period of ten years
constrain (verb)	force; compel; coerce	decease (verb)	die; pass away
constrict (verb)	reduce; become narrower	deceive (verb)	betray; mislead; dishonest
construct (verb)	build; put together	decipher (verb)	find the meaning; figure out
consult (verb)	ask for professional advice	decision (noun)	conclusion; outcome
consume (verb)	use up; utilize	decline (verb)	refuse; do not accept; repudiate
contact (noun)	communication	decrease (verb)	lessen; dwindle; subside
contemplate (verb)	meditate on; think deeply about	dedicate (verb)	devote; commit
contemporary (adj.)	modern; present-day	deduce (verb)	determine; figure out; infer
contemptible (adj.)	despicable; strong dislike for	deduct (verb)	subtract; discount; reduce
content (adj.)	satisfied; happy	defeat (verb)	overcome; win; beat
context (noun)	background information	defendant (noun)	accused person
contingency (noun)	emergency; possibility of happening	deficient (adj.)	inadequate; not enough
contract (noun)	agreement	deficit (noun)	shortage; inadequacy
contradict (verb)	dispute; refuse to accept	define (verb)	identify; describe; explain
contrary (adj.)	opposite; totally different	defraud (verb)	cheat; take what belongs to you
contrast (verb)	show differences	defy (verb)	disobey; oppose; resist

Word	Meaning	Word	Meaning
degenerate (verb)	deteriorate; worsen; decay	discard (verb)	reject; get rid of
deliberate (adj.)	intentional; planned	discipline (verb)	punish; penalize; chastise
delicate (adj.)	weak; easy to break	discount (noun)	reduction in price
delicious (adj.)	appetizing, pleasant taste	discreet (adj.)	careful; cautious; vigilant
delirious (adj.)	unable to speak sensibly; mentally unbalanced; confused	discriminate (verb)	separate; show bias
delegate (verb)	give duty to act on behalf of	disenchanted (adj.)	disillusioned; disappointed
deliver (verb)	hand over; convey; carry	disengage (verb)	set loose; extricate
demand (verb)	command; ask forcefully	disgrace (noun)	shame; lost of honor
demolish (verb)	destroy; dismantle	disillusion (noun)	chagrin; disappointment
demonstrate (verb)	explain; make clear	dislocate (verb)	disconnect; move out of position
deny (verb)	declare untrue; repudiate	disloyal (adj.)	untrue; untrustworthy
denote (verb)	indicate; stand for	dismantle (verb)	take apart
denounce (verb)	condemn; criticize severely	disparity (noun)	dissimilarity; difference
depart (verb)	leave; vacate; evacuate	disperse (verb)	scatter; spread in all directions
deplete (verb)	drain; use up; reduce	displace (verb)	put out of place; force out
deplore (verb)	condemn; disapprove of	display (verb)	exhibit; show to the public
deposit (verb)	store; put for safe keeping	dispose (verb)	get rid of; give away; discard
depreciate (verb)	reduce in value or price	dispute (verb)	argue; challenge; question
depress (verb)	sadden; discourage	disreputable (adj.)	having a bad reputation
deprive (verb)	withhold; take away	dissatisfied (adj.)	unhappy; not pleased; discontented
derelict (noun)	bum; beggar	dissent (verb)	differ in opinion or belief
derive (verb)	gain; figure out	dissident (noun)	rebel; holding different belief; protester
derogatory (adj.)	negative; dishonorable	dissipate (verb)	disperse; scatter
describe (verb)	explain; tell by writing or speaking	dissuade (verb)	advise against; deter
design (verb)	draw; devise	distinct (adj.)	clear; different from
designate (verb)	appoint; name; specify	distinction (noun)	excellence; special award; honor
desist (verb)	stop; refrain	distinguish (verb)	tell apart; tell difference
despair (noun)	hopelessness; melancholy	distort (verb)	twist; tell incorrectly; falsify
desperate (adj.)	urgent; hopeless	distress (noun)	trouble; extreme worry
despite (preposition)	in spite of; although	distribute (verb)	give out; dispense; disburse
despondent (adj.)	discouraged; depressed	disturb (verb)	irritate; interrupt
destination (noun)	end; place want to go	diurnal (adj.)	happening in the daytime
detest (verb)	hate	diverge (verb)	stray; going in different directions
devastate (verb)	destroy totally; demolish	diversity (noun)	variety; very different; heterogeneity
deviate (verb)	depart from normal path	docile (adj.)	obedient; easily controlled; quiet
devise (verb)	formulate; make up	domestic (adj.)	relating to the home
devoted (adj.)	dedicated; committed to	dominate (verb)	control; have power over
dexterous (adj.)	clever; skillful with hands	donate (verb)	give away
different (adj.)	unlike; dissimilar; diverse	donor (noun)	someone who gives something
differentiate (verb)	see a difference; tell apart	dormant (adj.)	inactive; passive
difficult (adj.)	hard to do; onerous	draft (verb)	sketch; write first version
digress (verb)	stray; get lost	drastic (adj.)	extremely severe
dilapidated (adj.)	decay; falling apart	drip (verb)	fall in small drops
dilemma (noun)	a difficult problem; crisis	dubious (adj.)	undecided; uncertain
diligent (adj.)	hardworking; conscientious	duration (noun)	time during which something happens
dilute (verb)	weaken; make thinner	dwindle (verb)	lessen; decrease; decline
dimensions (noun)	measurements	dynamic (adj.)	powerful; spirited; charismatic
diminish (verb)	decrease; reduce; curtail	eager (adj.)	anxious; avid; ardent; want very much
diplomacy (noun)	tact; a skill not to offend	earn (verb)	obtain; gain money
disagree (verb)	differ in opinion; do not accept		
disappear (verb)	vanish; go out of sight		

Word	Meaning	Word	Meaning
eccentric (adj.)	odd; strange; weird	entity (noun)	organization
economical (adj.)	thrifty; frugal; not wasteful	envy (noun)	jealousy; unhappy of one's success
ecstasy (noun)	joy; great happiness	equate (verb)	make equal; match
edit (verb)	correct mistakes	equip (verb)	provide with; supply
egocentric (adj.)	self-centered; thinks highly of oneself	equivalent (adj.)	equal; same
eject (verb)	expel; force to leave	equivocal (adj.)	vague; several meanings
elaborate (verb)	more details; amplify	eradicate (verb)	eliminate; get rid completely
elapse (verb)	pass by; lapse	erase (verb)	delete; rub out; destroy completely
elated (adj.)	extremely happy; excited	erratic (adj.)	uncertain; irregular ; inconsistent
elective (adj.)	optional; not required	erode (verb)	wear away; disintegrate slowly
elicit (verb)	evoke; bring out	error (noun)	mistake; something wrong
eligible (adj.)	suitable; qualified; preferable	erupt (verb)	explode; break out
eliminate (verb)	remove; omit; dispense	escalate (verb)	increase in intensity
elite (adj.)	most distinguished; powerful; rich	espionage (noun)	spying; undercover work
eloquent (adj.)	skillful with words	establish (verb)	organize; start; lay foundation
embarrass (verb)	disgrace; make someone feel ashamed	estate (noun)	property
embezzle (verb)	steal; pilfer	esteem (noun)	high respect; think highly of someone; revere
emerge (verb)	appear; come into view	estrange (verb)	separate; break up; leave
eminent (adj.)	famous; respected; renowned	eternal (adj.)	lasting forever; perpetual; endless
emit (verb)	discharge; send out	ethics (noun)	rules of behavior; principles; values
emotional (adj.)	excitable; passionate	ethnic (adj.)	relating to race or culture
empathy (noun)	sharing of another person's feelings	evacuate (verb)	leave empty; move out
emphasize (verb)	stress; place importance on	evaluate (verb)	examine; determine value; assess
employ (verb)	hire; give money for working	evasive (adj.)	dishonest; giving unclear answer
empower (verb)	give power or authority to	eventual (adj.)	resulting; in the end
enable (verb)	make possible; capacitate	evident (adj.)	clear; notice easily; obvious; apparent
encounter (noun)	unexpected meeting with	evolve (verb)	develop gradually; grow
encourage (verb)	support; give confidence; inspire	exacerbate (verb)	aggravate; make more intense
endeavor (noun)	attempt to do; undertaking	exaggerate (verb)	overstate; make more important than really is
endorse (verb)	sponsor; support; approve	exceed (verb)	go beyond; rise above
endowment (noun)	valuable gift to college	excel (verb)	surpass; superior; extremely well
endure (verb)	undergo; experience without giving up	exceptional (adj.)	outstanding; extraordinary; excellent
enemy (noun)	foe; someone that hates; adversary	excessive (adj.)	too much; exorbitant
energy (noun)	power; strength	excitement (noun)	thrill; pleasure
enforce (verb)	implement; carry out	exclude (verb)	keep out; repudiate; preclude
enhance (verb)	improve; strengthen; augment	exemplify (verb)	show as an example; epitomize
enigmatic (adj.)	baffling; puzzling; difficult to understand	exempt (verb)	exclude; excuse
enlarge (verb)	increase in size; magnify	exhaust (verb)	deplete; use up; expend
enlighten (verb)	educate; inform	exhibit (noun)	something shown publicly; display
enmity (noun)	hatred; antagonism	exhilarate (verb)	enliven; make very happy
enormous (adj.)	very large; humongous; mammoth	exonerate (verb)	declare blameless
entertain (verb)	amuse; give pleasure; enliven	exorbitant (adj.)	overpriced; extravagant
ensure (verb)	make certain it happens	expand (verb)	increase in size; enlarge
		expedite (verb)	speed up; accelerate; hasten
		expel (verb)	dismiss; get rid of
		expert (noun)	one with special skills
		explain (verb)	clarify; make clear
		explicit (adj.)	clear; definite; open
		exploit (verb)	take advantage of; abuse
		export (noun)	product sent to another country
		expose (verb)	reveal; make aware of
		extensive (adj.)	broad; wide range

Word	Meaning	Word	Meaning
exterior (adj.)	outside	feud (noun)	bitter; quarrel
external (adj.)	outer; extraneous	fever (noun)	abnormally high body temperature
extract (verb)	remove; take out	fiction (noun)	fantasy; not true
extraterrestrial (adj.)	beyond earth	fictitious (adj.)	imaginary; unreal
extraordinary (adj.)	special; remarkable	fidelity (noun)	faithfulness; loyalty
extravagant (adj.)	excessive; wasteful	fiduciary (adj.)	involving confidence and trust
extricate (verb)	set free from a difficulty	file (verb)	organize; put in order
extrinsic (adj.)	outside	finances (noun)	available money
extrovert (noun)	friendly; outgoing; sociable	final (adj.)	last; happening at the end
exuberant (adj.)	extremely joyful; exhilarated	finish (verb)	complete; reach the end
fabulous (adj.)	fantastic; exceptionally good	finite (adj.)	limited; has limitations
facade (noun)	pretense; deception	fit (adj.)	suitable; qualified; apt
facetious (adj.)	frivolous; not serious	flagrant (adj.)	conspicuously bad; notorious
facilitate (verb)	make easier; aid; expedite	flamboyant (adj.)	too showy; stylish; ostentatious
factor (noun)	something that produces results	flatter (verb)	compliment; praise excessively
fade (verb)	pale; lose brightness	flaunt (verb)	display; show off
fail (verb)	unsuccessful; unable to do	flaw (noun)	defect; weakness
faith (noun)	strong belief; confident in one's ability	flexible (adj.)	capable of bending
		flippant (adj.)	rude; disrespectful
fake (adj.)	false; unreal	flourish (verb)	prosper; successful; grow
fallacy (noun)	false idea or opinion	fluctuate (verb)	change continually; vacillate
fallible (adj.)	imperfect; can make mistakes	fluent (adj.)	well-versed; speak or write easily
false (adj.)	not true; fallacious; spurious	fluster (verb)	disturb
falter (verb)	waver; hesitate; stumble	focus (verb)	direct; concentrate on; aim; fixate
fame (noun)	renown; favorable reputation	foe (noun)	enemy; rival
familiar (adj.)	well-known	fond (adj.)	adore; loving; feel affection for
famine (noun)	period of starvation	foolproof (adj.)	assured; without fault
famished (adj.)	starving; extremely hungry; voracious	forecast (noun)	prediction; happening in future
		foremost (adj.)	principal; most important
famous (adj.)	well-known; eminent; renowned	forever (adj.)	always; everlasting; endless
fantastic (adj.)	awesome; superb	forfeit (verb)	lose; give up something
fantasy (noun)	daydream	forgive (verb)	excuse; grant pardon; absolve
farewell (noun)	leaving; departure	formal (adj.)	businesslike; official
fascinate (verb)	attract; hold interest; charm	formidable (adj.)	powerful; great strength
fasten (verb)	attach; join together	formula (noun)	plan; recipe
fastidious (adj.)	hard to please; quick to find fault	formulate (verb)	prepare
fatal (adj.)	deadly; can cause death; pernicious	forsake (verb)	abandon; stop helping
		forthcoming (adj.)	honest; happening soon
fatigue (noun)	mental tiredness; languor	fortitude (noun)	courage; mental strength
fatuous (adj.)	silly; foolish; absurd; ludicrous	forward (verb)	advance onward; move in front
fault (noun)	mistake; flaw; culpability	find (verb)	discover; recover
faulty (adj.)	imperfect; not working correctly	fraction (noun)	portion of something
favor (verb)	take a side; prefer	fragile (adj.)	easily broken; delicate; brittle
favorite (adj.)	preferred	fragrant (adj.)	sweet-smelling; aromatic
feasible (adj.)	possible; probable	framework (noun)	structure that forms support
feature (noun)	important part; characteristic	frank (adj.)	outspoken; truthful
feeble (adj.)	very weak; frail; ailing	frantic (adj.)	scared; uncontrolled emotion
ferocious (adj.)	fierce; cruel	fraternity (noun)	organization for males
fervent (adj.)	showing great intensity of feeling; sincere; ardent	fraud (noun)	trickery; deception
		frequent (adj.)	regular; recurring
festive (adj.)	merry; happy; jovial	frigid (adj.)	ice-cold
fetch (verb)	go and bring back	frivolous (adj.)	insignificant; of little value

Word	Meaning
frolic (noun)	having fun playing; gaiety
frugal (adj.)	not wasteful; stingy
frustrated (adj.)	discouraged; disappointed
fugitive (noun)	one fleeing from justice
fulfilling (adj.)	pleasing; happy; satisfied
fun (noun)	pleasure; enjoyment
function (noun)	purpose; role; responsibility
fund (verb)	provide for
fundamentals (noun)	basics; most important
furthermore (adverb)	also
fury (noun)	very strong anger
futile (adj.)	useless; unsuccessful
gait (noun)	way of walking
gallant (adj.)	brave; noble; magnanimous
gamut (noun)	complete range; area
gang (noun)	group with common interest
garrulous (adj.)	excessively talkative about trivial things
gather (verb)	collect; come together
gaudy (adj.)	lacking in good taste
general (adj.)	broad; comprehensive
gender (noun)	related to one's sex
generate (verb)	produce; create
generations (noun)	groups of people born at the same time
generous (adj.)	unselfish; altruistic; giving; benevolent
genesis (noun)	beginning; start
ghastly (adj.)	dreadful; horrible
gigantic (adj.)	huge; very large; massive; colossal
glamorous (adj.)	more attractive than others
glimpse (noun)	glance; brief look
globe (noun)	round object with world map
gloom (noun)	feeling of sadness and hopelessness
glucose (noun)	blood sugar
goal (noun)	something to achieve
gossip (noun)	hearsay; unverified information
gradual (adj.)	slow; change little by little
graphic (adj.)	colorful
gratitude (noun)	appreciation; thankfulness
gratuitous (adj.)	undesired; unnecessary; free
gregarious (adj.)	sociable; likes the company of others
grieve (verb)	mourn; feel sadness
grotesque (adj.)	weird; ugly; uncanny
guarantee (noun)	assurance; promise to do something
guest (noun)	visitor
guide (verb)	direct
guidelines (noun)	instructions
guilty (adj.)	culpable; at fault
gullible (adj.)	easily deceived

Word	Meaning
gush (noun)	sudden flow
habit (noun)	routine; regular basis
hallucinate (verb)	hear or see something that does not exist
halt (verb)	stop
hamper (verb)	hinder; prevent from happening
handsome (adj.)	attractive
handy (adj.)	convenient
haphazard (adj.)	random; without a plan
harass (verb)	molest; annoy; bother
hardship (noun)	difficulty
harm (verb)	hurt
harmonious (adj.)	agreeing
harmony (noun)	agreement
harsh (adj.)	cruel
hasty (adj.)	swift; acting quickly without much thought
hazardous (adj.)	dangerous
heinous (adj.)	hateful; wicked; horrifying
hence (adverb)	therefore
hesitate (verb)	pause; not certain
heterogeneous (adj.)	dissimilar
hide (verb)	conceal; cannot easily be seen
hierarchy (noun)	system with levels
highlight (verb)	emphasize
hilarious (adj.)	comical
hinder (verb)	stop; slow down
histology (noun)	study of cells
hoax (noun)	fraud; trick; deception
hobby (noun)	favorite pastime
homage (noun)	respect
homicide (noun)	murder; manslaughter
homogeneous (adj.)	similar
horrible (adj.)	terrible
hostile (adj.)	unfriendly
humane (adj.)	kind; compassion for people
humble (adj.)	simple; not proud
humiliate (verb)	embarrass; feeling ashamed or stupid
hurry (verb)	rush; go speedily
hurt (verb)	harm; cause to feel pain
hypersensitive (adj.)	over-sensitive; offended easily
hypertension (noun)	high blood pressure
hypothermia (noun)	lower-than-normal body temperature
hyperthyroidism (noun)	excessive activity of thyroid gland
hypocrite (noun)	one who pretends to be what he or she is not
hypoglycemia (noun)	abnormally low blood sugar

Word	Meaning	Word	Meaning
hypothesis (noun)	assumption; proposition; theory	impostor (noun)	charlatan; pretend to be someone else
hysterical (adj.)	emotionally uncontrolled; extremely upset	impractical (adj.)	unworkable; unrealistic
ideal (adj.)	perfect; excellent; exemplary	impression (noun)	feeling; opinion; sense
identical (adj.)	alike; exactly same	impromptu (adj.)	unrehearsed; unprepared
identify (verb)	recognize; distinguish; select	improper (adj.)	incorrect; rude; dishonest; unsuitable
idle (adj.)	inactive; lackadaisical; lazy	improve (verb)	develop; make better
ignoble (adj.)	disgraceful; low character	imprudent (adj.)	without thought of consequences
ignorant (adj.)	lack knowledge; foolish	impure (adj.)	unclean; poor quality
ignore (verb)	avoid; pay no attention; disregard	inaccessible (adj.)	unreachable; impassable; remote
illegal (adj.)	unlawful; against the law	inaccurate (adj.)	incorrect; untrue; fallacious
illegible (adj.)	unreadable; unclear; obscure	inadequate (adj.)	insufficient; incompetent
illicit (adj.)	forbidden; illegal	inadvertent (adj.)	unintentional; not planned
illiterate (adj.)	unable to read or write	inanimate (adj.)	lifeless; without life
illogical (adj.)	senseless; untenable	inappropriate (adj.)	unsuitable
illuminate (verb)	brighten	incarcerate (verb)	imprison
illustrate (verb)	explain; make clear; elucidate	incentive (noun)	encouragement
illustrious (adj.)	famous; eminent	incessant (adj.)	continuous; without stopping; perpetual
image (noun)	picture; idea	incident (noun)	occurrence; something that happens
imbecile (noun)	fool; idiot; stupid person	inclement (adj.)	stormy; severe
imitate (verb)	copy; impersonate	incline (noun)	slope
immaculate (adj.)	faultless; extremely clean; tidy	incognito (adj.)	disguised; hiding one's identity
immature (adj.)	underdeveloped; inexperience	incoherent (adj.)	inconsistent; unclear
immeasurable (adj.)	too large to measure	incompetent (adj.)	unfit; lacking ability
immense (adj.)	enormous; vast; huge	incomplete (adj.)	unfinished; lacking something
immerse (verb)	completely involved	incomprehensible (adj.)	cannot be understood
immigrate (verb)	enter a foreign area	inconsiderate (adj.)	thoughtless; disregard one's feeling
imminent (adj.)	approaching; about to happen	inconsistent (adj.)	disagreeing; varying
immoral (adj.)	unethical; wrongful	inconspicuous (adj.)	low-profile; not easily seen
immune (adj.)	resistant to something	incorporate (verb)	include; integrate
impact (noun)	effect; influence; impression	incredible (adj.)	unbelievable
impair (verb)	damage; weaken	inculcate (verb)	influence by persistent urging
impartial (adj.)	fair decision; unbiased; just	incurable (adj.)	untreatable; not able to be cured
impatient (adj.)	restless; do not want to wait	indelible (adj.)	unable to remove or forget
impeccable (adj.)	faultless; without flaw; perfect	indicate (verb)	show; point out
impede (verb)	hinder; block; obstruct	indifferent (adj.)	unconcerned; callous; unemotional
imperceptible (adj.)	negligible; too small to notice	indiscriminate (adj.)	unsystematic; random; haphazard
imperfection (noun)	fault; weakness	indispensable (adj.)	essential; absolutely necessary
impetuous (adj.)	acting with little thought	induce (verb)	cause to happen; bring about
implausible (adj.)	unbelievable; not likely to be true	inedible (adj.)	uneatable; unfit to eat
implement (verb)	carry out; start	inept (adj.)	incompetent; lack skill or aptitude
implicate (verb)	bring into connection	inevitable (adj.)	unavoidable; certain to happen
import (verb)	bring in from foreign country	inexorable (adj.)	cannot be influenced
important (adj.)	major; significant	infallible (adj.)	incapable of error; faultless
impose (verb)	enforce; force to accept	infamous (adj.)	wicked; bad reputation
implicit (adj.)	unexpressed		
implore (verb)	appeal; beg; beseech		
imply (verb)	hint; suggest; say indirectly		
impolite (adj.)	rude; bad manners; insolent		

Word	Meaning
infer (verb)	conclude; from evidence; guess; figure out
inferior (adj.)	of low grade
infidelity (noun)	unfaithfulness; marital disloyalty
inflame (verb)	increase intensity of
inflate (verb)	swell up; become bigger
influence (noun)	control; impact
ingenious (adj.)	clever; inventive
ingredient (noun)	component; part
inhabitant (noun)	occupant
inherent (adj.)	inborn; built-in
inhibit (verb)	prevent; hold back; restrain
inhospitable (adj.)	not offering protection or shelter; unwelcoming; unfriendly
inhuman (adj.)	heartless; very cruel
initial (adj.)	occurring at the beginning
initiate (verb)	introduce; start; commence
injure (verb)	wound; hurt; damage
inmate (noun)	person living in prison
innate (adj.)	inborn; inherited
innocent (adj.)	blameless; not guilty
innocuous (adj.)	not likely to cause harm
innovate (verb)	introduce new ideas and changes
innuendo (noun)	suggestion; hint
inquisitive (adj.)	curious; nosy; questioning
insatiable (adj.)	incapable of being satisfied
insidious (adj.)	more dangerous than seems evident
insignificant (adj.)	unimportant; trivial; negligible
insinuate (verb)	suggest; say indirectly
insolent (adj.)	rude; disrespectful
inspect (verb)	examine carefully
inspire (verb)	encourage; motivate
installment (noun)	one payment of several made at regular intervals
instigate (verb)	start; cause to happen; provoke
institute (verb)	create; start
instruct (verb)	teach; provide knowledge
integral (adj.)	essential; indispensable; fundamental
integrate (verb)	combine; become part of
integrity (noun)	honor; honesty; moral principles
intelligence (noun)	high mental capacity
intense (adj.)	very strong; profound; impassioned
intentional (adj.)	deliberate; on purpose
interact (verb)	work together; collaborate; communicate
intermediate (adj.)	middle
interminable (adj.)	endless; incessant; infinite
intermission (noun)	break between two parts of a show
intermittent (adj.)	periodic; irregular

Word	Meaning
internal (adj.)	inside; inner
interpretation (noun)	understanding; explanation
interrogate (verb)	question thoroughly
intervene (verb)	step in; interrupt; mediate
intimate (adj.)	closely acquainted; personal
intimidate (verb)	frighten; induce fear; threaten
intoxicate (verb)	make drunk; inebriate
intravenous (adj.)	taken through a vein
intricate (adj.)	complex; difficult to understand
intrinsic (adj.)	not dependent on external circumstances
introvert (noun)	someone shy or withdrawn
intuition (noun)	instinct; insight
inundate (verb)	overwhelm with a great amount; drown
invalid (adj.)	ineffective; worthless
invert (verb)	capsize; overturn
invest (verb)	commit money
investigate (verb)	inquire; examine thoroughly
invincible (adj.)	unbeatable
invite (verb)	request to do something
involve (verb)	include; take part in
invoke (verb)	call forth for help; appeal
irate (adj.)	angry; infuriated
irrelevant (adj.)	unrelated; unconnected
irreparable (adj.)	ruined; unable to correct
irresistible (adj.)	compelling; cannot avoid
irrevocable (adj.)	cannot be recalled; changed or reversed
irritate (verb)	annoy; anger; enrage; harass
isolate (verb)	separate; place apart; seclude
issue (noun)	unresolved matter
item (noun)	individual thing
jealous (adj.)	envious; angry because of one's advantages
jeopardize (verb)	risk; put in danger
jest (verb)	joke
job (noun)	work done for money
join (verb)	connect
journal (noun)	record of daily happening
journey (noun)	trip
jovial (adj.)	joyful; happy
judge (verb)	mediate; settle dispute
judicious (adj.)	having or showing sound judgment
jumble (noun)	mix together without correct order
junior (adj.)	younger
justify (verb)	prove; give a reason for
juvenile (adj.)	young
keen (adj.)	sharp; very intelligent
keep (verb)	hold in one's possession
kidnap (verb)	steal; taken by force
kin (noun)	relative

Word	Meaning	Word	Meaning
kindle (verb)	light or start a fire	lucrative (adj.)	profitable
kit (noun)	items kept together in a case	ludicrous (adj.)	laughable
kleptomaniac (noun)	person with an irresistible desire to steal	luminous (adj.)	glows in the dark
		lunar (adj.)	related to the moon
knock (verb)	hit for attention	lure (verb)	attract
label (verb)	mark; identify	luscious (adj.)	sweet and pleasant to taste
labor (verb)	struggle; work very hard	lustrous (adj.)	shiny
lacerate (verb)	tear; cut	luxury (noun)	prosperity; richness
lack (verb)	need; something missing	magnanimous (adj.)	kind and giving; generous
landlord (noun)	owner of real estate	magnificent (adj.)	splendid; wonderful
languid (adj.)	weak; little energy	magnify (verb)	enlarge
lapse (noun)	temporary decline	magnitude (noun)	greatness
large (adj.)	big; great	main (adj.)	chief; most important
latent (adj.)	hidden; present but invisible	maintain (verb)	keep or support
lateral (adj.)	sideways	majestic (adj.)	dignified; extremely beautiful
laugh (verb)	chuckle	major (noun)	main subject of study
lavish (adj.)	plentiful; extravagant	malady (noun)	sickness
layer (noun)	part that lies over another	malicious (adj.)	spiteful; hateful
lawyer (noun)	person schooled in law; attorney	malignant (adj.)	harmful or dangerous
lax (adj.)	careless	mammoth (adj.)	gigantic; huge
lazy (adj.)	inactive	mandate (noun)	authoritative command to act
lead (verb)	guide	mandatory (adj.)	compulsory
learn (verb)	comprehend; get information	mania (noun)	fixation; mental sickness
leave (verb)	depart	manipulate (verb)	control for one's benefit
lecture (noun)	period of verbal instruction	manslaughter (noun)	killing without intention
legal (adj.)	allowed; permitted by law	manual (adj.)	hand-operated
legible (adj.)	clear; easy to read	masculine (adj.)	related to males
legislate (verb)	make laws	massacre (verb)	kill large number of people violently
legitimate (adj.)	legal; acceptable by law	massage (verb)	stroke
leisure (noun)	spare time	maternal (adj.)	motherly
lenient (adj.)	lax; easy	matrimony (noun)	marriage
lethal (adj.)	fatal; can kill; deadly	mature (verb)	develop; fully-grown
lethargy (noun)	unenergetic; laziness	maximize (verb)	increase
levy (verb)	impose; force upon	maximum (adj.)	greatest
liable (adj.)	accountable	meander (verb)	twist; not in straight line
liberal (adj.)	tolerant; broad-minded	mechanism (noun)	mechanical part
license (noun)	permit	media (noun)	means of communication
lien (noun)	claim on a property	mediate (verb)	bring agreement to
light (adj.)	weighing little	medical (adj.)	relating to medicine
likewise (adverb)	the same	mediocre (adj.)	inferior; poor
limp (adj.)	drooping	medium (noun)	middle
linger (verb)	remain; stick around	melancholy (noun)	sadness; depression
link (noun)	connection	menace (noun)	threat; harm; danger
literate (adj.)	can read and write	mental (adj.)	relates to the mind
litigate (verb)	take legal action	merchandise (noun)	goods
load (verb)	pack; put large quantity in	merge (verb)	combine
locate (verb)	find	mesmerize (verb)	fascinate; hypnotize
logic (noun)	thinking; reasoning	message (noun)	communication
logical (adj.)	sensible	metamorphosis (noun)	change
loiter (verb)	idle; waste time	method (noun)	way of doing something
loquacious (adj.)	talkative	meticulous (adj.)	careful
lucid (adj.)	clear	migrate (verb)	move to another place

Word	Meaning
militant (noun)	activist
military (adj.)	relating to soldiers
miniature (adj.)	small; minute
minimal (adj.)	least
minimize (verb)	make small
minimum (adj,)	least amount
minor (adj.)	small; insignificant
minute (adj.)	tiny; very small; minuscule
miscellaneous (adj.)	mixed; diversified
mischievous (adj.)	disobedient
misery (noun)	sorrow
misfortune (noun)	tragedy
mishap (noun)	unfortunate accident
misinterpret (verb)	understand incorrectly
misplace (verb)	lose
mistake (noun)	error
mistreat (verb)	abuse
mitigate (verb)	make less severe or painful
mobile (adj.)	movable
mode (noun)	manner; way of doing
moderate (adj.)	average
modest (adj.)	shy; bashful; withdrawn
modify (verb)	change; convert; alter
monitor (verb)	watch carefully; supervise
monotonous (adj.)	having no variety
monumental (adj.)	massive; very great
moral (adj.)	respectable; honest
morale (noun)	spirit; confidence
morbid (adj.)	ghastly; frightful
more (adj.)	extra
motivate (verb)	encourage
motive (noun)	purpose; reason
mourn (verb)	grieve for the dead
multiple (adj.)	many
multiply (verb)	increase in number
murmur (verb)	whisper; continuous and low sound
mutual (adj.)	common; shared
nag (verb)	annoy
naive (adj.)	innocent; inexperienced
naked (adj.)	undressed; without clothing
nap (noun)	rest
narcotics (noun)	drugs
nausea (noun)	disgust; feel like throwing up
nebulous (adj.)	unclear
necessary (adj.)	required
negate (verb)	cause to be ineffective
negative (adj.)	discouraging
neglect (verb)	ignore; do not take care properly
negligent (adj.)	careless
negotiate (verb)	bargain; deal; discuss

Word	Meaning
nervous (adj.)	anxious; fearful
neurosis (noun)	nervous disorder
neutral (adj.)	impartial; not supporting any side
nevertheless (adverb)	however; even though
niche (noun)	place suitable for a person
nocturnal (adj.)	during the night
nod (verb)	move head up and down
nominal (adj.)	small
nonchalant (adj.)	easygoing
nonetheless (adverb)	anyway
norm (noun)	standard
nostalgia (noun)	longing for the past
notify (verb)	inform
notion (noun)	idea
notorious (adj.)	widely and unfavorably known
notwithstanding (prep.)	despite
novice (noun)	beginner; inexperienced
noxious (adj.)	harmful; poisonous
nuclear (adj.)	relating to atomic energy
nuisance (noun)	annoyance; causing problems
nullify (verb)	void; cancel; revoke
numerous (adj.)	many
nurture (verb)	care for
nutritious (adj.)	nourishing
obey (verb)	listen to; follow instruction
objective (adj.)	unprejudiced; fair
obligate (verb)	require; have to do
oblivious (adj.)	unaware; ignorant of
oblong (adj.)	elongated
obnoxious (adj.)	highly offensive; disgusting
obscene (adj.)	offensive; indecent
obscure (adj.)	unclear
obsequious (adj.)	too willing to serve or obey
observe (verb)	note; watch carefully
obsess (verb)	preoccupy; think about continuously
obsolete (adj.)	outdated; no longer in use
obstacle (noun)	barrier; in your way
obstinate (adj.)	stubborn; refuse to change
obstruct (verb)	block; difficult to pass
obvious (adj.)	understandable; easily seen
occasionally (adverb)	sometimes
occupy (verb)	take up; busy with something
occur (verb)	happen; take place
odd (adj.)	strange; weird
odor (noun)	scent; smell
offend (verb)	displease; insult; make angry
old (adj.)	antique; outdated; traditional
ominous (adj.)	threatening; fearful; evil
omit (verb)	leave out; exclude

Word	Meaning
omnipotent (adj.)	supreme; having complete power
omnivorous (adj.)	eating plants and animals
ongoing (adj.)	continuing
onset (noun)	beginning
opaque (adj.)	unclear; clouded
opponent (noun)	one taking opposite position
oppose (verb)	resist; speak against
optimistic (adj.)	hopeful; positive
optimum (adj.)	best
option (noun)	choice
optional (adj.)	voluntary
oral (adj.)	verbal
ordeal (noun)	difficult experience; trial
ordinary (adj.)	usual
organize (verb)	arrange
orient (verb)	direct; familiarize
orientation (noun)	introduction; direction
originate (verb)	begin; emerge; arise
orthopedics (noun)	related to bone and spine
oscillate (verb)	swing to and fro
ostensible (adj.)	clearly evident or apparent, but not necessarily true
ostentatious (adj.)	pretentious; showing off
ostracize (verb)	banish or exclude; throw out
outcome (noun)	result
output (noun)	amount produced
outrageous (adj.)	shocking
outstanding (adj.)	excellent; exceptional
overall (adj.)	in general
overlap (verb)	have the same parts
overseas (adverb)	across the ocean
overt (adj.)	done openly
overwhelm (verb)	overpower
owe (verb)	be liable
own (verb)	possess
pace (noun)	rate; speed
pacify (verb)	calm
pain (noun)	ache
palpitate (verb)	beat rapidly; throb
panacea (noun)	remedy
pandemonium (noun)	confusion; noise
panel (noun)	section
panic (noun)	fright; anxiety
panorama (noun)	wide view in all directions
parade (noun)	procession
paradigm (noun)	model for something
paragraph (noun)	section of a piece of writing
parallel (adj.)	similar; side-by-side
paralyze (verb)	disable
parameters (noun)	rules
paramount (adj.)	ranking higher than any other
pardon (verb)	forgive
partial (adj.)	incomplete
participate (verb)	take part
particular (adj.)	specific
partner (noun)	associate
passion (noun)	love
passive (adj.)	inactive; lifeless
pathetic (adj.)	pitiful
patience (noun)	tolerance
patron (noun)	customer
pedestrian (noun)	walker
penalize (verb)	punish
penalty (noun)	fine; punishment
pensive (adj.)	thoughtful
per diem (adverb)	by the day; daily
perceive (verb)	realize; become aware by senses
percent (noun)	one part in one hundred
percentage (noun)	proportion of one hundred
perceptive (adj.)	observant
perennials (noun)	plants that live year after year
period (noun)	length of time; duration
permanent (adj.)	lasting
pernicious (adj.)	damaging
perpetual (adj.)	lasting forever; eternal
perplexed (adj,)	confused; puzzled
persevere (verb)	endure; do not give up
persist (verb)	persevere; endure
perspective (noun)	view; outlook
perspicacious (adj.)	having keen judgment
persuade (verb)	convince; cause to do
pertain (verb)	relate; belong or relevant to
perturb (verb)	disturb; upset; confuse
petite (adj.)	small; miniature
phase (noun)	part; period; stage
phenomenon (noun)	something observed
philosophy (noun)	ideas; principles
phobia (noun)	persistent fear of something
physical (adj.)	relating to the body
pilfer (verb)	steal; embezzle
pious (adj.)	religious; righteous
pity (noun)	compassion; feeling of sympathy
placid (adj.)	calm; untroubled
plagiarize (verb)	take an idea and pass off as one's own
plague (noun)	contagious and deadly epidemic
plausible (adj.)	believable; likely to be true
pleasant (adj.)	pleasing
pledge (noun)	oath; promise
plentiful (adj.)	abundant; large amount
poignant (adj.)	emotionally touching or moving; feeling sad

Word	Meaning
poisonous (adj.)	toxic; harmful
policy (noun)	plan for decision making
polite (adj.)	courteous
pompous (adj.)	self-important
ponder (verb)	reflect; think about deeply
portion (noun)	part; share; allotment
pose (verb)	act; pretend to be
positive (adj.)	confident; certain
possess (verb)	own
possible (adj.)	likely; can be done
postpone (verb)	delay; later time
posture (noun)	stance
potent (adj.)	strong; powerful
potential (noun)	capability; ability to be successful
practice (verb)	prepare
practitioner (noun)	professional
prank (noun)	childish trick; hoax
precede (verb)	come before
precedent (noun)	example serving as a future rule
precious (adj.)	valuable; favorite
precise (adj.)	accurate
preclude (verb)	keep out or prevent
predict (verb)	foretell; tell what will happen
predominant (adj.)	principal; most important
prefer (verb)	favor; like better than
prejudice (noun)	discrimination; bias; partial
preliminary (adj.)	coming first; at the beginning
prelude (noun)	opening; introduction
premature (adj.)	early; coming too soon
preposterous (adj.)	foolish and unreasonable
prerequisite (adj.)	required; must be done before
preserve (verb)	maintain; keep
presume (verb)	take for granted
pretend (verb)	give false appearance
prevail (verb)	win; succeed
prevalent (adj.)	widespread
prevent (verb)	obstruct; stop from doing
previous (adj.)	earlier; prior; before
primary (adj.)	most important; main; chief
principal (noun)	chief; primary
principle (noun)	basic truth
priority (noun)	greatest importance
probation (noun)	period of testing or trial
procedure (noun)	sequence of steps
proceed (verb)	continue; move forward
process (noun)	series of actions
procrastinate (verb)	delay; put off; postpone
profanity (noun)	cursing; dirty language
professional (adj.)	skillful; highly qualified
proficient (adj.)	capable; adept; can do something well
profit (noun)	gain

Word	Meaning
profound (adj.)	deeply felt; very intense
prohibit (verb)	prevent; stop; forbid
project (noun)	task; specific work
prolong (verb)	continue; longer; lengthen
prominent (adj.)	well-known; noticeable
promote (verb)	make popular
promiscuous (adj.)	having many sexual partners
prompt (adj.)	punctual; on time
prone (adj.)	likely; having a tendency
proponent (noun)	one who supports a proposal
proposal (noun)	offer; plan or idea to consider
proportion (noun)	size; percentage
prosperous (adj.)	successful; rich; affluent
protest (verb)	complain; disapprove
protocol (noun)	certain rules of behavior
proud (adj.)	boastful; showing superiority
proverb (noun)	saying
provoke (verb)	irritate; annoy; make angry
prowess (noun)	exceptional aptitude, ability, and skill
prudent (adj.)	careful; cautious; wise
pseudopod (noun)	"foot" of an amoeba
psychic (noun)	fortuneteller; telling the future
psychology (noun)	study of the mind
publication (noun)	something printed
punctual (adj.)	prompt; on time
punish (verb)	scold; reprimand; suffer from wrong doing
purchase (verb)	buy
purpose (noun)	aim; reason for doing
purposeful (noun)	intentional; strong desire to get something
pursue (verb)	chase; go after
puzzle (verb)	perplex; confuse; think about
quadruple (adj.)	having four parts
quagmire (noun)	difficult situation; predicament
qualm (noun)	doubt; uneasy feeling
quandary (noun)	puzzle; state of uncertainty
quarrelsome (adj.)	bad-tempered; irritable; contentious
queer (adj.)	strange; weird
quell (verb)	calm; quiet; pacify
query (very)	question; ask; dispute
questionable (adj.)	open to doubt; uncertain; dubious
quiet (adj.)	still; no sound; peaceful
quirk (noun)	strange trait or mannerism
quit (verb)	discontinue; give up; stop doing
quiver (verb)	tremble; shake; vibrate
quiz (noun)	short examination
quota (noun)	proportion
quote (verb)	repeat something written or spoken
radiant (adj.)	shining; bright

Word	Meaning	Word	Meaning
radical (adj.)	extreme	reject (verb)	refuse
rage (noun)	extreme anger; fury	relapse (verb)	slip back
rancor (noun)	feeling of bitterness or spitefulness; hatred	relax (verb)	rest
		release (verb)	free
random (adj.)	unplanned; haphazard	relentless (adj.)	persistent; continuous
range (noun)	distance	relevant (adj.)	suitable
rank (noun)	position in something	reliable (adj.)	trustworthy
rapacious (adj.)	selfish or greedy behavior	relinquish (verb)	surrender or give up
rapid (adj.)	very quickly	relish (verb)	enjoy
ratify (verb)	confirm; approve	reluctant (adj.)	unwilling
ratio (noun)	relationship; proportion	rely (verb)	depend on
rational (adj.)	sensible; logical; sound; sane	remain (verb)	stay
ravage (verb)	damage; ruin	remarkable (adj.)	special
react (verb)	respond; answer back	remedial (adj.)	developmental
ready (adj.)	prepared; willing to	remedy (noun)	cure
refine (verb)	process; make pure; improve	remember (verb)	recall
region (noun)	area	remorse (noun)	sorrowful repentance
real (adj.)	true; genuine	remote (adj.)	distant; far from cities
rebuke (verb)	scold	remove (verb)	expel; erase; take away
recall (verb)	remember	render (verb)	perform; provide
recede (verb)	withdraw	repair (verb)	fix; restore; improve
receive (verb)	get	repeat (verb)	restate; do something again
recess (noun)	short period or break	replenish (verb)	renew; fill again
recession (noun)	a decline in economic activity	replete (adj.)	plentifully supplied; full of something
recipe (noun)	formula		
reciprocate (verb)	return	replicate (verb)	copy; duplicate
recite (verb)	repeat	reprehensible (adj.)	disgraceful; very bad
reckless (adj.)	careless	reprehend (verb)	find fault; criticize; disapprove
recognize (verb)	identify	representative (noun)	spokesperson; on behalf of
recollect (verb)	remember	reprimand (verb)	speak severely to
recommend (verb)	suggest; give approval	repudiate (verb)	forsake; abandon; reject
reconciliation (noun)	resolution; restore to harmony	repugnant (adj.)	disgusting; horrible
record (verb)	register; put down in writing	reputation (noun)	fame; trustworthiness
recover (verb)	get back	require (verb)	need; want; necessary
recruit (noun)	newcomer	rescue (verb)	save; free from danger
rectify (verb)	correct	research (verb)	investigate; find facts
recur (verb)	repeat	resentment (noun)	hatred; anger
reduce (verb)	lessen or decrease	reserve (verb)	keep for future use
redundant (adj.)	using more words than necessary	reside (verb)	live; stay
		resign (verb)	quit; leave; give up position
refrain (verb)	avoid; do without	resilient (adj.)	flexible; bend easily
refuge (noun)	shelter	resist (verb)	oppose; refuse to accept
refund (noun)	repayment	resolve (verb)	settle; find solution
refuse (verb)	reject	resourceful (adj.)	clever; intelligent
refute (verb)	disprove; prove false	resource (noun)	source of supply
register (verb)	sign up	respond (verb)	reply; react; answer
regress (verb)	go back	responsible (adj.)	reliable; trustworthy
regret (noun)	sorrow; sense of loss	restore (verb)	bring back
regular (adj.)	usual	restrain (verb)	control; hold back
regulate (verb)	adjust	restrict (verb)	control; regulate; put a limit
rehearse (verb)	practice	resume (verb)	continue; begin again
reinforce (verb)	strengthen	retain (verb)	hold on to; keep

Word	Meaning	Word	Meaning
retaliate (verb)	fight back; strike back	simulate (verb)	pretend to be
reticent (adj.)	quiet; saying little; secretive	sinister (adj.)	evil; harmful; wicked
retreat (verb)	withdraw; pull back; recede	site (noun)	location
retrospect (noun)	thinking of the past; think about afterward	skeptic (noun)	doubtful person; disbeliever
		solace (noun)	comfort; peace
reveal (verb)	disclose	solar (adj.)	related to the sun
reverse (verb)	backtrack; change to the opposite	sole (adj.)	only one; singular
revert (verb)	return; go back	solitude (noun)	isolation; loneliness
revise (verb)	improve; make better; edit	sorority (noun)	organization for females in college
revoke (verb)	cancel	source (noun)	thing or person that gives
revolution (noun)	act of overthrowing a government	spacious (adj.)	roomy; large; enormous
ridiculous (adj.)	foolish; stupid; silly	spank (verb)	beat; punish; smack
rigorous (adj.)	difficult; severe; thorough	specific (adj.)	particular; exact
role (noun)	part played	specify (verb)	name definitely
rough (adj.)	not smooth; uneven	speculate (verb)	guess what might happen
rupture (noun)	break or burst	spendthrift (noun)	extravagant person; waste money
rural (adj.)	relating to the countryside	sphere (noun)	round object
sabotage (verb)	undermine; deliberately destroyed	spontaneous (adj.)	unprepared; not planned
salient (adj.)	significant; important	sporadic (adj.)	irregular intervals; on and off
salute (verb)	honor; show respect	squander (verb)	misuse; wasteful
sane (adj.)	sensible; not mentally ill	stable (adj.)	steady; unchangeable
sarcastic (adj.)	mocking; saying the opposite of what one means	standstill (noun)	dead stop; stop completely
		stationary (adj.)	not moving; fixed
saturate (verb)	fill completely	stationery (noun)	writing materials
scandal (noun)	disgrace; say hateful things	statistics (noun)	facts; data; figures
scatter (verb)	disperse; spread over an area	status (noun)	position; rank
schedule (noun)	plan of things to be done	steal (verb)	pilfer; take without permission
scheme (noun)	clever plan to follow; plot	stereotype (noun)	fixed image
scope (noun)	extent of view	sterilize (verb)	disinfect; free from germs
scrupulous (adj.)	extremely careful	stimulate (verb)	arouse; encourage
scrutinize (verb)	examine closely	stingy (adj.)	cheap; unwilling to spend
scurrilous (adj.)	abusive; slanderous; vulgar	straightforward (adj.)	easy to understand
seal (verb)	close completely	strategy (noun)	plan to obtain something
section (noun)	a part; portion	strenuous (adj.)	hard work; difficult
sector (noun)	an area	stress (noun)	mental or physical tension
secure (verb)	protect; make safe	structure (noun)	the way something is organized or made
sedative (noun)	something that calms		
seduce (verb)	tempt; trick; bait	stubborn (adj.)	obstinate; determined
seek (verb)	search; look for	sturdy (adj.)	strong; durable
seldom (adverb)	rarely; not often	style (noun)	the way something is done
select (verb)	choose; make a choice	subjective (adj.)	biased; based on personal feeling
sensible (adj.)	wise; intelligent; judicious	subjugate (verb)	defeat or conquer
sensuous (adj.)	pleasing	submit (verb)	present; give in; comply
sentimental (adj.)	emotional; showing love; romantic	subordinate (adj.)	less important in position
separate (verb)	isolate; keep apart	subsequent (adj.)	following; afterward
serene (adj.)	peaceful; calm; quiet	subservient (adj.)	submissive; uncomplaining
serious (adj.)	important	subside (verb)	recede; sink to lower level
severe (adj.)	serious; harsh; difficult	substitute (verb)	replace; take the place of
shortage (noun)	insufficient amount; not enough	subtle (adj.)	indirect; not noticeable right away
shrewd (adj.)	smart; intelligent	succinct (adj.)	concise; express in few words
significant (adj.)	important	succulent (adj.)	juicy
similar (adj.)	alike; same	succumb (verb)	surrender; give in to

Word	Meaning	Word	Meaning
sufficient (adj.)	enough; adequate	text (noun)	printed matter
suitable (adj.)	acceptable; appropriate	theme (noun)	main subject
sullen (adj.)	unhappy; not cheerful	theory (noun)	an idea to explain something
sum (noun)	total amount	thesis (noun)	research project to earn a degree
summarize (verb)	condense; briefly explain	thorough (adj.)	complete; detailed
sumptuous (adj.)	costly; lavish	threaten (verb)	intimidate; warn; frighten
superb (adj.)	splendid; admirable; excellent	thrive (verb)	prosper; do well; successful
supercilious (adj.)	characterized by pride; think you are better than others	timid (adj.)	shy; lack courage; afraid
		tolerate (verb)	put up with; permit; allow
superficial (adj.)	shallow; without depth	topic (noun)	subject; theme
superfluous (adj.)	excessive; unnecessary	toxic (adj.)	noxious; poisonous
superior (adj.)	high-quality	trace (noun)	very small amount
superstition (noun)	belief based on ignorance	traditional (adj.)	old-fashioned; established a long time ago
supplement (noun)	addition; add to		
surpass (verb)	exceed; outperform; outdo	traditions (noun)	practices handed down
surplus (noun)	excess; more than needed	tragic (adj.)	devastating; extremely sad
surrender (verb)	submit; give up	trait (noun)	quality; characteristic
surreptitious (adj.)	acting in a secretive manner	tranquil (adj.)	peaceful; calm
survive (verb)	live through; remain alive	transfer (verb)	go from one place to another
susceptible (adj.)	affected by	transform (verb)	convert; change
suspend (verb)	postpone; delay; stop	transgress (verb)	go over a boundary; trespass
suspicious (adj.)	distrustful; cautious	transient (adj.)	passing; lasts for a short time
sustain (verb)	support; keep up; maintain	transmit (verb)	send; pass along
symbiosis (noun)	relationship that benefits both parties	translucent (adj.)	allowing light to shine through
		transparent (adj.)	clear; see-through
symbol (noun)	item that stands for something else	transpire (verb)	occur; happen; take place
symbolize (verb)	represent; stand for	transport (verb)	carry away from one place to another
synchronize (verb)	cause to happen at same time		
synthesize (verb)	combine; to form single unit	trauma (noun)	shock; severe mental stress
talent (noun)	natural ability to excel	treacherous (adj.)	dangerous
tangible (adj.)	seen, felt or noticed easily	treason (noun)	betrayal of one's country
tantrum (noun)	outburst of anger	tremendous (adj.)	vast; large; great in size
tape (noun)	thin sticky strip of material	tremor (noun)	vibration; shaking; quivering
targets (noun)	marks to shoot at	trend (noun)	current style; new; different
task (noun)	job; chore; something to do	trepidation (noun)	fear; apprehension; anxiety
taste (noun)	experience; try	trespass (verb)	intrude; enter without permission
teacher (noun)	one who instructs	trigger (noun)	set off; cause to happen
team (noun)	group of people	triumph (noun)	great success; victory; achievement
tear (verb)	rip; cut; pull apart		
technique (noun)	way of doing something	trivial (adj.)	insignificant; small; unimportant
technology (noun)	technical knowledge	trophy (noun)	prize; award
tedious (adj.)	dull; boring; monotonous	tumult (noun)	uproar; great confusion
temperamental (adj.)	moody; unpredictable	turmoil (noun)	disturbance; confusion; chaos
temporary (adj.)	short-lived; lasts for short while	ubiquitous (adj.)	seeming to be everywhere
tenacious (adj.)	stubborn; do not give up easily	ultimate (adj.)	final; last
tense (adj.)	anxious; uneasy; nervous	unanimous (adj.)	showing complete agreement; unified
tentative (adj.)	uncertain; not definite		
tenuous (adj.)	having little substance; weak	unbelievable (adj.)	incredible; amazing
tenure (noun)	permanent position as in academia	uncanny (adj.)	strange; mysterious; hard to explain
terminal (adj.)	deadly; cannot be cured	uncomfortable (adj.)	uneasy; disturbed
terminate (verb)	discontinue; put a stop to	unconscious (adj.)	unaware; not awake

Word	Meaning
undercover (adj.)	secret; covert; concealed
undermine (verb)	weaken; less secure
undergo (verb)	pass through; experience
underlying (adj.)	basic; important; vital
underrate (verb)	belittle; fail to recognize one's intelligence
undertake (verb)	agree to; take responsibility
unfair (adj.)	unjust; prejudiced; not right
unfit (adj.)	unsuitable
unforgettable (adj.)	lasting
uniform (adj.)	always the same
unify (verb)	bring together
unique (adj.)	distinctive; special; exceptional
universal (adj.)	worldwide
unreal (adj.)	imaginary; does not exist
unrest (noun)	uneasiness; disturbance
unscrupulous (adj.)	dishonest; without principles
unscathed (adj.)	unharmed; uninjured
unskilled (adj.)	inexperienced; without training
unstable (adj.)	unsteady; erratic; not fixed
untidy (adj.)	messy; not neat
uproar (noun)	chaos; noisy; disturbance
urban (adj.)	relating to a city
urge (noun)	longing; strong desire; yearning
urgent (adj.)	requiring immediate action
usual (adj.)	common; ordinary
utilize (verb)	spend; use
vacant (adj.)	empty; unoccupied
vacillate (verb)	go back and forth; waver; change mind
vague (adj.)	unclear; dubious; doubtful
valiant (adj.)	brave; courageous; audacious
valid (adj.)	genuine
validate (verb)	authorize; give approval to
vanish (verb)	disappear quickly
various (adj.)	many different; assorted
vary (verb)	change
vast (adj.)	immense; extremely large
vehement (adj.)	intense feeling; violent
velocity (noun)	speed; rate of movement
vengeance (noun)	retaliation; revenge
version (noun)	account; interpretation of something
verbal (adj.)	spoken
verdict (noun)	decision; finding
verify (verb)	support; make sure; confirm
versatile (adj.)	flexible; adapt easily
vertical (adj.)	erect; stand straight up
veto (verb)	reject
via (preposition)	by means of; through
viable (adj.)	able to live or survive
vicarious (adj.)	substitute; taking the place of another person or thing
vicinity (noun)	surrounding area
vicious (adj.)	cruel; corrupt; dangerous
victim (noun)	sufferer
vigilant (adj.)	alert; watchful; keen
vigorous (adj.)	full of energy; forceful; strong
vile (adj.)	offensive; unpleasant; disgusting
vindicate (verb)	clear of accusation
vindictive (adj.)	revengeful; hateful
virtue (noun)	goodness; integrity; honor
visible (adj.)	noticeable; can be seen
vital (adj.)	very important; essential; necessary
vivacious (adj.)	lively; full of life; exciting
vivid (adj.)	graphic; clear; bright
vociferous (adj.)	loud; noisy; boisterous
void (verb)	empty; devoid
volume (noun)	amount
voracious (adj.)	excessively eager; very greedy
vulgar (adj.)	obscene
vulnerable (adj.)	susceptible; unprotected; open to attack
wander (verb)	stray; walk around aimlessly; digress
warn (verb)	caution; make aware; notify
warp (verb)	bend out of shape
weak (adj.)	feeble; frail; not healthy
weed (noun)	undesirable plant
weep (verb)	sob; cry
weird (adj.)	strange; odd; eccentric
welcome (verb)	greet; gladly accept; congenial; cordial
whereas (conjunction)	while
whereby (adverb)	by which
whine (verb)	complain in annoying manner about something not important
whisper (verb)	speak with extremely soft voice with the breath
widespread (adj.)	spread out
withdraw (verb)	retreat; take back
yearn (verb)	crave; want or desire strongly
yell (verb)	shout loudly
yield (noun)	return; income from an investment
youth (noun)	youngster; before maturity
zeal (noun)	enthusiasm; zest
zoology (noun)	study of animals

SUGGESTION

Review the Word List and Word Parts tables before you proceed to chapter one.

Coming to America

Chapter 1

PRE-READING

About This Chapter from *Trial of Love*

- Read the names and descriptions of this chapter's main characters below.
    - Sonny Kumar: Husband of Rita Kumar
    - Rita Kumar: Wife of Sonny Kumar
    - Kamla Kumar: Daughter of Sonny and Rita
    - Fernandez: Smuggler of people across the border
    - Jaime: Helper in Fernandez's work

Story Vocabulary Exercise

- Before you begin reading this chapter, figure out the meanings of the unfamiliar **boldfaced** vocabulary words. You may use the Word List, Word Parts Chart, or your dictionary to assist you in finding their meanings.
- Look for the various types of context clues—synonyms, antonyms, general context, and examples—as you read.
- Write a word or phrase about the meaning of each **boldfaced** word in the margin.

Reading and Writing Exercise

- Skim the entire chapter and pay attention to the headings and the discussion questions that follow.
- Initial Response: Write a paragraph explaining, in your own words, what you think this chapter of the story will be about.
- Final Response: After you have read the entire chapter, compare your current understanding with your initial response above. If your initial response was accurate, you can simply write it again to fill in the blanks below. If it was not, then write a paragraph on what the chapter was really about instead.

Initial Response

This chapter **will** be about ____

____

____

____

Final Response

This chapter **was** about ____

____

____

____

COMING TO AMERICA

The bus stopped at a motel in the desert. The empty parking lot and rusted signs showed that it had been **abandoned** long ago.

The bus driver opened the door and said something in Spanish. The four Mexican passengers jumped to their feet and hurried off.

Kamla Kumar looked at her father, Sonny. He was **frowning** at the motel.

"You are sure this is the place?" Sonny asked.

The driver shouted in Spanish again and pointed at the open door.

"Let's go," Sonny said.

When the Kumars and the two other Indian passengers stepped off the bus, nobody remained inside but the driver. He shut the door and drove back toward the city.

The nine of them stood outside, waiting and fearing something **dreadful** might happen. Kamla Kumar ran about ten yards from their drop-off point to the entrance of the motel. She **peered inquisitively** through the broken glass window next to the main door. As she crept like a skillful thief to the next window, a black van suddenly appeared from the back of the motel. It drove into the parking lot and stopped **abruptly**. Everybody **dispersed**, running for a place to hide.

The driver **emerged** from the vehicle and called, "Stop! I'm Fernandez. I'm the man you've been waiting for."

"Why did you **frighten** us? Were you trying to **intimidate** us?" Kamla complained breathlessly. "What took you so long? Do you know we've been traveling for days now with hardly any sleep or food? We left India ten days ago and we still don't know if you can get the job done!"

Fernandez was **startled** by the **fury emanating** from her **distrustful** eyes. Most of the illegal immigrants he dealt with were too frightened to get so angry.

"You seem to be a **loquacious** but **perspicacious** young woman. You talk too much and love to be argumentative, but you're quick to figure things out. I like that in a person. You've got a future in America, my girl.

"Although I've had several years of experience with this sort of **risky** business, I'm not **adroit** at it. On my first trip, I made numerous mistakes because I was a **novice**. There were American agents working **discreetly** undercover. They posed **covertly** as Mexican businessmen who **smuggled illegal** items across the border. I didn't **comprehend** that this was a dirty trick until I was **apprehended** and imprisoned twenty years ago.

"**Clandestine** operations can land people in jail for life. Crossing illegal aliens is a **lucrative** business for Mexicans, but one has to plan **meticulously** to be successful. If you step into the motel, I'll **demonstrate** how I can determine if there are agents in this group."

Kamla realized it was useless, or **futile**, to argue with him, and reluctantly stepped into the motel.

"Do you see that thing over there?" Fernandez asked, pointing to an object in the far right corner of the room.

"Yes."

"What is it?"

"It looks like an **ancient**, worn-out leather coat on a **dilapidated** clothes rack."

"Right. Take a look under the coat."

"You're pretty **shrewd**. A security camera. Isn't that a monitor over there?" Kamla asked with **confidence** while pointing to a screen in the far corner of the room.

"Right again."

"Who taught you these **tricks**, Fernandez?"

"My grandfather owned an electronics store. He taught me several survival tricks that **entailed** the use of an **array** of electronic gadgets—microphones, cameras, and so on. When your group **comprised** of five Indians and four Mexicans arrived, I was inside on the second floor of the motel with the camera. It took only a few minutes to compare the image on the screen with the photographs I received earlier today from my agent who brought you here. However, I was **reluctant** to appear because I observed there were only nine of you. I expected eleven. I also **anticipated** a **mole** in the group who would **betray** me. Then I recalled that **unfortunate** incident in which two people died. That was a **shocking** and unfortunate **tragedy**."

"Just make sure it doesn't happen again," interrupted Sonny, who had just entered the **run-down** motel.

"Accidents are **inevitable**. They will always happen," replied Fernandez casually, as he motioned to Kamla to exit the room.

"Is rape included in the price? We didn't pay you an **exorbitant** sum of money to have our women **molested**," Sonny said with **immense animosity** and **hostility** in his voice. "Don't pretend you don't know that a very young woman from our group was raped by one of your **monstrous cronies**. She was from my village."

"I heard of the incident yesterday. Who raped her?"

"That **egotistical**, **arrogant** drunk who always thought he knew everything. He smelled worse than a **filthy** pig in a sty."

"Hey, wait a minute," Fernandez said. "That's no way to talk about my **pal**. Show some respect. Don't blame him if he's **addicted** to food and has an **insatiable** desire for liquor. He works best when he's **intoxicated**. Underneath that rough exterior, he's really not so bad. He was raised by pious, **compassionate**, nurturing nuns in an **orphanage**. Why didn't someone stop him?"

"Her fiancé tried to. Now they're both dead. Your pal shot them," replied Sonny.

Fernandez **quivered**, shaking with **uncontrollable** anger. He grabbed a chair and hurled it across the room, screaming, "I'll kill that man! He's **ruining** my business, my **reputation**, my dignity! Who will trust me now? I'm going to lose everything if this sort of thing continues!"

"Oh my God! Another **lunatic**, a madman," whispered Sonny fearfully to himself as he inched deliberately toward the door of the motel.

"Stop! Where do you think you're going?" shouted Fernandez.

Kamla and a few of the others rushed into the motel. They had heard the loud noise when Fernandez had thrown the chair.

More calmly, Fernandez said, "I promise it won't happen again. I can control him because he's my cousin. He's spent most of his teenage life in prison. As a matter of fact, he is wanted for armed robbery now. It's just a matter of time before the police **apprehend** him.

"Enough wasted time, my friends," Fernandez continued. "Let's prepare for the crossing. Tell everybody to get ready. It's almost time."

It was about 6:00 p.m. Kamla and the others felt anxious and fearful as they watched Fernandez disappear behind the motel. Minutes later, he returned in a dark blue van that appeared to be older than time. It seemed he wanted to keep his nice black one safe. He instructed them to board immediately.

Fernandez sped from the motel. Occasionally, he slowed down to dodge potholes. Each time he had to decrease his speed, his brows **furrowed** as he frowned. The passengers were packed like Norwegian sardines, but no one complained.

They traveled about ten miles toward the Mexican border without speaking. Just as the group began to relax, the **earsplitting** sound of a siren rang through the night. One of the Mexicans, Raul, shouted, "Traitor! You betrayed us. You're one of those rotten people. I'm going to kill you if you don't get us out of this **mess**."

Fernandez started to speak in Spanish at a very **rapid pace**. Sometimes he paused and bit his fingernails anxiously.

"Raul, what's he saying? Translate. Please translate," implored Kamla.

"He doesn't know how to handle the situation."

"But he should have planned for this, Raul," Sonny interjected. "He was **boasting** about his extensive experience in risky business and now he's sweating **profusely** at the sound of a siren. I can't believe he's so **incompetent**."

"My God!" cried Fernandez, as he pulled off onto the shoulder of the highway and turned off the engine. "Why is this happening to me?"

"Why did you stop the vehicle, traitor?" shouted Raul, as he reached forward to grab the collar of Fernandez's shirt and strike him.

"Leave him alone, Raul. You're hurting him," screamed Kamla.

"Why should I let him get away with this?"

"Don't be **ridiculous**, Raul. We need him. He's the only person able to take us across the border," said Kamla.

"Kamla," shouted her father, Sonny, "he's reaching for his gun!"

"Don't shoot, Fernandez!" yelled everybody in **unison**.

As Fernandez was about to pull his gun from where it was taped beneath the dashboard, a Mexican border patrol officer pulled in front of the van. Raul let Fernandez go. The siren stopped abruptly and the officer approached.

"May I see some identification, please?" the officer asked Fernandez in Spanish.

"Sure, Officer," Fernandez replied in the same language. He moved his hand from his gun to his wallet and nervously extracted his false driver's license, with the name of Hugo Perez on it.

"Here you are, sir. Is this OK?" Fernandez asked.

"Let me look at it," said the border patrol officer.

The officer shined his flashlight on the license and then on Fernandez's face.

"You shouldn't be out here so late. It's dangerous, especially since three murderers escaped from prison and are holding two prison guards **hostage**. That's why I'm patrolling the area." He turned his flashlight on the crowd in the back. "Well, well. We sure have a crowd in here." He pointed the light in each passenger's eyes, one at a time. "Where are the ten of you off to?"

"Nuevo Laredo, Officer," Fernandez said. "We're just on our way back from a wedding. My daughter-in-law is from India."

"All right. I'll let you guys get off easy tonight. I'd normally ask a few more questions to make sure you aren't making a run for the border, but these murderers are more important. Just be careful, Mr. Perez. Don't pick up any **hitchhikers**."

"Of course. Have a good night, Officer."

They drove in silence for thirty minutes. Everybody was frustrated and distrustful of Fernandez.

"We're almost there. My **informant**, Jaime, should appear any moment with instructions. Watch out for him," requested Fernandez politely.

"Stop, stop," commanded Kamla. "Is that the person?"

"Where is he?" inquired Fernandez anxiously.

"You've just passed him. Is he a short, slim fellow wearing a green cap?"

"That's him."

"Well, stop and wait for him."

"No. I've got to continue driving. If he's my informant, he'll get on the highway and flash his flashlight three times."

"Look, that's exactly what's he's doing," said Kamla.

"I can see him clearly now in the rear-view mirror." Fernandez breathed a sigh of relief. It was the end of the highway. He made a left turn onto a **trail** that continued where the highway left off and waited for his informant. In less than five minutes, Jaime approached them.

"Good news, my friends. All is clear on the American side of the border. But you must hurry," cautioned Jaime.

Jaime left to return to the American side of the border **via** his secret way. Then Fernandez instructed everybody to follow him after they **disembarked** from the van. They walked wearily down the lonely trail.

"How much longer do we have to **endure** this suffering, Fernandez?" asked Sonny.

Fernandez replied, "We're almost there. Just be patient."

They dragged themselves for another fifty yards before Fernandez stopped to give his final instructions. "Everybody, listen to me **attentively**. You need to hear every word I'm about to say because you must **adhere** to my instructions **meticulously**. If you make a mistake, the plan could be **thwarted** by the border patrol, and we'll be in big trouble."

"We're listening. Would you hurry?" said Kamla.

"Look over there. Can you see it?" Fernandez asked them while pointing to a ball of flashing light ahead.

"See what?" inquired Kamla.

"That bright, blinding light. It's the American border patrol's light. It's from a tower about twenty feet high. There are usually two patrolmen in the tower at all times. If you observe, it **rotates** slowly and shines on the Mexican side of the border once every forty-five seconds. As we get closer to the border, you'll see the river that separates Mexico and America. Connecting the two countries is a narrow twenty-foot wooden bridge. That light shines directly on the bridge. This means you must cross it within those forty-five seconds. The river is deep and is **infested** with crocodiles, so you must be extremely careful not to fall in. One person has to cross the bridge at a time. When you cross over to the other side, you'll be approached by my partner. Follow his instructions."

They walked down the trail with renewed energy and strength. In less than ten minutes, they saw the wooden bridge. Fernandez assured them that they would be able to cross without difficulties. He asked everybody to stand in single file.

Sonny was the first person to cross. He was followed by his wife, Rita, and then the others.

"That's beautiful. Number seven, go for it. Good lord! He fell. Get up! Get up!" commanded Fernandez.

"But he can't. He's hurt," whispered Kamla.

"Please hurry. Hurry, son. You have twenty seconds," encouraged Fernandez. Finally the young boy was able to get up and cross the bridge.

"Thank God he made it," said Kamla.

Fernandez was **furious** with the delay. He looked like he wanted to hit the boy. "Number eight. Get ready."

Kamla was number eight. She made it across without difficulty. There was only one person left to cross after her. Fernandez was not as **irritated** as before and urged the last person to cross.

"Stella, it's your turn. Good luck."

Stella started out slowly and appeared **reluctant** to cross. It seemed as if she knew something

dreadful would happen.

"Is something wrong, Stella?" inquired Fernandez.

"No."

"Don't you want to cross? Your husband and friends are waiting for you in America."

Stella finally began walking **briskly** over the bridge. Halfway across, she turned around and ran back to the Mexican side of the border. As she was about to **descend** the bridge, she turned back again and attempted to cross the bridge to enter America. The light struck her. An American border patrol officer was waiting on the other side for her.

Fernandez witnessed the incident but was helpless to **render** assistance at that moment. He wondered if the border guard had caught the others. It was too dark for him to see what was **transpiring** on the American side of the border.

"Come on, my darling. Don't be afraid," said the patrolman, who was standing on the bridge with folded arms.

As he approached Stella, she backed slowly away from him, hoping that Fernandez would rescue her.

"I know you want the American dream," the guard said **mockingly**.

Stella realized it was futile to resist him. He was six feet tall and muscular. She stopped backing away from him and threw herself down deliberately on the bridge. He tried to **drag** her toward the American side of the border, but Stella managed to hold on to one of the bridge's vertical supporting structures. She struggled to free herself from the guard's **grasp** without success. He lifted her up. She tried to run away, but he grabbed the sleeve of her blouse. It ripped and exposed her arm.

"You're hurting me. Please stop. Let me go," she pleaded.

He ignored her plea, but she wasn't prepared to **surrender** to him without a fight. To her advantage, he was tired to the point of collapse, as he had worked a double shift the day before. Stella **mustered** all her strength and kicked him in the groin. He groaned like a wounded animal and **collapsed** instantly.

"Freeze!" shouted a voice from the tower, and the enormous light pointed directly into Stella's eyes, blinding her. "You're under arrest!"

Stella heard Fernandez's friend, Jaime, shouting from the American side of the border. "Hurry! He won't shoot, and there are two vehicles approaching! We must leave before more officers arrive!"

Stella began to **panic** and ran. Despite Jaime's promise, she heard the sound of gunfire behind her. Jaime **revved** the engine impatiently as she approached the van and began moving as soon as she got near. Kamla slid the door open and pulled her inside, and Jaime stepped on the gas pedal and sped off toward Dallas, Texas.

EXERCISE 1

Applying the Words You Have Learned to Critical Thinking and Creative Writing

- Use the two questions in Section A below to discuss this chapter with your classmates. Be sure to apply your critical thinking skills.

- Write an essay about either question using the vocabulary words you know from real-life experiences and the new ones you have learned from this text.

Section A

Discussion Questions

1. What are some reasons why a person would want to leave his/her country?

2. Many people experience great physical and emotional pain when they try to enter another country illegally. Do you agree or disagree?

EXERCISE 2

Forming Synonyms

■ Fill in the blank(s) to complete the word that is similar in meaning to the **boldfaced** word.

1. **pace** sp__ __d
2. **palpitate** th__ __b
3. **patience** toler__ __ce
4. **persevere** en __u__e
5. **victim** suf__ __r__r
6. **prone** lik__ __y
7. **utilize** spe__d
8. **prevail** ab__ __nd
9. **posture** st__n__e
10. **provocative** irri__ __ __ing
11. **parade** proc__ __s__on
12. **penalize** pun__ __h
13. **pertain** r__ __ate
14. **pilfer** s__ __a__
15. **pity** com__ __ __ __ion
16. **poisonous** tox__ __
17. **pledge** o__ __h
18. **possess** __wn
19. **practice** pr__ __ __re
20. **prank** tr__ __k
21. **topic** s__ __j__ __t
22. **toxic** no__ __ __us
23. **treacherous** da__ __ __r__us
24. **trophy** p__ __ze

EXERCISE 3

Synonyms and Antonyms

■ Write the corresponding letter for the synonym and antonym of each **boldfaced** word.

	Synonym	Antonym			
1. **acquire**	______	______	**A.** gain	**B.** joy	**C.** lose
2. **admit**	______	______	**A.** consent	**B.** done	**C.** deny
3. **affection**	______	______	**A.** love	**B.** sit	**C.** dislike
4. **agile**	______	______	**A.** fast	**B.** jump	**C.** slow
5. **acknowledge**	______	______	**A.** tell	**B.** recognize	**C.** ignore
6. **achieve**	______	______	**A.** sing	**B.** accomplish	**C.** fail
7. **accuse**	______	______	**A.** blame	**B.** exonerate	**C.** rush
8. **accept**	______	______	**A.** approve	**B.** reject	**C.** run
9. **abstract**	______	______	**A.** concrete	**B.** theoretical	**C.** laughter
10. **abolish**	______	______	**A.** cancel	**B.** like	**C.** retain
11. **abhor**	______	______	**A.** listen	**B.** hate	**C.** love
12. **aloof**	______	______	**A.** upside	**B.** distant	**C.** friendly
13. **antagonize**	______	______	**A.** provoke	**B.** affect	**C.** soothe
14. **appease**	______	______	**A.** calm	**B.** irritate	**C.** fast
15. **affirm**	______	______	**A.** confirm	**B.** deny	**C.** fasten
16. **adept**	______	______	**A.** skillful	**B.** likely	**C.** unskillful
17. **aggravate**	______	______	**A.** soon	**B.** annoy	**C.** pacify
18. **ample**	______	______	**A.** taste	**B.** plenty	**C.** insufficient
19. **awkward**	______	______	**A.** clumsy	**B.** happen	**C.** graceful
20. **absurd**	______	______	**A.** foolish	**B.** mighty	**C.** sensible
21. **arrogant**	______	______	**A.** haughty	**B.** petty	**C.** humble
22. **audible**	______	______	**A.** clear	**B.** unclear	**C.** pause
23. **auspicious**	______	______	**A.** favorable	**B.** untimely	**C.** listless
24. **austere**	______	______	**A.** petite	**B.** harsh	**C.** soft
25. **available**	______	______	**A.** sustain	**B.** ready	**C.** inaccessible
26. **altruistic**	______	______	**A.** generous	**B.** simple	**C.** selfish

	Synonym	Antonym			
27. **attest**	______	______	**A.** verify	**B.** refute	**C.** tough
28. **adjust**	______	______	**A.** change	**B.** belittle	**C.** maintain
29. **adhere**	______	______	**A.** abhor	**B.** cling	**C.** detach
30. **absent**	______	______	**A.** detest	**B.** away	**C.** present
31. **abrupt**	______	______	**A.** sudden	**B.** gradual	**C.** yell
32. **adverse**	______	______	**A.** unfavorable	**B.** advantageous	**C.** youthful
33. **aspire**	______	______	**A.** desire	**B.** vacant	**C.** repudiate
34. **admonish**	______	______	**A.** warn	**B.** visit	**C.** praise
35. **attain**	______	______	**A.** weird	**B.** obtain	**C.** lose
36. **astute**	______	______	**A.** smart	**B.** calm	**C.** stupid
37. **apprehensive**	______	______	**A.** fearful	**B.** happen	**C.** brave
38. **assimilate**	______	______	**A.** integrate	**B.** isolate	**C.** weird
39. **attrition**	______	______	**A.** witty	**B.** decrease	**C.** increase
40. **bad**	______	______	**A.** salute	**B.** evil	**C.** good
41. **barren**	______	______	**A.** unfertile	**B.** speed	**C.** productive
42. **belated**	______	______	**A.** late	**B.** belittle	**C.** early
43. **belief**	______	______	**A.** adhere	**B.** trust	**C.** doubt
44. **beneficial**	______	______	**A.** helpful	**B.** dark	**C.** harmful
45. **better**	______	______	**A.** superior	**B.** full	**C.** worse
46. **bitter**	______	______	**A.** failure	**B.** unpleasant	**C.** pleasant
47. **borrow**	______	______	**A.** fair	**B.** take temporarily	**C.** return
48. **brave**	______	______	**A.** courageous	**B.** retard	**C.** cowardly
49. **break**	______	______	**A.** separate into pieces	**B.** mend	**C.** fair
50. **brief**	______	______	**A.** short	**B.** long	**C.** strange
51. **bright**	______	______	**A.** shining	**B.** sing	**C.** dull
52. **buy**	______	______	**A.** reject	**B.** purchase	**C.** sell
53. **baffle**	______	______	**A.** honor	**B.** puzzle	**C.** enlighten
54. **benefactor**	______	______	**A.** supporter	**B.** city	**C.** critic
55. **barrier**	______	______	**A.** obstacle	**B.** aid	**C.** quiet

	Synonym	Antonym			
56. **boss**	_______	_______	**A.** patron	**B.** supervisor	**C.** employee
57. **bother**	_______	_______	**A.** court	**B.** disturb	**C.** pacify
58. **boycott**	_______	_______	**A.** ban	**B.** success	**C.** acceptance
59. **brilliant**	_______	_______	**A.** bright	**B.** dull	**C.** scold
60. **burst**	_______	_______	**A.** explode	**B.** receive	**C.** implode
61. **convert**	_______	_______	**A.** change	**B.** maintain	**C.** confide
62. **concurrent**	_______	_______	**A.** simultaneous	**B.** lose	**C.** differing
63. **confiscate**	_______	_______	**A.** seize	**B.** saint	**C.** donate
64. **congenial**	_______	_______	**A.** scold	**B.** pleasant	**C.** unpleasant
65. **consensus**	_______	_______	**A.** agreement	**B.** conflict	**C.** distant
66. **constrict**	_______	_______	**A.** reduce	**B.** still	**C.** enlarge
67. **contemporary**	_______	_______	**A.** modern	**B.** decision	**C.** old-fashioned
68. **circumvent**	_______	_______	**A.** avoid	**B.** stick	**C.** confront
69. **cause**	_______	_______	**A.** reason	**B.** clamor	**C.** result
70. **concise**	_______	_______	**A.** try	**B.** brief	**C.** lengthy
71. **complain**	_______	_______	**A.** rim	**B.** protest	**C.** approve
72. **chief**	_______	_______	**A.** confirm	**B.** primary	**C.** secondary
73. **chance**	_______	_______	**A.** lose	**B.** risk	**C.** secure
74. **caution**	_______	_______	**A.** care	**B.** constant	**C.** recklessness
75. **cancel**	_______	_______	**A.** terminate	**B.** continue	**C.** confess

EXERCISE 4

More Practice with Synonyms

■ Circle the letter of the word or phrase that is most similar in meaning to the **boldfaced** word.

	A	B	C	D
1. **betray**	**A.** deceive	**B.** take	**C.** silent	**D.** try
2. **deliberate** move	**A.** intentional	**B.** reality	**C.** deliver	**D.** distant
3. **bankrupt**	**A.** abundant	**B.** financially ruined	**C.** tired	**D.** plenty
4. **demonstrate** a procedure	**A.** tell	**B.** show	**C.** trace	**D.** talk
5. bear a **burden**	**A.** hardship	**B.** battle	**C.** birth	**D.** beside
6. **deprive**	**A.** withhold	**B.** detain	**C.** give	**D.** assist
7. **deviate**	**A.** stand	**B.** depart from	**C.** return	**D.** resist
8. **brutal** enemy	**A.** kind	**B.** friendly	**C.** loyal	**D.** cruel
9. **detect** a movement	**A.** notice	**B.** neglect	**C.** pursue	**D.** follow
10. take the **blame**	**A.** praise	**B.** worth	**C.** fault	**D.** popularity
11. **desperate** plea	**A.** unusual	**B.** urgent	**C.** bad	**D.** silly
12. **boredom**	**A.** ennui	**B.** unhappiness	**C.** silence	**D.** death
13. **bourgeois**	**A.** famous	**B.** middle-class	**C.** rich	**D.** barely
14. **benign**	**A.** nightly	**B.** dangerous	**C.** harmless	**D.** fatal
15. a **brisk** walk	**A.** vigorous	**B.** brief	**C.** lazy	**D.** short
16. **buoyant**	**A.** sinking	**B.** floating	**C.** under	**D.** heavy
17. **categorize** the books	**A.** arrange	**B.** destroy	**C.** tear	**D.** collect
18. **cease**	**A.** begin	**B.** stop	**C.** quiet	**D.** fancy
19. **conscious** during surgery	**A.** sleepy	**B.** drowsy	**C.** awake	**D.** cheap
20. **considerable** amount	**A.** sizeable	**B.** little	**C.** small	**D.** change
21. **comparison**	**A.** likeness	**B.** familiar	**C.** dissimilar	**D.** unlike
22. a **convincing** liar	**A.** honest	**B.** persuasive	**C.** truthful	**D.** tough
23. a major **catastrophe**	**A.** victory	**B.** triumph	**C.** tragedy	**D.** trial
24. **conceited** millionaire	**A.** self-important	**B.** rich	**C.** risky	**D.** whole
25. **conclusion**	**A.** part	**B.** end	**C.** compose	**D.** extra
26. **compulsory**	**A.** trifle	**B.** betray	**C.** required	**D.** hope
27. boost his **confidence**	**A.** certainty	**B.** religion	**C.** concern	**D.** care
28. a **credible** witness	**A.** disloyal	**B.** believable	**C.** disturb	**D.** slept
29. a patient **collapsed**	**A.** stood	**B.** fell	**C.** fought	**D.** scored
30. earned a **compliment**	**A.** scold	**B.** ignore	**C.** praise	**D.** sweet
31. a **candid** remark	**A.** frank	**B.** silly	**C.** dirty	**D.** huge
32. a **dirty** room	**A.** unclean	**B.** neat	**C.** small	**D.** huge

EXERCISE 5

Word Meaning in Context: Set 1

■ Read each sentence and find the missing word in the box below. Fill in the blank with the correct *form* of that word.

boredom	**demonstrate**	**brutal**	**deprive**
betray	**blame**	**burden**	**deliberate**
bankrupt	**detect**	**desperate**	**deviate**

1. I will tell you a secret if you promise not to ___________ my confidence.
2. After ___________ for five hours, the jury found the defendant innocent.
3. In the end, his high-risk ventures ___________ the company.
4. It is preferable to have someone ___________ a technique than to read an instruction manual.
5. Having a child with disabilities is a difficult ___________ for most families to bear.
6. By ___________ herself of desserts for a month, she was able to lose ten pounds.
7. The rules at the school were strict, and anyone who ___________ from them was expelled immediately.
8. Because the murder was so ___________, the commissioner assigned twenty police officers to the case.
9. If you ___________ any odor of gas in your apartment, call the utility company immediately.
10. I was ___________ for the accident despite my protests that I was not even at work the day it happened.
11. Because he was so ___________ to buy drugs, he did not think twice before stealing money from his mother's wallet.
12. ___________ is often a factor when children drop out of school.

EXERCISE 6

Word Meaning in Context: Set 2

■ Read each sentence and find the missing word in the box below. Fill in the blank with the correct *form* of that word.

considerable	**cease**	**catastrophe**	**benign**
candid	**buoyant**	**bourgeois**	**conscious**
definite	**brisk**	**categorize**	**compulsory**

1. His ___________ childhood left him unprepared for the poverty in which he suddenly found himself.
2. To everyone's relief, the tumor was diagnosed as ___________.
3. As part of my exercise program, I take a ___________ walk for thirty minutes every day.
4. His mood was ___________ when he went to work in the morning, but his spirits sank when he discovered that someone else had been recommended for the promotion.
5. Linnaeus was the first to systematically ___________ members of the plant and animal kingdoms.
6. When the noise of the road repair finally ___________, quietness returned to the neighborhood.
7. Despite a severe blow to the head, the accident victim was still ___________ .

8. A ___________ number of people in the United States never exercise their right to vote.

9. Please give me your ___________ opinion of this essay.

10. While we hope to release the movie on August 15, this date is not ___________.

11. Physical education is a ___________ subject in most American high schools.

12. The earthquake was the greatest ___________ the country had ever experienced.

EXERCISE 7

Context Clues

- Select the word or phrase that most closely matches the meaning of the **boldfaced** word. *Note that replacing the **boldfaced** word with the right answer might not produce a grammatically correct sentence.*

1. Joining a military **academy** will help a soldier prepare to become a high-ranking officer.
   A. program **B.** dormitory **C.** club **D.** school

2. They will **accumulate** a great deal of wealth by investing carefully.
   A. build up **B.** steal **C.** forfeit **D.** adjust

3. It is important to be **accurate** when measuring the ingredients for a cake.
   A. generous **B.** quiet **C.** exact **D.** bold

4. Immigrating to a new country requires people to **adapt** to new traditions and cultures.
   A. produce **B.** battle **C.** confess **D.** adjust

5. A new shopping mall will be built **adjacent** to the highway to allow for easy access.
   A. over **B.** next to **C.** distant **D.** after

6. This new job requires that someone **administrate** the day-to-day operations of the human resources department, which includes assigning employees to tasks and supervising meetings.
   A. undermine **B.** verify **C.** supervise **D.** fix

7. Felicia refused to let her daughter go to the party when she heard there would be no **adults** present.
   A. grown-ups **B.** professionals **C.** adolescents **D.** actors

8. The city's decision to limit bus service will negatively **affect** families who depend on public transportation to travel to work and school.
   A. scare **B.** cripple **C.** deny **D.** influence

9. The new computer software program can **aggregate** monthly sales in a reliable, comprehensive format.
   A. lose **B.** distort **C.** put together **D.** create

10. The charity is asking for more donations and **aid** to feed the thousands of families who evacuated their homes during the hurricane.
    A. help **B.** votes **C.** change **D.** force

11. I took painkillers to **alleviate** the pain.

    A. worsen **B.** lessen **C.** forget **D.** dismiss

12. The insurance company is prepared to **allocate** the monies needed to pay back homeowners whose properties were damaged by recent flooding.

    A. distribute **B.** ask for **C.** collapse **D.** raise

13. We planned to go hunting, but we **altered** our plan and went skiing instead.

    A. got rid of **B.** changed **C.** upgraded **D.** forgot

14. The city council will have to **amend** the law if it wants to make employers pay workers the federal minimum wage.

    A. erase **B.** imagine **C.** revise **D.** veto

15. Stories are often used as **analogies** to explain difficult ideas.

    A. contrasts **B.** equations **C.** effects **D.** comparisons

16. The board of directors must approve the **annual** budget every year.

    A. weekly **B.** daily **C.** yearly **D.** monthly

17. The lawyers wanted to **append** a new section to the settlement to avoid future legal problems.

    A. add **B.** send **C.** write **D.** cancel

18. The marketing agent was careful in his **approach** to convince the new client to invest more money in advertising.

    A. idea **B.** lack of morals **C.** letter **D.** method

19. The new public recreation **area** will include a space that private companies can rent.

    A. section **B.** park **C.** business **D.** view

20. A different **aspect** of the plan was presented at the meeting.

    A. formula **B.** criticism **C.** part **D.** demonstration

21. Mike was skilled at reading instructions, so he was able to **assemble** the desk in less than half an hour.

    A. take apart **B.** place upright **C.** put together **D.** sell

22. Before the police could try to rescue the hostages, they first had to **assess** the safety of the people inside.

    A. improve **B.** give up on **C.** question **D.** evaluate

23. The new communications director had to **assign** new job responsibilities to her staff.

    A. give out **B.** allow **C.** oversee **D.** mention

24. Some experts believe people have become too **attached** to their cellphones and tablet computers.

    A. disgusted **B.** dependent **C.** accustomed **D.** uncomfortable

EXERCISE 8

Vocabulary Test

- Select the correct answer.
- Hint: Review the meanings of all the **boldfaced** words in this chapter before you take the test. This approach can help you to score 100 percent.
- Record the percentage of correct answers on the Master Self-Assessment table on page 397.

1 Another word for **pace** is:

A. spread **B.** speed

C. run **D.** slow

2 A synonym for **palpitate** is:

E. stationary **F.** vibrate

G. cough **H.** dancer

3 A **victim** is a:

A. writer **B.** seller

C. sufferer **D.** dancer

4 A synonym for **prone** is:

E. likely **F.** daring

G. seldom **H.** certain

5 To **utilize** means to:

A. unite **B.** dare

C. bare **D.** use

6 A synonym for **prevail** is:

E. come out on top **F.** stare

G. blow **H.** evade

7 To be **provocative** is to be:

A. silly **B.** funny

C. kind **D.** irritating

8 Another word for **pertain** is:

E. say **F.** sing

G. relate **H.** suggest

9 **Pilfer** means to:

A. demand **B.** comply

C. steal **D.** give

10 To **persevere** means to:

E. slow down **F.** give up

G. carry on **H.** return

11 A **prank** is a:

A. reward **B.** gift

C. trick **D.** compliment

12 **Noxious** means:

E. poisonous **F.** clean

G. healthy **H.** airy

13 A person who is **treacherous** is:

A. dangerous **B.** likeable

C. enduring **D.** friendly

14 An antonym for **admit** is:

E. deny **F.** consent

G. relay **H.** look at

15 An antonym for **agile** is:

A. fast **B.** jump

C. slow **D.** crawl

16 To **acknowledge** is to:

E. tell **F.** recognize

G. discuss **H.** deny

17 The opposite of **abstract** is:

A. concrete
B. theoretical
C. laughter
D. joy

18 To **abolish** is to:

E. put an end to
F. hate
G. love
H. promote

19 An **adept** worker is:

A. skillful
B. adorable
C. unskillful
D. punctual

20 To **abhor** someone is to:

E. hate
F. love
G. listen
H. enjoy

21 **Aloof** means:

A. upside-down
B. detached
C. friendly
D. secure

22 The opposite of **antagonize** is:

E. provoke
F. affect
G. soothe
H. stop

23 To **appease** means to:

A. calm
B. irritate
C. fight
D. enjoy

24 To **aggravate** is to:

E. molest
F. annoy
G. pacify
H. clear

25 An antonym for **absurd** is:

A. foolish
B. mighty
C. sensible
D. hasty

26 An antonym for **arrogant** is:

E. haughty
F. humble
G. petty
H. gentle

27 **Ample** means:

A. tasteful
B. healthy
C. plentiful
D. greedy

28 Someone who is **awkward** is:

E. clumsy
F. happy
G. graceful
H. dear

29 Another word for **austere** is:

A. appetite
B. harsh
C. soft
D. gentle

30 A person who is **altruistic** is:

E. generous
F. simple
G. selfish
H. alert

31 An antonym for **attest** is:

A. verify
B. refute
C. tough
D. simple

32 To **admonish** someone is to:

E. visit
F. warn
G. praise
H. abolish

33 **Astute** means:

A. smart
B. calm
C. foolish
D. silly

34 An antonym for **apprehensive** is:

E. stop
F. fearful
G. stupid
H. brave

35 An antonym for **assimilate** is:

A. weird
B. divide
C. isolate
D. integrate

36 Land that is **barren** is:

E. infertile
F. productive
G. fruitful
H. seasonal

37 A synonym for **baffle** is:

A. honor
B. enlighten
C. known
D. puzzle

38 A **benefactor** is a:

E. priest
F. city
G. critic
H. donor

39 A **barrier** is an:

A. author
B. entity
C. obstacle
D. aide

40 To **boycott** is to:

E. ban
F. succeed
G. accept
H. direct

41 **Concur** means to:

A. agree
B. lose
C. gain
D. disagree

42 To **confiscate** is to:

E. seize
F. donate
G. conquer
H. evaluate

43 A **congenial** person is:

A. unpleasant
B. friendly
C. scolding
D. active

44 To **circumvent** means to:

E. avoid
F. stick to
G. repair
H. adhere

45 A **parade** is a:

A. street fair
B. stroll
C. procession
D. jug

46 To **penalize** is to:

E. punish
F. care
G. show courage
H. weaken

47 A **trophy** is a:

A. calling
B. promise
C. prize
D. decision

48 An **abrupt** stop is:

E. sudden
F. gradual
G. grinding
H. sliding

49 **Adverse** weather conditions are:

A. favorable
B. unfavorable
C. rainy
D. humid

50 **Aspire** means to:

E. desire
F. vacate
G. repudiate
H. discard

51 **Attrition** is the process of:

A. increasing
B. decreasing
C. subtracting
D. withholding

52 An antonym for **belated** is:

E. late
F. belittle
G. early
H. soon

53 **Bitter** is a synonym for:

A. tasty
B. sweet
C. unpleasant
D. pleasant

54 To **convert** something is to:

E. maintain
F. upkeep
G. change
H. develop

55 To have a **consensus** is to have:

A. agreement
B. denial
C. joy
D. peace

56 A **cause** is a:

E. reason
F. result
G. clamor
H. decision

57 To be **concise** is to be:

A. lengthy
B. wordy
C. silent
D. brief

58 To **betray** someone is to:

E. be disloyal
F. praise
G. neglect
H. honor

59 A **deliberate** action is:

A. intentional
B. real
C. awkward
D. unknown

60 **Bankrupt** means:

E. plenty
F. abundant
G. surplus
H. financially ruined

61 To **demonstrate** a procedure is to:

A. tell
B. show
C. verify
D. advertise

62 A **burden** is a:

E. battle
F. birth
G. joy
H. hardship

63 To **deprive** someone of something is to:

A. withhold
B. give
C. assist
D. donate

64 When you **deviate** from a path, you:

E. stand
F. depart from
G. return
H. retire

65 A **brutal** enemy is:

A. kind
B. ugly
C. loyal
D. cruel

66 **Bourgeois** refers to the:

E. famous
F. middle class
G. innocent
H. poor

67 A **benign** tumor is:

A. fatal
B. dangerous
C. harmless
D. harmful

68 A **brisk** walk is:

E. short
F. long
G. brief
H. vigorous

69 **Buoyant** means:

A. floating
B. heavy
C. shallow
D. deep

70 A **catastrophe** is a:

E. victory
F. triumph
G. tragedy
H. trial

71 A **conceited** millionaire is:

A. self-important
B. famous
C. respectful
D. humble

72 **Compulsory** means:

E. significant
F. acceptable
G. required
H. unnecessary

73 A **credible** witness is:

A. disloyal
B. dishonest
C. unstable
D. believable

74 A **compliment** is a form of:

E. praise
F. scolding
G. score
H. prize

75 A remark that is **candid** is:

A. frank
B. silly
C. dirty
D. sweet

EXERCISE 9

Building a Stronger Vocabulary

- Review all the **boldfaced** words in this chapter before you proceed to the next exercise.
- Highlight the ones you are still having difficulty remembering.
- List them with their meanings on a table.
- Use them to compose your own sentences.
- Think of a synonym and an antonym for each word.
- Use checkmarks to indicate if each word you want to practice more has a prefix, suffix, and/or root.
- You may use the table below as a sample to write your answers in your notebook.

Word	Definition	Sentence	Synonym	Antonym	Prefix	Suffix	Root

EXERCISE 10

Creating My Own Powerful Word List

- Write the words and meanings from the above table on the **Creating My Own Powerful Word List** table on page 398. Review them often to build that super vocabulary you want to create for school, work, and everyday use.

Chapter 2 On Their Way to New York

PRE-READING

About This Chapter from *Trial of Love*

- Read the names and descriptions of this chapter's main characters below.
  - Sonny and his family
  - Jose: Fernandez's assistant
  - Dr. Joshi: Rita's brother
  - Errol: Taxi driver

Story Vocabulary Exercise

- Before you begin reading this chapter, figure out the meanings of the unfamiliar **boldfaced** vocabulary words. You may use the Word List, Word Parts Chart, or your dictionary to assist you in finding their meanings.
- Look for the various types of context clues—synonyms, antonyms, general context, and examples—as you read.
- Write a word or phrase about the meaning of each **boldfaced** word in the margin.

Reading and Writing Exercise

- Skim the entire chapter and pay attention to the headings and the discussion questions that follow.
- Initial Response: Write a paragraph explaining, in your own words, what you think this chapter of the story will be about.
- Final Response: After you have read the entire chapter, compare your current understanding with your initial response above. If your initial response was accurate, you can simply write it again to fill in the blanks below. If it was not, then write a paragraph on what the chapter was really about instead.

Initial Response

This chapter **will** be about ______________________________

____

____

____

Final Response

This chapter **was** about ______________________________

____

____

____

ON THEIR WAY TO NEW YORK

It was about midnight when Sonny, Kamla, and Rita were dropped off at the Bruno Inn in Dallas. For the first time in the two weeks since they had left India, they felt excited and **elated**. Coming to America was what they had **yearned** for their entire lives.

Jose, Fernandez's partner in Texas, had **reserved** a room for them at an inn, paying for it before they arrived. He left as soon as they entered their room.

Room 555 was very small. The walls were off-white and smelled moldy. The scent was so **offensive** that it could **induce** instant **nausea**. The room had almost no furniture, except for a huge green leather sofa, a single bed, and four chairs seated around a small oval-shaped table.

Sonny locked the door and walked over to the bed to rest briefly. In the meantime, Rita and Kamla began unpacking their bags. After everybody had a bath, the family sat at the table and enjoyed chicken sandwiches purchased by Jose. There was hardly any conversation while they **devoured** their sandwiches like starved tigers.

As Sonny was about to take his last bite, there was a sudden banging on the door. He whispered to his wife and daughter, asking them to be quiet. The loud noise seemed to have confused Rita. She looked **perplexed**. Kamla was visibly amazed. Rita **motioned** to Sonny to answer the door. He shook his head in **disbelief** and said quietly, "Who could it be at this hour?"

"I don't know," replied Rita. "It's 1:00 a.m. We've just checked in. Nobody knows we're here except the clerk. I can't believe this is happening to us."

"It's probably the immigration officers," remarked Kamla. Sonny became tense on hearing her guess.

"What should we do? It makes no sense to ignore the person at the door, Sonny," said Rita.

Sonny got out of the chair and tip-toed **stealthily** to the door without making a sound. He **peered** through the peephole cautiously.

"There's someone here," whispered Sonny, after looking through the hole in the door.

"We're aware of that, Dad. Who is it?"

"I can't see clearly. I think it's a woman."

Sonny **gestured** for them to hide in the closet, waving his hand toward it. Kamla frowned. She knew a closet was not the best place to hide. Her dad could see her unwillingness to obey him, and his eyes widened with anger at her **obvious reluctance**. Sonny did not like **defiance** or disobedience. He often lost his temper when people did not listen to him.

Someone inserted a key in the lock. Sonny signaled to them again to hide. Rita knew it was useless to disagree with him. She held Kamla's arm and pulled her forcefully into the closet. Suddenly, Kamla's eye caught a baseball bat that was sitting under the bed. She motioned to her dad to get it before shutting herself and her mother inside.

The door opened slowly as Sonny positioned himself behind it to attack with the baseball bat. A faint, feminine voice said, "Room service. I'll be back later." Without entering the room, the motel maid placed a bundle of towels on a small table next to the door. She closed it gently and left. Sonny felt relieved. He wondered what the maid had been thinking, coming up to an occupied room at this hour. Perhaps Jose had sent her.

The family could not keep their eyes open for another minute. Rita and Kamla went to sleep in the bed while Sonny fell asleep on the sofa.

Several hours later, Kamla was awakened by a loud noise. She was alone in the bed.

"Mom, where are you?"

There was no answer.

"Mom, are you there in the bathroom?"

When there was no response again, Kamla was suddenly **seized** by panic. She jumped out of bed and saw that her mother was sleeping next to her dad on the sofa.

Rita had not been able to sleep in the bed because of Kamla's **relentless** snoring. It just kept going all night long.

Kamla **tapped** her mother's shoulder repeatedly.

"Where are we? What time is it, Kamla?" her mother, Rita, asked when her eyes opened.

"It's 9:00 a.m. Mom, there's somebody at the door. You and Dad have to get dressed."

"It's probably room service again. Why don't you look through the peephole and see who's there? In the meantime, your dad and I will get dressed in the bathroom."

"Just a minute. I'm coming," responded Kamla as she heard the knock at the door again.

Kamla was **baffled** when she opened the door and saw Jose, who was wearing a serious look on his face. She invited him into their room and offered him a seat at the table. By that time, Sonny was fully dressed. He joined Jose at the table while Kamla went to shower.

"Jose, sorry I can't offer you coffee," said Sonny **apologetically**.

"It's OK. How is your family?"

"They're **coping**. They're trying to deal with the situation. What brings you here today, Jose?"

Jose was caught off-guard by Sonny's question.

"What did you say, Sonny?"

"I would like to know why you're here."

"I'm here for our money."

"What money?"

"You know, our fee for crossing you and your family. Twenty thousand dollars."

"I told your partner, Fernandez, that he'll get it within a few days. That was our agreement."

"I understand. But circumstances have changed. We think there'll be an investigation on the border patrolman's death. Did you read today's newspaper?"

"No."

Jose **whipped** a copy out of his briefcase and gave it to Sonny.

"Read it, my friend," insisted Jose.

"My God!" exclaimed Sonny. "According to this article, one of the patrolmen died from a gunshot wound. Stella didn't have a gun."

"But shots were fired."

"Yes. I remember. Stella isn't the murderer. She didn't kill anyone."

"Probably someone in the vehicles that were approaching us shot him."

"I don't think so."

"It's the police's job to find the killer, Sonny. My job is to get $20,000 from you and leave right away," said Jose in a very demanding tone.

Sonny observed that Jose was very tense. He felt that he was **untrustworthy**. Although the room was not warm, Jose was constantly wiping **huge beads** of perspiration from his forehead.

"Jose, I'll have to talk with my family about this matter."

"Hurry up. I don't have **ample** time, so I can't afford to sit around chatting with you. I have to collect our fees from the others before they leave. They are only staying **temporarily** at other motels in the area."

Sonny got up and went to the bathroom to talk with Rita and Kamla.

"We heard everything, Dad. We should telephone uncle Joshi. He said he'd have the money ready when I spoke with him back in India," Kamla reminded her father.

Moments later, Sonny and Kamla hurried to the telephone. Sonny dialed Joshi's number. He told them he had the money and would come to the Bruno Inn as quickly as he could.

Kamla hurried to the bathroom to share the good news with her mother. To her surprise, she wasn't there.

"Dad, could you please step in here for a second?" she called.

Sonny, who was speaking with Jose, detected the **agitation** in Kamla's voice. He immediately rushed to the bathroom.

"Your mother isn't here," he said as soon as he entered. "Where is she?"

"Maybe she's **summoning** the police."

"That's **ludicrous**! Don't make me laugh, Kamla. That's **absurd**. It's very foolish of her to call the police if that's what she's doing. We'll certainly be **deported** if she does that. We'll be sent home to India if the American immigration officers get involved in this matter."

While Sonny and Kamla were guessing Rita's **motive**, or intention, Jose was becoming more **restless** and **irritable**. He was pacing and behaving as if he had a hill's worth of angry ants trapped in his pants.

"Is everything OK, Sonny?" he asked loudly.

"Yes."

"I haven't seen your wife. Is she OK?"

"She's fine. I'll be out in a second."

Sonny instructed Kamla to be calm and lock the bathroom door. He also told her not to **intervene**, or come between him and Jose, if they got into an argument.

"The money will be here momentarily, Jose," said Sonny.

"I'm tired of waiting."

"It's not my fault. I didn't ask you to come—"

The conversation was interrupted by a knock on the door.

"Who's there?" inquired Sonny.

"It's me, Joshi."

Sonny opened the door and breathed a sigh of relief at the sight of his most **reliable** relative. Joshi was someone who would do whatever he said he was going to do.

"I'm sure glad to see you," said Sonny as he hugged Joshi.

"Sonny, I'm happy to see you too, after ten long years."

"You're a **savior**, Joshi," said Sonny with **genuine appreciation** in his voice. "Thanks for getting me out of this mess."

Sonny paid Jose the $20,000 and **escorted** him out of Room 555, where they were staying. To his amazement, Rita was standing outside the room in the hallway and had been listening attentively to the conversation. Her hands were behind her back.

As soon as Jose disappeared around the corner, she **revealed** that she had a pistol in her hand.

"What are you doing with that . . . that gun? Where did you get it?" asked Sonny angrily.

"I recalled that Jaime had a gun when he brought us to Dallas," Rita replied calmly, "and Fernandez had one too, remember? I wasn't **optimistic** about you being able to reach Joshi. If you hadn't, that would've made Jose angry and violent, and I thought he would have a gun too. So I climbed through the window to get help from the police. As I was about to dial their number from the payphone down the hall, Joshi arrived. I explained Jose's demand for money. Joshi gave me his gun and suggested that I use it only if Jose tried to hurt us."

Sonny was relieved that the **dispute** with Jose had been settled **amicably** and without violence. Shortly after, Joshi and Sonny and his family went to a nearby restaurant for breakfast and discussed their plans for living in America. They sat in a corner far from any other customers so they could speak in private.

"Sonny, why didn't you telephone me last night as soon as you arrived in Dallas?" asked Joshi.

"I thought about calling you, but I couldn't take the risk."

"What risk?"

"I didn't want anybody to know we have relatives in Dallas, particularly those **unscrupulous** men who brought us here. They could tell the immigration authorities that we're staying with you. You could get into trouble for **accommodating** illegal **aliens**. All of your efforts to get us into America would go to waste. I wish I hadn't been forced to call you over while Jose was there."

"Do not worry about it, Sonny. Our families are one. You should've spent the night with us"

Rita and Kamla were **ignoring** their conversation and paying more attention to the menu. Kamla ordered bacon, sausage, and waffles so she could **sample** things she had never tried before. Rita, on the other hand, was very **selective**. She chose only things that were familiar to her.

"We don't have all day to spend here," cautioned Rita. "We must leave shortly."

"Where are you going, Rita?" asked Joshi.

"To New York, of course."

"Why New York?"

"That's where the jobs are."

"What about Dallas? There's an **abundance** of jobs here as well. Remember, it's the illegal person's **paradise**. You can find plenty of high-paying jobs with excellent benefits. The standard of living is very high. It's the perfect place to raise a family."

"That might be true, but I read that people in Dallas are very **conservative**. They're not as **liberal** or broad-minded as New Yorkers, who readily welcome people to America and respect their cultural differences and traditions," said Rita with confidence.

Sonny added, "Joshi, you also have to consider that the investigation of the border patrolman's death is probably in **progress**. It might continue for a while. We really shouldn't take the risk of staying in Dallas."

"I just can't understand you, Sonny," remarked Joshi. "Why are you concerned about the investigation? You aren't involved."

"Maybe it's my concern," replied Sonny.

Sonny excused himself and went to the men's room. Joshi frowned and looked **puzzled** because he could not figure out, or **decipher**, what Sonny was worried about.

"Rita, my beautiful sister, what's on Sonny's mind?" whispered Joshi. "He sounds as if he had something to do with the murder."

"Impossible! He didn't have a gun."

"Rita, please, you must keep your voice down," Joshi said, looking up to make sure nobody had **overheard**.

"He did have that bag," interrupted Kamla.

"What bag?" inquired Joshi.

"He had a brown paper bag with something in it," said Rita reluctantly. "I think it was a small object that he intentionally **concealed** from us. He didn't want us to see it. When the officer was struggling with Stella, he became extremely angry and dashed out of the van to assist her. I remember he reached for the paper bag in his pocket while running like a deer to rescue her. Shots were fired. He didn't make it to the bridge because two vehicles were spotted and we yelled for him to return to the van."

"Who gave him the bag containing the object?"

"Fernandez," said Kamla.

"Who's Fernandez?"

"The Mexican **guy** whom we had the contract with."

"Why did he give him the bag? What did he say to your dad?"

Kamla hesitated, **recollecting** her thoughts. She remembered certain details about the incident.

"When it was Dad's turn to cross the bridge, Fernandez gave him the bag and told him he'd need it to protect his family."

"Did you see the contents of the bag, Kamla?"

"No."

"It appears that Sonny was given a gun. Who has the bag now?"

"Nobody. Dad **disposed** of it. He got rid of it before he returned to the van."

"Knowing that, it might be in your family's best interest to leave Dallas as soon as possible, Rita," encouraged Joshi.

"I agree."

They fell silent as the waitress approached. She inquired if they needed a refill of coffee. Joshi turned her down and paid the bill, and they waited patiently for Sonny to return.

"Joshi, we must leave now. I appreciate everything you have done for us. We'll phone you as soon as we arrive in—"

Joshi interrupted Sonny angrily. He reminded him that Rita was his sister, and he could not understand why he was treating him **formally** like a stranger. He **assured** Sonny that nothing terrible or **awful** was going to happen to him or his family in New York. Joshi walked with them to their room, where he discussed his plan to sponsor them to become permanent residents of America. He reviewed the three applications his attorney had prepared for them prior to their arrival in Dallas, and assured him that all of the other necessary paperwork had been filed.

After signing the applications, Sonny, Rita and Kamla took turns to bow down and touch Joshi's feet with **profound reverence** as a symbol of their deep respect, admiration and appreciation for Joshi's **initiatives**. **Affectionate** tears gently flowed down Rita's cheeks as they waved to him while he drove away to work at the Dallas Medical Center.

Rita slowly wiped away her tears. "My brother, you are the **angel** from **heaven** that **Bhagwan**, our **Almighty**, has sent," she whispered, kissing her handkerchief.

Parental Love and Sacrifice

Kamla was tall, slim and charming, with a fair complexion. Her silky dark hair reached to her waist. She enjoyed singing, and her voice was soft, **invigorating**, and **soothing**. It was full of energy, yet calm enough to put you to sleep. As she showered, she **hummed** the tunes of her favorite songs.

Sonny was unusually quiet while packing his clothes. Rita saw that he was **preoccupied**. He was thinking deeply about their new life in America. She walked over and gently kissed him on his cheek.

"What's the matter, my husband?" asked Rita lovingly as she kissed him again.

Sonny was surprised to hear her speak affectionately.

"Nothing. Nothing at all," he said quietly.

"Now, tell me what's on your mind. I know you well enough to tell that something is **bothering** you. You don't look as calm and **composed** as your usual self "

"It's just that I've been thinking about how we are going start over again in America. In India, we were well established. Suddenly, you dreamed up this bright idea of coming to America. You've **uprooted** our family in search of a perfect life. I just don't know what this perfect life is that you're seeking."

"Sonny, why are you blaming me? You agreed to come to America, didn't you?"

"Yes. But you **persuaded** me. You convinced me to come to America."

"That's just an excuse. You're just worrying unnecessarily, dear. Both of us will work **conscientiously** and before you know it, we'll be a happy family again. Hard work pays off. Just cheer up, Sonny. You know that Kamla is our **principal** reason for coming to America, don't you?"

Rita felt **fortunate** that she and Sonny had graduated with their Master of Science degrees. None of their parents had completed high school, yet they had been **determined** to work very hard as street vendors to support their children in their **pursuit** of higher education. They had believed that an advanced level of education was the primary key to breaking the vicious cycle of poverty. They had wanted their children and grandchildren to have better lives than they had been **enduring** at the time.

When Kamla was young, Rita worked part-time in sales while Sonny climbed the ranks as a security professional. Sonny eventually took on a high-paying management position. Once he was earning enough money to support their upper-class lifestyle on his own, he asked Rita to stop working out of respect for tradition. She **quit** her job the next day.

Kamla had taken the family's education level up another **notch**. As a young girl, she had **aspired** to become a medical scientist and work with poverty-stricken children and their parents in the slums of her country's major cities. She developed a love of reading science books at a very **tender** age. She was a gifted and talented student who **skipped** several grades when she was in high school. She felt that she had been born with a **silver spoon in her mouth**. Thanks to her family's high income, Kamla had been able to attend **prestigious** universities with superior academic programs. She had earned her doctoral degree in Medical Science at the age of twenty-five.

It was her dream to become a leading research scientist and win a Nobel Prize. After her graduation, she conducted research under the supervision of a **renowned** international **expert** on infectious diseases. Several years later, with the guidance of a group of scientists, Kamla developed a vaccine to treat Clonza, an infectious disease that mainly affects poor people because it is **confined** to **slums**. She won several awards for her outstanding **expertise** and became an instant **celebrity** in the medical field in India.

Rita and Sonny were **proud as peacocks**. They were enjoying their daughter's **accomplishments**. However, they knew that despite Kamla's success, her professional growth would be **retarded** because India had very limited research facilities **pertinent** to Kamla's expertise and interest. They sacrificed their comfortable upper-class lives so that one day their daughter would become a Nobel laureate. Even if coming to America **endangered** their lives, it was worth it, because it would give their daughter the opportunity to make her dream come true. Kamla's happiness was their happiness.

Never before did Kamla feel more blessed than when her parents agreed to come to America. Of course, if there was one weakness she had developed over years of having everything go her way, it was impatience. She had not been willing to wait the years it would take to get her green card properly. Now she had to face a lifetime of worrying that she would eventually be discovered as an illegal immigrant, and if her father really had murdered that guard. . . .

Kamla stopped humming and reached for a towel in silence.

Outside the bathroom, Rita was sitting at the edge of the bed while Sonny continued to pack.

"I wish I had your courage, **optimism**, and outlook on life, Rita," said Sonny proudly. "Your positive attitude and **perspective** make you a real **survivor**." He reached over to hug her.

"Oops! Tell me when you're done, **lovebirds**," said Kamla when she saw them hugging, hurrying back to the bathroom.

"Come back here. We're just talking about your grandmother," lied Sonny.

"I believe you," said Kamla **sarcastically**, letting him know that she didn't believe him at all. "What were you saying about Grandma, Dad?"

"She was ill when we left home, and I'm certain she's worried about us, particularly you. You're her only granddaughter. She raised you when I was studying in college, and she loves you dearly. I pray that her health improves rather than **deteriorates**."

"Actually, I've had **nightmares** about her. I didn't mention it for fear that I'd upset you and Mom," said Kamla.

"You don't have to worry about her. She'll be fine as long as she continues taking her medications, and she's very **faithful** when it comes to that," Sonny reassured her.

Sonny finished packing and urged Kamla and Rita to hurry, as their flight was leaving in less than two hours. While he had a bath, Kamla and Rita continued chatting.

"Mom, what should I wear? Would this pair of jeans and plain white blouse make me look sexy and attractive? Joshi brought them for me and said Aunt Roxy picked them out."

Rita was **startled** by her question. "Why this sudden **intense** interest in style? You never paid much attention to it before. All you wanted to wear were colorful Indian **saris** that made you look **elegant**. You always attracted upper-class men."

"That was when we were in India, Ma."

"It makes no difference where we are. I've observed certain **subtle** changes in you. I saw the intense **admiration** in your eyes for that **fellow**, the **farmhand**, who was leaning against you purposely in that crowded van. He was trying to get your attention. I wish you had known how **infuriated** I was. I was very angry and upset and felt like spanking you like I used to when you were a little girl. But I'm glad I didn't."

"He isn't a farmhand. Raul was a college student studying agriculture in Mexico. A year ago, he was forced to **discontinue** his studies because his father passed away. As the eldest son of the family, it was his responsibility to care for his younger **siblings**. In Mexico, it's almost impossible to find a job with a decent salary. Raul had no other **option** but to work on a ranch. His **meager** earnings were insufficient to make ends meet. He felt that coming to America would enable him to earn a **sufficient** amount of money to **rescue** his family from poverty. I admire his sense of responsibility."

"I bet you do. But he worked on a ranch, so he was still a farmhand."

Kamla was losing her patience and becoming **irritable**. She was annoyed about her mother's **overprotection** of her. She wished she had the freedom of other American women she read about in magazines in India. Kamla **detested** her mother's attitude toward her. She hated that her mother was treating her like a spoiled teenager rather than a mature woman. It was customary for parents in India to treat their children the way Rita and Sonny were treating Kamla, regardless of their age or education level, and that was one thing Kamla had hoped to escape in the United States.

"Mother, you're behaving like Dad. I'm surprised at you."

"Frankly, you embarrassed me when you **permitted** that man to hold your hand. I saw your eyes **glowed** with **lust** when he attempted to kiss you."

"How do you know these **minute** details? Were you **spying** on me?"

"Not at all. The brightness of your eyes filled with pleasure spoke more words than the stars in the heavens."

"I've always been honest and **candid** with you. To tell you the truth, it was a great feeling to know that a man noticed and appreciated me. Ma, I hope I experience this feeling again. Soon."

Rita was **stunned** at her daughter's **candor**. She hadn't expected a response of that nature from her.

Sonny seemed to take forever to bathe. Finally, as he entered the living room, Rita and Kamla discontinued their conversation. Without delay, Rita telephoned for a taxi to take them to the airport. In less than fifteen minutes, a tall, muscular man **emerged** from the taxi that arrived.

"Where to?" he asked after stepping out of the taxi. He had a strong French accent.

"To the airport," replied Kamla.

The driver loaded their **meager belongings** in the trunk in less than a minute. They traveled for about a mile before he stopped suddenly.

"Which airport?" he asked. "There are two in Dallas."

After a moment's **hesitation**, Kamla took airline tickets that Joshi had purchased for them from her handbag and showed them to the driver. He flipped the pages and smiled as he drove to Dallas International Airport.

There was complete and **utter** silence for a while. Nobody spoke a word. Eventually, the driver attempted to **initiate** a conversation with the family, but only Kamla responded. Rita and Sonny were **skeptical** of him because they were wondering if he was an immigration officer working **undercover** and pretending to be a taxi driver. Besides, they had read **countless** horrible stories in India about taxi drivers in America.

"Where're you from?" asked the driver.

Nobody responded, but he was determined to start an ongoing conversation with his passengers. He continued talking, hoping someone would reply.

"My name is Errol, by the way. My boss is from India. He owns this taxi company. I like him very much because he is kind to me. When I came to Dallas with my family, I was almost **penniless**. I didn't have friends or relatives in this city. I had only a few dollars in my pocket. We stayed at a **shelter**, but had to leave after two weeks. That was the **maximum** time we could have stayed there. I remember **vividly** that rainy night five years ago when I met him. I was purchasing milk for my child at a convenience store when he entered. The clerk told me I was short nine cents, and he couldn't give me the milk. I explained I was homeless, but he laughed at me. Then this gentleman paid him with a hundred-dollar bill for the milk and told him to give me the change. He left the store and waited for me in his car in the parking lot. I am grateful that he hired me for this job. I was able to start a new life with my family in Dallas because of him."

"Where're you from?" inquired Kamla, after listening to his emotional experience.

"From Haiti."

"How did you get to Dallas?"

"It's a long story. In those days many families were **desperate** to escape Papa David, Haiti's **notorious dictator**. Papa David was **infamous** for his cruelty toward certain people, and for successfully controlling the entire island for thirty years without ever winning an election. The police and military personnel were his **thugs**. They **tortured** and imprisoned people who spoke against corruption and attempted to overthrow his government. After a while, a large number of families were frustrated by the political **turmoil** in Haiti and escaped to Miami in small fishing boats. Several were successful. Others **perished** in the **perilous** and **furious** ocean when their boats **capsized**. My family was **fortunate**. My boat overturned when waves more than forty feet high attacked it. It was a **miracle** that two American fishermen who were living in Dallas rescued me and my family. They brought us here secretly after narrowly escaping the American coast guards in Miami. It's very comforting to know that our world still has many **good Samaritans**," said Errol, the taxi driver.

"Why were you left in a shelter?" asked Kamla.

"I insisted on staying at the shelter, hoping we'd receive long-term care from the government. But things did not work out as I planned."

"What a sad story! But I admire your **fortitude** and bravery. You had the guts to stand up to those **mighty** waves," said Kamla. "I guess all immigrants have a story to tell."

"Thank God we're here in America. This is the greatest country God made," said Errol gratefully as he tried to hold back his tears of joy.

Rita and her family **disembarked** from the taxi when it arrived at the airport. After getting out, Sonny and the driver carried their belongings to the check-in counter. They boarded their flight to New York an hour later.

EXERCISE 1

Applying the Words You Have Learned to Critical Thinking and Creative Writing

- Use the two questions in Section A below to discuss this chapter with your classmates. Be sure to apply your critical thinking skills.

- Write an essay about either question using the vocabulary words you know from real-life experiences and the new ones you have learned from this text.

Section A

Discussion Questions

1. What did Rita mean when she said that her brother, Joshi, was an angel?

2. Do you predict that Kamla and her parents will argue frequently in this story?

EXERCISE 2

Matching Meanings

- Match each word with its meaning.

_____ 1. university	**A.** a treasurer or financial officer of a school
_____ 2. tenure	**B.** all the teachers of a college or school
_____ 3. dean	**C.** a measurement of completion for a unit or course of study
_____ 4. faculty	**D.** an individual who counsels and advises students
_____ 5. registrar	**E.** profession or occupation
_____ 6. bursar	**F.** an administrative officer of a school, college, or university
_____ 7. counselor	**G.** educational institution of the highest level
_____ 8. coach	**H.** a trial period because of low grades
_____ 9. credit	**I.** a trainer
_____ 10. course	**J.** an office that registers students and maintains records
_____ 11. major	**K.** a college organization for men
_____ 12. career	**L.** a college organization for women
_____ 13. elective	**M.** a room for experimentation or research
_____ 14. laboratory	**N.** holding one's position on a permanent basis
_____ 15. cafe	**O.** a unit of instruction in a subject
_____ 16. probation	**P.** an optional course
_____ 17. suspension	**Q.** a small restaurant or coffee house
_____ 18. fraternity	**R.** a person on a trial period before initiation into a fraternity or sorority
_____ 19. sorority	**S.** temporary barring from school
_____ 20. pledge	**T.** a field of study in which a student specializes and earns a degree

EXERCISE 3

Forming Synonyms

■ Fill in the blank(s) to complete the word that is similar in meaning to the **boldfaced** word.

1. **alternative** op__ __ __n
2. **acquaint** fam__ __ __ __ __ize
3. **accompany** e__co__t
4. **access** __ntry
5. **analyze** ex__ __ __ne
6. **alien** forei__ __
7. **ascertain** con__ __rm
8. **astute** __lev__r
9. **attain** acco__ __ __ __sh
10. **boundary** bo__ __er
11. **browse** sk__ __
12. **bundle** pac__ __ge
13. **concise** b__ __ef
14. **compensate** p__y
15. **classify** cate__ __ __ __ze
16. **confide** trus__
17. **chubby** st__ __ky
18. **chore** t__sk
19. **cherish** tr__ __ __ure
20. **change** conv__rt
21. **predict** for__ __ __ __ __
22. **pretend** as__ __me
23. **profanity** cur__ __ng
24. **pursue** __hase

EXERCISE 4

Synonyms: Multiple Choice

■ Circle the letter of the word that is most similar in meaning to the **boldfaced** word.

1. **abundant**	**A.** little	**B.** less	**C.** some	**D.** plentiful
2. **calm**	**A.** rowdy	**B.** noisy	**C.** angry	**D.** quiet
3. **adequate**	**A.** large	**B.** enough	**C.** last	**D.** far
4. **annual**	**A.** yearly	**B.** weekly	**C.** everyday	**D.** yesterday
5. **beneficiary**	**A.** cousin	**B.** inheritor	**C.** uncle	**D.** aunt
6. **boast**	**A.** show off	**B.** ail	**C.** lie	**D.** sleep
7. **eager**	**A.** anxious	**B.** first	**C.** serious	**D.** settled
8. **chilly**	**A.** cool	**B.** hot	**C.** humid	**D.** calm
9. **ailment**	**A.** health	**B.** disease	**C.** temperature	**D.** fever
10. **famous**	**A.** silly	**B.** sick	**C.** well-known	**D.** loyal
11. **internal**	**A.** under	**B.** above	**C.** below	**D.** inside
12. **finish**	**A.** start	**B.** begin	**C.** rest	**D.** complete
13. **hesitate**	**A.** hurry	**B.** haste	**C.** pause	**D.** speed
14. **joy**	**A.** happiness	**B.** sadness	**C.** anger	**D.** perfection
15. **harass**	**A.** bother	**B.** kiss	**C.** honor	**D.** talk
16. **insane**	**A.** smart	**B.** crazy	**C.** intelligent	**D.** scholarly
17. **final**	**A.** excellent	**B.** last	**C.** fair	**D.** poor
18. **laugh**	**A.** frown	**B.** argue	**C.** speak	**D.** chuckle
19. **main**	**A.** side	**B.** lateral	**C.** chief	**D.** evident
20. **nap**	**A.** rest	**B.** jog	**C.** tap	**D.** ache

EXERCISE 5

More Practice with Synonyms

■ Circle the letter of the word or phrase that is most similar in meaning to the **boldfaced** word.

1. **accompany**	**A.** to go with	**B.** delay	**C.** dare	**D.** fight
2. earned **distinction**	**A.** excellence	**B.** marks	**C.** pointers	**D.** extinction
3. **accelerate**	**A.** speed up	**B.** slow	**C.** crawl	**D.** creep
4. **determine** the cost	**A.** tell	**B.** calculate	**C.** ask	**D.** note
5. **apparent**	**A.** invisible	**B.** apart	**C.** clear	**D.** distort
6. in **dormancy**	**A.** fastness	**B.** swiftness	**C.** consciousness	**D.** inactivity
7. **appropriate** amount	**A.** suitable	**B.** unsuitable	**C.** enormous	**D.** low
8. **disloyal** employee	**A.** faithful	**B.** untrue	**C.** fearless	**D.** dependable
9. **affiliated** with	**A.** unrelated	**B.** located	**C.** associated	**D.** failed
10. **dislocate**	**A.** unite	**B.** disconnect	**C.** locate	**D.** join
11. **abduct** a child	**A.** take by force	**B.** comfort	**C.** protect	**D.** care for
12. **dissatisfied** customer	**A.** grateful	**B.** regular	**C.** dependable	**D.** unhappy
13. **disillusion**	**A.** disappointment	**B.** positivity	**C.** posterior	**D.** encouragement
14. **abnormal** behavior	**A.** usual	**B.** strange	**C.** normal	**D.** friendly
15. **discount** in the price	**A.** reduction	**B.** increase	**C.** raise	**D.** sale
16. **devastated**	**A.** honored	**B.** obeyed	**C.** destroyed	**D.** vast
17. **absent-minded** professor	**A.** forgetful	**B.** tough	**C.** easy	**D.** lazy
18. **distinguish**	**A.** bring together	**B.** burden	**C.** tell apart	**D.** create
19. **donate** used clothes	**A.** give away	**B.** accept	**C.** keep	**D.** take
20. a **derogatory** remark	**A.** uncertain	**B.** negative	**C.** complimentary	**D.** kind
21. **aggressive** behavior	**A.** quiet	**B.** pushy	**C.** careless	**D.** harmless
22. **dominate** the discussion	**A.** control	**B.** ignore	**C.** interrupt	**D.** conclude
23. to **disperse**	**A.** convince	**B.** encourage	**C.** break up	**D.** satisfy
24. an **anonymous** caller	**A.** well-known	**B.** dishonest	**C.** friendly	**D.** unidentified
25. **exploited** the workers	**A.** liked	**B.** respected	**C.** accepted	**D.** took advantage of
26. to **exaggerate**	**A.** ignore	**B.** overlook	**C.** overstate	**D.** hasten
27. to **abbreviate**	**A.** shorten	**B.** increase	**C.** deviate	**D.** dissipate
28. **digress**	**A.** stick to	**B.** stray	**C.** clear	**D.** unknown
29. a **dynamic** speaker	**A.** poor	**B.** noisy	**C.** disrespectful	**D.** powerful
30. **charismatic** leader	**A.** appealing	**B.** selfish	**C.** loyal	**D.** caring
31. imprisoned the **dissident**	**A.** friend	**B.** relative	**C.** rebel	**D.** lawyer
32. **disappear** into the woods	**A.** camp	**B.** sleep	**C.** hunt	**D.** go away
33. **discreet**	**A.** careful	**B.** constant	**C.** honest	**D.** habitual

EXERCISE 6

Antonyms

■ Match each word with its antonym.

_____	1. betray	**A.** prosperous
_____	2. deliberate	**B.** return
_____	3. bankrupt	**C.** defend
_____	4. demonstrate	**D.** remain
_____	5. burden	**E.** accidental
_____	6. deprive	**F.** exonerate
_____	7. deviate	**G.** aristocratic
_____	8. brutal	**H.** malignant
_____	9. detect	**I.** ease
_____	10. blame	**J.** conceal
_____	11. boredom	**K.** overlook
_____	12. bourgeois	**L.** begin
_____	13. benign	**M.** humane
_____	14. brisk	**N.** unconscious
_____	15. buoyant	**O.** discouraging
_____	16. cease	**P.** excitement
_____	17. conscious	**Q.** beginning
_____	18. considerable	**R.** heavy
_____	19. convincing	**S.** modest
_____	20. conceited	**T.** trivial
_____	21. conclusion	**U.** lethargic
_____	22. compulsory	**V.** doubt
_____	23. confidence	**W.** evasive
_____	24. compliment	**X.** criticism
_____	25. candid	**Y.** voluntary

EXERCISE 7

Word Meaning in Context: Set 1

■ Read each sentence and find the missing word in the box below. Fill in the blank with the correct *form* of that word.

abduct	**affiliate**	**determine**	**appropriate**
discount	**accompany**	**dislocate**	**disillusion**
abnormal	**accelerate**	**disloyal**	**apparent**

1. If you have time, I would like you to __________ me to the doctor's office this afternoon.
2. Once he found a Japanese girlfriend, his progress in learning the language __________.
3. The best way to __________ how much to tip a server in a restaurant is to double the tax.
4. It was __________ to everyone except his parents that he was using drugs.
5. Jeans are not __________ attire for an office with a formal dress code.
6. Even though he was cheating on his wife, he did not see himself as __________.
7. Our company is in no way __________ with the similarly named company down the block.
8. His attempt to lift a 200-pound weight caused him to __________ his shoulder.
9. The town was horrified because the child had been __________ in broad daylight.
10. Although he immigrated with high hopes, he became __________ when he failed to find work within his first two weeks.
11. __________ sensitivity to light is just one symptom of the virus.
12. If you pay cash, there is a __________ of 5 percent.

EXERCISE 8

Word Meaning in Context: Set 2

■ Read each sentence and find the missing word in the box below. Fill in the blank with the correct *form* of that word.

charismatic	**donate**	**abbreviate**	**dynamic**
derogatory	**disappear**	**devastate**	**exaggerate**
discreet	**dominate**	**aggressive**	**distinguish**

1. She was __________ when she found out that she had failed the college entrance examination and all her friends had passed.
2. Because the symptoms are the same, it is hard to __________ between the flu and certain more serious illnesses.
3. If you __________ $100 or more to our radio station, you will receive a free tote bag.
4. Because he made __________ remarks about every proposal presented, he was not popular with his co-workers.
5. A tendency to be __________ can be a problem in a house pet but useful in a guard dog.
6. Although the computer company initially __________ the market, it was soon overshadowed by a host of competitors.
7. Fishermen are known to __________ when telling stories of their experiences at sea.
8. In formal writing, it is best not to __________ phrases such as "do not."

9. When the previous head of our brainstorming committee stopped coming up with new ideas, we fired him and found someone more ____________.

10. John F. Kennedy was one of the most ____________ U.S. presidents.

11. If something is not done in the next few years, the rainforests of the Amazon basin could ____________.

12. Because Thomas was very ____________ about his personal life, everyone was very surprised when the paper announced that he had been arrested for having several wives.

EXERCISE 9

Context Clues

■ Select the word or phrase that most closely matches the meaning of the **boldfaced** word. *Note that replacing the **boldfaced** word with the right answer might not produce a grammatically correct sentence.*

1. After dozens of counseling sessions, the **attitude** and behavior of the married couple changed, making them fall back in love.

   A. way of thinking **B.** religion **C.** popularity **D.** finances

2. When writing a report, it is essential to **attribute** information and statistics to their sources in order to give recognition.

   A. fake **B.** bring to life **C.** personalize **D.** give credit

3. To become a successful **author**, one must be passionate about the subject one is writing about.

   A. writer **B.** inventor **C.** attorney **D.** clerk

4. Politicians are people of **influence**.

   A. kindness **B.** power **C.** clarity **D.** servitude

5. Computers can **automate** simple tasks, such as locking doors or turning on lights.

   A. perform without human input **B.** invent
   C. finish **D.** violate the laws of physics

6. It is important to be **aware** of one's surroundings when in a new place.

   A. prejudiced **B.** absentminded **C.** attentive **D.** forecasting

7. The writer was unable to attend the ceremony, so he sent his agent to accept the award on his **behalf**.

   A. command **B.** against one's will **C.** for someone else **D.** for pleasure

8. A fundraiser to build a new hospital wing will **benefit** surrounding communities that are in need of medical services.

   A. help **B.** grow **C.** hurt **D.** irritate

9. Building a **bond** with people at the office can make the work experience more rewarding.

   A. inside joke **B.** relationship **C.** new office **D.** stock portfolio

10. In today's retail stores, buying in **bulk** means purchasing large quantities of food and household products that can last many months.

    A. large amounts **B.** small amounts **C.** warehouses **D.** mail orders

11. Companies prefer hiring **capable** workers who already have the skills the position requires.

    A. scholarly **B.** wealthy **C.** skilled **D.** bankrupt

12. Tennis players who wanted to compete in the tournament had to select a **category** based on their age and gender.
    A. group **B.** field **C.** school **D.** job

13. They sailed through the **channel** between two islands.
    A. storm **B.** waterway **C.** fog **D.** port

14. Consumers want to buy food that does not contain harmful **chemicals** that can make them sick.
    A. substances **B.** textures **C.** plants **D.** animal products

15. As I evaluated my **circumstance**, I realized that if I did not make a decision, the situation would get worse.
    A. grief **B.** condition **C.** mood **D.** building

16. When a museum exhibits the work of an artist, it must **cite** the name of the artist and the sponsor who commissioned the work.
    A. remove **B.** mention **C.** change **D.** correct

17. A society is measured by its **civil** laws that recognize the rights of its people.
    A. relating to citizens **B.** in the workplace **C.** dealing with politics **D.** concerning a jury

18. She preferred to buy **classic** clothing rather than follow the flashy styles that changed every season.
    A. casual **B.** traditional **C.** risky **D.** low quality

19. It is always wise to read each **clause** in a contract, including the part of the document that is written in small print.
    A. page **B.** word **C.** proper name **D.** separate section

20. A new dress **code** was approved by the school, but the students were upset by the policy.
    A. room for changing **B.** uniform **C.** set of standards **D.** pattern

21. After a lengthy court process, lawyers for both parties were happy to reach a settlement that **coincided** with the wishes of their clients.
    A. went along **B.** argued against **C.** paid for **D.** betrayed

22. A co-worker and professional **colleague** recommended I contact a job recruiter who specializes in our field.
    A. intern **B.** associate **C.** student **D.** employer

23. You should buy all the materials you will need before **commencing** work on a new project.
    A. ending **B.** avoiding **C.** starting **D.** advising

24. The guest speaker made informative remarks and **comments**.
    A. spoken statements **B.** physical movements
    C. warnings **D.** accusations

EXERCISE 10

Vocabulary Test

- Select the correct answer.
- Hint: Review the meanings of all the **boldfaced** words in this chapter before you take the test. This approach can help you to score 100 percent.
- Record the percentage of correct answers on the Master Self-Assessment table on page 397.

1 An **alternative** is an option.

A. True B. False

2 To **acquaint** means to familiarize.

E. True F. False

3 To **accompany** means to escort.

A. True B. False

4 **Analyze** does not mean to examine.

E. True F. False

5 Something that is **alien** is foreign.

A. True B. False

6 To **ascertain** means to learn with certainty.

E. True F. False

7 Another word for **astute** is clever.

A. True B. False

8 To **attain** is to accomplish.

E. True F. False

9 A **boundary** is not a border.

A. True B. False

10 **Tenure** means holding one's position on a permanent basis.

E. True F. False

11 A **coach** is a trainer.

A. True B. False

12 To **disappear** means to go away.

E. True F. False

13 A synonym for **distinction** is excellence.

A. True B. False

14 Something **calm** is:

E. rowdy F. noisy
G. angry H. quiet

15 **Adequate** means:

A. all B. enough
C. scarce D. insufficient

16 To **boast** is to:

E. show off F. be sick
G. lie H. sleep

17 A **chilly** night is:

A. hot B. cool
C. humid D. windy

18 An **ailment** is a:

E. fruit F. disease
G. biopsy H. fever

19 An artist who is **famous** is:

A. well-known B. unknown
C. humid D. windy

20 To **finish** a task is to:

E. start F. continue
G. begin H. complete

21 To **hesitate** means to:

A. hurry
B. hasten
C. pause
D. accelerate

22 **Internal** refers to:

E. under
F. above
G. below
H. inside

23 **Insane** means:

A. smart
B. crazy
C. scholar
D. intelligent

24 Another word for **final** is:

E. excellent
F. last
G. speechless
H. few

25 A **nap** is a:

A. condition
B. rest
C. teacher
D. nest

26 Something **apparent** is:

E. invisible
F. concealed
G. clear
H. windy

27 **Dormancy** refers to:

A. fastness
B. swiftness
C. consciousness
D. inactivity

28 Companies that are **affiliated** are:

E. equal
F. associated
G. unrelated
H. different

29 A **dislocated** shoulder is:

A. sharp
B. disconnected
C. joined
D. connected

30 To **abduct** a child is to:

E. take by force
F. comfort
G. protect
H. care for

31 A **dissatisfied** customer is likely to be:

A. selfish
B. greedy
C. unhappy
D. friendly

32 A synonym for **disillusion** is:

E. disappointment
F. disagreement
G. happiness
H. encouragement

33 A behavior that is **abnormal** is:

A. quick
B. strange
C. normal
D. kind

34 A price that is **discounted** is:

E. reduced
F. increased
G. stable
H. unchanged

35 **Devastation** refers to:

A. erosion
B. unrest
C. destruction
D. calmness

36 **Distinguish** means to:

E. bring together
F. tell apart
G. burden
H. create

37 To **donate** clothes is to:

A. give away
B. accept
C. keep
D. take

38 A **derogatory** remark is:

E. encouraging
F. persuasive
G. negative
H. supportive

39 **Aggressive** means:

A. quiet

B. pushy

C. careless

D. care for

40 To **dominate** the discussion is to:

E. control

F. ignore

G. interrupt

H. conclude

41 The opposite of **deviate** is:

A. stay on course

B. follow

C. serve

D. change direction

42 A **brutal** attack is:

E. cruel

F. painless

G. noisy

H. humane

43 Another word for **detect** is:

A. misplace

B. find

C. conceal

D. overlook

44 A **burden** is something that is:

E. important

F. light

G. smooth

H. worrisome

45 The opposite of **boredom** is:

A. excitement

B. anger

C. distress

D. uneasiness

46 To **convince** means to:

E. defend

F. discourage

G. persuade

H. accept

47 A synonym for **betray** is:

A. disloyal

B. believe

C. esteem

D. mistake

48 An antonym for **aggressive** is:

E. hostile
F. calm
G. careless
H. threatening

49 A **deliberate** act is:

A. accidental
B. firm
C. careless
D. purposeful

50 **Disperse** means to:

E. convince
F. encourage
G. break up
H. satisfy

51 A caller who is **anonymous** is:

A. well-known
B. dishonest
C. famous
D. unidentified

52 To **exploit** workers means to:

E. respect
F. accept
G. take advantage of
H. praise

53 To **exaggerate** means to:

A. ignore
B. overlook
C. overstate
D. hasten

54 To **abbreviate** is to:

E. shorten
F. lengthen
G. deviate
H. dissipate

55 **Digress** means to:

A. stick to
B. stray
C. clear
D. unknown

56 **Dynamic** means:

E. powerless
F. inactive
G. dull
H. powerful

57 Someone who is **charismatic** is:

A. charming

B. selfish

C. loyal

D. caring

58 A **dissident** is a:

E. friend

F. relative

G. rebel

H. lawyer

59 **Discreet** means:

A. careful

B. constant

C. honest

D. careless

60 An antonym for **compulsory** is:

E. deliberate

F. voluntary

G. forced

H. prevalent

EXERCISE 11

Building a Stronger Vocabulary

- Review all the **boldfaced** words in this chapter before you proceed to the next exercise.
- Highlight the ones you are still having difficulty remembering.
- List them with their meanings on a table.
- Use them to compose your own sentences.
- Think of a synonym and an antonym for each word.
- Use checkmarks to indicate if each word you want to practice more has a prefix, suffix, and/or root.
- You may use the table below as a sample to write your answers in your notebook.

Word	Definition	Sentence	Synonym	Antonym	Prefix	Suffix	Root

EXERCISE 12

Creating My Own Powerful Word List

- Write the words and meanings from the above table on the **Creating My Own Powerful Word List** table on page 398. Review them often to build that super vocabulary you want to create for school, work, and everyday use.

PRE-READING

About This Chapter from *Trial of Love*

- Read the names and descriptions of this chapter's main characters below.
  - Sheila: Rita's sister in New York
  - Conchita: Sheila's best friend in New York
  - Shelly Strongfellow: Director at T&T Security Agency
  - Billy Burger: President of Maxi Cosmetics
  - Sonny and his family

Story Vocabulary Exercise

- Before you begin reading this chapter, figure out the meanings of the unfamiliar **boldfaced** vocabulary words. You may use the Word List, Word Parts Chart, or your dictionary to assist you in finding their meanings.
- Look for the various types of context clues—synonyms, antonyms, general context, and examples—as you read.
- Write a word or phrase about the meaning of each **boldfaced** word in the margin.

Reading and Writing Exercise

- Skim the entire chapter and pay attention to the headings and the discussion questions that follow.
- Initial Response: Write a paragraph explaining, in your own words, what you think this chapter of the story will be about.
- Final Response: After you have read the entire chapter, compare your current understanding with your initial response above. If your initial response was accurate, you can simply write it again to fill in the blanks below. If it was not, then write a paragraph on what the chapter was really about instead.

Initial Response

This chapter **will** be about ____

____

____

____

Final Response

This chapter **was** about ____

____

____

____

THE HUNT FOR EMPLOYMENT

The flight started off smoothly, and the first hour went by without a problem. Kamla and her father talked about their plans for New York as they rose above the clouds. Just as they were beginning to relax and enjoy the ride, the aircraft began moving in a wave-like manner. Suddenly, the captain lost control, and the plane started to dive with its nose down while continuing to **undulate**. There was **incessant** yelling and screaming for several minutes. Children cried and clung to their mothers' bosoms. Several passengers fought for life jackets. Flight attendants could not **pacify** or calm them. Fortunately, the aircraft emerged victoriously from the wicked air pocket that had **engulfed** and trapped it. **Tranquility** returned to the cabin. The calmness was welcomed by the passengers and crew.

"Thank God we survived," Sonny said to his family with a sigh of relief.

Kamla had stayed calm during the commotion, but now she felt foolish. When they had been packing for the journey to America, her grandmother had told them never to fly on certain days of the year. This was one of those days. "Dad, we **neglected** grandmother's warning," she said. "She **sternly** warned that we should never fly on certain Fridays of the year because we're likely to experience air **disasters**."

Sonny said, "She's a **superstitious** elderly woman. Sometimes you have to **ignore** her, because she believes in things that are not true."

"But she was **precise**, Dad. Her priest **predicted** this **mishap**."

"She pays too much attention to his predictions."

"The next time we fly, I'll consult with her or her **astrologer**."

"I'm surprised you take these predictions seriously, Kamla," said Sonny.

Their flight arrived promptly at 6:30 p.m. in New York. Everybody **cheered** when the aircraft landed safely on the runway. Rita's sister, Sheila, was anxiously waiting to greet them.

"How's Mother, Rita?" asked Sheila, after hugging her and Kamla affectionately.

"She's doing well for her age. When you left home, she became ill for more than a month. She has never been the same since you **departed** from India. You're her eldest and favorite daughter. Mother misses you dearly."

"It really wasn't easy for me, either. When I first came to New York, I cried for several nights because I was lonely and **homesick**. I was missing her and all my friends in the village."

Kamla was bored listening to their **sentimental** conversation. She excused herself to help her dad with their belongings. Sonny was waiting for the bags when Kamla joined him. Moments later, they loaded their belongings in the trunk of Sheila's car.

"Sonny, you haven't changed a bit," said Sheila as she embraced Sonny. "You look just the same as when I last saw you in India."

"My goodness, Sheila! You've changed **remarkably**."

"For better or worse?"

"Better, of course. You've lost a lot of weight. What have you done to become so slim? What diet did you follow to **reduce** your weight?"

"I'm now a **vegetarian**. I eat tons of fruits and vegetables and work out at the gym every day. My yoga instructor also insists that I **meditate** daily to **eliminate** stress from my life.

"Sonny, you've made my day," Sheila continued. "Thank you."

Sheila's house was very small and could not **accommodate** Sonny's family comfortably. Nevertheless, she insisted that they live with her for at least a month or two while **adjusting** to life in New York. Rita eventually rented a house in the **suburbs** just a few streets away from Sheila's residence. Sheila was delighted to pay for their living expenses but felt hurt when Rita mentioned that she would **reimburse** her as soon as they started to work. Sheila's culture had taught her that it was her **duty** and **obligation** to care for her sister and her family until they became **self-sufficient** and could provide for themselves. She thought it strange that Rita acted as if she had not been raised to have the same beliefs.

Sonny on a Job Interview

Sonny went for a job interview at T&T Security Agency a week after he arrived in New York. He was about six feet tall, very muscular, and strong. He gave the impression that he was a tough guy who should be taken seriously.

"Excuse me, sir. May I help you?" asked the receptionist as Sonny **cautiously** opened the door and entered the office.

"A friend of mine mentioned that you have a **vacancy** for a private investigator. I'd like to apply for it."

"Do you have experience as an investigator?"

"Sure."

"Have a seat and complete these forms, please," said the receptionist politely as she handed him an application.

Sonny completed the application and **submitted** it to her. She suggested to Sonny that he should wait in the office because today was the final day for interviews. Sonny had no problem waiting because he needed a job to support his family. He was very nervous, though, because this would be his first job interview in America. He did not know what to expect from the interviewer.

After waiting in the conference room for about thirty minutes, Sonny was approached by an employee from the agency. "Hello, I'm Shelly Strongfellow," she said. "Welcome to T&T Security Agency. I'm the Director of Field Operations."

"I'm Sonny Kumar. Thanks for your warm welcome," said Sonny.

"Sonny, why did you seem surprised when I entered the room?" asked Shelly.

"I was expecting. . . ."

"You were expecting a male instead of a female, if I guess correctly. I get that reaction from people most of the time." Shelly glanced down at the papers in her hand. "I see from your application that you're from India. That explains it," she said, with a smile on her face.

"What're you talking about, madam?" asked Sonny with a frown.

"Maybe in India it's not customary for women to hold security positions."

"Absolutely correct."

"You have to get used to the fact that women are just as capable as men of working as private investigators. Sonny, you're in America now. We do things differently here!"

Sonny was silent. Shelly reviewed Sonny's application carefully. Occasionally, she sipped her coffee.

"You have a wealth of experience as a private investigator in Mumbai, India, Sonny. Looks like you are just as good at managing operations from the office as you are at working on the streets, too."

Sonny nodded in agreement.

"I notice you received several security medals from the governor of your state in India. You must be very good at your job."

"Does this mean you'll hire me?" asked Sonny excitedly.

"I see you don't have any experience in America. But I'm **confident** I can train you."

"You won't regret hiring me. I'm good at my profession."

"Really. Really good?"

Shelly smiled. Sonny looked **perplexed** at her **vague** question.

"When should I start working?"

"Oops! You forgot to write your social security number on your application. Also, are you a citizen or permanent resident of America? I see that you didn't answer these questions either."

"I don't have a social security number. To be honest, I'm not a citizen or permanent resident of America."

"Sonny, you know the rules. I can't hire you if you don't meet these requirements. Our company can be fined by the government if I hire someone who is here illegally."

"But many companies do it, Shelly."

"I'm aware of that. They hire them because they pay low wages and subject them to poor working conditions. I don't have the heart to do that. Furthermore, I will never break the laws of our country."

"I wish you were more sensitive to my **predicament**," said Sonny. He **restrained** his anger, but it was still visible to Shelly.

"And what's that predicament?" asked Shelly curiously.

Sonny got out of the chair and walked to the door. "I have a wife and daughter to . . . never mind . . . you won't understand . . . you're an American."

Sonny opened the door and left after thanking Shelly for the interview. Shelly felt sad that she could not hire him.

Rita was anxiously awaiting Sonny's return home. She knew he had not gotten the job because he looked disappointed when he entered the house.

Could Rita Handle Her First Job?

It was around 7:00 p.m. when Sheila phoned Rita to inquire how she and her family were doing. Rita was very happy to hear from Sheila because she needed someone to talk with about Sonny's attitude.

"Sheila, I need your help to deal with Sonny. He recently started feeling **depressed**," said Rita sadly. "He has been **rejected** every time he has gone for a job interview. He is **contemplating** returning to India."

"Did he say why he keeps getting turned down?"

"Nobody wants to hire him because he does not have a green card and a social security number."

"Tell him to cheer up. Everybody goes through this phase of disappointment and rejection when they first come to America. It does not matter if you have a green card or not. It is not easy to find work nowadays. As a matter of fact, many Americans want foreigners to return to their home countries because they feel they are taking their jobs away by being willing to work for very low wages. Rita, I hope you aren't feeling as down as Sonny. You have to be strong for your family. Things will definitely get better. I'm confident he will change his mind about going back to India after hearing the good news I have for you."

"Good news. Really! Girl, I certainly need some now."

"Don't be a **perennial pessimist** like your husband, Rita. I'm positive your **crybaby** will be happy when you tell him you have a job," teased Sheila.

"Me? A job?"

"Yes. Working at the company where I'm at."

"I can't believe it, Sheila," said Rita. "How did you manage to **orchestrate** this? I'm **curious** as to how you pulled this off."

"My manager has been dating my best friend, Conchita, for several months. He's passionately in love with her."

"What's the connection between your friend, the job, and your manager?"

"My manager is a married man. Conchita threatened to tell his wife about their **illicit** affair if he doesn't hire you."

"But that is **blackmail**!" said Rita.

"Not really. Conchita would never do that to him. She was only kidding when she mentioned his wife to him. He has agreed to hire you because he is a foreigner too. He had experiences similar to those you and your family have been having when he came to America. The job is yours if you want it. Let me know early in the morning if you change your mind."

It was difficult for Rita to sleep that night. Sonny detected her restlessness in bed and **confronted** her.

"I'm tired of depending on my sister for financial support, Sonny. One of us must find a job soon," said Rita.

"I agree, Rita."

"Does that mean that I can work if I find a job? Ever since you made me **quit** my job in India, you've been against the idea."

"There's a need now, Rita," said Sonny, with deep concern.

"There was always a need. It's just that you've always been a slave to tradition," scolded Rita, before drifting off into sleep.

More than 150 employees were working at the garment factory on Canal Street in New York City. They were **predominantly** foreign-born females ranging in age from their late teens to mid-sixties. Very few were **fluent** in English. This made it difficult for them to communicate with their fellow employees.

Rita was assigned to work with Conchita during her training. Conchita was a very caring and **compassionate** woman. Her mother had died from a heart attack at the factory several years ago. Conchita began working at the factory because her siblings, who were in elementary school, depended on her for financial support. Their father had abandoned them when Conchita was two years of age.

Rita experienced a great deal of difficulty **coping** with her job. She was expected to **sew** seventy-five blouses per day, but could not even complete fifty. This **enraged** her supervisor. However, Conchita encouraged her to **ignore** him. She was supportive of Rita's efforts.

Sonny was not against Rita working. It was her frequent complaints of headaches, eye fatigue, and swollen feet, the symptoms of her **tedious** job, that displeased him immensely. Rita **battled** these problems bitterly, but her health did not permit her to continue beyond the second week.

Rita knew her college degrees from Henderson University in India entitled her to a professional job. She examined the classified advertising section of the newspaper daily. After two weeks of **aggressive** job hunting, she thought she had gotten lucky. She telephoned Billy Burger, President of Maxi Cosmetics Corporation. She later regretted making that call.

What Did Billy Do to Rita?

Rita rang the doorbell. Billy opened the door and invited Rita in.

"Am I at the right place for the interview for the administrative assistant position?" asked Rita nervously when she stepped inside. This felt wrong. She had expected to meet in an office in the city, not a house in the suburbs.

"Of course. But I'm positive you're qualified for the international sales manager position."

"What exactly does it **entail**?"

"It requires **substantial** travel, including trips to London, Paris, Frankfurt, and several other cities, to train sales representatives. Maxi Cosmetics is the world's fastest-growing company in cosmetology."

"I've never traveled to those cities."

"That's fine. You'll be traveling with me."

"With you, alone? I have a husband and a daughter."

"What does that have to do with the job?"

"Everything. I can't leave them and fly with you around the **globe**. My husband won't **approve** of it."

"Does he have to approve of your job?"

Rita looked perplexed. "Of course."

Billy got out of his chair and stood behind her.

"This is an opportunity of a lifetime," he whispered in her ear. He gently placed his hands on her shoulders.

"Billy, I would prefer the job as the administrative assistant in New York," said Rita as she removed his hand from her right shoulder.

He ignored what she was saying and let his other hand drift down to touch her inappropriately. She removed his hand in disgust and anger. Standing, she raised her hand to slap him, but he caught both of her arms and gripped them tightly.

"Honey, you'll enjoy our relationship," Billy said with an evil glint in his eyes. "You've got a bright future at this company."

In Search of Rita

It was approaching 8:00 p.m. and Sonny was becoming restless. Rita was not at home.

"Is Rita with you?" asked Sonny when he telephoned Sheila.

"No, Sonny. Didn't she say where she was going?"

"When I left home in the morning to look for work, she was still sleeping."

"Look around the house for a note. Check on the door of the refrigerator. That's the most common place to leave messages."

"Good gracious! You're right. I can see a note from where I'm standing."

"What does it say?"

"Gone for an interview at 121 Myrtle Road."

"Oh, no! Get a cab. We have to get over there immediately. She's probably in danger. That's a **residential** area, not a business one."

Sheila was at Sonny's house in the blink of an eye. They told the cabbie they'd pay him double if he got them to Myrtle Road in five minutes. The cab sped like a racecar. Sonny **leaped** out before it came to a **halt** and ran to the house. He heard Rita crying for help.

With his iron fists, Sonny smashed the glass window next to the main entrance door of the house. He pushed his hand through the window to open the door from the inside, but Billy grabbed it forcefully.

"No. Sonny, stop! He has a knife!" Rita yelled.

As Billy attempted to stab Sonny's hand, Rita crawled on the floor and **grabbed** a wine bottle that had fallen and **shattered** during her struggle. She pierced Billy's buttocks with all her **might**. He groaned with pain as blood **gushed** out of the wound.

Billy turned around instantly to attack Rita. He was unsuccessful. Sheila had just entered the house through the back door, and she struck him on his knees with a baseball bat. Slowly, he collapsed on the floor. Sonny returned to the cab and sat in the back seat.

"What on Earth are you doing here?" asked Sheila angrily while helping Rita to get up.

"I called his office this morning to inquire if the position he advertised in the newspaper was available," Rita sobbed. "He said it was still open. I took a taxi here. I swear I didn't know this was his home address. Sister, I'm so ashamed of myself. Billy planned the evening carefully. He was almost drunk before I arrived. Dinner was already prepared before I came. When I resisted his sexual advances, he became angry. Like a wild tiger, he ripped my dress and was about to rape me when you and Sonny arrived."

"Let's go home."

Rita entered the cab after she regained her **composure**. She sat next to her husband with her head

bowed in **shame**.

"We should call the police," the driver said.

"No," Sonny said. "Take us back." He feared that police intervention might lead to his family's deportation to India. They'd just have to hope that Billy would be too scared of getting caught for his own crime to report them.

"But this looks like you attacked him! I could get arrested as a getaway driver!"

"We'll double your pay again," Sheila said.

The cabbie hesitated a moment, then hit the accelerator.

As soon as they arrived at home, Rita rushed to the bathroom. She stared at herself in the mirror and broke down in tears. It was difficult for her to **comprehend** what she had experienced. She wanted to go to bed and then wake up the following morning and pretend she had never had that dreadful and **humiliating** experience.

When Sonny did not come to bed, Rita **confronted** him in the living room. He was lying on the couch. "Sonny, why aren't you sleeping in bed with me? The sofa is not as comfortable."

"You **lewd** woman, don't speak—"

Before he completed his sentence, Rita slapped him on his right cheek. He didn't expect the blow.

"Don't you dare disrespect me again," Sonny growled. He leaped out of the sofa and grabbed the collar of her nightgown. He was about to strike her when Kamla entered the house.

"Stop it, Daddy," she shouted. "Why can't you show some understanding and give her support?"

Sonny let go of Rita, and she ran to Kamla and hugged her. Kamla hugged and kissed her.

"Mother, I couldn't believe it when Aunt Sheila told me about the incident. I'm very sad for you."

Sonny went to the kitchen and poured a cup of tea. He lit a cigarette and sipped his tea at the table.

Kamla slept with her mother that night.

The following morning, Rita was greeted with good news on the telephone. Joshi called to inform her that he had received their green cards from the United States immigration department. Rita felt **exhilarated** and **jubilant**. It was the first time she had experienced so much joy and happiness since she had come to America. With **dogged** determination, she put behind all the painful and **traumatic** experiences she and her family had **endured** in their **quest** for a better life in America. She felt fortunate that the immigration department had awarded them their permanent residency status based on the **merit** of her brother's sponsorship and their graduate degrees and work experience in India.

Later that day, Sonny begged Rita to **forgive** him for his **outrageous** behavior and insensitive attitude following her **ordeal** with Billy. He had come to understand that it was a **nightmare** she would never forget. Afterwards, Rita shared the good news with him and Kamla about their green cards.

With his green card in hand, Sonny was finally hired by Shelly at T&T Security Agency.

Rita accepted a sales manager position at the garment factory where she had initially worked. Her experience in a similar position in India qualified her for this job.

Kamla was hired as a science professor at Rollins University in New York City. She was confident now that her dream of becoming a Nobel laureate could come true.

EXERCISE 1

Applying the Words You Have Learned to Critical Thinking and Creative Writing

- Use the two questions in Section A below to discuss this chapter with your classmates. Be sure to apply your critical thinking skills.

- Write an essay about either question using the vocabulary words you know from real-life experiences and the new ones you have learned from this text.

Section A

Discussion Questions

1. What did Rita mean when she said Sonny was a slave to tradition?

____

____

____

____

____

____

____

____

2. How do you feel about Billy Burger's behavior toward Rita?

____

____

____

____

____

____

____

EXERCISE 2

Matching Meanings

■ Match each word with its meaning.

_____	1. court	**A.**	one who is guilty of a crime
_____	2. judge	**B.**	a member of a jury
_____	3. jail	**C.**	one who owns and rents real estate
_____	4. defendant	**D.**	the killing of one person by another
_____	5. criminal	**E.**	the study and investigation of crime and criminals
_____	6. homicide	**F.**	a hall where trials are held
_____	7. juror	**G.**	one who settles a dispute
_____	8. litigation	**H.**	one who passes judgment in a court of law
_____	9. tenant	**I.**	an order to appear in court
_____	10. rent	**J.**	betrayal of one's country
_____	11. jailbreak	**K.**	a building where convicted people are confined
_____	12. landlord	**L.**	a lawsuit
_____	13. summons	**M.**	a person accused
_____	14. bailiff	**N.**	one who maintains order in a courtroom
_____	15. arbitrator	**O.**	one who pays to occupy part or all of a building
_____	16. criminology	**P.**	one who is often put in jail
_____	17. treason	**Q.**	breaking out of jail by force
_____	18. cop	**R.**	payment for occupying part or all of a building
_____	19. jailbird	**S.**	imprison
_____	20. incarcerate	**T.**	police officer

EXERCISE 3

Synonyms: Multiple Choice

■ Circle the letter of the word or phrase that is most similar in meaning to the **boldfaced** word.

1. **frugal** **A.** not wasteful **B.** smart **C.** old **D.** young
2. **gentle** **A.** soft **B.** tough **C.** hard **D.** hardy
3. **general** **A.** broad **B.** narrow **C.** constricted **D.** limited
4. **extraordinary** **A.** special **B.** stale **C.** useless **D.** void
5. **difficult** **A.** easy **B.** hard **C.** helpful **D.** dismissive
6. **habit** **A.** chore **B.** routine **C.** honesty **D.** holiness
7. **consistent** **A.** erratic **B.** unsteady **C.** steady **D.** uneasy
8. **adversary** **A.** friend **B.** family **C.** enemy **D.** folly
9. **fashion** **A.** age **B.** novelty **C.** routine **D.** style
10. **elated** **A.** normal **B.** abnormal **C.** just **D.** happy
11. **alias** **A.** title **B.** address **C.** alarm **D.** nickname
12. **compare** **A.** differ **B.** distance **C.** match **D.** dislike
13. **envy** **A.** guilt **B.** shame **C.** jealousy **D.** fear
14. **assertive** **A.** bossy **B.** smart **C.** outlying **D.** unlawful
15. **chastise** **A.** punish **B.** congratulate **C.** admire **D.** assist
16. **challenge** **A.** obey **B.** confront **C.** respect **D.** laugh
17. **expedite** **A.** slow down **B.** speed up **C.** extend **D.** use
18. **assist** **A.** neglect **B.** help **C.** avoid **D.** refuse
19. **ban** **A.** permit **B.** stay **C.** allow **D.** prohibit
20. **constant** **A.** tolerant **B.** helpful **C.** steady **D.** aloud

EXERCISE 4

More Practice with Synonyms

■ Circle the letter of the word or phrase that is most similar in meaning to the **boldfaced** word.

1. guilty of **manslaughter**	**A.** killing	**B.** theft	**C.** rape	**D.** burglary
2. **heterogeneous**	**A.** dissimilar	**B.** agreeable	**C.** disagreeable	**D.** genius
3. **hazardous** materials	**A.** dangerous	**B.** safe	**C.** chemical	**D.** expensive
4. a bad **habit**	**A.** routine	**B.** sleep	**C.** time	**D.** object
5. **hamper** construction of	**A.** hinder	**B.** assist in	**C.** study	**D.** dislike
6. **decision** to remain	**A.** conclusion	**B.** anxiety	**C.** want	**D.** dread
7. **internal** bleeding	**A.** inside	**B.** outside	**C.** open-air	**D.** mental
8. **intervene** on my behalf	**A.** save	**B.** step in	**C.** help	**D.** ignore
9. to **illustrate** a point	**A.** conceal	**B.** make clear	**C.** fall	**D.** cancel
10. first **impression**	**A.** attempt	**B.** job	**C.** feeling	**D.** press
11. **inept** employee	**A.** honorable	**B.** worthy	**C.** heroic	**D.** incompetent
12. during the **intermission**	**A.** movie	**B.** performance	**C.** play	**D.** break
13. **impartial** decision	**A.** favorite	**B.** fake	**C.** fair	**D.** partial
14. **influence** his decision	**A.** tell	**B.** control	**C.** guess	**D.** forecast
15. **inhabitant** of an island	**A.** occupant	**B.** enemy	**C.** friend	**D.** governor
16. **intentional** remark	**A.** deliberate	**B.** petty	**C.** harsh	**D.** encouraging
17. **inferior** materials	**A.** high-quality	**B.** low-grade	**C.** expensive	**D.** rare
18. **interpret** the passage	**A.** dislike	**B.** like	**C.** understand	**D.** read
19. to **investigate** a case	**A.** examine thoroughly	**B.** assist in	**C.** partake	**D.** observe
20. **illegible** handwriting	**A.** clear	**B.** legitimate	**C.** unreadable	**D.** best
21. an **incredible** story	**A.** sad	**B.** true	**C.** unbearable	**D.** unbelievable
22. **initiate** a conversation	**A.** end	**B.** argue	**C.** participate in	**D.** start
23. an **introvert**	**A.** a shy person	**B.** unhappy	**C.** outgoing	**D.** vivacious
24. **instigate** a riot	**A.** cease	**B.** stop	**C.** control	**D.** start
25. **intermittent** rain showers	**A.** constant	**B.** heavy	**C.** plenty	**D.** periodic
26. **intimidate** his enemy	**A.** play with	**B.** respect	**C.** frighten	**D.** fight
27. an **irate** student	**A.** bright	**B.** smart	**C.** angry	**D.** popular
28. first-aid **kit**	**A.** pens	**B.** package	**C.** equipment	**D.** story
29. **kidnap** the baby	**A.** care for	**B.** take by force	**C.** silence	**D.** hit
30. **legible** handwriting	**A.** dirty	**B.** easy to read	**C.** small	**D.** large
31. **lien** on the property	**A.** claim	**B.** payment	**C.** price	**D.** purchase
32. **logical** conclusion	**A.** stupid	**B.** sensible	**C.** humorous	**D.** incorrect
33. to **locate** something	**A.** conceal	**B.** find out where it is	**C.** hide	**D.** sell
34. **maintain** his average	**A.** keep	**B.** lower	**C.** increase	**D.** decrease
35. **maximum** sentence	**A.** best	**B.** greatest	**C.** lowest	**D.** correct
36. **minimum** sentence	**A.** harsh	**B.** lenient	**C.** tough	**D.** least

EXERCISE 5

Synonyms and Antonyms

■ Write the corresponding letter for the synonym and antonym of each **boldfaced** word.

	Synonym	Antonym			
1. **offend**	______	______	**A.** tender	**B.** displease	**C.** please
2. **often**	______	______	**A.** thrifty	**B.** frequently	**C.** seldom
3. **old**	______	______	**A.** antique	**B.** modern	**C.** extensive
4. **onset**	______	______	**A.** beginning	**B.** end	**C.** remarkable
5. **opaque**	______	______	**A.** unclear	**B.** easy	**C.** transparent
6. **oppose**	______	______	**A.** resist	**B.** habitual	**C.** agree
7. **ordinary**	______	______	**A.** consistent	**B.** usual	**C.** rare
8. **pacify**	______	______	**A.** norm	**B.** calm	**C.** provoke
9. **particular**	______	______	**A.** specific	**B.** friend	**C.** general
10. **passive**	______	______	**A.** inactive	**B.** old	**C.** forceful
11. **pernicious**	______	______	**A.** damaging	**B.** title	**C.** harmless
12. **petite**	______	______	**A.** differ	**B.** small	**C.** big
13. **plausible**	______	______	**A.** slow	**B.** believable	**C.** improbable
14. **pleasant**	______	______	**A.** appealing	**B.** unfavorable	**C.** guilt
15. **plentiful**	______	______	**A.** abundant	**B.** scarce	**C.** obedient
16. **polite**	______	______	**A.** courteous	**B.** rude	**C.** permitted
17. **potent**	______	______	**A.** strong	**B.** tolerant	**C.** weak
18. **possible**	______	______	**A.** smart	**B.** likely	**C.** unattainable
19. **precious**	______	______	**A.** valuable	**B.** inexpensive	**C.** tough
20. **prejudice**	______	______	**A.** discrimination	**B.** impartiality	**C.** enough
21. **premature**	______	______	**A.** stole	**B.** early	**C.** late
22. **previous**	______	______	**A.** narrow	**B.** earlier	**C.** following
23. **profit**	______	______	**A.** gain	**B.** hard	**C.** loss
24. **proud**	______	______	**A.** boastful	**B.** humble	**C.** practical
25. **prudent**	______	______	**A.** careful	**B.** careless	**C.** unsteady
26. **prowess**	______	______	**A.** aptitude	**B.** inability	**C.** family

	Synonym	Antonym			
27. **punctual**	______	______	**A.** prompt	**B.** late	**C.** abnormal
28. **quarrelsome**	______	______	**A.** bad-tempered	**B.** shame	**C.** peaceful
29. **queer**	______	______	**A.** distant	**B.** strange	**C.** normal
30. **quell**	______	______	**A.** outsmart	**B.** calm	**C.** incite
31. **query**	______	______	**A.** question	**B.** answer	**C.** confrontation
32. **question**	______	______	**A.** ask	**B.** respond	**C.** assist
33. **quick**	______	______	**A.** fast	**B.** tiring	**C.** slow
34. **quiet**	______	______	**A.** still	**B.** noisy	**C.** hurried
35. **radiant**	______	______	**A.** shining	**B.** steady	**C.** dull
36. **rage**	______	______	**A.** anger	**B.** difficulty	**C.** calmness
37. **rapid**	______	______	**A.** quick	**B.** old	**C.** slow
38. **rational**	______	______	**A.** sensible	**B.** foolish	**C.** useless
39. **ravage**	______	______	**A.** damage	**B.** restore	**C.** stay
40. **ready**	______	______	**A.** prepared	**B.** unprepared	**C.** confront
41. **real**	______	______	**A.** helpful	**B.** true	**C.** false
42. **rebuke**	______	______	**A.** rival	**B.** scold	**C.** praise
43. **recall**	______	______	**A.** remodel	**B.** remember	**C.** forget
44. **recede**	______	______	**A.** withdraw	**B.** alarm	**C.** advance
45. **receive**	______	______	**A.** obtain	**B.** match	**C.** give
46. **reckless**	______	______	**A.** careless	**B.** careful	**C.** outlay
47. **recover**	______	______	**A.** get back	**B.** lose	**C.** admire
48. **refrain**	______	______	**A.** avoid	**B.** respect	**C.** indulge
49. **refuse**	______	______	**A.** reject	**B.** slow down	**C.** accept
50. **refute**	______	______	**A.** disprove	**B.** agree	**C.** admire
51. **regular**	______	______	**A.** usual	**B.** avoid	**C.** irregular
52. **reinforce**	______	______	**A.** strengthen	**B.** allow	**C.** weaken
53. **release**	______	______	**A.** free	**B.** hold	**C.** comply
54. **relevant**	______	______	**A.** suitable	**B.** hardy	**C.** unnecessary
55. **relish**	______	______	**A.** avoid	**B.** enjoy	**C.** dislike

	Synonym	Antonym			
56. **remain**	_______	_______	**A.** limit	**B.** stay	**C.** leave
57. **remember**	_______	_______	**A.** recall	**B.** forget	**C.** return
58. **remarkable**	_______	_______	**A.** special	**B.** holy	**C.** ordinary
59. **repair**	_______	_______	**A.** fix	**B.** break	**C.** facilitate
60. **responsible**	_______	_______	**A.** foolish	**B.** reliable	**C.** undependable
61. **retreat**	_______	_______	**A.** style	**B.** withdraw	**C.** advance
62. **reveal**	_______	_______	**A.** disclose	**B.** nickname	**C.** hide
63. **ridiculous**	_______	_______	**A.** foolish	**B.** abhorrent	**C.** sensible
64. **rigorous**	_______	_______	**A.** severe	**B.** lenient	**C.** fearful
65. **rough**	_______	_______	**A.** helpful	**B.** unsmooth	**C.** gentle
66. **saturate**	_______	_______	**A.** fill	**B.** outlaw	**C.** empty
67. **scatter**	_______	_______	**A.** disperse	**B.** gather	**C.** laugh
68. **scrupulous**	_______	_______	**A.** extremely careful	**B.** typical	**C.** negligent
69. **seal**	_______	_______	**A.** close	**B.** open	**C.** refuse
70. **seldom**	_______	_______	**A.** previously	**B.** rarely	**C.** often
71. **sensible**	_______	_______	**A.** wise	**B.** senseless	**C.** aloud
72. **separate**	_______	_______	**A.** isolate	**B.** unite	**C.** traumatize
73. **serene**	_______	_______	**A.** peaceful	**B.** confusing	**C.** disturbed
74. **serious**	_______	_______	**A.** important	**B.** unessential	**C.** emotional
75. **shrewd**	_______	_______	**A.** smart	**B.** envious	**C.** dull-witted

EXERCISE 6

Antonyms

■ Match each word with its antonym.

_____ 1. hamper	**A.** biased
_____ 2. inept	**B.** believable
_____ 3. impartial	**C.** conclude
_____ 4. interpret	**D.** help
_____ 5. illegible	**E.** misunderstand
_____ 6. incredible	**F.** dexterous
_____ 7. initiate	**G.** rough
_____ 8. instigate	**H.** preserve
_____ 9. intermittent	**I.** gloom
_____ 10. hot	**J.** harmless
_____ 11. maximum	**K.** readable
_____ 12. gentle	**L.** dissuade
_____ 13. emotional	**M.** boredom
_____ 14. enmity	**N.** extravagant
_____ 15. eliminate	**O.** minimum
_____ 16. excitement	**P.** constant
_____ 17. enough	**Q.** cold
_____ 18. fun	**R.** internal
_____ 19. frugal	**S.** calm
_____ 20. fluctuate	**T.** apathy
_____ 21. erratic	**U.** goodwill
_____ 22. external	**V.** flawless
_____ 23. fervor	**W.** consistent
_____ 24. fatal	**X.** stabilize
_____ 25. faulty	**Y.** shortage

EXERCISE 7

Word Meaning in Context: Set 1

■ Read each sentence and find the missing word in the box below. Fill in the blank with the correct *form* of that word.

inept	**inferior**	**impartial**	**hazardous**
interpret	**illustrate**	**hamper**	**influence**
intermission	**intervene**	**intentional**	**heterogeneous**

1. Unlike Japan, where almost everyone is of Japanese ancestry, the population of the United States is ___________.
2. To ___________ my point, I will give several examples from recent history.
3. Do not let only the question of money ___________ your decision to take the new job.
4. Walking in an open field during a thunderstorm can be ___________.
5. Despite being ___________ in all aspects of business, the supervisor's nephew was hired as the new office manager.
6. Please, forgive me. If I offended you, it was certainly not ___________.
7. Lack of a college degree ___________ Catherine in her job search.
8. Because the movie is over three hours long, there will be an ___________ after the first ninety minutes.
9. A lower price for an item sometimes reflects ___________ quality.
10. Although she usually remained neutral, the seriousness of the fight between the two brothers forced their mother to ___________.
11. Although teachers claim to be ___________, studies have shown that they pay more attention to boys than girls in the classroom.
12. Your handwriting is so bad that I am having a difficult time trying to ___________ it.

EXERCISE 8

Word Meaning in Context: Set 2

■ Read each sentence and find the missing word in the box below. Fill in the blank with the correct *form* of that word.

irate	**incredible**	**logical**	**instigate**
maximum	**illegible**	**locate**	**intermittent**
introvert	**investigate**	**intimidate**	**legible**

1. Ten detectives ___________ the case, but they never found the missing child.
2. When we discovered that $50,000 was missing, we immediately ___________ a search.
3. After one hundred years in the attic of the house, the handwriting on the letter was barely ___________.
4. Some doctors have such bad handwriting that the prescriptions they write are ___________.
5. The meteorologist predicted ___________ showers throughout the day, with the occasional hour or two of sunshine in between.
6. Scientists and mathematicians must think in a ___________ way.
7. Nowadays, if a letter arrives one day after it was mailed, people regard it as ___________.

8. Because Billy was six inches taller than his classmates, he was able to ___________ them.

9. Bus stations always seem to be ___________ in the worst areas of big cities.

10. ___________ should consider a career other than sales.

11. When the check he deposited two weeks before still had not cleared, the customer became ___________.

12. The ___________ speed limit on certain highways in the United States is sixty-five miles per hour.

EXERCISE 9

Context Clues

■ Select the word or phrase that most closely matches the meaning of the **boldfaced** word. *Note that replacing the **boldfaced** word with the right answer might not produce a grammatically correct sentence.*

1. The sales agent earned a **commission** of $100 for selling the home entertainment system.
   A. low payment **B.** check **C.** share of the profit **D.** vacation

2. She carefully deliberated the pros and cons of her decision before she **committed** her savings to the new stockbroker.
   A. took away **B.** entrusted **C.** told about **D.** threw

3. The healthcare company encouraged senior citizens to buy its new **commodity** by offering it at a reduced price.
   A. action **B.** product **C.** plan **D.** calendar

4. It is not easy to reveal one's needs and **communicate** them to an employer.
   A. leave out **B.** intensify **C.** express **D.** examine

5. Elected government officials have learned that communicating with their **community** is essential if they want to be re-elected.
   A. workers **B.** extended family
   C. medical professionals **D.** people living in a specific place

6. The online dating service had a proven track record of matching men and women who were **compatible**.
   A. able to go together **B.** work-oriented **C.** outgoing **D.** overachievers

7. In order to **compensate** the family for its losses, the insurance company had to pay more than they were willing to.
   A. give money **B.** punish **C.** investigate **D.** elect to office

8. Before seeing his tax preparer, the man **compiled** all his papers and documents.
   A. stole **B.** falsified **C.** erased **D.** put together

9. The science students learned how to identify different **compounds** and elements.
   A. combinations of parts **B.** demonstrations of skill
   C. changes in state **D.** details

10. The housing developers created a package **comprised** of attractive photos and information about the homes they were selling.
   A. made up **B.** repeated **C.** omitted **D.** deleted

11. The total savings from their shopping trip were **computed** with a calculator.

  A. determined **B.** written **C.** improved **D.** turned into a program

12. When he first presented his vision to colleagues, it seemed impossible to **conceive** that one day his invention would make him a millionaire.

  A. say **B.** imagine **C.** prove **D.** deny

13. I find it hard to **concentrate** if the room is noisy.

  A. focus **B.** spell **C.** talk **D.** withdraw

14. The class ended when the instructor **concluded** her lecture.

  A. finished **B.** yawned **C.** timed **D.** recorded

15. His new job schedule ran **concurrently** with his classes at the college. It was impossible for him to be in two places at once.

  A. at the same time **B.** in different ways **C.** near **D.** in the same town

16. The principal told the parents that if their daughter did not **conduct** herself more respectfully, she would be disciplined.

  A. speak **B.** behave **C.** dress **D.** do homework

17. Before the business deal could be approved, both parties had to **confer** on the smaller details of the contract.

  A. discuss **B.** place **C.** achieve **D.** swear

18. The prisoners were **confined** to their cells until officers could restore order to the jail.

  A. praised **B.** restricted **C.** freed **D.** destroyed

19. There was a **conflict** between the parents, and they began shouting at each other.

  A. loud song **B.** heavy object **C.** argument **D.** river

20. The school had to receive parental **consent** before the children could go on the school trip.

  A. approval **B.** business **C.** signatures **D.** attention

21. The group of boys had to face the **consequences** of their poor behavior.

  A. results **B.** path **C.** cause **D.** victim

22. Water **consists** of two atoms of hydrogen and one atom of oxygen.

  A. is made up **B.** is held together **C.** is kept hidden **D.** is worth

23. It could take more than a year to **construct** a six-family building.

  A. leave **B.** build **C.** buy **D.** destroy

24. Yen always **consulted** with her supervisor before taking a day off from work.

  A. fight **B.** intimidate **C.** sulk **D.** checked

EXERCISE 10

Vocabulary Test

- Select the correct answer.
- Hint: Review the meanings of all the **boldfaced** words in this chapter before you take the test. This approach can help you to score 100 percent.
- Record the percentage of correct answers on the Master Self-Assessment table on page 397.

1 **Frugal** means:

A. not wasteful
B. smart
C. old
D. young

2 A **gentle** voice is:

E. soft
F. tough
G. hard
H. hardy

3 A **general** statement is:

A. broad
B. narrow
C. constricted
D. weak

4 An **extraordinary** festival is:

E. stale
F. special
G. useless
H. void

5 A synonym for **habit** is:

A. normal
B. routine
C. honest
D. holy

6 To be **consistent** is to be:

E. frugal
F. steady
G. unsteady
H. uneasy

7 An **adversary** is:

A. a friend
B. a family
C. an enemy
D. an ant

8 A new **fashion** is a:

E. dance
F. routine
G. rarity
H. style

9 A person **elated** to win something is:

A. entitled
B. dedicated
C. happy
D. justified

10 An **alias** is:

E. a title
F. an address
G. an alarm
H. a nickname

11 A synonym for **envy** is:

A. guilt
B. shame
C. jealousy
D. blame

12 An **assertive** manner is:

E. bossy
F. loyal
G. rough
H. illegal

13 To **chastise** someone is to:

A. punish
B. congratulate
C. admire
D. assist

14 **Expedite** means to:

E. slow down
F. speed up
G. decrease
H. change

15 To **assist** is to:

A. neglect
B. help
C. avoid
D. refuse

16 To **ban** a product is to:

E. permit
F. alter
G. allow
H. disallow

17 A **constant** speed is:

A. slow
B. high
C. steady
D. irregular

18 A person guilty of **manslaughter** is guilty of:

E. killing someone
F. rape
G. theft
H. burglary

19 **Heterogeneous** means:

A. dissimilar
B. agreeable
C. disagreeable
D. similar

20 To **hamper** construction is to:

E. hinder
F. assist
G. study
H. dislike

21 To **intervene** on behalf of someone is to:

A. save
B. step in
C. support
D. represent

22 To **illustrate** something is to:

E. conceal
F. explain using examples
G. tell
H. cancel

23 A first **impression** is:

A. an attempt
B. a job
C. a feeling
D. an idea

24 **Inept** means:

E. good
F. able
G. unhappy
H. incompetent

25 An **intermission** is a:

A. movie
B. performance
C. message
D. break

26 An **impartial** decision is:

E. favorable
F. illegal
G. fair
H. incomplete

27 To **influence** a decision is to:

A. argue with
B. have control over
C. guess
D. forecast

28 An **inhabitant** is:

E. an occupant
F. an enemy
G. a friend
H. a governor

29 **Intentional** remarks are:

A. deliberate
B. petty
C. harsh
D. encouraging

30 **Inferior** materials are:

E. of high quality
F. of low grade
G. expensive
H. inexpensive

31 To **interpret** a passage is to:

A. dislike
B. approve
C. understand
D. read

32 An **incredible** story is:

E. sad
F. true
G. unbearable
H. unbelievable

33 To **initiate** a conversation is to:

A. end
B. start
C. participate in
D. argue

34 An **introvert** is someone who is:

E. shy
F. careful
G. unusual
H. vivacious

35 To **instigate** a riot is to:

- **A.** cease
- **B.** stop
- **C.** control
- **D.** encourage to begin

36 **Intermittent** rain showers are:

- **E.** constant
- **F.** heavy
- **G.** plentiful
- **H.** periodic

37 To **intimidate** an enemy is to:

- **A.** play with
- **B.** respect
- **C.** frighten
- **D.** fight

38 An **irate** student is:

- **E.** bright
- **F.** smart
- **G.** angry
- **H.** popular

39 A first-aid **kit** has:

- **A.** pens
- **B.** hardware
- **C.** medical supplies
- **D.** software

40 To **kidnap** a baby is to:

- **E.** care for
- **F.** seize by unlawful force
- **G.** silence
- **H.** hit

41 To place a **lien** on a property is to make:

- **A.** a claim
- **B.** a payment
- **C.** a price
- **D.** an offer

42 A **logical** conclusion is:

- **E.** stupid
- **F.** sensible
- **G.** wrong
- **H.** illegal

43 To **locate** a street is to:

- **A.** find
- **B.** walk
- **C.** pass by
- **D.** sweep

44 To **maintain** means to:

E. keep
F. lower
G. increase
H. decrease

45 **Maximum** means:

A. least
B. greatest
C. lowest
D. fastest

46 To **offend** someone is to:

E. embrace
F. displease
G. satisfy
H. prod

47 An antonym for **often** is:

A. thrifty
B. frequently
C. seldom
D. never

48 An antonym for **onset** is:

E. beginning
F. end
G. security
H. severity

49 **Opaque** means:

A. not bright or unclear
B. easy
C. clear
D. white

50 To **oppose** means to:

E. resist
F. help
G. agree
H. assess

51 To **pacify** is to:

A. scold
B. calm
C. prolong
D. irritate

52 A **particular** person is:

E. specific
F. friendly
G. ordinary
H. uneasy

53 A **passive** person is:

A. inactive
B. old
C. forceful
D. sleepy

54 A synonym for **pernicious** is:

E. damaging
F. eager
G. harmless
H. cruel

55 A **pleasant** outing is:

A. enjoyable
B. calming
C. guilty
D. tiring

56 An antonym for **petite** is:

E. different
F. small
G. big
H. fat

57 An antonym for **plentiful** is:

A. abundant
B. scarce
C. obedient
D. lean

58 **Polite** means:

E. courteous
F. rude
G. cunning
H. permissive

59 A **potent** mixture is:

A. strong
B. heavy
C. weak
D. sweet

60 A **possible** task is:

E. smart
F. attainable
G. challenging
H. simple

61 **Precious** jewelry is:

A. of great value
B. inexpensive
C. gaudy
D. shiny

62 Another word for **prejudice** is:

E. discrimination
F. pride
G. glory
H. decision

63 A **premature** baby is:

A. coming too soon
B. ready
C. late
D. punctual

64 Another word for **profit** is:

E. gain
F. money
G. loss
H. income

65 A person who is not **prudent** is:

A. careful
B. careless
C. unsteady
D. reliable

66 The gymnast showed great **prowess** or:

E. skill
F. fear
G. weakness
H. loyalty

67 **Punctual** for class means:

A. prompt or on time
B. tardy
C. delayed
D. absent

68 A **quarrelsome** person is:

E. bad-tempered
F. shameful
G. peaceful
H. agreeable

69 A synonym for **queer** is:

A. distant
B. strange
C. normal
D. careful

70 To **quell** a riot is to:

E. outsmart
F. calm
G. incite
H. engage

71 To **query** means to:

A. question

B. seek

C. reject

D. accept

72 To **question** is to:

E. answer

F. ask

G. help

H. see

73 A **quick** act is:

A. fast

B. risky

C. slow

D. sudden

74 Another word for **rage** is:

E. anger

F. sadness

G. joy

H. happiness

75 **Radiant** means:

A. dull

B. hot

C. shining

D. cloudy

EXERCISE 11

Building a Stronger Vocabulary

- Review all the **boldfaced** words in this chapter before you proceed to the next exercise.
- Highlight the ones you are still having difficulty remembering.
- List them with their meanings on a table.
- Use them to compose your own sentences.
- Think of a synonym and an antonym for each word.
- Use checkmarks to indicate if each word you want to practice more has a prefix, suffix, and/or root.
- You may use the table below as a sample to write your answers in your notebook.

Word	Definition	Sentence	Synonym	Antonym	Prefix	Suffix	Root

EXERCISE 12

Creating My Own Powerful Word List

- Write the words and meanings from the above table on the **Creating My Own Powerful Word List** table on page 398. Review them often to build that super vocabulary you want to create for school, work, and everyday use.

PRE-READING

About This Chapter from *Trial of Love*

- Read the names and descriptions of this chapter's main characters below.
  - Kathy Precious Armstrong: Kamla's best friend
  - Mark Edison Hubbard: A professor of pre-law
  - Cindy Singh: A laboratory assistant
  - Sonny and his family

Story Vocabulary Exercise

- Before you begin reading this chapter, figure out the meanings of the unfamiliar **boldfaced** vocabulary words. You may use the Word List, Word Parts Chart, or your dictionary to assist you in finding their meanings.
- Look for the various types of context clues—synonyms, antonyms, general context, and examples—as you read.
- Write a word or phrase about the meaning of each **boldfaced** word in the margin.

Reading and Writing Exercise

- Skim the entire chapter and pay attention to the headings and the discussion questions that follow.
- Initial Response: Write a paragraph explaining, in your own words, what you think this chapter of the story will be about.
- Final Response: After you have read the entire chapter, compare your current understanding with your initial response above. If your initial response was accurate, you can simply write it again to fill in the blanks below. If it was not, then write a paragraph on what the chapter was really about instead.

Initial Response

This chapter **will** be about ____

____

____

____

Final Response

This chapter **was** about ____

____

____

____

KAMLA AT ROLLINS UNIVERSITY

It was about 2:00 a.m. when Rita made her way downstairs to the sitting room. She was surprised that Kamla was still watching television, and that she did not **acknowledge** her presence when she sat beside her on the sofa.

"Is something bothering you? You haven't slept much for the past two nights."

Kamla didn't **respond**.

"I'm your mother. You should feel comfortable **confiding** in me, Kamla."

"Today will be my first day teaching at an American university. I'm very nervous, Mother. I don't know anybody there. I'll feel **awkward** and out of place."

"There's nothing to worry about. Feeling awkward is natural. We're in a foreign country with a culture that's **alien** to us. We'll adjust to it slowly."

"That's not all. I am not sure I will be able to teach American students. They are not the same as Indian students."

"You're a brilliant and **talented** researcher. You received numerous awards for your outstanding professional work when you were in India. I'm positive you'll **excel** at Rollins, too. You always worry unnecessarily."

Kamla felt somewhat relaxed after talking with her mother. She threw her arm around her in anticipation of a hug.

"Mother, why do I always feel better after talking with you about things that bother me?"

Rita said, "I guess it's because I'm your mother." She returned the hug. "Let's get some sleep."

Kamla's Meeting with Her Boss

Kamla didn't recall the room number of the science department at Rollins. She was reading the signs on the doors of the offices in the east wing of the science building. As she was about to knock on one of the doors, a very friendly voice interrupted her.

"Are you a new faculty member?"

"Yes, I am. I'm Kamla Kumar."

"What a beautiful name!" said Kathy.

"So is yours. Kathy Precious Armstrong," said Kamla, reading from the identification badge on Kathy's lab coat.

"I'm the department's laboratory assistant," Kathy said. "I guess we will be working together. I was assigned to all your classes in the lab. At our last staff meeting, our chairperson mentioned that you would be joining our faculty."

"Thanks for telling me."

"Are you from India?"

"Yes," replied Kamla.

"I miss India."

"When were you there?" asked Kamla excitedly.

"Actually, I was raised in India. My stepfather was a diplomat who worked in New Delhi. We returned home a few years ago. I miss the colorful festivals, the vast **array** of foods with their **pungent** smells and **aromas**. I **yearn** to hear the **gurus chanting** at **dawn** every day. I miss the slow-paced lifestyle and peaceful **tranquility**. The people were warm, sensitive and caring. They embraced me as their Indian sister and not as a white girl and the daughter of the American Consul General."

As soon as Kathy completed her last sentence, Kamla anxiously asked if she could **accompany** her to meet the chairperson of their department. Kamla had never met her chairperson. She had been hired by the president of Rollins University, an international **scholar** on infectious diseases. He had chosen to hire Kamla because he had read about her research in India. Her findings had been published in several scientific journals worldwide.

Kathy thought Kamla was stunningly beautiful. She **envied** her charm. She invited Kamla to join her for lunch in the faculty cafeteria, and the pair became so caught up in conversation that they almost forgot about Kamla's meeting with the chairperson. Kathy hurriedly led Kamla to the chairperson's office and wished her good luck.

Dr. Elsie Penelope had been the chairperson of the science department for more than a decade. When Kamla arrived in her office, she discussed Kamla's research plans with her and pledged to support her goals. Professor Penelope told Kamla that she hoped she would invent more vaccines to cure other deadly diseases.

Kamla felt pressured by her expectations. Nevertheless, she expressed her **gratitude** for the confidence Professor Penelope had in her abilities and **expertise**. She left her office after receiving her teaching schedule from her.

Kamla needed a friend at Rollins University. It was still a challenge for her to **adjust** to a new way of life in America, and she felt left out because there were no Indian faculty members on Rollins University's staff. Kathy was the only person on campus who understood her cultural background. Kamla felt **compelled** to establish a close friendship with her, even though they did not share common academic interests at the professorial level.

After the meeting, Kamla and Kathy enjoyed coffee and dessert in the cafeteria. Kathy gave Kamla an excellent **orientation** to Rollins University. They talked about its faculty, staff, administration, and student population. As they were chatting, Cindy, one of Kathy's friends, dropped by to say hello to her. Kathy introduced her to Professor Kamla. After lunch, Kamla returned to teach her afternoon classes.

Kamla's Bad Attitude

Rita was preparing dinner when Kamla returned from school. She had been thinking about her all day at work. Kamla uttered a few words to her before going to her room to prepare her lessons for the next day's classes. Less than one hour later, Sonny returned home from work. Rita was still in the kitchen. When he attempted to embrace her, she pushed him away.

"Keep your hands to yourself," she said with a smile.

Sonny was taken aback by her reaction.

"What's the matter with you today? Aren't you in the mood for . . . ?"

"Don't you have respect for your daughter?"

"Sure. But she isn't around. Are we still married or what?"

"Sonny, I always feel uncomfortable displaying affection openly when Kamla is at home."

"You talk like an old village woman! Anyway, yell when dinner is ready."

"Sure. Neither of you cares to help in the kitchen."

"Sorry. I'll return to assist you as soon as I finish bathing."

"Never mind. Dinner is almost ready."

Rita observed that Kamla was very **irritable** at dinner. Sonny did not notice, though, and he was **curious** about her experience at school.

"How was your first day, Kamla?" he asked.

"Fine," she **snapped**.

Sonny paused for a second before continuing the conversation.

"Did you make any friends?"

"Yes," said Kamla reluctantly. "I met Kathy, my lab assistant."

Rita observed that Kamla wasn't eating much of her food. Meanwhile, Sonny was **devouring** his chicken **biryani**, a rice dish, with an **insatiable** appetite.

"Don't you like the food, Kamla?" asked Rita.

"I'm tired of eating the same Indian food day after day."

"What's your **preference**?"

"American dishes."

Sonny choked momentarily at her response.

"Kamla, I don't know how to prepare American dishes."

"Then you should learn, Mother."

Rita felt disappointed and was quiet. Sonny stared at Kamla with piercing eyes.

"Your mother doesn't have to learn to cook American dishes," said Sonny angrily. "If that's your preference, then you should learn to prepare them."

The telephone rang and Rita answered the call. It was Kathy calling for Kamla. Kamla thanked Kathy for making her feel comfortable and welcome at Rollins University.

Kamla went to bed after their conversation, but could not fall asleep easily. She regretted her bitter **disrespect** toward her parents at the dinner table.

During the next several weeks, Kathy and Kamla's friendship grew stronger. Kathy felt very comfortable talking about anything with Kamla. She had a very strong, sisterly love for her.

Kathy observed that Kamla was spending very long hours at work every day. She would rush to her private lab to conduct research the same way she had when she was in India. She was working almost fifteen hours per day. Kathy knew that her long hours of work were **detrimental** to her health and were the result of not having a social life.

Kathy had a plan for her best friend, Kamla. She revealed it to her the following evening at dinner at the Fung Yu restaurant in midtown Manhattan.

"Kamla, don't you want to take a break from your **rigid** work schedule?" asked Kathy cautiously.

"What do you mean?" asked Kamla.

"I think you should take a break from your work to relax, especially on weekends. I mean, you should go out and have a good time like most Americans do," replied Kathy.

"I really don't need a guy in my life now, if that's what you are **insinuating**, Kathy. Thanks for your concern. I'm proud to have a friend like you who is looking out for my best interest. I'm truly blessed!"

"Just be quiet, Kamla. Save your academic reasoning for someone else. I've got the perfect guy for you. You must meet him."

"Sorry, I'm not interested, Kathy."

"Don't lie to me. I'm quite **adept** at lying and can tell when somebody's trying to **deceive** me. I know you Indian women **intimately** and can see through the **pretentiousness** of foreigners quite easily. I know how lonely you are when you come to America. The first thing you do when you arrive is look for the closest McDonald's so you can dig into that juicy burger. Then you **discard** your **traditional attire** and **embark** on a wild chase for the hottest nightclubs in town to get down and let loose. Don't think you can **trick** me, my dear. I saw the way you were secretly admiring some of the male faculty members in the lounge last week. You seem to be the type that will do **naughty** things behind closed doors. Don't worry. I have your back covered."

Suddenly, Kathy became apologetic. "Don't mind my street talk. I can **switch** gears if you want me to, Professor. Pardon me if I am too **forthright**."

"Be quiet, you **chatterbox**. All foreigners are not like that, but I'm positive you're not a **biased** idiot, my friend. I do not have time for a man at this stage of my life. I only want to concentrate, to **focus**, on my career," lied Kamla. "By the way, who is the guy you're talking about?"

"Ah ha! Now we are getting somewhere. I have Mark Edison Hubbard in mind for you."

"Who?" inquired Kamla with **ardent zeal** and **fervent enthusiasm**.

"Mark. He's the pre-law professor. He is very tall and handsome. He has small pale eyes, and dark russet hair. It is his **aspiration** to become an attorney."

"Kathy Precious, why are you so kind to me? You're going out of your way to make me feel happy."

Kathy said, "You and Mark will make an **ideal** couple."

Kamla pretended that she did not hear her and changed the subject.

"Incidentally, I **bumped** into your pal today."

"Who?" asked Kathy without interest.

"Cindy. She's a really **weird** girl."

"She's into **astrology**. Strange **rituals** and who knows what else," said Kathy.

It was around 8:30 when they finished dinner. Kamla thanked Kathy for inviting her out for an enjoyable evening. She went home feeling very relaxed.

EXERCISE 1

Applying the Words You Have Learned to Critical Thinking and Creative Writing

- Use the two questions in Section A below to discuss this chapter with your classmates. Be sure to apply your critical thinking skills.

- Write an essay about either question using the vocabulary words you know from real-life experiences and the new ones you have learned from this text.

Section A

Discussion Questions

1. Do you believe Kamla is becoming Americanized?

____

____

____

____

____

____

____

____

2. Do you predict that Kamla might develop a personal relationship with Mark?

____

____

____

____

____

____

____

EXERCISE 2

Matching Meanings

■ Match each word with its meaning.

_____	1. advocate	**A.** praise or approval
_____	2. apprentice	**B.** an informative talk
_____	3. audit	**C.** amount of money needed for a specific purpose
_____	4. lecture	**D.** a person against another; an adversary
_____	5. credit	**E.** having qualities of men or boys
_____	6. corpse	**F.** examine and verify correctness of financial transactions
_____	7. budget	**G.** happening in the night
_____	8. bilingual	**H.** a person who tells jokes
_____	9. opponent	**I.** that which brings about or hastens a result
_____	10. lunar	**J.** publicly recommend or support
_____	11. solar	**K.** having qualities of women or girls
_____	12. masculine	**L.** the dead body of a person
_____	13. feminine	**M.** ability to speak two languages
_____	14. universe	**N.** a beginner acquiring a trade or skill
_____	15. sedative	**O.** relating to the moon
_____	16. nocturnal	**P.** relating to the sun
_____	17. century	**Q.** a period of 100 years
_____	18. catalyst	**R.** a drug that decreases irritation or nervousness
_____	19. diurnal	**S.** happening in the daytime
_____	20. comedian	**T.** a domain

EXERCISE 3

Forming Synonyms

■ Fill in the blank(s) to complete the word that is similar in meaning to the **boldfaced** word.

1. **naïve** inn__ __ent
2. **nag** an__ __y
3. **niche** pl__c__
4. **nurture** c__re
5. **nonchalant** easyg__ __ __g
6. **negotiate** b__rga__n
7. **nod** mot__on
8. **ominous** thr__ __ten__ __g
9. **orientation** intr__du__ __ __ __ __n
10. **obsess** preo__ __ __py
11. **obstacle** barr__ __r
12. **offend** ins__ __t
13. **occasionally** some__ __ __es
14. **odor** sc__ __t
15. **omnipotent** su__reme
16. **ordeal** tr__al
17. **outcome** re__ __lt
18. **owe** lia__le
19. **own** po__ __ess
20. **panacea** rem__ __y
21. **tangible** concr__ __e
22. **tantrum** outb__ __s__
23. **task** ch__re
24. **temperamental** m__ody

EXERCISE 4

Synonyms: Multiple Choice

■ Circle the letter of the word or phrase that is most similar in meaning to the **boldfaced** word.

1. **assume**	**A.** reject	**B.** accept	**C.** retain	**D.** retry
2. **dilapidate**	**A.** reward	**B.** decay	**C.** strong	**D.** rigid
3. **extrinsic**	**A.** outside	**B.** internal	**C.** exceptional	**D.** fluent
4. **docile**	**A.** passion	**B.** obedient	**C.** arguable	**D.** disobedient
5. **brevity**	**A.** conciseness	**B.** elaboration	**C.** length	**D.** behavior
6. **annual**	**A.** yearly	**B.** sporadic	**C.** slow	**D.** frequent
7. **indicate**	**A.** show	**B.** hide	**C.** conceal	**D.** congest
8. **excited**	**A.** indifferent	**B.** gloomy	**C.** distant	**D.** thrilled
9. **animosity**	**A.** friendship	**B.** warmth	**C.** hatred	**D.** glory
10. **malice**	**A.** affection	**B.** love	**C.** ennui	**D.** hate
11. **tranquil**	**A.** noisy	**B.** crowded	**C.** peaceful	**D.** plenty
12. **dispose**	**A.** save	**B.** get rid of	**C.** retain	**D.** revive
13. **exclude**	**A.** keep out	**B.** include	**C.** disappear	**D.** exhibit
14. **inhuman**	**A.** heartless	**B.** kind	**C.** sad	**D.** polite
15. **articulate**	**A.** sloppy	**B.** well-spoken	**C.** organized	**D.** generous
16. **multiple**	**A.** many	**B.** few	**C.** major	**D.** one
17. **dispute**	**A.** agreement	**B.** friendship	**C.** fatality	**D.** argument
18. **smile**	**A.** frown	**B.** scowl	**C.** grin	**D.** stare
19. **mediocre**	**A.** humble	**B.** superior	**C.** inferior	**D.** excellent
20. **anticipate**	**A.** expect	**B.** reject	**C.** guide	**D.** assist

EXERCISE 5

More Practice with Synonyms

■ Circle the letter of the word or phrase that is most similar in meaning to the **boldfaced** word.

	A	B	C	D
1. country is in a **recession**	**A.** decline in economic activity	**B.** progression	**C.** war	**D.** drought
2. **reduce** the amount	**A.** lessen	**B.** increase	**C.** delete	**D.** add
3. **resourceful** student	**A.** clever	**B.** angry	**C.** lazy	**D.** talkative
4. a good **reputation**	**A.** fame	**B.** dignity	**C.** notoriety	**D.** loneliness
5. **repeat** the lesson	**A.** omit	**B.** restate	**C.** delete	**D.** teach
6. obtain a **refund**	**A.** down payment	**B.** repayment	**C.** discount	**D.** fine
7. **register** for my courses	**A.** delete	**B.** select	**C.** sign up	**D.** drop
8. **respond** to my request	**A.** reject	**B.** deny	**C.** confirm	**D.** reply
9. **revise** the first draft	**A.** add	**B.** mail	**C.** type	**D.** improve
10. **regulate** the flow	**A.** lower	**B.** observe	**C.** adjust	**D.** stop
11. **remedial** courses	**A.** developmental	**B.** difficult	**C.** easy	**D.** long
12. **reserve** something	**A.** keep for future use	**B.** take	**C.** discard	**D.** overtake
13. **rely** on his parents	**A.** work with	**B.** depend on	**C.** disobey	**D.** assist
14. **resume** working	**A.** stop	**B.** discontinue	**C.** begin	**D.** continue
15. **restrict** movement	**A.** encourage	**B.** stop	**C.** control	**D.** initiate
16. **removed** from school	**A.** stay	**B.** remain	**C.** expelled	**D.** failed
17. **reject** the proposal	**A.** consider	**B.** refuse	**C.** study	**D.** take
18. a **remote** village	**A.** distant	**B.** friendly	**C.** war-like	**D.** lonely
19. **revert** to her bad habits	**A.** return	**B.** reply	**C.** ignore	**D.** support
20. a **rigid** schedule	**A.** fixed	**B.** unstable	**C.** difficult	**D.** changing
21. **rural** area	**A.** city	**B.** suburban	**C.** country	**D.** urban
22. **recommend** the person	**A.** give approval	**B.** hire	**C.** fire	**D.** discourage
23. **relapse** into a coma	**A.** slip back	**B.** recover	**C.** enter	**D.** come out
24. **fast** asleep	**A.** sound	**B.** light	**C.** wide	**D.** little
25. **trip** on the bump	**A.** fall	**B.** cover	**C.** stain	**D.** step

EXERCISE 6

Word Meaning in Context

■ Read each sentence and find the missing word in the box below. Fill in the blank with the correct *form* of that word.

rigid	**refund**	**recession**	**revert**
replace	**restrict**	**respond**	**reduce**
reputation	**resourceful**	**revise**	**register**

1. As the interest rates began to rise, the economy slipped into a ____________.
2. If a person faints, the first thing to do is to loosen all clothing that ____________ breathing.
3. Only the most ____________ people can find a taxi in the rain.
4. Charlie's customers did not mind waiting for their repairs, as he had the ____________ of being the best car mechanic in town.
5. If you file your tax return electronically, you will get your ____________ in less than a month.
6. One hundred people had ____________ for the conference, but only fifty showed up because of the snowstorm.
7. If you do not ____________ to this notice in thirty days, your case will be canceled.
8. After hearing that it was going to rain, they __________ their plans to include more indoor activities and less time outside.
9. The military decided to pull its troops back from the border in hopes of __________ tensions with the neighboring country.
10. After losing fifty pounds on the diet, he ____________ to his old eating habits and gained it all back.
11. The Browns sent their son to the military school because they thought its ____________ schedule would help him become more disciplined.
12. It is wise to ____________ the battery in a smoke detector once a year.

EXERCISE 7

Context Clues

■ Select the word or phrase that most closely matches the meaning of the **boldfaced** word. *Note that replacing the **boldfaced** word with the right answer might not produce a grammatically correct sentence.*

1. The more unhealthy foods one **consumes**, the more likely it is that one will have to go on a diet.

   A. eats　**B.** hates　**C.** makes　**D.** enjoys

2. She called her friend to get in **contact** with her mother.

   A. a car　**B.** a fight　**C.** housing　**D.** communication

3. The textbook offered a **context** that helped students understand the lesson.

   A. background information　**B.** picture
   C. question　**D.** unfamiliar words

4. The engineer signed a **contract** stating the price and length of the project before she began working.

   A. demand　**B.** piece of art　**C.** autograph　**D.** agreement

5. Opinions were expressed that were **contrary** to traditional beliefs.
   A. timely **B.** opposite **C.** vulgar **D.** central

6. To show **contrasting** points of view, students were asked to write down their own ideas on gun control, even if their friends disagreed.
   A. very different **B.** closely held **C.** unique **D.** bad

7. **Contributing** money to a charity could improve the well-being of the poor.
   A. giving **B.** reducing **C.** taking **D.** lending

8. After the **controversy** got out of hand, a fight broke out.
   A. resentment **B.** question **C.** dispute **D.** investigation

9. The city council members had to **convene** with sanitation officials to discuss emergency flooding plans.
   A. listen **B.** meet **C.** plan ahead **D.** leave

10. The office workers had to **cooperate** to complete the project.
   A. work together **B.** make amends **C.** keep guard **D.** send mail

11. To organize a recreational program, team leaders had to **coordinate** volunteers.
   A. organize **B.** send away **C.** leave alone **D.** ask a favor from

12. Police said the **core** of complaints from residents was about loud parties in the neighborhood at night.
   A. least common **B.** central part **C.** most frequent **D.** unimportant

13. The **corporate** headquarters of the company was a desirable place to work.
   A. evil in nature **B.** expensive **C.** distant **D.** relating to business

14. Job applicants must **correspond** with employers through the Internet if they want to learn about future job openings.
   A. communicate **B.** reason **C.** deceive **D.** argue

15. The man and woman were considered an ideal **couple**.
   A. pair **B.** advisor **C.** citizen **D.** neighbor

16. To **create** a new recipe for apple pie, the baker added cinnamon and raisins.
   A. sell **B.** steal **C.** avoid burning **D.** make

17. Even though he had hardly worked on the project, Chris took all the **credit**.
   A. recognition **B.** earnings **C.** conditions **D.** materials

18. The job had a long list of difficult **criteria** for completion.
   A. standards **B.** lessons **C.** challenges **D.** employment

19. It is **crucial** that all parents attend the parents' association meeting this week.
   A. voluntary **B.** indecent **C.** outrageous **D.** important

20. This weekend's international festival will highlight various **cultural** celebrations, such as Chinese New Year and the Indian festival of Diwali.

    A. relating to a group of people
    B. famous
    C. televised
    D. attended by many people

21. Only U.S. **currency** will be accepted at the airport's exchange booths.

    A. credit cards
    B. tickets
    C. money
    D. luggage

22. Many people born to poor parents have trouble getting an education, which would let them break the **cycle** of poverty.

    A. trap
    B. repeated set of events
    C. college degree
    D. motorcycle

23. After leaving in the 1980s, the father finally returned to see his son almost a **decade** later, in the 1990s.

    A. ten years
    B. one year
    C. ten days
    D. one generation

24. She **declined** her invitation to the wedding because she hated the family.

    A. corrected
    B. compared
    C. repeated
    D. refused

EXERCISE 8

Vocabulary Test

- Select the correct answer.
- Hint: Review the meanings of all the **boldfaced** words in this chapter before you take the test. This approach can help you to score 100 percent.
- Record the percentage of correct answers on the Master Self-Assessment table on page 397.

1 An **advocate** pleads the cause of another.

A. True
B. False

2 An **apprentice** is a beginner acquiring a trade or skill.

E. True
F. False

3 An accountant's **audit** involves examining and verifying the correctness of financial transactions.

A. True
B. False

4 A **lecture** is an informative talk.

E. True
F. False

5 His success earns him **credit**.

A. criticism
B. praise
C. disapproval
D. money

6 A **corpse** in a coffin is:

E. a dead body
F. bones
G. burial clothing
H. a zombie

7 A company's **budget** refers to:

A. mission statement
B. financial investment
C. standard procedure
D. amount of money needed for a purpose

8 **Bilingual** means:

E. being unable to speak
F. speaking two languages
G. being unable to read
H. speaking many languages

9 An **opponent** is:

A. a giant
B. one who takes an opposite position
C. a teammate
D. an animal

10 **Lunar** refers to the:

E. moon
F. sun
G. galaxy
H. eclipse

11 **Solar** refers to the:

A. moon
B. sun
C. shadows
D. stars

12 **Masculinity** refers to:

E. having talent
F. having male qualities
G. being human
H. being very strong

13 **Femininity** refers to:

A. being sorry
B. having strength
C. being an adult
D. having female qualities

14 **Universal** means:

E. the planet
F. the sky
G. worldwide
H. the neighborhood

15 A **sedative**:

A. generates excitement
B. calms nervousness or excitement
C. protects from disease
D. fertilizes plants

16 **Nocturnal** relates to:

E. nighttime
F. weekend
G. brightness
H. daytime

17 A **century** is a period of:

A. ten years
B. twenty-five years
C. one hundred years
D. inactivity

18 A **catalyst**:

E. adds volume
F. analyzes the behavior of felines
G. increases time
H. brings about or hastens a result

19 **Diurnal** refers to:

A. moonlight
B. daytime
C. darkness
D. morning

20 A **comedian**:

E. tells jokes
F. is a serious person
G. is a fan
H. makes people cry

21 When you **assume** responsibility, you:

A. decline it
B. accept it
C. reject it
D. retry it

22 A **dilapidated** building is:

E. rebuilt
F. decayed
G. strong
H. rigid

23 **Extrinsic** means:

A. outside
B. internal
C. inside
D. evasive

24 A **docile** animal is:

E. angry
F. disobedient
G. obedient
H. sleepy

25 **Brevity** refers to:

A. conciseness
B. boredom
C. clarity
D. frequency

26 An **annual** meeting is:

E. yearly
F. quarterly
G. weekly
H. daily

27 To **indicate** is to:

A. hide
B. conceal
C. congest
D. show

28 When **excited**, you show:

E. indifference
F. gloom
G. fear
H. enthusiasm

29 **Animosity** means:

A. friendship
B. apathy
C. warmth
D. hatred

30 A synonym for **malice** is:

E. affection
F. confusion
G. hate
H. loyalty

31 Being **tranquil** is:

A. noisy
B. crowded
C. peaceful
D. valuable

32 **Dispose** means:

E. save
F. get rid of
G. hide
H. retain

33 To **exclude** is to:

A. keep out
B. include
C. remain
D. excite

34 To be **inhuman** is to be:

E. kind
F. heartless
G. confused
H. polite

35 An **articulate** person is:

A. sloppy
B. well-spoken
C. well-read
D. disorganized

36 **Multiple** times means:

E. few
F. always
G. many
H. never

37 To **dispute** is to:

A. agree
B. argue
C. discuss
D. think

38 A **smile** is a:

E. grin
F. frown
G. nod
H. sign

39 **Mediocre** work is:

A. sensible
B. superior
C. inferior
D. excellent

40 To **anticipate** success is to:

E. expect it
F. reject it
G. decline it
H. abandon it

41 A person who is **obsessed** with something is:

A. worried
B. preoccupied
C. lazy
D. insane

42 To **offend** is to:

E. insult
F. fight
G. compliment
H. soothe

43 When someone is **naïve**, he or she is:

A. wise
B. nostalgic
C. innocent
D. confused

44 An **ominous** situation is:

E. threatening
F. superior
G. optimistic
H. smelly

45 A synonym for **rigid** is:

A. strenuous
B. rightful
C. angry
D. fixed

46 Something that happens **occasionally** occurs:

E. during a scheduled time
F. once a year
G. sometimes
H. frequently

47 A **niche** is a:

A. place suitable for a person or thing
B. schedule
C. type of bird
D. nest

48 An **omnipotent** being:

E. feels angry
F. eats both plants and animals
G. is stubborn
H. is supreme

49 Something **tangible** is:

A. vague
B. aggressive
C. off topic
D. concrete

50 To **nurture** is to:

E. care for
F. worry
G. garden
H. cook

EXERCISE 9

Building a Stronger Vocabulary

- Review all the **boldfaced** words in this chapter before you proceed to the next exercise.
- Highlight the ones you are still having difficulty remembering.
- List them with their meanings on a table.
- Use them to compose your own sentences.
- Think of a synonym and an antonym for each word.
- Use checkmarks to indicate if each word you want to practice more has a prefix, suffix, and/or root.
- You may use the table below as a sample to write your answers in your notebook.

Word	Definition	Sentence	Synonym	Antonym	Prefix	Suffix	Root

EXERCISE 10

Creating My Own Powerful Word List

- Write the words and meanings from the above table on the **Creating My Own Powerful Word List** table on page 398. Review them often to build that super vocabulary you want to create for school, work, and everyday use.

Chapter 5

What Was Mark Doing at Kamla's Home When Her Parents Were at Work?

PRE-READING

About This Chapter from *Trial of Love*

- Read the names and descriptions of this chapter's main characters below.
  - Sonny and his family
  - Swami Venkat: A priest
  - Mark Edison Hubbard: A professor of pre-law
  - Agatha Noel: A campus nurse

Story Vocabulary Exercise

- Before you begin reading this chapter, figure out the meanings of the unfamiliar **boldfaced** vocabulary words. You may use the Word List, Word Parts Chart, or your dictionary to assist you in finding their meanings.
- Look for the various types of context clues—synonyms, antonyms, general context, and examples—as you read.
- Write a word or phrase about the meaning of each **boldfaced** word in the margin.

Reading and Writing Exercise

- Skim the entire chapter and pay attention to the headings and the discussion questions that follow.
- Initial Response: Write a paragraph explaining, in your own words, what you think this chapter of the story will be about.
- Final Response: After you have read the entire chapter, compare your current understanding with your initial response above. If your initial response was accurate, you can simply write it again to fill in the blanks below. If it was not, then write a paragraph on what the chapter was really about instead.

Initial Response

This chapter **will** be about ______________________________

____

____

____

Final Response

This chapter **was** about ______________________________

____

____

____

WHAT WAS MARK DOING AT KAMLA'S HOME WHEN HER PARENTS WERE AT WORK?

Kamla's left arm was swollen. It was beginning to hurt, but she attempted to **conceal** the pain from Mark. He deliberately held it and applied just enough pressure to show her that she was hurt. Her eyes filled with tears of pain and she withdrew her arm from his **grip**.

"Come on," Mark said. "You need to see a nurse."

Kamla reluctantly agreed, and he **escorted** her to the nursing office on campus.

"Hello, Mark, what brings you to the nursing office?" asked Nurse Agatha Noel curiously.

"I've brought Kamla, a new faculty member. She needs **emergency** care."

"Where's the professor?"

"She's standing outside your office."

"Ask her to come inside."

Mark walked to the door and motioned to Kamla to step inside. Kamla was very nervous.

"How did this happen?" inquired Agatha while examining Kamla's swollen arm.

"She fell in the gymnasium while she was jogging," Mark said quickly.

"Did you **slip**, Kamla?" asked Agatha.

"Yes," replied Mark.

"Mark, would you please allow Kamla to answer my questions? I'm positive she's **fluent** in English."

"Sorry, Agatha. I was trying to be helpful," said Mark.

Agatha gave Kamla an aspirin and recommended that she return home to rest her arm. In Agatha's professional opinion, Kamla's arm was not broken.

"Do you need assistance to get home?" asked Agatha.

Kamla paused before replying. She was staring at Mark.

"Yes, ma'am."

"I'll have a student **accompany** you on your way home."

"I'm free for the rest of the afternoon," said Mark eagerly. "I've just finished teaching for the day. I don't mind accompanying her."

"Are you certain you want to do this, Mark?" inquired Agatha.

"Yes, it's no problem at all."

Mark seemed excited to accompany Kamla home. In the taxi, Kamla remembered what Kathy had said about Mark. Reflective silence reigned only for a fleeting moment.

"How long have you been teaching at Rollins, Mark?" asked Kamla.

"About a year."

"You look young to be a professor."

"I recently graduated from college."

"How old are you, if you don't mind?"

Mark hesitated before replying. He had not expected Kamla to be so **assertive**, and he was wondering why she was asking such personal questions. He was **surprised** that she had agreed to allow him to **escort** her home. It was unusual for an Indian woman, from his **vast** experience, to agree to have a stranger bring her home. He was **reluctant** to draw conclusions about Kamla's attitude toward him. He felt that he was being **pursued** by a female, something he had never experienced in his entire **adventurous** life.

"I'm twenty-nine," Mark replied with **deliberate** hesitation.

"I'm twenty-nine too," Kamla remarked. "I understand that you're attending Rexford Law School in the evenings and weekends."

"Who told you I'm in law school?"

"My friend, Kathy. Wasn't she supposed to mention it?"

Mark did not answer her. Moments later, the taxi came to a **halt** at the entrance to her residence.

"Thanks for escorting me home, Mark. I'll see you tomorrow at school if I feel better," said Kamla.

Mark looked perplexed. He couldn't believe Kamla expressed no interest in inviting him into the house. "Are you certain you'll be fine alone at home?" he asked.

"I'm a big girl! I can take care of myself," replied Kamla.

"I'm positive you can. But wouldn't you like for me to come inside and have a cup of coffee before I leave?"

Kamla smiled. She **detected** his desire to spend some time with her, so she invited him in.

When the clock **promptly** struck four, Kamla asked Mark to leave for fear that her parents would not **comprehend** his reason for being in the house alone with her. Unfortunately, on his way out of the yard, Mark was **confronted** by her father, Sonny, who was returning home from work.

"What are you doing in my house, Mr. Whoever-You-Are?"

Mark replied nervously, as his heart was **palpitating uncontrollably**, "You must be Kamla's father."

"Who are you?" asked Sonny with **vehemence** and **venom** in his **acrid** voice.

"Her **colleague** at Rollins University," replied Mark.

"Is Rollins teaching classes at my house now?" asked Sonny **sarcastically**.

"Sir, I know what you're thinking, but I'm not **guilty** of it. Please believe me. I'm **innocent**, sir."

"There is nothing innocent about you. You look like someone who's adept at **flirting**—someone who knows how to act like he's in love. Why are you here?"

"It's best you talk with Kamla, sir."

Mark left and Sonny ran up the stairs. He knocked impatiently on Kamla's bedroom door. Kamla hesitated before opening it.

"Is this what you do when we aren't at home?" yelled Sonny as he entered her room and **slammed** the door shut.

"Please control your anger, Daddy. One of these days you might have a **massive** heart attack," cautioned Kamla. "You have to get a grip on your stress level. Taking anger management classes might be an excellent **option** for **preserving** your mental health."

"What was he doing here?"

"He brought me home because I hurt myself at school."

"How long was he here with you?"

"Does it really matter?"

"Of course it does."

"Why can't you trust me?" yelled Kamla. "Am I not capable of taking care of myself? When will you start trusting me? You don't even give me room to breathe."

"My little princess, I have **utmost** trust in you," assured Sonny.

"That's the problem, Daddy. You feel I'm still a little girl. Why can't you accept the fact that I'm a grown-up woman now?"

"Sweetheart, it's just that I'm afraid of losing you. We're in a foreign country that isn't as safe as India. You've already made several **drastic** changes in your lifestyle."

"There you go again. What changes are you referring to now?"

"Look at the way you dress. You've discarded the traditional Indian clothes that **accentuate** your grace and beauty. For the first time in your life, I've seen you using **excessive** makeup. I can't even see the real you beneath it all."

"I've made these changes so I could fit in with other teachers at the university. It's painful to feel left out. I'm experiencing immense pressure to **conform**, Daddy."

"But you don't have to conform, Kamla. Be yourself, and if they're really your friends they'll accept you just the way you are."

"Daddy, I hate when you're so **rational**. Young people don't think the same way their parents do."

"Kamla, I sincerely understand that you're torn between two cultures. Somehow, we have to **cope** and live **harmoniously** as a close-knit family."

It was 5:15 p.m. when Rita returned from work. When she saw that Sonny seemed upset, she suspected that he had had another argument with Kamla, which seemed to be his daily **norm**.

"Why were you **verbally abusing** my daughter again? Aren't you tired of **arguing** with her almost every day?"

"Rita, I suggest you stay out of this. My daughter and I are having a **candid** and **amiable** discussion."

"It's hard to imagine you **resolving** a conflict with a friendly conversation. It's not in your **genetic** makeup to be **non-confrontational**, Sonny. You were born angry."

"Why don't you ask her?"

Rita decided to do just that.

"Mom, Dad is correct," Kamla lied. "He wasn't yelling and screaming as he usually does."

Kamla just wanted her parents to stop bothering her about Mark. She feared things would only get worse if they got in a fight over her relationship with him.

Kamla resumed grading the test she had **administered** to her students during the **previous** class session. Sonny and Rita went to the kitchen and **sipped** tea as they discussed Kamla.

"I'm surprised at what Kamla did today, Sonny," said Rita. "I never expected her to invite a man to our house while we were at work. I can imagine the **vicious gossiping** our neighbors will engage in now. This could be **detrimental** to our efforts to get a suitable marriage **proposal** for her."

"My fear is that she might become pregnant, Rita."

"Kamla will never have sex before marriage. Our culture, tradition, and religion **prohibit** us from engaging in that sort of **risky** behavior."

"I wish I could believe that, Rita. People seem to be more **promiscuous** in this country. They're **tolerant** of almost everything. They even accept it when people do dangerous things that might result in their personal **demise**."

"Be cautious about **vague generalizations**, Sonny. This country believes in **democracy**, **tolerance**, and **respect** for individuals' rights. People have the freedom to choose how they want to live their lives even if their **ultimate** decisions are **detrimental** to their well-being. Still, we have nothing to worry about. I know Kamla very well, Sonny. Don't forget, I'm her mother."

"Maybe the two of you should discuss sex and other **pertinent** healthcare practices that the schools in our home country failed to **include** in their curricula," advised Sonny. "We are college-educated parents and yet we haven't talked with our daughter about our **paranoia** that she might engage in certain practices like drug use or unsafe sex, which could **ruin** her life and embarrass our family. Rita, don't forget that Kamla has never had a boyfriend and is very **naïve** when it comes to dealing with personal relationships with men."

"Don't forget that it's your responsibility to communicate with her as well, Sonny," encouraged Rita. "Doing so will reduce **conflict** and the odds of a **confrontation** with her. It will help us have a harmonious, rather than an **adversarial**, relationship with our daughter."

Sonny ignored her last statement and walked over to the stove to pour another cup of tea. Rita was too tired to cook, so they had leftovers for dinner.

Kamla Worried about the Astrologer's Predictions

Kathy was looking forward to having lunch with Kamla. She was eager to learn what had **transpired** during Mark's visit to Kamla's home, as she was an **inquisitive** woman by nature. She remembered Kamla mentioning that she was not interested in having a relationship with a man. This proved that Kathy had been right when she told Kamla that life in America would change her ways.

"You're the luckiest, or most **fortunate**, prof at Rollins, Kamla," said Kathy. "Many of the female faculty members want to know what **tricks** you pulled to get Mark over to your house."

"Tricks and **pranks** are **deceptive** practices that I do not **subscribe** or **resort** to. I guess the stars are in my favor," said Kamla with confidence.

"Stars! What have they got to do with your friendship?"

"Everything. I'm an **avid** believer in **astrology**."

"Don't be **ridiculous**!"

"I'm a **Hindu** and I believe in astrology and rituals. They're **vital** aspects of my culture. I wish I were in India now."

"Why?"

"So that I could consult with my **swami**, my spiritual guide, about my friendship with Mark."

"You don't have to go to India to see a swami."

Kamla followed Kathy's eyes to the entrance of the faculty cafeteria. Cindy and two of her friends had just entered.

"This is your lucky day, Kamla," said Kathy, smiling. "I know someone who could be helpful."

"Who?"

"Cindy Singh."

"Are you crazy? You must be **insane**, Kathy."

"She may dress **weirdly** and do **ludicrous** things, but she will never **let the cat out of the bag**. She can keep a secret. If it's okay with you, I'll ask her to introduce you to her swami."

"Does she have a swami?"

"Of course. Whether you choose to believe it or not, she has some things in common with you. She is an Indian from Guyana. She is a Hindu as well. Interestingly, her father is a Muslim and her mother is a Christian. I'm not sure how Cindy turned out to be a Hindu, but I heard this sort of thing is very common in her country and on the Caribbean island of Trinidad."

"Are you certain I can **confide** in her about Mark?"

"You have my word."

Later that day, they cautiously climbed the stairs to the second floor of the temple, where Swami Venkat was **meditating**. The smell of the incense was soothing. Kathy was reluctant to enter the room where he was **chanting** peacefully. He wore a **dhoti**, a long loincloth, and his pot belly was plain to see since he wore no shirt. His beard was long and grey. Around his neck was a chain of small, brownish beads that were of immense religious significance to him.

With crossed legs, Swami Venkat was sitting on the carpeted floor in front of his **altar**. Placed around the room were **statues** of various gods and goddesses. **Interspersed** between the statues on the altar were **assorted** colorful flowers.

Swami Venkat continued to chant for about ten minutes before he **acknowledged** his visitors. "Is that you, Cindy?" he asked with his eyes closed.

They were barefoot and seated on the floor directly behind him. Kathy was amazed that he knew Cindy was there. None of them had telephoned to say they were coming over to see him.

"Your friends shouldn't feel uncomfortable. Come sit next to me, the three of you."

Cindy sat closest to him while Kathy stayed the farthest away. It was the first time in Kathy's entire life that she had gone to a swami.

Kathy inquired anxiously, "Swami, how did you know it was us?"

"The power of the gods, my child."

"How do you get this power from them?"

"It's **inexplicable**. Nobody understands how. Not even I could explain it."

"Swami Venkat," said Cindy, "my friend, Kamla, wants to consult with you about—"

The swami interrupted her.

"Kamla wants to know the future of her friendship with Mark."

"Yes, Swami," replied Cindy.

Kathy's eyes widened in disbelief at his knowing the **precise** reason for their visit. The swami asked Kamla a few personal questions while thumbing through the pages of a book on religious astrology.

"The man you fell in love with at first sight is very brilliant," said the swami.

"That's correct," said Kamla.

"He has an analytical mind, but seldom expresses his true feelings."

"Does that mean he isn't really in love with me?"

"That's not what I'm saying. He fell in love with you the minute he saw you."

"Is he **sincere** about his feelings for me?"

"Presently, he's madly in love with you. Your beauty and charm impress him most."

"That's all?"

"Be patient. I'm still concentrating," said Swami Venkat. He appeared to be studying hard as he read the pages **meticulously**.

"Hurry, please," said Kamla, biting her fingernails.

"Kamla, I'm **obligated** to convey what the stars are telling you."

Kamla thought that if he was only telling her because he had to, it meant he had bad news. "I don't want to hear it if it's bad."

"If it's not in your favor, there are certain rituals I can perform to **modify** things to your advantage."

"Will he marry me?"

"That's not what I'm concerned about."

Kamla said, "But that's what matters most to me."

"I understand your feelings."

"Could you please be frank with me?"

"The stars indicate you'll be given an enormous amount of money by someone wicked and **vindictive**. Someone who likes to get even with people."

"Money. That's great!" exclaimed Kathy. "I hope she shares it with us."

"You won't be in possession of it for long," warned Swami Venkat.

"Really?" asked Kamla.

"Yes. Because you'll get it dishonestly. But the good news is that once you **dispose** of it, you'll experience a lifetime of happiness."

"This is encouraging. Please continue, Swami," said Kamla with excitement.

He continued reading again. Kathy was very attentive to each word he uttered.

"I have to perform a ritual on your behalf."

"Do you really have to, Swami?" interjected Cindy, who had been very quiet while Kathy and Kamla were talking with Swami Venkat. Cindy knew from experience that whenever he decided to perform a ritual for her, it meant a **life-threatening** incident was **inevitable** and that she could possibly die. She knew something bad would certainly happen to Kamla. Neither Swami Venkat nor Cindy revealed this to Kamla and Kathy, but Kamla already knew its significance.

With tears in her eyes, Kamla sadly asked the swami, "What sort of ritual is it?"

"You won't understand the **intricacy** or complexity of it if I tell you. Don't worry, my child. Don't be scared. I've performed hundreds of these rituals. I'll do it for you. Go home. Everything will be all right."

Kathy breathed a sigh of relief when he closed his book.

When they were about to leave, Cindy and Kamla **bowed** while facing him with **clasped** hands. They both left Swami Venkat's place feeling very uneasy, though Kathy just seemed confused.

Kamla sensed that the need for the ritual meant that not everything was fine in her life. She could not figure out what the purpose of the ritual was, yet she did not question the swami about it. The three of them walked down the street outside his temple on their way to the bus stop.

"What was all that bowing for?" inquired Kathy, after a minute or two of silence.

"It's an expression of respect for his **spirituality**, an **acknowledgement** of his **innate** ability to **interpret** our religious astrological **scripture**," replied Kamla.

"That's interesting. I wish our American culture had some sort of belief system similar to yours."

"Each culture has its own strengths and weaknesses. People bring their unique cultures and traditions to the U.S. from around the globe, and that makes America the greatest **melting pot** of the world," stated Kamla. "So don't **complain**, my dear Kathy."

Kamla spoke little for the next few minutes. It was **obvious** that she was **disturbed** by certain things Swami Venkat had **revealed** about her future.

"Do you really take him seriously, Kamla?" questioned Kathy when they were on the bus. Kamla did not answer.

"Cheer up, my friend. These swamis don't know what they're talking about most of the time. They're merely guessing about the future," said Kathy.

Cindy ignored Kathy's **nonchalant** attitude toward the predictions. She strongly believed the swami's reading was accurate.

When Kathy realized neither Kamla nor Cindy was paying attention to her, she quit talking. Before they departed the bus for their respective homes, though, she reminded Kamla and Cindy not to mention to her friends on campus that she had accompanied them on a visit to an astrologer. She feared they would **humiliate** and **mock** her.

Kamla was beginning to wonder if she would die if the swami did not perform the ritual. She spent the night awake in bed, mentally replaying everything that Swami Venkat had predicted.

EXERCISE 1

Applying the Words You Have Learned to Critical Thinking and Creative Writing

- Use the two questions in Section A below to discuss this chapter with your classmates. Be sure to apply your critical thinking skills.

- Write an essay about either question using the vocabulary words you know from real-life experiences and the new ones you have learned from this text.

Section A

Discussion Questions

1. How do you feel about Kamla, a very intelligent professor, believing in astrology?

2. Do you feel Swami Venkat's predictions for Kamla will come true?

EXERCISE 2

Matching Meanings

■ Match each word with its meaning.

_____ 1. dictator	**A.** flesh-eating
_____ 2. extrovert	**B.** choosing between undesirable alternatives
_____ 3. diversity	**C.** feeding on plants
_____ 4. buffet	**D.** abnormally sensitive
_____ 5. blemish	**E.** a beginner
_____ 6. carnivorous	**F.** abnormal fear of being in a small place
_____ 7. herbivorous	**G.** blood relatives
_____ 8. omnivorous	**H.** abnormal fear of something
_____ 9. dilemma	**I.** difference or variety
_____ 10. extraterrestrial	**J.** eating both animal and plant foods
_____ 11. hypersensitive	**K.** one who is expressive
_____ 12. fugitive	**L.** a part of a debt
_____ 13. novice	**M.** meal where guests serve themselves
_____ 14. kin	**N.** a person who has run away to avoid arrest
_____ 15. installment	**O.** one who has complete authority and power
_____ 16. subsidy	**P.** outside the limits of the earth
_____ 17. phobia	**Q.** a spot, stain or scar
_____ 18. claustrophobia	**R.** a grant of money
_____ 19. capitalism	**S.** system where businesses are privately controlled
_____ 20. communism	**T.** system where economic activities are controlled by government

EXERCISE 3

Synonyms: Multiple Choice

■ Circle the letter of the word or phrase that is most similar in meaning to the **boldfaced** word.

1. **velocity**	**A.** speed	**B.** city	**C.** stillness	**D.** upset
2. **verdict**	**A.** victim	**B.** question	**C.** decision	**D.** retreat
3. **yell**	**A.** belittle	**B.** quiet	**C.** shout	**D.** whisper
4. **wander**	**A.** adhere	**B.** run	**C.** think	**D.** stray
5. **lustrous**	**A.** dark	**B.** black	**C.** unattractive	**D.** shiny
6. **youth**	**A.** senior	**B.** relative	**C.** youngster	**D.** newborn
7. **triumph**	**A.** failure	**B.** success	**C.** trial	**D.** hardship
8. **vacant**	**A.** full	**B.** empty	**C.** simple	**D.** short
9. **verify**	**A.** neglect	**B.** disobey	**C.** support	**D.** avoid
10. **sinister**	**A.** angelic	**B.** saintly	**C.** heavenly	**D.** evil
11. **yield**	**A.** give in	**B.** lose	**C.** oppose	**D.** decrease
12. **abandon**	**A.** leave	**B.** crowded	**C.** care	**D.** careless
13. **quiver**	**A.** nod	**B.** tremble	**C.** revive	**D.** strengthen
14. **qualm**	**A.** certainty	**B.** confidence	**C.** confession	**D.** doubt
15. **subsequent**	**A.** late	**B.** rearranged	**C.** following	**D.** retested
16. **subjective**	**A.** fair	**B.** biased	**C.** honest	**D.** free
17. **weird**	**A.** strange	**B.** well	**C.** lucky	**D.** wasteful
18. **rehearse**	**A.** sing	**B.** play	**C.** practice	**D.** work
19. **welcome**	**A.** reject	**B.** greet	**C.** chase	**D.** disown
20. **salute**	**A.** honor	**B.** scold	**C.** criticize	**D.** fall

EXERCISE 4

More Practice with Synonyms

■ Circle the letter of the word or phrase that is most similar in meaning to the **boldfaced** word.

1. **tentative** plan	**A.** sudden	**B.** not definite	**C.** urgent	**D.** small
2. **motivate** his students	**A.** encourage	**B.** discourage	**C.** attack	**D.** assist
3. a **negative** remark	**A.** discouraging	**B.** honest	**C.** dishonest	**D.** funny
4. feeling of **nausea**	**A.** disgust	**B.** anger	**C.** happiness	**D.** affection
5. a **nutritious** meal	**A.** complete	**B.** enjoyable	**C.** tasty	**D.** nourishing
6. **numerous** remarks	**A.** few	**B.** two	**C.** many	**D.** three
7. feeling **nervous**	**A.** anxious	**B.** prepared	**C.** playful	**D.** unconcerned
8. **negotiate** a deal	**A.** resist	**B.** simplify	**C.** bargain	**D.** fasten
9. selling **narcotics**	**A.** drugs	**B.** nuggets	**C.** snacks	**D.** beverages
10. **oral** report	**A.** written	**B.** verbal	**C.** usual	**D.** illegible
11. **outrageous** incident	**A.** excited	**B.** fancy	**C.** shocking	**D.** happy
12. **optional** assignment	**A.** voluntary	**B.** compulsory	**C.** important	**D.** difficult
13. **odd** teacher	**A.** tired	**B.** cheerful	**C.** happy	**D.** strange
14. **occurred** at midnight	**A.** happened	**B.** disappeared	**C.** lasted	**D.** placed
15. a **positive** attitude	**A.** strange	**B.** confident	**C.** negative	**D.** harmful
16. a **pious** preacher	**A.** happy	**B.** inspired	**C.** boring	**D.** religious
17. a risky **procedure**	**A.** sequence of steps	**B.** set of lessons	**C.** jump	**D.** environment
18. careless **pedestrian**	**A.** walker	**B.** cyclist	**C.** jogger	**D.** runner
19. **untidy** room	**A.** clean	**B.** messy	**C.** organized	**D.** small
20. urgent **message**	**A.** distress	**B.** massage	**C.** communication	**D.** mess
21. **obscene** language	**A.** indecent	**B.** clean	**C.** clear	**D.** confusing
22. **omit** details	**A.** include	**B.** leave out	**C.** observe	**D.** adopt
23. a strong **opponent**	**A.** giant	**B.** soldier	**C.** opposite position	**D.** friend
24. **persuade** him to go	**A.** convince	**B.** assist	**C.** help	**D.** please
25. **obstruct** his view	**A.** block	**B.** clear	**C.** facilitate	**D.** assist
26. a **passion** for sports	**A.** love	**B.** contempt	**C.** eye	**D.** ability
27. **observe** her behavior	**A.** suspend	**B.** note	**C.** react to	**D.** avoid
28. **prolong** the suspense	**A.** strengthen	**B.** continue	**C.** avoid	**D.** notice
29. a **loud** uproar	**A.** noisy	**B.** musical	**C.** quiet	**D.** calm
30. **urban** area	**A.** dirty	**B.** clean	**C.** city	**D.** country
31. **ultimate** decision	**A.** surprise	**B.** final	**C.** urgent	**D.** hasty

32. **undermine** their efforts	**A.** weaken	**B.** encourage	**C.** strengthen	**D.** applaud
33. **tolerate** his mannerisms	**A.** disapproving	**B.** dislike	**C.** note	**D.** put up with
34. **terminal** disease	**A.** deadly	**B.** not serious	**C.** rare	**D.** short
35. **stubborn** child	**A.** excited	**B.** angry	**C.** sad	**D.** obstinate
36. a **skeptic** is	**A.** doubtful	**B.** positive	**C.** agreeable	**D.** disloyal
37. a weekly **quiz**	**A.** debate	**B.** short examination	**C.** trip	**D.** tour

EXERCISE 5

Synonyms and Antonyms

■ Write the corresponding letter for the synonym and antonym of each **boldfaced** word.

	Synonym	Antonym			
1. **capacity**	_______	_______	**A.** capital	**B.** capability	**C.** inability
2. **cite**	_______	_______	**A.** want	**B.** indicate	**C.** plagiarize
3. **coherent**	_______	_______	**A.** consistent	**B.** disjointed	**C.** honest
4. **compel**	_______	_______	**A.** practice	**B.** force to act	**C.** stop
5. **comparable**	_______	_______	**A.** chosen	**B.** alike	**C.** different
6. **comfortable**	_______	_______	**A.** relaxed	**B.** penalized	**C.** restless
7. **competent**	_______	_______	**A.** upset	**B.** efficient	**C.** inept
8. **comply**	_______	_______	**A.** retreat	**B.** follow	**C.** disobey
9. **concede**	_______	_______	**A.** admit	**B.** argue	**C.** deny
10. **confirm**	_______	_______	**A.** verify	**B.** stray	**C.** question
11. **consequence**	_______	_______	**A.** result	**B.** cause	**C.** decision
12. **conservative**	_______	_______	**A.** traditional	**B.** senile	**C.** liberal
13. **clandestine**	_______	_______	**A.** secret	**B.** hard	**C.** overt
14. **collaborate**	_______	_______	**A.** control	**B.** cooperate	**C.** disagree
15. **contingency**	_______	_______	**A.** emergency	**B.** certainty	**C.** choice
16. **coincide**	_______	_______	**A.** disappear	**B.** correspond	**C.** disagree
17. **compose**	_______	_______	**A.** create	**B.** litter	**C.** destroy
18. **contradict**	_______	_______	**A.** dispute	**B.** agree	**C.** wonder
19. **confront**	_______	_______	**A.** challenge	**B.** admit	**C.** avoid
20. **controversy**	_______	_______	**A.** conflict	**B.** doubt	**C.** agreement

	Synonym	Antonym			
21. **callous**	______	______	**A.** free	**B.** cruel	**C.** sensitive
22. **capability**	______	______	**A.** ability to perform	**B.** growth	**C.** incompetence
23. **capture**	______	______	**A.** arrest	**B.** free	**C.** waste
24. **care**	______	______	**A.** assurance	**B.** protection	**C.** neglect
25. **charming**	______	______	**A.** naive	**B.** pleasing	**C.** obnoxious
26. **cheap**	______	______	**A.** inexpensive	**B.** possessive	**C.** costly
27. **clarify**	______	______	**A.** explain	**B.** fall	**C.** confuse
28. **clean**	______	______	**A.** pure	**B.** internal	**C.** dirty
29. **combine**	______	______	**A.** hinder	**B.** mix	**C.** separate
30. **commotion**	______	______	**A.** disturbance	**B.** order	**C.** judgment
31. **compassion**	______	______	**A.** sympathy	**B.** agreement	**C.** harshness
32. **complex**	______	______	**A.** complicated	**B.** simple	**C.** safe
33. **confess**	______	______	**A.** dread	**B.** admit	**C.** deny
34. **conform**	______	______	**A.** agree	**B.** distort	**C.** dissent
35. **convenient**	______	______	**A.** disturbing	**B.** suitable	**C.** inappropriate
36. **counterfeit**	______	______	**A.** fake	**B.** frantic	**C.** real
37. **courteous**	______	______	**A.** polite	**B.** rude	**C.** expensive
38. **deduct**	______	______	**A.** subtract	**B.** disagree	**C.** add
39. **defy**	______	______	**A.** conceal	**B.** disobey	**C.** follow
40. **depart**	______	______	**A.** leave	**B.** attempt	**C.** arrive
41. **demolish**	______	______	**A.** destroy	**B.** move	**C.** restore
42. **deposit**	______	______	**A.** save	**B.** tell	**C.** withdraw; take out
43. **desist**	______	______	**A.** stop	**B.** continue	**C.** deliberate
44. **destroy**	______	______	**A.** ruin	**B.** analyze	**C.** repair
45. **detain**	______	______	**A.** delay	**B.** dislike	**C.** release
46. **different**	______	______	**A.** unlike	**B.** alike	**C.** careful
47. **difficult**	______	______	**A.** hard	**B.** sad	**C.** easy
48. **diminish**	______	______	**A.** decrease	**B.** increase	**C.** withdraw

	Synonym	Antonym			
49. **dilute**	______	______	**A.** weaken	**B.** cease	**C.** strengthen
50. **discard**	______	______	**A.** reject	**B.** keep	**C.** constrain
51. **distinct**	______	______	**A.** clear	**B.** indefinite	**C.** calm
52. **distress**	______	______	**A.** anguish	**B.** comfort	**C.** harshness
53. **drastic**	______	______	**A.** severe	**B.** least	**C.** mild
54. **dwindle**	______	______	**A.** lessen	**B.** keep	**C.** increase
55. **dynamic**	______	______	**A.** oppressed	**B.** spirited	**C.** dull
56. **eager**	______	______	**A.** confused	**B.** anxious	**C.** unconcerned
57. **ecstasy**	______	______	**A.** tasty	**B.** joy	**C.** unhappiness
58. **eject**	______	______	**A.** expel	**B.** fake	**C.** include
59. **elated**	______	______	**A.** overjoyed	**B.** controlling	**C.** unhappy
60. **elder**	______	______	**A.** older	**B.** younger	**C.** adult
61. **eligible**	______	______	**A.** suitable	**B.** petty	**C.** unqualified
62. **emit**	______	______	**A.** offer	**B.** discharge	**C.** receive
63. **encourage**	______	______	**A.** give support	**B.** reveal	**C.** dissuade
64. **enhance**	______	______	**A.** improve	**B.** stop	**C.** worsen
65. **enlarge**	______	______	**A.** exhaust	**B.** increase	**C.** reduce
66. **entire**	______	______	**A.** correct	**B.** complete	**C.** partial
67. **enormous**	______	______	**A.** large	**B.** loyal	**C.** tiny
68. **erratic**	______	______	**A.** uncertain	**B.** sold	**C.** constant
69. **evacuate**	______	______	**A.** leave an area	**B.** decrease	**C.** enter
70. **eternal**	______	______	**A.** forever	**B.** timely	**C.** temporary
71. **evident**	______	______	**A.** upset	**B.** clear	**C.** vague
72. **excess**	______	______	**A.** extra	**B.** amount	**C.** lack
73. **exterior**	______	______	**A.** outside	**B.** start	**C.** interior
74. **explicit**	______	______	**A.** clear	**B.** unclear	**C.** amazing
75. **extravagant**	______	______	**A.** excessive	**B.** observable	**C.** meager

EXERCISE 6

Word Meaning in Context: Set 1

■ Read each sentence and find the missing word in the box below. Fill in the blank with the correct *form* of that word.

nervous	**pious**	**optional**	**outrageous**
oral	**numerous**	**odd**	**tentative**
negotiate	**nausea**	**motivate**	**negative**

1.The couple set a ___________ date of June 5, 2025 for their wedding.

2. No threats or bribes could ___________ Henry to get a summer job; he preferred visiting his family in Jamaica.

3. ___________ feedback caused Edith to give up on her idea of opening a vegetarian restaurant.

4. The _________ began as soon as she stepped aboard the boat and continued to make her miserable throughout the voyage.

5. Because of ___________ complaints from customers, the automobile manufacturer completely redesigned the car's cooling system.

6. Lisa often felt ___________ for no good reason, so she decided to consult a therapist.

7. That bicycle is not worth $400. Try to ___________ a better price.

8. To get a doctoral degree, one must pass both ___________ and written examinations.

9. The price you have set for this property is ___________—I will not buy it.

10. The travel package included one week in Honolulu; trips to the other islands were ___________.

11. People from other countries find the American custom of treating pets like children very ___________.

12. My grandmother was extremely ___________; she went to church every Sunday morning throughout her life.

EXERCISE 7

Word Meaning in Context: Set 2

■ Read each sentence and find the missing word in the box below. Fill in the blank with the correct *form* of that word.

obscene	**skeptic**	**opponent**	**pedestrian**
ultimate	**procedure**	**persuade**	**obstruct**
untidy	**tolerate**	**message**	**omit**

1.Please explain again the ___________ for applying for a driver's license.

2. Being a ___________ in cities with few traffic lights is taking your life in your hands.

3. Although her desk appeared ___________, she was actually a very organized person.

4. At the sound of the tone, please leave a short ___________.

5. The school board declared the novel ___________ and removed all copies from the shelves of the library.

6. When addressing the envelope, do not ___________ the zip code.

7. The high school gym was packed for the game against Central High, their chief ____________ in the district.

8. No matter how hard we tried, we could not ____________ him to taste the pickled pigs' feet.

9. Twenty years ago, there was a clear view of the river. Now the view is ____________ by high-rise apartment buildings.

10. I think the idea for your book is good; however, the __________ decision of whether it will be published lies with the editor.

11. People from rural areas find it difficult to ____________ the noise level in big cities.

12. Even after reading several firsthand accounts of abductions by space aliens, he remained a ____________.

EXERCISE 8

Context Clues

- Select the word or phrase that most closely matches the meaning of the **boldfaced** word. *Note that replacing the **boldfaced** word with the right answer might not produce a grammatically correct sentence.*

1. The doctors finally **deduced** how the virus spread after spending several weeks trying to figure out what made people sick.

   A. determined **B.** cured **C.** prevented **D.** postponed

2. The science students were asked to **define** the plants and their geographical origin.

   A. nurture **B.** create **C.** avoid **D.** identify

3. Strong winds and dark clouds **denote** a storm heading towards the coastline.

   A. cause **B.** speed up **C.** indicate **D.** hide away

4. The man who was arrested **denies** he was near the crime scene, contradicting police accounts.

   A. declares untrue **B.** controls the media **C.** delivers a truth **D.** protects a family

5. The news of their mother's illness **depressed** the family.

   A. saddened **B.** sustained **C.** invigorated **D.** illuminated

6. Antivenin is **derived** from the same poison it is meant to cure.

   A. stored **B.** made **C.** misunderstood **D.** shipped

7. Architects have started to **design** new buildings that encourage people to use the stairs instead of elevators.

   A. draw **B.** undermine **C.** demolish **D.** publicize

8. **Despite** knowing that consuming too much sugar can cause diabetes, he continued to drink three sodas daily.

   A. for health **B.** due to ignorance **C.** regardless of **D.** after arguing

9. Pari is a **devoted** Hindu and regularly goes to India for religious festivals.

   A. non-believing **B.** admitted **C.** dedicated **D.** manipulated

10. At the medical emergency training course, technicians learned how to **differentiate** between the symptoms of a heart attack and an anxiety attack.
    A. recognize differences **B.** make a plan **C.** activate a machine **D.** provide a remedy

11. The carpenter wrote down the **dimensions** of the room's width and height before cutting the beams.
    A. materials **B.** colors **C.** textures **D.** measurements

12. The attack forced thousands to flee, **displacing** them from their homes.
    A. putting out of place **B.** trapping inside **C.** showing **D.** tricking

13. The Christmas show was festive and the light **display** was colorful, bringing cheer to the children.
    A. dedication **B.** exhibit **C.** celebration **D.** generation

14. Workers reorganized the warehouse and **disposed** of the old machines.
    A. got rid **B.** held onto **C.** made repairs **D.** added features

15. His poor research **distorted** the true meaning of what happened when the famous steamship, Titanic sank in the Atlantic Ocean.
    A. explained **B.** identified **C.** revealed **D.** twisted

16. Volunteers **distributed** thousands of bottles of water to the marathon runners.
    A. gave out **B.** stole **C.** mailed **D.** removed

17. The school enrolled many students who spoke different languages and were from **diverse** cultural backgrounds.
    A. wealthy **B.** pleasant **C.** similar **D.** different

18. The original **document** was more valuable than the copied article.
    A. safe **B.** jewelry **C.** wood **D.** manuscript

19. Some fathers choose **domestic** work and stay home to take care of their children.
    A. household **B.** overseas **C.** charitable **D.** evening

20. The play included scenes of **drama** and suspense, but it also made the audience laugh.
    A. action **B.** seriousness **C.** dreams **D.** love

21. The game went into overtime, thereby extending the **duration** of the match.
    A. reach **B.** gear **C.** time **D.** place

22. The country's financial system kept the **economy** on a steady course of recovery.
    A. exchange of goods and services **B.** international relations
    C. people fighting wars **D.** illegal activities

23. The English teacher urged the students to **edit** and proofread their essays to make sure they eliminated spelling and grammar errors.
    A. describe **B.** observe **C.** elaborate **D.** correct

24. An **element** of surprise in the book's ending caused students to argue whether it was the best part.
    A. chapter **B.** trick **C.** moment **D.** aspect

EXERCISE 9

Vocabulary Test

- Select the correct answer.
- Hint: Review the meanings of all the **boldfaced** words in this chapter before you take the test. This approach can help you to score 100 percent.
- Record the percentage of correct answers on the Master Self-Assessment table on page 397.

1 A **dictator** does not have complete authority or power.

A. True **B.** False

2 An **extrovert** is someone who is not expressive.

E. True **F.** False

3 **Diversity** means difference or variety.

A. True **B.** False

4 A **buffet** is a meal where guests serve themselves.

E. True **F.** False

5 A **blemish** is a spot.

A. True **B.** False

6 **Carnivores** are flesh-eating mammals.

E. True **F.** False

7 Anteaters are **herbivores**.

A. True **B.** False

8 A **kin** is a good friend.

E. True **F.** False

9 **Omnivores** eat both animal and plant foods.

A. True **B.** False

10 A **phobia** is an abnormal liking of something.

E. True **F.** False

11 Being in a **dilemma** is:

A. being in a pool

B. having to choose between equally undesirable alternatives

C. having a dime

D. being in a contest

12 **Extraterrestrial** is:

E. on the earth

F. in the air

G. in the sea

H. outside the limits of the earth

13 One who is **hypersensitive** to light:

A. sees far distances

B. is abnormally sensitive to light

C. is nearsighted

D. lacks sensitivity to light

14 The **fugitive**:

E. ran away from justice

F. is in jail

G. is out on bail

H. has joined the military

15 A **novice** is a:

A. rebel

B. veteran

C. beginner

D. reader

16 **Claustrophobia** is:

E. a fear of clothes

F. a fear of snakes

G. a fear of spiders

H. an abnormal fear of being in small spaces

17 **Capitalism** is a system where:

A. people rent businesses

B. businesses are privately controlled

C. there are no businesses

D. businesses are publicly controlled

18 The **velocity** of a boat refers to its:

E. speed

F. direction

G. crew

H. time

19 To **yell** is to:

A. belittle
B. cry
C. shout
D. cook

20 A **lustrous** surface is:

E. dark
F. smooth
G. unattractive
H. shiny

21 **Triumph** means:

A. failure
B. success
C. difficulty
D. three attempts

22 To **verify** is to:

E. neglect
F. call into question
G. disobey
H. prove the truth

23 Something that is **sinister** is:

A. evil
B. heavenly
C. angelic
D. perfect

24 A **qualm** is a:

E. question
F. quality
G. doubt
H. certainty

25 **Subsequent** means:

A. prior
B. before
C. following
D. returning

26 An object that is **weird** is:

E. strange
F. triangular
G. rectangular
H. normal

27 To **rehearse** for a show is to:

A. practice
B. appear
C. clarify
D. study

28 To **salute** soldiers is to:

E. scold
F. honor
G. criticize
H. persuade

29 A plan that is **tentative** is:

A. sudden
B. uncertain
C. urgent
D. small

30 To **motivate** is to:

E. discourage
F. encourage
G. deter
H. observe

31 **Nausea** is a feeling of:

A. disgust
B. anger
C. happiness
D. hatred

32 To **negotiate** a deal is to:

E. bargain
F. ignore
G. reject
H. refuse

33 **Narcotics** are:

A. snacks
B. drugs
C. missiles
D. toys

34 **Dispose** means:

E. save
F. get rid of
G. hide
H. retain

35 **Oral** refers to something that is:

A. spoken

B. written

C. posted

D. memorized

36 An **outrageous** report is:

E. revealing

F. excellent

G. shocking

H. dull

37 Something that is **optional** is:

A. compulsory

B. voluntary

C. important

D. mandatory

38 Someone who is **pious** is:

E. unrighteous

F. sincere

G. religious

H. skinny

39 A **procedure** refers to a:

A. sequence of steps

B. set of lessons

C. high temperature

D. headache

40 To **omit** details is to:

E. leave out

F. include

G. saturate

H. recant

41 To **obstruct** a view is to:

A. find

B. clear

C. uncover

D. block

42 To have **passion** for something is to have:

E. animosity

F. hatred

G. love

H. respect

43 **Urban** refers to the:

A. suburbs
B. farm
C. country
D. city

44 A decision that is **ultimate** is:

E. final
F. reliable
G. acceptable
H. urgent

45 **Terminal** diseases cause:

A. longevity
B. uncertainty
C. death
D. recovery

46 Someone who is **obstinate** is:

E. argumentative
F. excited
G. angry
H. stubborn

47 A **skeptic** is someone who is:

A. doubtful
B. positive
C. confident
D. disloyal

48 A synonym for **coherent** is:

E. consistent
F. inconsistent
G. wavering
H. flexible

49 A worker who is **inept** is:

A. competent
B. incompetent
C. dependable
D. reliable

50 **Comply** means to:

E. follow
F. reject
G. refute
H. ignore

51 To **concede** defeat is to:

A. accept

B. deny

C. respect

D. reject

52 To **confirm** an appointment is to determine if it is:

E. rescheduled

F. canceled

G. uncertain

H. definitely true

53 Another word for **clandestine** is:

A. overt

B. secretive

C. liberal

D. conservative

54 **Contingency** relates to:

E. emergency

F. certainty

G. conflict

H. complexity

55 An antonym for **contradict** is:

A. dispute

B. agree

C. care for

D. oppose

56 To **confront** someone is to:

E. challenge

F. ignore

G. avoid

H. control

57 A **vacant** house is:

A. empty

B. full

C. occupied

D. abundant

58 To **compose** is to:

E. litter

F. disintegrate

G. destroy

H. create

59 A **controversy** is a:

A. dispute
B. riot
C. doubt
D. war

60 A statement that is **callous** is:

E. sensitive
F. insensitive
G. cordial
H. affectionate

61 To **clarify** something is to:

A. explain
B. contradict
C. digress
D. disregard

62 A **commotion** is a:

E. procession
F. celebration
G. disturbance
H. feeling

63 Another word for **compassion** is:

A. hostility
B. sympathy
C. agility
D. animosity

64 If something is **dwindling**, it is:

E. lessening
F. increasing
G. accelerating
H. expanding

65 **Ecstasy** refers to a feeling of:

A. sadness
B. extreme happiness
C. loyalty
D. disdain

66 To **evacuate** the flooded area is to:

E. stay
F. leave
G. protest
H. barricade

67 **Eternal** means:

A. rigid

B. forever

C. transient

D. mortal

68 If something is **evident**, it is:

E. clear

F. vague

G. unclear

H. hidden

69 Another word for **exterior** is:

A. inside

B. outside

C. above

D. below

70 An **extravagant** person is:

E. thrifty

F. frugal

G. carefree

H. excessive or wasteful

EXERCISE 10

Building a Stronger Vocabulary

- Review all the **boldfaced** words in this chapter before you proceed to the next exercise.
- Highlight the ones you are still having difficulty remembering.
- List them with their meanings on a table.
- Use them to compose your own sentences.
- Think of a synonym and an antonym for each word.
- Use checkmarks to indicate if each word you want to practice more has a prefix, suffix, and/or root.
- You may use the table below as a sample to write your answers in your notebook.

Word	Definition	Sentence	Synonym	Antonym	Prefix	Suffix	Root

EXERCISE 11

Creating My Own Powerful Word List

- Write the words and meanings from the above table on the **Creating My Own Powerful Word List** table on page 398. Review them often to build that super vocabulary you want to create for school, work, and everyday use.

Chapter 6

PRE-READING

About This Chapter from *Trial of Love*

- Read the names and descriptions of this chapter's main characters below.
  - Kathy Precious Armstrong: Kamla's best friend
  - Mark Edison Hubbard: A professor of pre-law
  - Cindy Singh: A laboratory assistant
  - Sonny and his family

Story Vocabulary Exercise

- Before you begin reading this chapter, figure out the meanings of the unfamiliar **boldfaced** vocabulary words. You may use the Word List, Word Parts Chart, or your dictionary to assist you in finding their meanings.
- Look for the various types of context clues—synonyms, antonyms, general context, and examples—as you read.
- Write a word or phrase about the meaning of each **boldfaced** word in the margin.

Reading and Writing Exercise

- Skim the entire chapter and pay attention to the headings and the discussion questions that follow.
- Initial Response: Write a paragraph explaining, in your own words, what you think this chapter of the story will be about.
- Final Response: After you have read the entire chapter, compare your current understanding with your initial response above. If your initial response was accurate, you can simply write it again to fill in the blanks below. If it was not, then write a paragraph on what the chapter was really about instead.

Initial Response

This chapter **will** be about ____

____

____

____

Final Response

This chapter **was** about ____

____

____

____

WHY IS MARK'S MOTHER IN A NURSING HOME?

It was about 7:30 a.m. and Kamla had some time before her first lecture. She was the first person to enter the gymnasium to work out.

As she exercised, Kamla could not stop thinking about Swami Venkat's predictions and their **impact** on her personal life. From time to time, she **reflected** on their **validity**. She wasn't entirely sure they were accurate. However, she knew she could not ignore them. Eventually, she stopped working out and sat down to focus on her problems.

Mark was **astonished** to see her looking **preoccupied** and sitting on a bench in the gym. He had not seen her the previous day and had been starting to feel lonely. Kamla was beginning to bring happiness to his life, something he had desperately **craved** for years.

"Good morning," he said, greeting her with **jubilation**. He was very excited to see her.

Kamla was taken aback because she hadn't expected to see him in the gym at such an early hour. She felt like embracing him, but **concealed** the pleasure she was experiencing.

"I didn't see you yesterday. I thought your dad had probably **confined** you to your house and that you couldn't leave," he said jokingly.

"I'm sorry he was **rude** and **obnoxious** to you, Mark."

"I expected that sort of reaction from him."

"What makes you say that?"

"Seeing a stranger leaving my house, I probably would've reacted similarly."

"I expected him to be more **cordial** to a stranger."

"I didn't. Parents, especially those from your cultural background, usually behave in an **overprotective** manner when their daughters engage in things **contrary** to their culture."

"What do you know about my culture?"

"People from your culture are very **conservative** and **traditional**. They're usually old-fashioned and find it very difficult to change their ways."

"That's a generalization."

"Sure. But it's applicable to your parents."

"What about me?"

Mark replied, "You're an exception. You're a woman who's in tune with **modern** times."

"I'm not a modern woman."

"But you have a modern **perspective**."

"Is that good or bad?"

"I love women who're partially conservative like you."

"Your reason, may I ask?"

"They're usually **faithful**. You can count on them. My **instinct** tells me you know how to make someone feel desirable and special. And that's why I'm crazy about you, Kamla," Mark **confessed** sincerely.

"Mark, I hope you mean every word you say. Every word you **utter** means a lot."

"Kamla, don't you trust me?"

"Yes. It's just that I am very **fond** of you, and I don't want to get hurt. I was attracted to you the moment our eyes met," said Kamla happily.

"Nothing will come between us. I promise."

"I believe you, Mark," said Kamla, whose heart was **throbbing** faster and faster. It seemed loud enough to be heard a million miles away.

Mark glanced at the clock on the wall. It was almost 7:50. He invited Kamla to his office for a **beverage**.

Kamla sipped orange juice while he poured water into the coffeemaker.

"I can help you with that if you wait a second, Mark," said Kamla.

"I can manage, but thank you for your kind **gesture**."

"It seems as if you can do everything for yourself, Mark. You're **self-reliant**. I like that in a guy."

"Fortunately, my mother, Dorothy, taught me every **conceivable** household **chore** you could think of."

"Where's your mother, dear? Students on campus often mention that you live alone."

He was surprised at her question, as living alone was normal for an unmarried American of his age. He **pretended** not to hear her.

"Where's your mother?" repeated Kamla.

"In a nursing home," Mark replied.

"She can't be living in a nursing home. She isn't that old."

Mark said, "You don't have to be old to live in a nursing home."

"What's the matter with her, Mark?"

Suddenly, tears flooded his eyes. Kamla walked up behind him and threw her arms around his shoulders. He **grasped** them as if it they were his only **solace**.

"Kamla, I wish you knew how sad I feel about my mother's condition. She had an accident and can't move as freely as she desires. I couldn't leave her alone at home while I went to work. She needs **copious** care around the clock. The nursing home isn't the best place for her, but that's all I can provide for her now."

"What about your father?"

"I don't know if I should love or hate him."

"Everybody at school says that you're a terrific guy. I'm positive your dad isn't the type of man to **abandon** his family and run away."

"Neither my mother nor I know if he's alive or dead. I wish I weren't the only child. Sometimes I **crave** a brother or a sister who could **alleviate** the **excruciating** pain I'm feeling from the depth of my **fragile** heart. Sometimes it's too much for me to handle. Sometimes I feel like screaming when I wake up in the middle of the night and think of my mother. My heart weeps for her."

"I truly understand what it's like not to have a brother or sister to **mitigate** the **pangs** of loneliness. I wish I had a **sibling**, too. **Solitude** can be a terrifying experience, even if it's **transient** and only visits periodically. It's not easy to live alone, especially in a situation like yours."

"I hope your **steadfast** love will **sustain** me over the years. You're **precious** to me, Kamla," Mark said affectionately. "I'm looking forward to an **enduring** relationship that will withstand the **vicissitudes** of life. I know there are always ups and downs, and I'm prepared to deal with them."

It sounded like Mark was about to **propose**, but Kamla wasn't sure she was ready for marriage. They hugged each other tightly and then went to teach their classes.

Swami Venkat and His Ritual

Kamla met Kathy in the hallway shortly after lunch and chatted for a while.

"Kamla, why didn't you call me after our visit to Swami Venkat?" complained Kathy.

"I was too tired. By the way, where's Cindy?" asked Kamla with great concern.

"I don't know. But I hope you aren't **preoccupied** with those predictions."

"I thought about them seriously. They're accurate. Swami Venkat is a **genius**, Kathy," said Kamla.

"Then he should be a professor and scientist like you," teased Kathy.

"Shame on you if you think the guy is a **fake**," said Kamla.

"I'm **disturbed** that an intelligent professor like you can be so **superstitious**, Kamla."

"I know you can't understand my **rationale** for doing certain things. Kathy, some things in life are **inexplicable**. There aren't always rational explanations for the things we do, yet we believe in doing them in the hopes that the end result will be beneficial."

"I hate when you get **philosophical**, Kamla."

"No. You hate when I make sense. I'm positive I can't **convince** you to share my beliefs at this moment, but I'll remind you when these predictions come to **fruition**, Kathy."

"And that will be the day the sun rises in the west and sets in the east," said Kathy with confidence.

Kamla was very **disheartened** because Kathy didn't believe Swami Venkat's astrological predictions.

Kathy mentioned that Cindy had confirmed that the swami would perform the ritual on her behalf. She said it in a way that made it sound silly, and Kamla left angrily because she felt that Kathy was **mocking** her.

EXERCISE 1

Applying the Words You Have Learned to Critical Thinking and Creative Writing

- Use the two questions in Section A below to discuss this chapter with your classmates. Be sure to apply your critical thinking skills.

- Write an essay about either question using the vocabulary words you know from real-life experiences and the new ones you have learned from this text.

Section A

Discussion Questions

1. Do you believe that the love Kamla and Mark expressed for each other is genuine?

2. Does Mark sincerely love his mother?

EXERCISE 2

Matching Meanings

■ Match each word with its meaning.

_____	1. kilometer	**A.**	has nine angles and nine sides
_____	2. radius	**B.**	increase in number or amount
_____	3. circumference	**C.**	has ten angles and ten sides
_____	4. ton	**D.**	a small part of a whole
_____	5. square	**E.**	has seven angles and seven sides
_____	6. multiply	**F.**	three feet
_____	7. triangle	**G.**	has eight angles and eight sides
_____	8. quadrangle	**H.**	has three sides and three angles
_____	9. foot	**I.**	a straight line from the center of a circle to the circumference
_____	10. pentagon	**J.**	has six angles and six sides
_____	11. hexagon	**K.**	outer boundary of a circle
_____	12. heptagon	**L.**	has four equal sides
_____	13. octagon	**M.**	a unit of weight; 2.2046 pounds
_____	14. nonagon	**N.**	equal to one thousand meters
_____	15. decagon	**O.**	two thousand pounds
_____	16. percentage	**P.**	has four sides and four angles
_____	17. fraction	**Q.**	twelve inches
_____	18. yard	**R.**	has five angles and five sides
_____	19. kilogram	**S.**	a rate or proportion per hundred
_____	20. angle	**T.**	the space between two lines diverging from a common point

EXERCISE 3

Forming Synonyms

■ Fill in the blank(s) to complete the word that is similar in meaning to the **boldfaced** word.

1. **cab** ta__i

2. **calculate** fig__ __e

3. **camouflage** di__gui__e

4. **candidate** ap__ __icant

5. **capsize** over__ __ __n

6. **caress** f__ __dle

7. **converse** c__ __t

8. **calamity** dis__ __ter

9. **charisma** ch__ __m

10. **comprehensive** e__ten__ive

11. **constitute** com__ __ __se

12. **contemplate** m__ditat__

13. **recipe** form__ __a

14. **curtail** s__ __rten

15. **cheat** r__b

16. **chastise** re__ __ke

17. **caution** ad__ __se

18. **coerce** fo__ __e

19. **compensate** __ay

20. **consecutive** cont__ __ __ous

21. **purpose** __im

22. **quantity** amo__ __t

EXERCISE 4

Synonyms: Multiple Choice

■ Circle the letter of the word or phrase that is most similar in meaning to the **boldfaced** word.

1. **intrinsic**	**A.** inherent	**B.** outside	**C.** intended	**D.** painful
2. **insinuate**	**A.** suggest	**B.** deny	**C.** detain	**D.** hear
3. **impromptu**	**A.** unrehearsed	**B.** prepared	**C.** promised	**D.** prompted
4. **manipulate**	**A.** control	**B.** move	**C.** linger	**D.** pretend
5. **mammoth**	**A.** gigantic	**B.** tiny	**C.** microscopic	**D.** heavy
6. **majestic**	**A.** major	**B.** dignified	**C.** minor	**D.** holy
7. **leisure**	**A.** labor	**B.** laughter	**C.** daytime	**D.** spare time
8. **latent**	**A.** active	**B.** alert	**C.** hidden	**D.** late
9. **lucid**	**A.** loose	**B.** difficult	**C.** clear	**D.** cloudy
10. **nocturnal**	**A.** mighty	**B.** nightly	**C.** daily	**D.** negative
11. **lavish**	**A.** little	**B.** meager	**C.** few	**D.** extravagant
12. **loiter**	**A.** leave	**B.** idle	**C.** depart	**D.** lose
13. **obvious**	**A.** unseen	**B.** uneasy	**C.** understandable	**D.** invisible
14. **objective**	**A.** unprejudiced	**B.** subjective	**C.** biased	**D.** favorite
15. **quota**	**A.** quote	**B.** allocation	**C.** economy	**D.** number
16. **obsolete**	**A.** modern	**B.** showy	**C.** outdated	**D.** current
17. **passive**	**A.** alive	**B.** energetic	**C.** active	**D.** inactive
18. **psychic**	**A.** fortune teller	**B.** phony	**C.** psychiatrist	**D.** scientist
19. **proverb**	**A.** saying	**B.** praise	**C.** verb	**D.** noun
20. **provoke**	**A.** pacify	**B.** irritate	**C.** calm	**D.** boast

EXERCISE 5

More Practice with Synonyms

■ Circle the letter of the word that is most similar in meaning to the **boldfaced** word.

1. **principal** investigator	**A.** assistant	**B.** older	**C.** chief	**D.** elderly
2. to **protest** against someone	**A.** celebrate	**B.** act	**C.** complain	**D.** occur
3. **pursue** the thief	**A.** apprehend	**B.** catch	**C.** arrest	**D.** chase
4. a **permanent** job	**A.** difficult	**B.** seasonal	**C.** tedious	**D.** lasting
5. a **prelude** is an	**A.** opening	**B.** end	**C.** entity	**D.** operation
6. **prominent** politician	**A.** well-known	**B.** unpopular	**C.** rude	**D.** incompetent
7. to **procrastinate** over a task	**A.** delay	**B.** hasten	**C.** change	**D.** hurry
8. **prosperous** business	**A.** greedy	**B.** successful	**C.** dishonest	**D.** famous
9. **punish** the child	**A.** love	**B.** notice	**C.** scold	**D.** nurture
10. **outstanding** job	**A.** excellent	**B.** unsatisfactory	**C.** disappointing	**D.** creative
11. **unstable** mental condition	**A.** stable	**B.** acceptable	**C.** smart	**D.** unsteady
12. **traditional** lifestyle	**A.** modern	**B.** daily	**C.** old-fashioned	**D.** lavish
13. earth **tremor**	**A.** latitude	**B.** longitude	**C.** vibration	**D.** mechanic
14. a **tragic** accident	**A.** minor	**B.** devastating	**C.** recent	**D.** harmless
15. **reliable** friend	**A.** trustworthy	**B.** able	**C.** sincere	**D.** wicked
16. **remedy** for a headache	**A.** formula	**B.** solution	**C.** chemical	**D.** cure
17. **reduce** my payment	**A.** increase	**B.** postpone	**C.** decrease	**D.** accept
18. **reluctant** to leave	**A.** ready	**B.** unwilling	**C.** incapable	**D.** apt
19. to **replicate** something	**A.** copy	**B.** hide	**C.** picture	**D.** invent
20. union **representative**	**A.** friend	**B.** thief	**C.** enemy	**D.** spokesperson

EXERCISE 6

Word Meaning in Context

■ Read each sentence and find the missing word in the box below. Fill in the blank with the correct *form* of that word.

prelude	**replicate**	**reliable**	**pursue**
prosperous	**tragic**	**prominent**	**unstable**
reluctant	**principal**	**procrastinate**	**protest**

1. What is the ____________ reason you do not want to see this movie?

2. You can ____________ all you want; the boss is not going to change the work schedule just for you.

3. The police had to ____________ the robber for six blocks before they finally caught up with him.

4. The announcement of a ten o'clock curfew was only the __________ of worse things to happen under the rule of the dictator.

5. Because he was a ____________ name in the field of criminal law, he was able to charge fees of $1,000 per hour.

6. Because of her tendency to ____________, Molly always found herself rushing to meet deadlines.

7. With the discovery of oil, the small country became ____________.

8. The kids built their own treehouse, but it was so ____________ that their father had to tear it down and rebuild it.

9. The hit-and-run deaths of the mother and child were ____________.

10. Unless we find ____________ workers, our company will never succeed.

11. The manager was ____________ to give Ms. Campbell the loan because the business she wanted to start seemed very risky.

12. The scientists were excited by the experiment at first, but they became frustrated when they tried again and were unable to ____________ the results.

EXERCISE 7

Context Clues

■ Select the word or phrase that most closely matches the meaning of the **boldfaced** word. *Note that replacing the **boldfaced** word with the right answer might not produce a grammatically correct sentence.*

1. The teacher **emphasized** the importance of reading the chapter because it would be on the final examination.
   A. reduced **B.** denied **C.** stressed **D.** enhanced

2. Relying on experiments, the doctors could offer an **empirical** study on sleep deprivation.
   A. relevant **B.** based on observation
   C. disagreeable **D.** informational

3. He **enabled** his brother's gambling by giving him money whenever he asked.
   A. reported **B.** pleaded with **C.** made possible **D.** attacked

4. When the longtime friends ran into each other, the unexpected **encounter** surprised both of them.
   A. collision **B.** parting **C.** talk **D.** meeting

5. Conserving **energy** by using less electricity will help reduce pollution.
   A. water **B.** the environment **C.** money **D.** power

6. Police should **enforce** a curfew that requires teenagers between the ages of thirteen and sixteen to stay in after 10:00 p.m.
   A. implement **B.** delay **C.** ignore **D.** undermine

7. To determine if employees were eligible for health insurance, the company had to **ensure** they were fulltime workers.
   A. mislead **B.** make certain **C.** claim **D.** explain

8. In the Middle Ages, church and state were combined into one **entity**.
   A. building **B.** agreement **C.** organization **D.** story

9. We are learning that we must protect the **environment** from pollution so that it can continue to provide clean air and water.
   A. surroundings **B.** pipes **C.** laborers **D.** clouds

10. The job applicant turned down the position when she realized the salary would be **equivalent** to that of her present employment.

    A. lower **B.** attractive **C.** humble **D.** equal

11. Climate change is producing higher sea levels that are causing beaches to **erode**, forcing city planners to build sand dunes to stop the beaches from being destroyed.

    A. wear away **B.** grow **C.** become rocky **D.** have too many visitors

12. His computer programming **error** resulted in severe consequences, causing the website he was working on to crash.

    A. feedback **B.** virus **C.** mistake **D.** theft

13. He became wealthy when he inherited his father's **estate**.

    A. business **B.** stock portfolio **C.** life insurance **D.** property

14. Every corporation should have a code of **ethics** to help employees understand their responsibilities.

    A. rules of behavior **B.** focus on health **C.** meeting customers **D.** making payments

15. Violent conflicts between different **ethnic** groups are scattered across the African continent.

    A. relating to politics **B.** relating to education **C.** relating to culture **D.** relating to money

16. The accountants had to **evaluate** the numbers to assess whether the company's financial records were accurate.

    A. examine **B.** invent **C.** delay **D.** deny

17. The company was once prosperous, but it **eventually** went bankrupt because its executives made bad decisions.

    A. reluctantly **B.** in the end **C.** sadly **D.** luckily

18. The lawyers for the defendant said it was **evident** that their client was not guilty of the charges made against him.

    A. wrong **B.** foggy **C.** questionable **D.** clear

19. The school improved its academic reputation, but it took time for its athletic department to **evolve**.

    A. appreciate **B.** develop **C.** fall behind **D.** concentrate

20. The high salary and benefits package **exceeded** her expectations, so she gladly accepted the job offer.

    A. went above **B.** cut in half **C.** fell short of **D.** steadied

21. He dropped out of college because he was **excluded** from the basketball team.

    A. questioned **B.** assisted **C.** kept out of **D.** attacked

22. The museum **exhibit** showed the paintings of Leonardo da Vinci, whose works were displayed throughout the summer.

    A. booklet **B.** display **C.** website **D.** performance

23. The shopping mall was renovated to **expand** its selection of luxury retail stores.

    A. liquidate **B.** increase **C.** involve **D.** decrease

24. She decided to seek out an **expert** who was more knowledgeable about her illness.

    A. one with special skills **B.** one who relies on others

    C. one who acts dramatically **D.** one who states a case

EXERCISE 8

Vocabulary Test

- Select the correct answer.
- Hint: Review the meanings of all the **boldfaced** words in this chapter before you take the test. This approach can help you to score 100 percent.
- Record the percentage of correct answers on the Master Self-Assessment table on page 397.

1 A **triangle** has three sides and three angles.

A. True **B.** False

2 A **quadrangle** has four sides and three angles.

E. True **F.** False

3 A **foot** is twelve inches.

A. True **B.** False

4 **Majestic** means stately.

E. True **F.** False

5 Another word for **lucid** is unclear.

A. True **B.** False

6 Another word for **latent** is hidden.

E. True **F.** False

7 Anteaters are **herbivores**.

A. True **B.** False

8 A **kilometer** is:

E. three meters **F.** one thousand meters

G. one yard **H.** one thousand feet

9 A circle's **radius** is:

A. around the circumference **B.** a line through the circumference

C. the circle's diameter **D.** a straight line from the circle's center to its circumference

10 A **circumference** is:

E. a quarter circle
F. the outer boundary of a circle
G. a half circle
H. one half the circle's diameter

11 A **ton** is equivalent to:

A. 2,300 pounds
B. 3,000 pounds
C. 2,000 pounds
D. 5,000 pounds

12 A **square** has:

E. uneven sides
F. four equal sides
G. five equal sides
H. 45° angles

13 **Multiply** means to:

A. subtract
B. increase in number
C. decrease in number
D. solve the derivative

14 A **pentagon** has:

E. four angles
F. four sides
G. five angles and five sides
H. two angles

15 A **hexagon** has:

A. six angles and six sides
B. five angles and four sides
C. a sum of 180 degrees
D. six angles and seven sides

16 A **heptagon** is a figure:

E. of seven angles
F. of seven angles and seven sides
G. of ten sides and angles
H. half the size of a hexagon

17 An **octagon** is a figure of:

A. four angles and sides
B. eight angles and eight sides
C. six angles
D. nine sides

18 A **nonagon** is a figure of:

E. nine faces
F. three angles
G. ten sides
H. nine sides and nine angles

19 A figure of ten angles and ten sides is a:

A. square **B.** triangle

C. decagon **D.** nonagon

20 A **yard** is:

E. a percentage **F.** a hectare

G. three feet **H.** one mile

21 A **kilogram** is:

A. 2.2046 pounds **B.** 1.500 pounds

C. 4.4092 pounds **D.** 3.333 pounds

22 **Curtail** means to:

E. lengthen **F.** shorten

G. cease **H.** increase

23 **Intrinsic** means:

A. built-in **B.** outside

C. outlawed **D.** painful

24 To **insinuate** is to:

E. suggest **F.** deny

G. detain **H.** hear

25 An **impromptu** speech is:

A. prepared **B.** well rehearsed

C. well received **D.** done without preparation

26 To **manipulate** something is to:

E. deny it **F.** control it

G. incite it **H.** seize it

27 **Mammoth** refers to:

A. tiny

B. heavy

C. great or gigantic

D. microscopic

28 Workers enjoy **leisure** time:

E. nap

F. spare time

G. labor

H. morning

29 **Nocturnal** animals come out:

A. during the day

B. during the full moon

C. at noon

D. during the night

30 Another word for **lavish** is:

E. meager

F. little

G. excessive or extravagant

H. cheap

31 **Loiter** around the cafeteria:

A. leave

B. idle

C. stop

D. study

32 Something **obvious** is:

E. unseen

F. easily seen

G. dirty

H. tiny

33 An **objective** decision is:

A. unprejudiced

B. subjective

C. rude

D. dull

34 A **quota** refers to:

E. a quote

F. a quarter

G. a number

H. an allocation

35 An **obsolete** design is:

A. modern
B. obvious
C. outdated
D. current

36 A **passive** attitude is:

E. alive
F. energetic
G. active
H. inactive

37 A synonym for **psychic** is:

A. fortune teller
B. doctor
C. mechanic
D. scientist

38 A **proverb** is a:

E. saying
F. compliment
G. story
H. song

39 To **provoke** someone is to:

A. pacify
B. anger
C. pay
D. quiet

40 The **principal** investigator is:

E. a deputy
F. an elder
G. an assistant
H. a chief

41 To **pursue** means to:

A. chase
B. strike
C. ignore
D. recommend

42 A **prelude** is an:

E. opening
F. ending
G. interval
H. intermission

43 A **prominent** scientist is:

A. unknown
B. well known
C. well spoken
D. stubborn

44 To **procrastinate** over an assignment is to:

E. delay
F. complete
G. hurry
H. ignore

45 When you **scold** a child, you:

A. love
B. find fault with
C. care for
D. notice

46 A **traditional** lifestyle is:

E. modern
F. contemporary
G. old-fashioned
H. lavish

47 A **tragic** accident is:

A. not serious
B. devastating
C. unsafe
D. safe

48 A **remedy** is a:

E. formula
F. chemical
G. cure
H. rejection

49 Being **reluctant** to do something is being:

A. ready
B. incapable
C. unwilling
D. afraid

50 To **replicate** something is to:

E. copy
F. print
G. increase
H. reduce

EXERCISE 9

Building a Stronger Vocabulary

- Review all the **boldfaced** words in this chapter before you proceed to the next exercise.
- Highlight the ones you are still having difficulty remembering.
- List them with their meanings on a table.
- Use them to compose your own sentences.
- Think of a synonym and an antonym for each word.
- Use checkmarks to indicate if each word you want to practice more has a prefix, suffix, and/or root.
- You may use the table below as a sample to write your answers in your notebook.

Word	Definition	Sentence	Synonym	Antonym	Prefix	Suffix	Root

EXERCISE 10

Creating My Own Powerful Word List

- Write the words and meanings from the above table on the **Creating My Own Powerful Word List** table on page 398. Review them often to build that super vocabulary you want to create for school, work, and everyday use.

PRE-READING

About This Chapter from *Trial of Love*

- Read the names and descriptions of this chapter's main characters below.
  - Dr. Azeez: The village medical doctor in India
  - Rita Kumar
  - Sosheila: Rita's mother
  - Shastri: Rita's cousin

Story Vocabulary Exercise

- Before you begin reading this chapter, figure out the meanings of the unfamiliar **boldfaced** vocabulary words. You may use the Word List, Word Parts Chart, or your dictionary to assist you in finding their meanings.
- Look for the various types of context clues—synonyms, antonyms, general context, and examples—as you read.
- Write a word or phrase about the meaning of each **boldfaced** word in the margin.

Reading and Writing Exercise

- Skim the entire chapter and pay attention to the headings and the discussion questions that follow.
- Initial Response: Write a paragraph explaining, in your own words, what you think this chapter of the story will be about.
- Final Response: After you have read the entire chapter, compare your current understanding with your initial response above. If your initial response was accurate, you can simply write it again to fill in the blanks below. If it was not, then write a paragraph on what the chapter was really about instead.

Initial Response

This chapter **will** be about ______________________________

____

____

____

Final Response

This chapter **was** about ______________________________

____

____

____

WHY DID RITA SUDDENLY RETURN TO INDIA?

Rita didn't expect Sonny or Kamla to be up at 5:30 a.m.

"Who's in there?" asked Kamla, knocking impatiently on the bathroom door.

"What do you want?" replied Rita angrily.

"Nothing, Mom. But why are you taking a bath so early?"

"Kamla, go back to sleep."

"I can't."

"Well, then think of the good times you've been spending with Mark in his apartment, and you'll slowly **drift** into sweet sleep," said Rita **sarcastically**.

"Is that what's annoying you, Mother?"

"Annoying me? Honey, it's your life. Do as you please."

Rita then stepped out of the bathroom. She was clothed in a light blue robe. Kamla followed her downstairs to the kitchen, where she had a cup of tea and a few slices of toasted rye bread. Rita ignored her as she ate hurriedly.

"Mother, who told you I've been spending time with Mark in his apartment?"

"Kamla, I wasn't born yesterday. Lying is a **vice** and not a **virtue**. I didn't expect you to **indulge** in it. I don't know if I should continue trusting you. I also know what you did with him in his apartment. And it was not cooking dinner for him," Rita said firmly.

"Please understand my feelings, Mother. I don't regret spending time with Mark. I'm beginning to fall deeply in love with him. I want to know him better because I hope one day he'll be my faithful life partner."

"I've had enough of this daily **bickering** and **squabbling**. I must get out of here before I go **insane**. Your father is so fed up with our family life that he has started drinking again."

"Please don't blame me for it, Mother."

"Kamla, your dad hasn't touched a drink for the past ten years. But recently I've observed how frustrated and depressed he has become. I won't **permit** your social life to ruin him. Sonny has always been a good and loyal husband and father. I'm not about to let him destroy himself because of you. He needs my help."

"Will running away solve our family **crisis**?" asked Kamla.

"I'm not running away."

"Then where are you going?"

Rita got up from the dining table and placed the dirty dishes in the sink. She got dressed and then telephoned for a taxi.

"Mother, if you leave now, this family will fall apart. You're our only hope for keeping it **intact**."

"In case you didn't notice, it's already falling apart."

"Why are you making me feel guilty? It's unfair to blame my relationship with Mark for our family problems."

Sonny was aware that Rita and Kamla were arguing downstairs in the kitchen, but he did not get out of bed.

At 6:30, the taxi arrived at their residence. The driver **tooted** the horn to remind Rita he was waiting for her outside their house. Rita got Kamla's attention just before she entered the taxi.

"I received a call from India last night asking that I return home immediately. It's an emergency," said Rita.

Kamla asked, "Is Grandmother ill?"

Rita did not reply. She hurriedly got into the taxi and set out for the airport.

For the next few minutes, Kamla sat on the veranda of their house and wept bitterly, because her mother had ignored her when she **waved** good-bye.

Twenty-four hours later, Rita was in India.

Rita Arrives in Her Village

Mumbai International Airport in India was not air conditioned. It was hot and humid. Rita was sweating **profusely** outside the airport's terminal. She appeared to be at a loss. Suddenly, a man appeared from behind her and tapped her gently on her shoulder. When he got her attention, he **scrutinized** her closely while glancing at the photograph he was carrying.

"Are you Rita?" he asked uncertainly.

"Yes, I am. Who are you?"

"That's not important."

"How did you get my photograph?" Rita asked him suspiciously after she saw it in his hand.

"Your mother asked me to pick you up at the airport."

"OK. Is she feeling well?"

"She's strong for an elderly woman. I wouldn't worry about her health."

He loaded her luggage into the trunk and sped away from the airport to her home. He was a careless driver who ignored all the traffic rules.

Gangaram was a very small **rural** village about one hundred miles from the airport. Most of the villagers **earned** their living working on sugarcane and rice plantations. These plantations were owned by a very wealthy **local** businessman who resided in the village. Rita was eager to return. She missed her friends very much.

News of her arrival had already spread like wildfire in the village.

"Good gracious, what's the occasion, driver? Why are the streets so beautifully decorated?"

"We're having a celebration."

"It's about time we had a village wedding."

"Village wedding? Yes! We're having a village wedding," he lied bravely.

"Who's getting married?"

"I can't remember her name."

"You ought to be ashamed of yourself. All the villagers are supposed to know each other."

"Sorry, ma'am. Her name **evades** my mind at this moment."

As he drove through the entry gates of Gangaram, a **procession** began. The villagers began beating drums, singing, and dancing to their traditional music. Those who lined the streets showered fresh-scented camellia flowers on the driver's car. Rita broke down in tears.

The driver stopped his car at the village leader's home. When Rita stepped out, a beautiful eight-year-old girl put a **garland** of flowers around her neck. It was the villagers' way of welcoming her back home. Then Rita's mother, Sosheila, **emerged** from the crowd and **embraced** her affectionately.

"My daughter, I wish you knew how much I missed you. I'm very happy you've returned."

"I was worried about you, Mother. But I can see you're doing just fine."

"Thank God for the villagers. We're like one big family. They've given me the best care you could possibly imagine."

Rita hugged and kissed the villagers as she **mingled** with them. Her friends **gossiped** and shared the rumors of the village with her. All the villagers were appreciative of the presents she brought them from New York.

Why Is Rita Inquiring about Dr. Azeez?

The following morning, Rita questioned her mother about the driver. She had been tempted to do so as soon as she arrived, but felt it was **inappropriate** to talk about him first.

"Mother, who's the driver you sent to the airport?"

"I meant to ask you last night about why you're paying such **keen** attention to him," said Rita's mother, Sosheila.

"I haven't expressed interest in him, Mother."

"A few people were **gossiping** about it."

"You know the villagers better than I do. They're **gossipmongers**. They have nothing else to do after **dusk**, when the sun sets. They love to talk about the private affairs of other people."

"Rita, to set the record straight, he's not a driver by **profession**."

"I can guess that."

"He's not a plantation worker, either."

"Get to the point, Mother. Stop beating around the bush—I hate **circumlocution**. What does he do for a living?"

"You mean, what is his **occupation**? He's a doctor, Rita."

"When did our village doctor pass away?"

"He's still alive," said Sosheila. "The driver is a medical doctor and not a village **witch** doctor."

"I must admit, he doesn't **impress** me as a doctor."

"Dr. Azeez is the best doctor this village has ever had."

"If he's so good, why has he chosen to work in Gangaram?" asked Rita.

"He isn't here to become rich off the villagers."

"Then why did he choose to work in our village?"

"Dr. Azeez is the **epitome** of a good doctor. He's truly dedicated to helping people. He has **accomplished** a lot here. If you recall, during the years before you left, the villagers were dying from easily **curable** diseases. He has **reversed** that situation. The elderly are even living longer because of his medical care."

"It seems as if things have changed **drastically** since I left the village."

"The doctor is a very intelligent man. We're very close friends," said Sosheila.

"You seem to have a lot of **trust** and **confidence** in him."

"He **confides** in me. He tells me many of his secrets because he knows that I'll never let the cat out of the bag."

"Is he married?"

"Rita, why are you asking me so many personal questions about him?"

"I . . . I just want to know him better."

"Why?" her mother asked angrily. "You have a husband who loves you dearly. Dr. Azeez is at least fifteen years younger than you are."

"Age doesn't matter, Mother."

"What has gotten into your head, Rita? I didn't expect you would've changed so much after going to America."

"I don't know why you're accusing me of wanting this man, Mother."

Rita's mother left her home in anger. She went to visit her best friend, who lived a few streets away.

Rita went to the kitchen and prepared a sandwich. It was a lovely day, so she went outside to enjoy it.

When she was about to take the last bite of her sandwich, she saw Dr. Azeez approaching their house on his bicycle. From a distance, he **pretended** not to see her. Rita was not prepared to let him go without

initiating a conversation, though.

"Dr. Azeez, do you have a minute to spare?"

"Well, of course, Rita."

He **dismounted** his bicycle and leaned it against the fence of the yard. Slowly, he walked to the veranda of the house, where Rita was rocking in her **hammock**.

"I'm sorry I didn't have the opportunity to thank you privately for the ride from the airport."

"Rita, that's **unnecessary**. And you don't have to be so **formal**."

"But that is the proper thing to do, Dr. Azeez."

"It was my pleasure to receive you at the airport. That's the least I could've done for your mother."

"And she's **eternally** grateful for the favor. She'll never forget it."

"Rita, I'm **indebted** to your mother. I owe her a lot."

"How's that so?"

"When I first came to Gangaram, the villagers were very **suspicious** of me."

"Why?"

"I don't know for sure. I guess they regarded me as an **outsider** whom they should **keep at arm's length**."

"You must have felt left out."

"That's correct. Initially, I felt rejected. But later, I became the village **hero**," he boasted.

"You must've done something **incredible**, a **courageous** act, maybe like a Bollywood movie star."

"Not really. It had nothing to do with courage. It required **competence** and experience."

"What exactly have you done to earn your popularity?" asked Rita.

"Do you remember the little girl, Shanta?"

Rita replied, "Who could forget that little angel? She has been **confined** to her bed since birth because of a rare disease."

"You have a good memory. When I arrived the first day, there was a **monsoon**, a terrible storm. Huge expanses of black rainclouds were hanging over the village. It rained heavily for the next five days. The entire village was flooded. Many residents were **trapped** inside their homes and had very little food to eat. It was exactly midnight when I heard someone knocking at my door. Frankly, I was somewhat **terrified** to answer. But moments later, I opened the door. There were two elderly women who were **drenched** in rain and trembling **uncontrollably**. One of them was carrying a little girl in her arms. The girl was tightly wrapped in a blanket and protected only by a **tattered** umbrella."

"Was it Shanta?" asked Rita.

Dr. Azeez replied, "Yes. She had an **abnormally** high temperature and couldn't breathe with ease. The women thought she was in need of **urgent** medical care and wouldn't survive another hour without help."

"Sometimes, the villagers have the tendency to **overreact**. Did her condition really **warrant** emergency care?"

"Definitely. She would've died if they hadn't gotten her help that night," answered Dr. Azeez.

"So you're a hero."

"It's my job to help people recover from their illnesses."

"What did you do to **enable** her to recover?"

"I gave her an injection to help her breathe normally. In addition, I made sure she swallowed the antibiotics I **administered**. To think about it, Shanta is a very lucky girl."

"Why do you say that?"

"When I was packing to come to the village, I purposely left my medical kit to be shipped later with other **necessities**. As I was about to leave home, my father insisted I carry it with me. I'm glad I **obeyed** him. The kit had the medication Shanta needed."

"Dr. Azeez became popular among the villagers because he saved Shanta's life. Am I correct?"

"Absolutely."

"I'm curious to know who those two older women were."

Dr. Azeez smiled. "I'll give you one guess."

"My mother and Shanta's mother."

"Correct. To make a long story short, your mother was the only person who went out of her way to help me **adjust** to life in this village."

"I'm very proud of her, Dr. Azeez. She enjoys making people happy. She's an **incredible** and **awesome** woman."

Dr. Azeez glanced at his watch. He told Rita he had to return to the health clinic shortly because he had scheduled several appointments to see his patients. When he was about to leave, Rita **realized** he had spent his entire lunch break **conversing** with her.

"Could you please step inside the house for a minute, Dr. Azeez?"

"Sorry, I can't stay longer."

"Please, I insist, Dr. Azeez."

"Why do I have to step inside?"

"If I tell you, you won't come in. Why are you reluctant, Dr. Azeez?"

"I don't want the villagers to spread a **rumor** about us having an affair because we're alone in the house."

"Please **disregard** such **trivial assumptions**. Don't pay attention to small things."

"It's not petty. My job will become more difficult because I'll lose their trust and confidence."

Rita knew she could not ignore his concern about maintaining a sense of professionalism. She stopped asking him to come in and wished him a good day.

As Dr. Azeez was about to ride away to the clinic, Rita's mother caught his attention. She was returning from her friend's house.

"What's the rush, Doctor?" inquired Sosheila.

"It'll be a busy afternoon."

"Let me prepare a sandwich for you to take."

"I'm not hungry."

Rita added, "I invited him inside for the same reason, but he refused."

"I promise, I'll see you in the evening," assured Dr. Azeez as he hurried away on his bicycle.

When Dr. Azeez left, Rita's mother entered the house without **uttering** a word. Rita followed closely and offered to prepare her lunch.

"Mother, what would you like to eat?"

"I can help myself."

"I'm aware of that. But I want to prepare something special for you."

"You're here on vacation. Why don't you visit your friends? I'm sure you have a lot to talk about," encouraged Sosheila.

"I'm not here on vacation. Maybe Kamla is correct. I'm running away from problems in New York."

"Problems? What problems? Rita, what's going on?" she inquired with deep concern.

"Nothing to worry about, Ma."

Sosheila sat at the kitchen table and gazed at Rita for a minute before speaking. "Rita, as soon as I saw you yesterday, I knew your life was in **turmoil** again."

"Was it that **obvious**?"

"A mother can tell. She has that **maternal instinct** that tells her when something isn't right with her children. You tried to **conceal** your unhappiness with your broad, **cheerful** smile. When I observed you **covertly** admiring Dr. Azeez, my suspicion that something was wrong with your personal life was **confirmed**."

"Sonny has started drinking again, Mother."

"What **triggered** it, Rita?"

"I'm not sure, but I've a strong feeling that he can't **cope** with the stress and the **rapid** pace of life in America."

"Does he have friends?"

"A few," replied Rita.

"More than likely he isn't drinking because of stress. There must be other reasons. Are you hiding anything else from me, Rita?"

"I've never **concealed** anything from you, Mother. I've no secrets whatsoever."

"Are you having a relationship with someone in New York, Rita?"

"What sort of a woman do you think I am, Mother?" Rita demanded.

"Are you?"

"No. No. Please don't **disrespect** me." Tears **oozed** from her eyes.

"What are you doing about his drinking?"

"Nothing. It's all your **fault**, Mother."

"How is it my fault?"

"You insisted that I marry him."

"How was I supposed to know he would turn out to be a **chronic alcoholic**?"

"I've always hated arranged marriages. I regret having gone along with your choice."

"Rita, would you have selected someone better than Sonny for a husband?"

"You know the answer, Mother."

"I do. You were madly in love with that **moron**, Prakash. He was never good enough for you. Do you know where he is today?"

"Enjoying life with his **spouse** and kids, I guess," replied Rita.

"You know better than that, Rita. Prakash is in jail for armed robbery."

"Why do you have to remind me, Mother?"

"You brought up the subject. You should thank your lucky stars that Sonny isn't a **criminal**."

"You're right. Sonny is a **terrific** guy. Please ignore what I've said. I'm too upset to think clearly." Even as Rita spoke, though, she thought of the gun in the brown paper bag, and the newspaper story about the dead border guard.

"Sonny will **quit** drinking eventually. He has that **dogged** determination. Be patient, Rita."

Rita wiped her tears away and went to her room. An hour later, she went to visit her friends in the village for a few hours before returning home. Her mother was planning the menu in **anticipation** of Dr. Azeez's arrival.

Dr. Azeez Has Dinner at Sosheila's Home

Dr. Azeez arrived dressed as if he were going to a formal dinner. He looked **handsome** in his light-grey suit. Rita and her mother were surprised that he wasn't wearing a **lungi**, his favorite traditional Indian outfit.

The dishes were **delicious** and **sumptuous**. It had been a while since he had enjoyed cooking that tasted almost like his mother's, and even longer since someone had taken the time to make a meal look so good.

"These **chapattis** are great. I love the curried chicken too," he said, **complimenting** his **hosts**.

"I'm glad you're enjoying them," replied Rita. "Mother loves cooking. She never gets tired of it."

"What else can an old woman do around here?" interjected her mother. "I've taught Kamla to cook everything I can. She has **compiled** dozens of recipes, and she took them with her to New York."

"Who's Kamla?" asked Dr. Azeez.

Rita excused herself while they were eating and searched for her purse. It took her a while to find it because she didn't remember where she had left it. The purse was sitting in her handbag in the closet.

"This is Kamla," said Rita, pointing to her daughter in a photograph.

"She's a beauty, Rita!" said Dr. Azeez. "I wish I'd met her before she left for New York."

"I can arrange for her to meet you," assured Rita.

"Impossible," Dr. Azeez said.

"I mean it," replied Rita.

"Just how are you going to do that?" asked Dr. Azeez.

"Simple. Kamla has been wanting to visit her grandmother. Maybe she'll be here sooner than you expect," Rita said.

Rita's mother wasn't paying attention to them. After she finished eating, she went to the living room to watch her favorite shows on television. Rita and Dr. Azeez were still picking at their food at the dinner table while conversing on an **extensive range** of topics.

"Mother tells me that you're very busy at the clinic," Rita stated.

"Sometimes it's so busy that I don't even have a minute for a cup of tea."

"Doctor, you shouldn't be working so hard."

"I don't have a choice. There's nobody to assist me in the clinic."

"Not even a nurse or a nurse's aide?" asked Rita.

"As you're aware, the Department of Health, like other government agencies, is highly **inefficient** thanks to its **unique bureaucracy**. My boss promised to **assign** a nurse to me several months ago, but I still don't have one."

"This is unfair to you. Isn't there someone in the village whom you can train in the meantime?"

"The villagers are reluctant to serve as **volunteers**."

"When I was in college, I took several first-aid courses. If you have no objection, I'd be willing to volunteer to work in the clinic while I'm here, Dr. Azeez."

"Rita, that's very **generous** of you, but you're on vacation and I don't want to **impose** on you."

"You won't be taking advantage of me. I can't think of anything better than working side by side with you."

"I bet," said Dr. Azeez suspiciously.

His remark caught her off guard. She was convinced that he felt she was trying to **seduce**, or come on to, him.

Dr. Azeez suddenly felt uncomfortable and asked Rita to watch television with him and her mother. Around 8:30, he left for home.

Rita and her mother stayed up late to talk about their family members in America, Sheila and Joshi.

Fire in the Village the Following Day

Very early the following day, Rita was awakened by her cousin, Shastri. He had run from the clinic with a message from Dr. Azeez.

"Please help us. Dr. Azeez wants you to come to the clinic immediately," begged Shastri as he gasped for breath.

"What's the matter, what's the matter?" asked Rita as she jumped out of bed.

"Fire, fire."

"Is he hurt?"

"No. There's a fire at the sugarcane plantation. Not in the clinic. Many workers are severely burned."

"Where are they now?"

"In the clinic. Dr. Azeez wants you to help him."

"Tell him I'll be there shortly."

Shastri took off for the clinic like a jet.

Rescue workers had already brought in about thirty villagers. Less than twenty minutes after the fire struck, a majority of the villagers **congregated** at the clinic to find out if their family members or relatives were hurt. When Rita arrived, she was successful in **convincing** over fifteen persons to help her and Dr. Azeez. The team worked **conscientiously** under his supervision to provide care for the **victims**. Fortunately, most of them only suffered from smoke inhalation. Nobody died in the accident.

Rita Hosts a Party for the Villagers

The night before Rita returned to New York, she hosted a party for the villagers. They were sad that she was leaving again. Dr. Azeez had grown **fond** of her after she had started assisting him at the clinic. It was **evident** that they had established a strong relationship. When most of the villagers left the party, the couple went for a **stroll** in the park next to her residence.

"I'm going to miss you, Rita," said Dr. Azeez.

"I'll miss you too, my friend."

"I hope you'll return soon," he whispered.

"I'll be waiting for you. . . . Dr. Azeez, can I ask you an embarrassing question?"

"Go ahead. You don't need my permission, Rita."

"Would you consider marrying . . . ?"

"I was expecting that question from you a while ago."

"Does that mean you **approve**?"

"Rita, you're a married woman with a beautiful family. How can I . . . ?"

"Dr. Azeez, you've misunderstood me."

"In what manner?"

"I'm not asking you to marry me."

"Who do you have in mind?"

"My daughter, Kamla."

"Rita, you know how I feel about **arranged** marriages and **dowries**. I prefer dating someone before making that lifelong **commitment**."

"It won't exactly be an arranged marriage."

"What would it be?"

"I'm positive Kamla would also prefer to date you before making a **commitment**. The two of you can date when she returns from New York."

"That makes more sense."

Kamla and Mark

Dr. Azeez walked Rita back to the house from the park, and she kissed him before he left. Her mother looked confused when she saw Rita kissing him on his cheek.

"Rita, I think we should go to bed early so you won't miss your flight tomorrow."

"I agree, Mother. Mother, I want to make a **confession** before we go to bed."

"I know what it is, Rita."

"Are you certain?" asked Rita.

"Positive. You're in love with Dr. Azeez."

"I suspected that's what you were thinking, Mother."

"Tell me I'm wrong, Rita."

"You're incorrect."

"Then what is it that you want to **confess**?" Sosheila asked curiously.

"Mother, I told Kamla that I was returning home upon your request. I probably gave her the impression that you're very ill."

"Why did you suddenly come home?"

"It's about Kamla."

"Is she in trouble?"

"I don't know what has gotten into her head, Mother. She has been dating someone in New York."

"Why aren't you happy about it? Isn't he a decent Indian fellow?"

"Mark is an American. Caucasian. Neither Sonny nor I approve of the relationship. She ignores us and everything we believe in, even our cultural values. That is why Sonny began drinking again."

"I don't believe you, Rita. My granddaughter wouldn't do such a thing."

"I returned home hoping that I'd find an educated man for her."

"Now I understand why you've been trying to get close to Dr. Azeez."

"Dr. Azeez would be the perfect husband for Kamla."

"But will he marry her? Would Kamla approve of him?" asked Sosheila.

"We won't know the **outcome** until Kamla returns to India."

"I think you've made the right decision, Rita. Let's hope things work out between Kamla and Dr. Azeez."

Rita's mother could not sleep **soundly** that night. She felt disappointed and hurt that Kamla was **disobeying** her parents in New York. Kamla had never done anything without her parents' approval when she lived in India.

Sosheila woke very early in the morning to see Rita off. When the plane **departed** for New York, she broke down in tears, and Dr. Azeez **consoled** her.

EXERCISE 1

Applying the Words You Have Learned to Critical Thinking and Creative Writing

- Use the two questions in Section A below to discuss this chapter with your classmates. Be sure to apply your critical thinking skills.

- Write an essay about either question using the vocabulary words you know from real-life experiences and the new ones you have learned from this text.

Section A

Discussion Questions

1. Do you believe in arranged marriages?

____
____
____
____
____
____
____
____

2. Do you feel that Kamla will marry Dr. Azeez if she returns to India?

____
____
____
____
____
____
____

EXERCISE 2

Matching Meanings

■ Match each word with its meaning.

_____	1. thermostat	**A.**	front part of the brain
_____	2. thermometer	**B.**	back part of the brain
_____	3. barometer	**C.**	measures temperature
_____	4. chronometer	**D.**	makes microorganisms look larger
_____	5. telescope	**E.**	indicates speed of a motor vehicle
_____	6. microscope	**F.**	measures atmospheric pressure
_____	7. manometer	**G.**	may cause paralysis of parts of the body
_____	8. ambulance	**H.**	measures time
_____	9. lateral	**I.**	mental or physical tension
_____	10. speedometer	**J.**	regulates temperature
_____	11. stethoscope	**K.**	an organ that produces eggs in a woman's body
_____	12. sphygmomanometer	**L.**	an open sore
_____	13. cerebellum	**M.**	makes distant objects appear nearer and larger
_____	14. therapeutic	**N.**	belly or abdomen
_____	15. intravenous	**O.**	inject serum to create or boost immunity
_____	16. laryngitis	**P.**	sideways
_____	17. influenza	**Q.**	vehicle for transporting the sick
_____	18. inflamed	**R.**	measures the pressure of gases
_____	19. inoculate	**S.**	temporary loss of voice
_____	20. cerebrum	**T.**	measures blood pressure
_____	21. ulcer	**U.**	directly into a vein
_____	22. ovary	**V.**	feverish and swollen
_____	23. stroke	**W.**	used to listen to sounds in the body
_____	24. stress	**X.**	curative
_____	25. stomach	**Y.**	inflammation of respiratory tract caused by a virus

EXERCISE 3

Forming Synonyms

■ Fill in the blank(s) to complete the word that is similar in meaning to the **boldfaced** word.

1. **cohesive** con__ __ __ted
2. **convey** tra__ __ __it
3. **constituent** com__ __ __ent
4. **content** sa__ __ __fied
5. **criteria** mea__ __re
6. **commitment** pro__ __se
7. **component** s__gment
8. **crisis** emer__ __ __cy
9. **draft** ske__ch
10. **detract** d__ __tract
11. **decipher** inter__ __et
12. **derive** g__ __n
13. **destination** en__
14. **devise** form__ __ __te
15. **discriminate** sepa__ate
16. **diverge** st__ __y
17. **derelict** __um
18. **designate** app__ __ __t
19. **devastate** d__ __troy
20. **discipline** pun__sh
21. **diplomacy** ta__t
22. **reciprocate** ret__ __n
23. **recur** r__pea__
24. **refuge** she__ __er

EXERCISE 4

Synonyms: Multiple Choice

■ Circle the letter of the word that is most similar in meaning to the **boldfaced** word.

1. **squander**	**A.** save	**B.** hoard	**C.** sell	**D.** misuse
2. **reject**	**A.** accept	**B.** take	**C.** covet	**D.** refuse
3. **penalty**	**A.** add	**B.** reward	**C.** honor	**D.** fine
4. **militant**	**A.** politician	**B.** teacher	**C.** aide	**D.** activist
5. **subside**	**A.** rise	**B.** lessen	**C.** float	**D.** activate
6. **invincible**	**A.** unbeatable	**B.** weak	**C.** lazy	**D.** feeble
7. **harmony**	**A.** agreement	**B.** discord	**C.** hatred	**D.** harm
8. **criticize**	**A.** judge	**B.** praise	**C.** support	**D.** cry
9. **copious**	**A.** few	**B.** faulty	**C.** abundant	**D.** little
10. **speculate**	**A.** know	**B.** doubt	**C.** spend	**D.** guess
11. **cry**	**A.** laugh	**B.** sob	**C.** excite	**D.** enjoy
12. **perceptive**	**A.** negligent	**B.** ignorant	**C.** observant	**D.** sleepy
13. **innuendo**	**A.** suggestion	**B.** paper	**C.** report	**D.** assertion
14. **revoke**	**A.** accept	**B.** cancel	**C.** keep	**D.** restore
15. **possess**	**A.** disown	**B.** retreat	**C.** own	**D.** rest
16. **sustain**	**A.** neglect	**B.** support	**C.** stagnate	**D.** embarrass
17. **convince**	**A.** discourage	**B.** distance	**C.** trust	**D.** persuade
18. **assurance**	**A.** doubt	**B.** fault	**C.** guarantee	**D.** note
19. **concur**	**A.** deny	**B.** agree	**C.** detest	**D.** avoid
20. **proposal**	**A.** paper	**B.** story	**C.** book	**D.** offer

EXERCISE 5

More Practice with Synonyms

■ Circle the letter of the word or phrase that is most similar in meaning to the **boldfaced** word.

1. a **trauma** is a	**A.** shock	**B.** fiction	**C.** myth	**D.** tale
2. **eradicate** the disease	**A.** get rid completely	**B.** keep	**C.** control	**D.** treat
3. an **emotional** speech	**A.** fine	**B.** excitable	**C.** short	**D.** cold
4. **enmity** between them	**A.** joy	**B.** fate	**C.** fear	**D.** hatred
5. to **appreciate** someone	**A.** like	**B.** limit	**C.** propose	**D.** propel
6. filled with **excitement**	**A.** gloom	**B.** dismay	**C.** fervor	**D.** problems
7. **enough** food	**A.** little	**B.** sufficient	**C.** tasty	**D.** tasteless
8. drank **excessive** alcohol	**A.** too much	**B.** dangerous	**C.** expensive	**D.** too little
9. likes **fun**	**A.** enjoyment	**B.** jogging	**C.** fighting	**D.** boredom
10. a **frugal** man	**A.** harmful	**B.** stingy	**C.** harmless	**D.** dangerous
11. the price **fluctuates**	**A.** changes	**B.** stagnates	**C.** stays	**D.** remains
12. **erratic** thinking	**A.** stable	**B.** predictable	**C.** irregular	**D.** unjust
13. **guilty** verdict	**A.** sad	**B.** innocent	**C.** criminal	**D.** culpable or at fault
14. **external** porch	**A.** outer	**B.** broad	**C.** narrow	**D.** restricted
15. **fervor** in her heart	**A.** honor	**B.** boredom	**C.** ennui	**D.** enthusiasm
16. a **fatal** accident	**A.** harmless	**B.** deadly	**C.** emotional	**D.** insignificant
17. to **generate**	**A.** sell	**B.** distribute	**C.** produce	**D.** show
18. **faulty** device	**A.** perfect	**B.** accurate	**C.** expensive	**D.** imperfect
19. expressed **gratitude**	**A.** appreciation	**B.** taste	**C.** distrust	**D.** disdain
20. **eminent** citizen	**A.** unpopular	**B.** famous	**C.** sane	**D.** sick
21. **homogenous** class	**A.** similar	**B.** dissimilar	**C.** talented	**D.** generous
22. **frolic** in the park	**A.** fun	**B.** fright	**C.** fear	**D.** fighting
23. burning **fury**	**A.** shame	**B.** satisfaction	**C.** anger	**D.** tension
24. **frequent** interruptions	**A.** intermittent	**B.** short	**C.** single	**D.** regular
25. **hostile** behavior	**A.** unfriendly	**B.** acceptable	**C.** tolerable	**D.** thoughtful
26. **fictitious**	**A.** real	**B.** imaginary	**C.** tangible	**D.** touchable
27. **superstition** is a	**A.** fear	**B.** attack	**C.** bad habit	**D.** belief based on ignorance
28. **fulfilling** experience	**A.** disturbing	**B.** filling	**C.** pleasing	**D.** tiring
29. **facetious** conversation	**A.** serious	**B.** concerned	**C.** desperate	**D.** lacking seriousness
30. a **frustrated** student	**A.** discouraged	**B.** satisfied	**C.** brilliant	**D.** talkative
31. looks **perplexed**	**A.** honest	**B.** puzzled	**C.** afraid	**D.** disturbed
32. a slow **gait**	**A.** fatigue	**B.** gate	**C.** speech	**D.** way of walking
33. a **generous** teacher	**A.** careless	**B.** selfish	**C.** giving	**D.** tough
34. run the **gamut**	**A.** channel	**B.** range	**C.** machine	**D.** time
35. a **vivid** imagination	**A.** graphic	**B.** precise	**C.** simple	**D.** important

EXERCISE 6

Antonyms

■ Match each word with its antonym.

_____	1. accompany	**A.** unclear
_____	2. distinction	**B.** active; awake
_____	3. accelerate	**C.** disassociated
_____	4. apparent	**D.** increase
_____	5. dormant	**E.** known
_____	6. appropriate	**F.** abandon
_____	7. disloyal	**G.** insignificance
_____	8. affiliated	**H.** regular
_____	9. abduct	**I.** expand
_____	10. disillusion	**J.** slow down
_____	11. abnormal	**K.** passive
_____	12. discount	**L.** unsuitable
_____	13. donate	**M.** understate
_____	14. derogatory	**N.** true; faithful
_____	15. disperse	**O.** retain
_____	16. anonymous	**P.** delight
_____	17. exaggerate	**Q.** return
_____	18. abbreviate	**R.** repulsive; unexciting
_____	19. digress	**S.** complimentary
_____	20. dynamic	**T.** appear; emerge
_____	21. charismatic	**U.** gather
_____	22. disappear	**V.** careless
_____	23. discreet	**W.** stay
_____	24. recession	**X.** inept
_____	25. resourceful	**Y.** recovery

EXERCISE 7

Word Meaning in Context: Set 1

■ Read each sentence and find the missing word in the box below. Fill in the blank with the correct *form* of that word.

trauma	**fluctuate**	**frugal**	**erratic**
guilty	**eradicate**	**enmity**	**fervor**
appreciate	**enough**		

1. The ___________ between the two families lasted for twenty years, even though no one could recall the original source of the hatred.
2. After six months, she still had not recovered from the ___________ of the tornado.
3. I would ___________ it if you did not talk during the movie.
4. With the discovery of the Salk vaccine, polio was ___________.
5. They were such big eaters that a pound of spaghetti was barely ___________ for the two of them.
6. Because she lived on a fixed pension, Diane was forced to be ___________.
7. The price of gold has ___________ very little in the past five years, neither rising nor falling by a significant amount.
8. Because of his ___________ driving patterns, the policeman stopped him and asked if he had been drinking.
9. Although all the evidence pointed against him, the defendant insisted that he was not ___________.
10. Her lack of ___________ at the football game went unnoticed by her boyfriend, who immediately promised to buy her a ticket to the next game.

EXERCISE 8

Word Meaning in Context: Set 2

■ Read each sentence and find the missing word in the box below. Fill in the blank with the correct *form* of that word.

eminent	**fury**	**hostile**	**fictitious**
superstition	**gratitude**	**frolic**	**generate**
homogeneous	**frequent**	**fatal**	**faulty**

1. Smoking causes many diseases, some of which are ___________.
2. Keeping your money in a savings account is safe, but will not ___________ much interest.
3. The inspector traced the cause of the fire to ___________ wiring.
4. When the policewoman brought the lost child home, the relieved mother expressed her ___________.
5. Dr. Carter has received several awards and is one of the most ___________ physicians in town.
6. More people of different ethnicities have begun moving to South Korea where the population is mostly ___________.
7. The children loved to watch the lambs ___________ in the field.
8. No one had witnessed a hurricane with as much ___________ as this one; not one house was left undamaged.

9. Most airlines offer bonuses to ___________ flyers.

10. A clean kitchen is a ___________ environment for most cockroaches.

11. When the editor discovered that every detail in the shocking news story was ___________, she fired the reporter who had written it.

12. Due to a ___________, many buildings do not have a thirteenth floor.

EXERCISE 9

Context Clues

■ Select the word or phrase that most closely matches the meaning of the **boldfaced** word. *Note that replacing the **boldfaced** word with the right answer might not produce a grammatically correct sentence.*

1. The man's **export** business, which sold American furniture overseas, became a huge success.
   A. home improvement **B.** products sent to another country
   C. wooden products **D.** souvenir

2. Federal investigators **exposed** the corruption of a Wall Street financial firm, resulting in the arrest of several vice presidents.
   A. enhanced **B.** supported **C.** revealed **D.** mentioned

3. Rescue workers had to **extract** the driver from the passenger seat before they could clear the car from the highway.
   A. remove **B.** treat **C.** awaken **D.** talk to

4. The director **facilitated** John's visit to Washington, DC.
   A. slowed down **B.** assigned detention **C.** made easier **D.** shed tears

5. She refused to travel abroad for years; one **factor** was her fear of contracting diseases.
   A. an element of disguise **B.** anything that hides intention
   C. something that influences a result **D.** something that gets in the way

6. An additional **feature** in her European travel package was a visit to Paris that became the highlight of her trip.
   A. reason **B.** fate **C.** part **D.** season

7. The **Federal** Reserve Commission is the central banking system in the U.S.
   A. keeping full of money **B.** detaining a fugitive
   C. relating to central government **D.** a committee of rebels

8. The secretary had to **file** hundreds of folders that had been scattered throughout the office during the burglary.
   A. replace **B.** destroy **C.** hide **D.** organize

9. When the **finances** of the country begin to affect the personal lives of people, consumers stop spending.
   A. weather **B.** descending status **C.** available money **D.** increasing interest

10. If an entrepreneur's view of the future is too **finite**, the bank might not approve his business loan application; it wants to know if he will succeed down the road.
    A. limited **B.** treacherous **C.** endless **D.** scandalous

11. She wanted a pair of stretchy pants that would allow her to be **flexible** when she exercised.
    A. capable of bending **B.** fixed in position **C.** attractive **D.** warm

12. The spotlight was **focused** on the Brazilian dance troupe, whose lively samba dance captured the flavor of Rio de Janeiro's Mardi Gras carnival.
    A. glowing **B.** directed **C.** pointed away **D.** shut off

13. A late-night talk show adopted a new **format** to stand out from its competitors, removing the desk and couch so the host and his guests could sit at a table together.
    A. name **B.** time slot **C.** design **D.** space

14. The football coach needed to invent a new **formula** for victory so his team could surprise the competition and win the game.
    A. promotion **B.** lie **C.** player **D.** plan

15. The child was not **forthcoming** about his side of the story, which made it difficult for the teacher to get direct answers.
    A. willing to inform **B.** peaceful **C.** malicious **D.** enthusiastic

16. The **foundation** of the home cracked during the earthquake.
    A. pictures **B.** bottom structure **C.** wooden parts **D.** blueprint

17. The man was relieved when he **found** his wallet that was stolen last week.
    A. recovered **B.** was given **C.** lost **D.** bought

18. The building's steel **framework** was strong enough to survive any disaster.
    A. basement **B.** plumbing **C.** supporting structure **D.** garden

19. The primary **function** of the new browser software was to give consumers a more meaningful way to search the Internet.
    A. display **B.** purpose **C.** feeling **D.** suggestion

20. The charity needs more financial support to **fund** its mission, which is to help the elderly receive in-home medical care.
    A. confuse **B.** provide money for **C.** withdraw from **D.** symbolize

21. The fourth-grade music class was learning the **fundamentals** of playing the guitar.
    A. basics **B.** strings **C.** chords **D.** costs

22. The thief must perform community service; **furthermore**, he will be required to pay back all of the money he stole.
    A. without **B.** under **C.** in addition **D.** slyly

23. Society often defines certain feminine and masculine **gender** roles as right or wrong. For example, it is considered acceptable for a woman to be a stay-at-home parent and for a man to be a plumber, but the opposite is often seen as shocking.
    A. related to one's sex **B.** related to a crime **C.** related to faith **D.** related to one's past

24. Television commercials use music and fashion to target different **generations** so they can sell their products to these specific age groups.
    A. parts of society **B.** media such as magazines
    C. groups of people born at the same time **D.** parents with disposable income

EXERCISE 10

Vocabulary Test

- Select the correct answer.
- Hint: Review the meanings of all the **boldfaced** words in this chapter before you take the test. This approach can help you to score 100 percent.
- Record the percentage of correct answers on the Master Self-Assessment table on page 397.

1 A **thermostat** regulates temperature.

A. True **B.** False

2 A **thermometer** tells temperature.

E. True **F.** False

3 A **barometer** measures atmospheric pressure.

A. True **B.** False

4 A **chronometer** measures time.

E. True **F.** False

5 A **telescope** makes distant objects appear smaller.

A. True **B.** False

6 A **manometer** measures the pressure of gases.

E. True **F.** False

7 A **stethoscope** is used to listen to sounds in the body.

A. True **B.** False

8 A **speedometer** indicates the speed of a motor vehicle.

E. True **F.** False

9 **Blood pressure** is measured by a sphygmomanometer.

A. True **B.** False

10 The **cerebellum** is:

E. near the brain **F.** the brain

G. the back of the brain **H.** on top of the brain

11 The **cerebrum** is:

A. the front of the brain
B. the back of the brain
C. the nervous system
D. the center of the brain

12 To **squander** money is to:

E. use
F. save
G. spend wastefully
H. hide

13 To **reject** a proposal is to:

A. refuse it
B. accept it
C. revise it
D. advance it

14 A **penalty** is a:

E. reward
F. sum
G. recognition
H. punishment

15 A **militant** is:

A. a politician
B. a rogue
C. a soldier
D. an activist

16 To **subside** is to:

E. be silent
F. sink to lower level
G. float
H. be loud

17 An **invincible** thing is:

A. unbeatable
B. weak
C. lazy
D. feeble

18 **Copious** refers to:

E. few
F. faulty
G. plentiful
H. large

19 **Speculate** means to:

A. know
B. salute
C. calculate
D. guess

20 Someone who is **perceptive** is:

E. negligent
F. ignorant
G. observant
H. sleepy

21 An **innuendo** is a:

A. suggestion
B. nightmare
C. report
D. story

22 To **revoke** a contract is to:

E. accept
F. cancel
G. delay
H. restore

23 To **possess** something is to:

A. disown
B. retrieve
C. own
D. damage

24 **Sustain** means to:

E. neglect
F. support
G. stagnate
H. leave

25 To **convince** someone is to:

A. discourage
B. trust
C. destroy
D. persuade

26 A synonym for **assurance** is:

E. doubt
F. fault
G. guarantee
H. agreement

27 To **concur** means to:

A. deny
B. agree
C. detest
D. avoid

28 A **proposal** is an:

E. act
F. extension
G. entry
H. offer

29 A **trauma** is:

A. an alias

B. an alien

C. an aid

D. a severe shock or something very upsetting

30 To **eradicate** a disease is to:

E. destroy completely

F. maintain

G. control

H. treat

31 To **generate** wealth is to:

A. achieve

B. distribute

C. produce

D. transfer

32 **Enmity** refers to:

E. love

F. fear

G. fate

H. hatred

33 To **fluctuate** is to:

A. change

B. stagnate

C. remain stationary

D. flood

34 A heartbeat that is **erratic** is:

E. stable

F. strong

G. irregular

H. faint

35 **Fervor** means:

A. curiosity

B. sadness

C. rudeness

D. enthusiasm

36 A **fatal** accident is:

E. deadly

F. serious

G. safe

H. harmless

37 To express **gratitude** is to show:

A. appreciation

B. anger

C. distrust

D. disdain

38 An **eminent** writer is:

E. unknown

F. inexperienced

G. unpopular

H. famous

39 **Homogeneous** means:

A. dissimilar

B. genuine

C. similar

D. fake

40 Another word for **frolic** is:

E. fight

F. fun

G. fear

H. suspicion

41 A synonym for **fury** is:

A. shame

B. satisfaction

C. violent anger

D. tension

42 A **hostile** behavior is:

E. unfriendly

F. acceptable

G. tolerable

H. thoughtful

43 A story that is **fictitious** is:

A. real

B. truthful

C. not real

D. magic

44 A **superstition** is a:

E. proverb

F. story

G. attack

H. false belief

45 A remark that is **facetious** is:

A. serious

B. urgent

C. funny

D. insensitive

46 **Perplexed** means:

E. honest

F. puzzled

G. frightened

H. disturbed

47 **Gait** is:

A. a manner of walking
B. fish food
C. an opening
D. an illness

48 **Gamut** means:

E. party
F. range
G. property
H. machine

49 **Vivid** means:

A. lively
B. dull
C. burning
D. lethargic

50 To **accompany** someone is to:

E. ignore
F. neglect
G. go with
H. abandon

51 **Distinction** means:

A. deficiency
B. special recognition
C. difference
D. popularity

52 The opposite of **accelerate** is:

E. increase
F. slow down
G. wait
H. speed

53 **Dormancy** refers to:

A. inactivity
B. activity
C. agility
D. energy

54 A person who is **seized** and taken by force is:

E. accepted
F. rejected
G. abducted
H. released

55 Another word for **disillusion** is:

A. disappointment
B. recognition
C. fame
D. confidence

56 If something is **abbreviated**, it is:

E. lengthened

F. shortened

G. separated

H. enlarged

57 To **exaggerate** means to:

A. minimize

B. underestimate

C. overemphasize

D. reduce

58 A synonym for **discreet** is:

E. careful

F. careless

G. articulate

H. considerate

59 **Excessive** drinking is:

A. too much

B. expensive

C. too little

D. dangerous

60 A device that is **faulty** is:

E. perfect

F. accurate

G. expensive

H. imperfect

EXERCISE 11

Building a Stronger Vocabulary

- Review all the **boldfaced** words in this chapter before you proceed to the next exercise.
- Highlight the ones you are still having difficulty remembering.
- List them with their meanings on a table.
- Use them to compose your own sentences.
- Think of a synonym and an antonym for each word.
- Use checkmarks to indicate if each word you want to practice more has a prefix, suffix, and/or root.
- You may use the table below as a sample to write your answers in your notebook.

Word	Definition	Sentence	Synonym	Antonym	Prefix	Suffix	Root

EXERCISE 12

Creating My Own Powerful Word List

- Write the words and meanings from the above table on the **Creating My Own Powerful Word List** table on page 398. Review them often to build that super vocabulary you want to create for school, work, and everyday use.

Chapter 8

Who Shot the American Border Patrol Officer in Texas?

PRE-READING

About This Chapter from *Trial of Love*

- Read the names and descriptions of this chapter's main characters below.
  - Sonny and his family
  - Dr. Joshi and his family

Story Vocabulary Exercise

- Before you begin reading this chapter, figure out the meanings of the unfamiliar **boldfaced** vocabulary words. You may use the Word List, Word Parts Chart, or your dictionary to assist you in finding their meanings.
- Look for the various types of context clues—synonyms, antonyms, general context, and examples—as you read.
- Write a word or phrase about the meaning of each **boldfaced** word in the margin.

Reading and Writing Exercise

- Skim the entire chapter and pay attention to the headings and the discussion questions that follow.
- Initial Response: Write a paragraph explaining, in your own words, what you think this chapter of the story will be about.
- Final Response: After you have read the entire chapter, compare your current understanding with your initial response above. If your initial response was accurate, you can simply write it again to fill in the blanks below. If it was not, then write a paragraph on what the chapter was really about instead.

Initial Response

This chapter **will** be about ______________________________

____

____

____

____

Final Response

This chapter **was** about ______________________________

____

____

____

____

WHO SHOT THE AMERICAN BORDER PATROL OFFICER IN TEXAS?

Joshi, his wife Roxy, and their children were **eager** to visit New York from Texas. It was their first visit and they were looking forward to their vacation. Kamla and Sonny went to meet them at La Guardia Airport while Rita was preparing dinner at home.

"Sonny, it's wonderful to see you again," said Joshi, embracing him.

"I've never forgotten the kind **deed** you did for us in Texas," replied Sonny.

"Have you seen Jose again?" asked Joshi.

"No. More than likely, he's in Mexico now. He's probably in jail," replied Sonny.

Joshi replied, "No way. He and his partners are too **shrewd** to be caught by the American law enforcement officials."

"I don't think so, Joshi. The immigration department has **undercover** agents who work around the clock to arrest people who **engage** in this sort of business."

"I bet they rarely **apprehend** them," said Joshi.

"Why do you say that?" asked Sonny.

"There is very little that a **handful** of border patrol officers can **accomplish**. They need to hire more people if they want to get anything done."

"You don't really need too many agents for this purpose. Besides, they're very **efficient** and **competent** at their job," said Sonny.

"If they are, why are so many people crossing the border successfully from Mexico, Canada, and other countries without being **detected**?" asked Joshi.

"The border is a large area to **patrol**," replied Sonny. "At night, there's very little that the agents can do successfully. People view this time as an opportunity to gain entry into America."

"I agree," said Joshi. "Sonny, I read in the *Dallas Informer*, a very **reputable** newspaper, that thirty-six people from Central and South America were caught last month when they attempted to enter the country illegally through Mexico. It must've been the agents' luckiest day."

"It was not really luck, Joshi. The agents were successful because they were **tipped** off by their **informants**."

"Informants? Who are they?" asked Joshi innocently.

Sonny replied, "They're usually **street people** who **spy** on their friends and neighbors to find out if they are engaged in illegal activities. It doesn't only have to **pertain** to immigration. Informants usually gather information on **illicit** drug activities as well. When they learn of something **substantive**, they report it to the agents."

"I'm surprised people would discuss their private affairs with strangers or even their neighbors," Joshi said.

"Some people have the tendency to trust everybody," Sonny told Joshi. "I've heard of instances where relatives have even reported their illegal family members to the Immigration Department to have them deported from the country. This happens frequently in New York. A few days ago, one of my friends at work told me of a fellow who reported a woman with whom he was **cohabitating** to the Immigration Department."

"You aren't serious, Sonny. How could someone report the woman he was living with?"

"I'm not kidding, Joshi."

Joshi asked, "Why would he **commit** such a **reprehensible** act? I can't believe a person would **stoop** so low as to do something so evil, hateful, and **malicious**."

"Have you heard of the 'business' or 'convenient' marriage?" asked Sonny. "It has been a practice for a while in New York and other parts of the country."

Joshi said, "This sounds interesting. I can't wait to hear about it."

"It's very simple. A person who is living in America illegally and wants a green card pays someone who's either a legal resident or an American citizen to marry him or her for an agreed sum of money. The unfortunate thing about this arrangement is that the person who needs the green card is often **blackmailed**," said Sonny, with a feeling of pity and sadness.

"Why the blackmailing, Sonny?"

"For money in addition to the sum initially agreed upon. Sometimes the woman is blackmailed for sex by the man whom she married for the green card, especially if they aren't living together in the same **dwelling**. There are women as well who would do likewise to men."

"How shameful! How **despicable**! How people could **resort** to such a **demeaning** and **disgraceful** act is beyond my comprehension," said Joshi with surprise.

"Some people don't have **shame**, **pride**, or **dignity**, Joshi. They'd do anything for money. I'm truly **indebted** to you for getting us our green cards, the 'passports' to work legally in America. Thank God you used our work experience and graduate degrees from India as the bases of our green card applications. You're our hero," said Sonny appreciatively.

Rita and Kamla Argue about Mark

Kamla and Roxy and her children were returning from the hot dog stand when Sonny motioned to Joshi to proceed to the baggage claim area of the airport. Surprisingly, they waited only a few moments for their baggage. There had not been many passengers on their flight from Dallas to New York.

On their arrival, Rita welcomed their guests to her home. Then she served dinner. While they were dining, the telephone rang. Kamla excused herself from the dining room to answer the call. Sonny and Rita glanced at each other when she left. They suspected Kamla was talking with Mark.

"Hi Kamla, how have you been?" Sheila asked. "I haven't heard from you in a while."

"I'm just busy at school. I'm **overburdened** with research," Kamla said with **disgust**.

"Are you OK?"

"Yes. I'm fine, Sheila."

"It seems you don't feel like talking with me, Kamla."

"I'm expecting a call from my friend," replied Kamla.

"Who? Mark?" Sheila inquired.

"Who's Mark?" Kamla asked with **pretense**.

"Ask your dad if you've had a sudden attack of **amnesia** and can't remember anything," replied Sheila.

Kamla angrily placed the telephone receiver on the table and shouted for her mother to take the call. Meanwhile, she went upstairs and locked herself in her room. She felt hurt by Sheila's response to her question.

"Rita, you have a **rude** daughter," remarked Sheila.

"Ignore Kamla. All young women behave like that when they're in love. If you can **recall**, you behaved in a similar manner when you were secretly dating Harry in our village."

Rita changed the subject of the conversation because whenever she talked about Sheila's ex-husband, Harry, who had died in an automobile accident, Sheila got very emotional. She had never overcome the **shock** of his death.

"Roxy and her family are here," Rita reminded Sheila.

"I want to invite them for supper tomorrow," said Sheila

"I'll ask Roxy to telephone you after dinner," Rita replied.

"Thanks. I'll see you later."

Rita returned to finish her dinner. Joshi, Sonny, and the children watched television afterwards. Roxy insisted on helping Rita with the dishes. Afterwards, they **proceeded** to the living room.

"Sonny, you'll love me forever for what I'm about to tell you," said Roxy, who was sitting next to him on the sofa.

"Surprise me, surprise me!" he said.

Joshi dropped his cup of tea on the coffee table. He was taken aback by Sonny's childish exclamation of surprise.

"Do you remember those sleepless nights you had when you first came to New York?" asked Roxy.

"Yes. I had a series of **traumatizing** nightmares whenever I recalled the shooting involving the border patrol officer. I always wondered who shot the officer."

"It was Fernandez," answered Roxy. "He was arrested in Dallas."

"Impossible! He wasn't there," said Sonny.

"He didn't have to be in America to shoot the patrolman. Fernandez fired shots from the Mexican side of the border. He was hiding behind the bushes with a **sniper** rifle to protect your family and his other **clients**."

"I don't know whether to call him a fool and a murderer or be grateful for what he did," Sonny said seriously. "Either way, it's for the best that he's in jail." A moment of tense silence passed before he continued. "I'm amazed, Roxy, at how much you know about the incident, even though you weren't there."

"If you ask Joshi, he'll tell you how **meticulously** I read the newspaper. Recently, an article about the incident was written in our local paper. Sonny, were you aware that a detective from Dallas was following you in New York when you first came?"

"No. Is this something you **conjured** up?"

"No. I didn't make this up. Just ask your **better half**, Rita."

"The detective was always parked across the street from our house," Rita interjected. "I didn't tell you about him for fear that you would **overreact** and become **hysterical** about something **trivial**."

Sonny felt relieved, though he did wonder what that detective had been doing on the day of the incident with Billy Burger.

When everybody **retired** to bed that night, Rita **surreptitiously** entered Kamla's room. She tried to be **discreet** about the entry, but to her surprise, Kamla was still awake. She was in bed **gazing** at a photograph she had in her hand. Rita was speechless and **dumbfounded** for a few seconds because she had not expected her to have that photo in her possession.

"Where did you get that photograph, Kamla?" asked Rita.

"It was in your handbag. Who's this man, Mother?"

"Dr. Azeez."

"Where did you meet him?"

"He's our new village medical doctor."

"He looks young to be a doctor."

"He's somebody you should meet."

"Why?"

"He's handsome, charming, and educated. Any woman would dream of having him for a husband."

"I agree that he's handsome."

"How do you feel about him, Kamla?"

"Mother, that's a **silly** question. What answer are you **anticipating**? What do you expect me to say? I've never met the guy. Besides, you know how I feel about Mark."

"Kamla, don't even mention Mark," Rita said **lividly**, suddenly **enraged**. She **hastened** to **exit** Kamla's room.

"Please wait a second, Mother. Why are you in such a hurry to leave? We have to talk."

"There's nothing to talk about, Kamla."

"Why do you and Daddy **disrespect** my feelings for Mark? Is it because he's an American?"

"We only want what's best for you. I'm certain Mark is a terrific man. But that's not a good enough reason to marry him. You have to think about cultural differences. You're **underestimating** how negatively these differences can **impact** a marriage. When **conflict** arises later, how will you deal with it, Kamla? Don't take these differences for granted. They can strike a severe **blow** to a marriage or a relationship."

"What conflict? What disagreements? There wouldn't be any conflict," assured Kamla.

"A **fantasy** is not a **reality**. Stop living in a dream world. Mark will leave you for another woman in a heartbeat if the two of you can't **resolve** conflicts or work out your differences."

"You should be an astrologer, Mother. It seems as if the future is crystal clear to you."

"Experience is something that I have and you don't. Mark is a **Caucasian**. Simply put, he's a white guy with a certain way of life that's **alien** to you. Your **puppy love** for him has **blinded** you and **paralyzed** your ability to **rationalize** intelligently. You want him so badly that you can't see the truth, and you aren't thinking." Rita spoke **sternly**, just like Kamla's **strict**, old-fashioned grandmother, Sosheila.

"Please stop it, Mom. This isn't childish or adolescent love that I'm feeling for Mark. I don't want to continue this conversation. It's **futile** to discourage me from dating him. Furthermore, it's useless to try to convince me that Mark would be an unsuitable husband or **life partner** for me."

"Whether you like it or not, you've no other **prerogative** but to consider Dr. Azeez your possible **spouse**," Rita said. "That's all I have to say to you, young woman. Do not dare to forget that you're an Indian and not an American. Just remember that a zebra cannot change its stripes. You can change anything in life but your Indian **identity** and **heritage**."

"For your information, I'm going to our college's graduation dance with Mark tomorrow night."

"You will do no such thing. That's final," said Rita threateningly.

Rita was upset by Kamla's **fierce determination** to marry Mark. If this marriage should take place, Rita feared that her relatives and friends, **locally** as well as **abroad**, would look down on her and her family because her only daughter would have married someone outside her culture. Rita and her family would earn a lifetime of disrespect. Later that night, she wished she had not spoken with Kamla about her affair with Mark, because she could not sleep well afterwards.

Kamla and Mark at the Graduation Dance

The following day, Joshi and his family went to visit Sheila. They spent the night at her house. When Rita and Sonny returned from work, Kamla was already home from the university. She spent most of the evening preparing for her date with Mark. At approximately eight o'clock, she telephoned him.

"I'm looking forward to going to the dance with you, honey," Kamla said affectionately.

"I can't wait to see you, my princess," he replied.

"Mark, please pick me up at home at 9:30 sharp. Please be **prompt**. Be on time."

"You can count on me, my dear," said Mark excitedly.

When the clock struck 8:45, Kamla came downstairs. Sonny and Rita were astonished at her **attire**. She was dressed in a beautifully designed peach evening gown. Her makeup and jewelry matched her **clear** complexion and **accentuated** her beauty. She looked **gorgeous**.

"Mom and Dad, I'm going to the graduation dance tonight," said Kamla politely and respectfully.

"Kamla, didn't your mother say that you can't go?" reminded Sonny.

"Yes."

"Why are you disobeying her?"

"She's being unreasonable, Dad."

"How?"

"All the students I've taught at Rollins are graduating this semester. I've been their **academic** and **extracurricular** activities **mentor** and **advisor**. This might be the last time I'll see most of them."

"I understand, Kamla. Your mother wants you to go and enjoy yourself at the dance. But she's afraid you'll once again be spending the night with Professor Hubbard in his apartment. You and I know that you and Mark aren't grading students' tests whenever you visit him at his apartment. You are **cognizant** that our culture **prohibits** females from engaging in this sort of **conduct**. It considers it a **demeaning** and **degrading** act that should not be **tolerated**, especially if the woman is **intimate** with someone before marriage. Kamla, it's our parental **duty** to **ensure** that these values are **observed** by our daughter. That's just the way it is, whether you like it or not, Kamla. There are no exceptions, regardless of **prestige** or **profession**, **wisdom** or **wealth**."

"Please ignore her, Dad. Mom's always suspicious of my intentions."

"She has reasons to be. The changes in your lifestyle are **overwhelming** us. Your mother and I feel that things with you are getting out of control. You aren't the same daughter we had back home in India, Kamla."

"Whose side are you on, Dad?"

"Nobody's."

"Are you saying I can't go to the dance, Dad?"

"I'm afraid so."

Kamla burst into tears, ran up the stairs and slammed the door to her room loudly. Shortly after, Sonny's **sullen** expression caught Rita's eyes.

"Why are you making me feel guilty, Sonny?" Rita asked angrily.

"I think you're being too tough on Kamla. You've **ruined** her evening."

"Sonny, you're the one who's worried about her relationship with Mark."

"I agree. But can't you see how lovely and **innocent** she looks?"

"Sonny, stop being a **sentimental** fool. Your daughter is putting on an act. I bet she's up to something naughty and **devious**. Don't forget that I carried her in my belly for nine months. I know my daughter **intimately**."

"Rita, this might be a **traumatic** experience for her."

"Don't be **naive**, Sonny. Let's watch television."

"That's all we do around here, Rita."

"Then why don't you take me out to a movie or a restaurant for a change, Sonny?"

"A great idea, Rita."

Rita and Sonny went to see an Indian movie at the local cinema a few blocks from their home. They went to a restaurant for dinner afterwards. They had a great evening and **vowed** to go out more frequently. Once a month was the **pledge** Sonny made to Rita.

Kamla Ignores Her Parents

Mark arrived promptly at 9:30 p.m. at Kamla's home. He gave her a **fabulous** bouquet of red roses and showered her with **compliments** on how terrific she looked. Mark observed that she was a bit uneasy and gently **confronted** her about it. He listened attentively to what she had to say.

"Honey, I'm so afraid. I don't know what will happen to me," Kamla said nervously as she sat close to him in the car.

"What's the matter, Kamla?" asked Mark.

"You don't know what I'm experiencing at home with my parents, Mark. There is an argument concerning you almost every day."

"I suspect your parents are **forbidding** you to date me, and I understand their reasons."

"You do understand, Mark?"

"Of course. What was tonight's argument about?"

"My parents don't want me to go to the dance for fear that I might spend the night with you."

"Are they at home now?"

"No. I **overheard** them making plans to go out for the evening," replied Kamla.

"Are they aware that you are going to the dance with me now?"

"No. I don't care how they feel about our relationship anymore. Mark, let's not talk about my parents. We're very young and **tender** at heart. We must enjoy ourselves during every minute we spend with each other.

"Do you promise me an unforgettable night, Mark?" said Kamla like a **seductive temptress**. "My heart yearns for moments with you that time will never erase."

"Anything for you," Mark whispered as he drove toward the hotel where the dance was being held.

The dance was everything Kamla had imagined. She remembered her parents' concerns about her spending time at Mark's apartment, yet she stayed with him there until 5:00 a.m. She was prepared to face the consequences for disobeying her parents. She did not mind, because she had fulfilled her dream of **intimacy** with Mark.

EXERCISE 1

Applying the Words You Have Learned to Critical Thinking and Creative Writing

- Use the two questions in Section A below to discuss this chapter with your classmates. Be sure to apply your critical thinking skills.

- Write an essay about either question using the vocabulary words you know from real-life experiences and the new ones you have learned from this text.

Section A

Discussion Questions

1. Do you agree or disagree with Kamla's parents for wanting to uphold their cultural values with regard to Kamla having a relationship with Mark?

2. How do you think Kamla's parents will react when she returns home after spending the night with Mark?

EXERCISE 2

Forming Synonyms

■ Fill in the blank(s) to complete the word that is similar in meaning to the **boldfaced** word.

1. **data** fa__ __s
2. **decease** d__e
3. **susceptible** vulner__ __ __ __
4. **dedicate** de__ __te
5. **defeat** over__ __ __e
6. **deficient** i__adeq__ __ __e
7. **delicious** tas__ __
8. **demand** com__ __ __d
9. **describe** ex__ __ __in
10. **explain** __ __ __rify
11. **exempt** exc__ __ __ed
12. **elicit** ev__ __e
13. **rank** po__ __tion
14. **endeavor** a__te__ __ __
15. **recite** re__ __at
16. **enhance** str__ __gt__en
17. **escalate** i__crea__e
18. **equate** equ__ __
19. **embezzle** __teal
20. **equip** pro__ __de

EXERCISE 3

Synonyms and Antonyms

■ Write the corresponding letter for the synonym and antonym of each **boldfaced** word.

	Synonym	Antonym			
1. **erase**	______	______	**A.** delete	**B.** preserve	**C.** greedy
2. **establish**	______	______	**A.** organize	**B.** apprehend	**C.** dissolve
3. **fallible**	______	______	**A.** difficult	**B.** imperfect	**C.** perfect
4. **facilitate**	______	______	**A.** delay	**B.** assist	**C.** hinder
5. **futile**	______	______	**A.** useless	**B.** greedy	**C.** effective
6. **fabulous**	______	______	**A.** fantastic	**B.** terrible	**C.** love
7. **faith**	______	______	**A.** belief	**B.** stable	**C.** doubt
8. **fantasy**	______	______	**A.** daydream	**B.** modern	**C.** reality
9. **fatigue**	______	______	**A.** tiredness	**B.** energy	**C.** latitude
10. **fault**	______	______	**A.** mistake	**B.** formula	**C.** merit
11. **festive**	______	______	**A.** increased	**B.** merry	**C.** gloomy
12. **flourish**	______	______	**A.** prosper	**B.** decline	**C.** prepare
13. **fluster**	______	______	**A.** disturb	**B.** copy	**C.** compose
14. **foremost**	______	______	**A.** most important	**B.** least	**C.** older
15. **forever**	______	______	**A.** always	**B.** seldom	**C.** never
16. **forsake**	______	______	**A.** act	**B.** abandon	**C.** keep
17. **grieve**	______	______	**A.** mourn	**B.** rejoice	**C.** hasten
18. **grotesque**	______	______	**A.** ugly	**B.** beautiful	**C.** acceptable
19. **graphic**	______	______	**A.** colorful	**B.** special	**C.** dull
20. **gang**	______	______	**A.** group	**B.** party	**C.** individual
21. **glimpse**	______	______	**A.** brief look	**B.** postpone	**C.** stare
22. **guest**	______	______	**A.** worker	**B.** visitor	**C.** host
23. **halt**	______	______	**A.** stop	**B.** continue	**C.** complain

	Synonym	Antonym			
24. **hilarious**	_______	_______	**A.** comical	**B.** chief	**C.** serious
25. **immaculate**	_______	_______	**A.** criminal	**B.** faultless	**C.** flawed
26. **implausible**	_______	_______	**A.** tedious	**B.** unbelievable	**C.** credible
27. **implicit**	_______	_______	**A.** unexpressed	**B.** spoken	**C.** plenty
28. **incentive**	_______	_______	**A.** encouragement	**B.** change	**C.** hindrance
29. **incoherent**	_______	_______	**A.** entity	**B.** inconsistent	**C.** understandable
30. **incorporate**	_______	_______	**A.** include	**B.** scold	**C.** exclude
31. **inquisitive**	_______	_______	**A.** curious	**B.** uninterested	**C.** dishonest
32. **intricate**	_______	_______	**A.** uneasy	**B.** complex	**C.** simple
33. **illuminate**	_______	_______	**A.** brighten	**B.** scold	**C.** darken
34. **impair**	_______	_______	**A.** damage	**B.** improve	**C.** eliminate
35. **initiate**	_______	_______	**A.** start	**B.** revise	**C.** conclude
36. **intense**	_______	_______	**A.** strong	**B.** weak	**C.** dormant
37. **inevitable**	_______	_______	**A.** detrimental	**B.** unavoidable	**C.** avoidable
38. **innate**	_______	_______	**A.** incapable	**B.** inherited	**C.** learned
39. **isolate**	_______	_______	**A.** separate	**B.** include	**C.** decrease
40. **illicit**	_______	_______	**A.** forbidden	**B.** incapable	**C.** authorized
41. **imminent**	_______	_______	**A.** fateful	**B.** about to happen	**C.** distant
42. **intimate**	_______	_______	**A.** innermost	**B.** incidental	**C.** public
43. **identify**	_______	_______	**A.** recognize	**B.** mistake	**C.** change
44. **idiot**	_______	_______	**A.** stupid person	**B.** genius	**C.** criminal
45. **implore**	_______	_______	**A.** appeal	**B.** hurry	**C.** refuse
46. **include**	_______	_______	**A.** attend	**B.** involve	**C.** exclude
47. **indiscriminate**	_______	_______	**A.** unsystematic	**B.** concerned	**C.** orderly
48. **inherent**	_______	_______	**A.** built-in	**B.** acquired	**C.** famous
49. **inquisitive**	_______	_______	**A.** unsteady	**B.** curious	**C.** uninterested
50. **invite**	_______	_______	**A.** request	**B.** collect	**C.** reject
51. **irrevocable**	_______	_______	**A.** cannot be recalled	**B.** lavish	**C.** reversible

	Synonym	Antonym			
52. **indelible**	______	______	**A.** harmless	**B.** not removable	**C.** temporary
53. **inconspicuous**	______	______	**A.** low-profile	**B.** pictured	**C.** noticeable
54. **inanimate**	______	______	**A.** lifeless	**B.** cured	**C.** active
55. **irrelevant**	______	______	**A.** unconnected	**B.** wicked	**C.** vital
56. **inform**	______	______	**A.** ask	**B.** tell	**C.** conceal
57. **involve**	______	______	**A.** include	**B.** cure	**C.** exclude
58. **irresistible**	______	______	**A.** compelling	**B.** acceptable	**C.** repulsive
59. **isolate**	______	______	**A.** separate	**B.** include	**C.** invent
60. **jealous**	______	______	**A.** envious	**B.** trusting	**C.** annoyed
61. **jeopardize**	______	______	**A.** manifest	**B.** risk	**C.** safeguard
62. **lucrative**	______	______	**A.** profitable	**B.** latent	**C.** unprofitable
63. **lenient**	______	______	**A.** imposing	**B.** lax	**C.** strict
64. **liberal**	______	______	**A.** broad-minded	**B.** conservative	**C.** lengthy
65. **labor**	______	______	**A.** struggle	**B.** operate	**C.** leisure
66. **lack**	______	______	**A.** need	**B.** have	**C.** object
67. **lapse**	______	______	**A.** decline	**B.** evolve	**C.** increase
68. **lure**	______	______	**A.** measure	**B.** attract	**C.** repulse
69. **learn**	______	______	**A.** labor	**B.** grasp	**C.** forget
70. **linger**	______	______	**A.** stick around	**B.** leave	**C.** deny
71. **mandatory**	______	______	**A.** compulsory	**B.** optional	**C.** difficult
72. **mobile**	______	______	**A.** movable	**B.** alert	**C.** stationary
73. **manage**	______	______	**A.** linger	**B.** control	**C.** follow
74. **manual**	______	______	**A.** hand-operated	**B.** complicated	**C.** automatic
75. **maintain**	______	______	**A.** support	**B.** abandon	**C.** bias

EXERCISE 4

Matching Meanings: Set 1

■ Match each word with its meaning.

_____	1. authenticate	**A.** indirect reference; indirect way
_____	2. irrevocable	**B.** work well together; get along well
_____	3. casual	**C.** hateful; evil; wicked
_____	4. allude	**D.** not likely to cause damage or harm; harmless
_____	5. disengage	**E.** a fraud or trick; deception
_____	6. conspire	**F.** sociable; likes the company of others
_____	7. compatible	**G.** verify as represented; reliable
_____	8. gregarious	**H.** not planned; happening by chance
_____	9. heinous	**I.** person with an irresistible impulse to steal
_____	10. hoax	**J.** set loose; detach
_____	11. innocuous	**K.** act together secretly
_____	12. kleptomaniac	**L.** cannot be recalled

EXERCISE 5

Matching Meanings: Set 2

■ Match each word with its meaning.

_____	1. adamant	**A.** vague; not clear
_____	2. aristocrat	**B.** not giving in; inflexible
_____	3. ambiguous	**C.** using vulgar or indecent language
_____	4. acrimonious	**D.** upper-class; privileged person
_____	5. scurrilous	**E.** stubborn; holding firmly
_____	6. subservient	**F.** take revenge; fight back
_____	7. tenacious	**G.** without interruption; continuous
_____	8. trepidation	**H.** act with little thought
_____	9. retaliate	**I.** bitter, especially in speech and manner
_____	10. redundant	**J.** anxious; fearful; apprehensive
_____	11. incessant	**K.** using more words than necessary
_____	12. impetuous	**L.** submissive; useful in an inferior capacity

EXERCISE 6

Word Meaning in Context: Set 1

■ Read each sentence and find the missing word in the box below. Fill in the blank with the correct *form* of that word.

hoax	**gregarious**	**allude**	**casual**
conspire	**innocuous**	**authenticate**	**heinous**
irrevocable	**kleptomaniac**	**disengage**	**compatible**

1. Before he would buy the Picasso painting, Mr. Fredericks called in an expert to ___________ it.
2. The decision to give up his citizenship was ___________, so he had to think long and hard.
3. Their first date was ___________, but the ones that followed became more serious.
4. Although she never directly stated her net worth, Ms. Watkins __________ to her wealth many times during our conversation.
5. A mechanical error caused the train car to ___________ while the train was moving, resulting in a serious accident.
6. Benedict Arnold was considered guilty of treason for ___________ with the enemy.
7. After a few years of marriage, many couples find that they are not ___________, resulting in divorce.
8. Unlike her older sister, who was shy and unsociable, Judy was quite ___________.
9. Murder is considered one of the most ___________ of crimes.
10. The radio announcer stated that Martians had landed, but when people began to call the station, he was forced to tell his listeners that it was a ___________.
11. Megadoses of vitamin C may help to prevent colds; at worst, they are ___________.
12. After her fourth arrest for shoplifting, a psychiatrist diagnosed her as being a ___________.

EXERCISE 7

Word Meaning in Context: Set 2

■ Read each sentence and find the missing word in the box below. Fill in the blank with the correct *form* of that word.

incessant	**impetuous**	**scurrilous**	**adamant**
trepidation	**retaliate**	**subservient**	**acrimonious**
redundant	**ambiguous**	**tenacious**	**aristocrat**

1. When asked if she would try skydiving, she refused so ___________ that nobody ever asked her again.
2. Although she was not from a royal family, many people considered Jacqueline Onassis a true ___________.
3. The directions for assembling this bicycle are so ___________ that I have put parts in the wrong places three times.
4. After a particularly ___________ argument with his neighbor, Mr. Miller decided to build a fence between their yards.
5. The conservative newspaper made a ___________ attack on the liberal president, hoping to damage his chances of being re-elected.

6. Tired of being ___________ to her employer, Jane quit her job as housekeeper.

7. Because habits are so ___________, they are often hard to change.

8. Not being a strong swimmer, Bill stepped into the sea with ___________.

9. The United States entered World War II to ___________ against the bombing of Pearl Harbor.

10. Many people find the term "free gift" to be ___________.

11. The new father was unable to cope with the baby's ___________ crying.

12. Although she thought of herself as a free spirit, her friends thought she was simply ___________.

EXERCISE 8

Context Clues

- Select the word or phrase that most closely matches the meaning of the **boldfaced** word. *Note that replacing the **boldfaced** word with the right answer might not produce a grammatically correct sentence.*

1. The little boy put his new **globe** on his desk and spun it around so he could see all the continents.
   A. a fish tank on a rotating platform
   B. a clear cube
   C. a hot lamp
   D. a round object with a map of the Earth

2. My **goal** is to lose ten pounds before the beginning of summer.
   A. past remembrance
   B. something to avoid
   C. something to achieve
   D. terrible fate

3. The honor student was concerned that if her **grades** were not good enough, she would not qualify for a college scholarship.
   A. work experience
   B. performance in sports
   C. marks of accomplishment
   D. essays and applications

4. The leaders of the non-profit organization were grateful for the **grant** they received to pay for their project.
   A. small amount of money
   B. money given for a specific purpose
   C. giant donation
   D. loan

5. The product came with a satisfaction **guarantee** that promised a full refund if the customer found even a single flaw.
   A. assurance
   B. deceit
   C. hope
   D. application

6. The instructor presented **guidelines** that students needed to obey if they wanted to complete the project successfully.
   A. instructions
   B. a book
   C. a treatment
   D. a contract

7. After he got married, he started making bad decisions and **hence** ended up divorced.
   A. lovingly
   B. accidentally
   C. therefore
   D. in spite of

8. It is important for newly hired firefighters to understand the **hierarchy** of the department and follow the chain of command.
   A. a system with levels of importance **B.** a measure of success
   C. a call to arms **D.** a clear target

9. A large flat-screen television **highlighted** the main points of the speaker's presentation.
   A. created a buzz **B.** emphasized **C.** confused **D.** explained

10. After extensive research, the students were ready to offer a **hypothesis** that made a convincing argument in support of their theory.
    A. possible explanation **B.** caption **C.** apparatus **D.** territory

11. We are taught to respect others' **ideologies** even if they go against our own views.
    A. residences **B.** wealth **C.** beliefs **D.** territories

12. The history professor presented several **images** created by artists during the French Revolution.
    A. pictures **B.** parcels **C.** sculptures **D.** lockets

13. His involvement with the drug dealer could **implicate** him in the crime as well.
    A. force into eviction **B.** remove from office
    C. assist in emancipation **D.** bring into connection

14. The doctor **imposed** strict dietary restrictions on her patient because of her obesity.
    A. recommended **B.** forced to accept **C.** asked about **D.** denied

15. The police reported three **incidents** of drunk driving this week.
    A. arrests **B.** court cases **C.** occurrences **D.** deaths

16. The **incline** of the mountainside made it difficult to climb.
    A. slope **B.** plants **C.** ice **D.** loose sand

17. The **income** earned by the business showed a 3 percent increase in profits.
    A. ideals **B.** money **C.** contract **D.** promise

18. The college campus directory also offered an **index** that made it easier to locate faculty offices.
    A. phone number list **B.** presentation **C.** calendar **D.** guide

19. This job requires an **individual** with great communication skills and management experience.
    A. professional **B.** person **C.** supervisor **D.** older worker

20. Doctors had to **induce** labor so the mother could deliver a healthy baby.
    A. cause to happen **B.** delay **C.** halt **D.** pay for

21. Voters asked the candidates how much taxpayer money would be spent on improvements to the region's **infrastructure**, particularly its bridges and roads.
    A. for passengers **B.** basic installations **C.** scenic overlook **D.** rivers and valleys

22. John corrected his answer after he realized his **initial** response had been incorrect.
    A. occurring at the beginning **B.** happening last
    C. with increasing difficulty **D.** poorly chosen

23. After he failed to **initiate** work on the project within the first three days, his employer canceled the contract.
    A. begin **B.** procrastinate **C.** deteriorate **D.** improve

24. When emergency medical technicians arrived at the home, they immediately realized that the **injured** woman had to be taken to a hospital.
    A. healed **B.** scared **C.** wounded **D.** deranged

EXERCISE 9

Vocabulary Test

- Select the correct answer.
- Hint: Review the meanings of all the **boldfaced** words in this chapter before you take the test. This approach can help you to score 100 percent.
- Record the percentage of correct answers on the Master Self-Assessment table on page 397.

1 **Deceased** means:

A. deceived **B.** alive

C. depressed **D.** dead

2 Being **susceptible** to a disease means you are:

E. likely to be affected **F.** resistant

G. affected **H.** unlikely to be affected

3 **Deficient** means:

A. adequate **B.** inadequate

C. surplus **D.** gifted

4 **Exempted** from a class is to be:

E. included **F.** excluded

G. accepted **H.** rejected

5 A synonym for **elicit** is:

A. request
B. evoke or bring out
C. discourage
D. beg

6 A person's **endeavor** is a(n):

E. attempt
F. opportunity
G. strength
H. weakness

7 To **recite** a poem is to:

A. respect
B. say aloud
C. release
D. reveal

8 To **enhance** something is to:

E. strengthen
F. weaken
G. destroy
H. imitate

9 The argument **escalated** suggests that it:

A. increased
B. decreased
C. stopped
D. paused

10 To **embezzle** money is to:

E. borrow
F. return
G. steal
H. earn

11 **Fallible** means:

A. might be difficult
B. likely to make a mistake
C. needs to be true
D. can be perfect

12 You **facilitate** an effort when you:

E. assist
F. desist
G. delay
H. hinder

13 A **futile** effort is:

A. welcome
B. helpful
C. hopeful
D. useless

14 The antonym for **fluster** is:

E. disturb
F. copy
G. compose
H. frustrate

15 Something that is **grotesque** is:

A. ugly
B. beautiful
C. acceptable
D. unacceptable

16 **Graphic** pictures are:

E. colorful
F. colorless
G. intricate
H. blurry

17 A **glimpse** of something is a:

A. consideration
B. glance or brief look
C. stare
D. thought

18 A **hilarious** show is:

E. serious
F. sad
G. comical
H. scary

19 Someone **immaculately** dressed is:

A. flawless
B. flawed
C. in rags
D. plain

20 An **implausible** excuse is:

E. tedious
F. unbelievable
G. credible
H. possible

21 An **incoherent** story is:

A. clear

B. meaningless

C. unclear

D. easy to understand

22 An **inquisitive** child is:

E. curious

F. dishonest

G. uninterested

H. truthful

23 An **intricate** plot is:

A. basic

B. complex

C. easy

D. simple

24 To **illuminate** is to:

E. brighten

F. open

G. obscure

H. increase

25 An **inevitable** result is:

A. sincere

B. avoidable

C. favorable

D. unavoidable

26 **Intimate** feelings are those that are:

E. casual

F. incidental

G. innermost

H. impersonal

27 **Implore** means to:

A. appeal

B. hurry

C. demand

D. explore

28 An **irrevocable** decision is:

E. reversible

F. irreversible

G. impossible

H. possible

29 **Indelible** means:

A. removable

B. authentic

C. impartial

D. not removable

30 If something is **inconspicuous**, it is:

E. valuable

F. obvious

G. unnoticeable

H. supernatural

31 An **inanimate** object is:

A. lifeless

B. healing

C. cursed

D. full of life

32 An antonym for **irrelevant** is:

E. unconnected

F. wicked

G. disjointed

H. connected

33 If something is **irresistible**, it is:

A. compelling

B. reasonable

C. forgettable

D. acceptable

34 To **jeopardize** is to:

E. manifest

F. put into danger

G. confirm

H. surrender

35 A **lucrative** business is:

A. failing

B. profitable

C. attacked

D. latent

36 A synonym for **lenient** is:

E. soft

F. hard

G. lax

H. tense

37 A person who is **liberal** is:

A. broad-minded
B. conservative
C. fair
D. traditional

38 **Indiscriminate** means:

E. selective
F. unsystematic
G. intolerant
H. prejudiced

39 To **lure** someone is to:

A. attack
B. repulse
C. attract
D. chase

40 If attendance is **mandatory**, it is:

E. compulsory
F. optional
G. unnecessary
H. voluntary

41 If something is **mobile**, it is:

A. alert
B. stationary
C. movable
D. electronic

42 To **authenticate** a document is to:

E. disprove
F. verify as represented
G. publish
H. challenge

43 A synonym for **data** is:

A. research
B. machine
C. opinion
D. facts

44 To **allude** to something is to:

E. make an indirect reference
F. make a direct reference
G. illustrate
H. ascertain

45 To **disengage** means to:

A. bring together
B. detach
C. strengthen
D. relax

46 To **conspire** to commit a crime is to:

E. act alone
F. plan publicly
G. pretend
H. act together secretly

47 **Compatible** team members:

A. compete
B. fight each other
C. work well together
D. disagree

48 A **gregarious** person is:

E. sociable
F. antisocial
G. unfriendly
H. private

49 A **heinous** crime is:

A. recent
B. simple
C. horrifying
D. harmless

50 **Innocuous** means:

E. careful
F. not likely to cause harm
G. dangerous
H. lacking substance

51 A **kleptomaniac** is someone who has:

A. an urge to tell lies
B. an urge to shop
C. an urge to overeat
D. an irresistible desire to steal

52 **Adamant** means:

E. not giving in
F. yielding
G. extremely cautious
H. compliant

53 An **ambiguous** answer is:

A. clear
B. unclear
C. compromised
D. unkind

54 **Acrimonious** means:

E. kind
F. nasty or bitter in speech or behavior
G. very polite in manner
H. extremely hot

55 A **scurrilous** attack on a politician is:

A. friendly and engaging
B. violent and physically harmful
C. abusive and slanderous
D. neither harmful nor offensive

56 A **subservient** person is:

E. extremely submissive
F. very strong
G. aggressive
H. unyielding

57 **Tenacious** means:

A. gracious
B. determined or persistent
C. evil
D. submissive

58 A feeling of **trepidation** means:

E. anxiety or fear
F. blissful happiness
G. depression
H. sadness

59 To **retaliate** is to:

A. forgive
B. compromise
C. accept with kindness
D. take revenge

60 **Redundant** means:

E. precise
F. using more words than necessary
G. using few words
H. satisfactory

61 **Incessant** noise from a construction site:

A. stops and starts

B. is consistently loud

C. stops suddenly

D. continues without interruption

62 An **impetuous** person:

E. acts without thinking

F. is petite

G. is impolite

H. is harsh

63 An **innate** response is:

A. inappropriate

B. learned

C. inborn or inherited

D. collective

64 **Imminent** danger is:

E. approaching

F. retreating

G. past

H. declining

65 To **isolate** is to:

A. include

B. separate

C. involve

D. join

EXERCISE 10

Building a Stronger Vocabulary

- Review all the **boldfaced** words in this chapter before you proceed to the next exercise.
- Highlight the ones you are still having difficulty remembering.
- List them with their meanings on a table.
- Use them to compose your own sentences.
- Think of a synonym and an antonym for each word.
- Use checkmarks to indicate if each word you want to practice more has a prefix, suffix, and/or root.
- You may use the table below as a sample to write your answers in your notebook.

Word	Definition	Sentence	Synonym	Antonym	Prefix	Suffix	Root

EXERCISE 11

Creating My Own Powerful Word List

- Write the words and meanings from the above table on the **Creating My Own Powerful Word List** table on page 398. Review them often to build that super vocabulary you want to create for school, work, and everyday use.

Did Kamla Run Away from Home after the Dance?

Chapter 9

PRE-READING

About This Chapter from *Trial of Love*

- Read the names and descriptions of this chapter's main characters below.
  - Dorothy: Mark's mother
  - Ashana Castro: A nurse at the nursing home
  - Piccolo: A former student of Mark's
  - Agatha Tellford: Mark's ex-girlfriend

Story Vocabulary Exercise

- Before you begin reading this chapter, figure out the meanings of the unfamiliar **boldfaced** vocabulary words. You may use the Word List, Word Parts Chart, or your dictionary to assist you in finding their meanings.
- Look for the various types of context clues—synonyms, antonyms, general context, and examples—as you read.
- Write a word or phrase about the meaning of each **boldfaced** word in the margin.

Reading and Writing Exercise

- Skim the entire chapter and pay attention to the headings and the discussion questions that follow.
- Initial Response: Write a paragraph explaining, in your own words, what you think this chapter of the story will be about.
- Final Response: After you have read the entire chapter, compare your current understanding with your initial response above. If your initial response was accurate, you can simply write it again to fill in the blanks below. If it was not, then write a paragraph on what the chapter was really about instead.

Initial Response

This chapter **will** be about ______________________________

____

____

____

Final Response

This chapter **was** about ______________________________

____

____

____

DID KAMLA RUN AWAY FROM HOME AFTER THE DANCE?

Mark did not see or hear from Kamla after the graduation dance. It was unusual for her not to telephone him. He knew Kamla would be **scolded** by her parents for visiting him at his apartment on the day of the dance. He was afraid that her dad might verbally abuse him if he called. Even so, his burning desire to hear Kamla's voice **propelled** his fingers to **dial** her phone number. He did not care if Sonny or Rita **insulted** him when he called.

"Sir, may I speak with Kamla?" Mark pleaded when Sonny picked up the phone.

"Sorry, I know nothing about Kamla's **whereabouts**," said Sonny angrily. "You should know best because she was with you the entire night. Furthermore, please don't dial my telephone number again."

After Mark hung up the phone, he had a feeling that Sonny was telling him the truth when he said that he did not know where Kamla was. He was very upset and needed someone to talk with about his feelings for Kamla. He felt Agatha Tellford was the best person to **confide** in because he had dated her prior to meeting Kamla. She could be insensitive at times, though. Agatha was not a **tactful** person. Nevertheless, he telephoned her.

"It has been a while since you called me, Mark," Agatha said excitedly.

"Why do you seem surprised?" Mark asked.

"This is the first time you have called since you **terminated** our relationship."

"To tell you the truth, I'm calling because I don't know where Kamla is."

"Kamla? You mean that Indian girl you're dating now? What do you mean you don't know where she is?"

"The night of the graduation dance was the last time I saw or heard from her."

"Did her parents report her missing?"

"How would I know?"

"Just relax. Don't be so **uptight**. Take it easy, Mark. Kamla is somewhere. Try calling her parents."

"I did. Her dad said he had no idea where she was. I have no reason to **doubt** him, Agatha."

"Is Kamla worth the headache you're experiencing? Why can't you date another woman if you don't want to be with me again?"

Mark was so **irate** at her suggestion that he hung up on her. He felt that rather than having a conversation with Agatha, he had just received a **scolding** from her.

Mark became more depressed as each day **elapsed**. Not for a second had he **envisioned** the marked toll the deprivation of Kamla's love would have on his health. Not even for a fleeting moment had he thought Kamla's absence would cause **irreparable** damage to his will to live or threaten his mere existence. He became more helpless daily and began neglecting his personal hygiene.

Mark in a Bar

"Professor Mark, what are you doing here?" asked Piccolo as he entered the bar.

"Who are you?"

"Don't you know me, sir? I was your student at Rollins University a while ago. I also lived next door when I was a kid. You showed me how to put the chain back on my bike one day."

"Sorry, I can't **recollect** much of anything from before the last couple months. I don't remember you," said Mark. He stumbled and barely managed to **regain** his balance in time to avoid falling.

"Sir, what brings you to this **crummy** bar? It's no place for a professor like you. I hope you're not working **undercover** for the cops as some teachers do during their summer vacation. I know many teachers don't mind **moonlighting** to make a few extra **bucks** to **supplement** their meager salary. There are better ways to earn more **dough**, though."

Mark's eyelashes fluttered like a bird's wings. Then he collapsed on the floor. Piccolo, his **former** student, rushed to his assistance and sat him on a chair.

"I'm fine. I'll be just fine. Leave me alone," Mark shouted at Piccolo.

"Sir, you're **intoxicated**. You've had too much to drink."

"How do you know that? Watch your words before I punch you, young man."

"I've been moonlighting as a bartender long enough to tell. I've been working here part-time while studying just to pay my **tuition** and other fees. You must get a **grip** on yourself, man. You have to exercise self-control."

"Shut up! Shut up before I make you **swallow** your teeth. I'll knock them right down your throat!"

Mark was so drunk that he would miss the wall if he tried to punch it, and Piccolo was not worried about his threats. He said, "I can't believe an **intellectual**, a university professor, like you would **consume** so much hard liquor without **restraint**."

"I just love the feeling. It makes me forget everything in life," Mark **muttered**.

Piccolo said angrily, "You've got to stop drinking that stuff. It's **potent**." He looked closely at Mark's eyes and frowned deeply. "Are you using drugs, too? You'll die if you continue like this, Professor."

"I want to die," Mark cried as he **collapsed** again.

"Don't be silly. You have everything going for you. You're a professor and you are studying to become a lawyer. Why do you want to die?" asked Piccolo. He lifted Mark with the help of his co-worker and sat him on a sofa.

"I want to die. I want to die right now. My woman walked out on me."

"Impossible. No woman in her right mind would do such an idiotic thing to you. You're a **remarkable** guy. I've known you and your family since my childhood." Piccolo hoped Mark would start to remember who he was, but Mark's mind had been **ravaged** by the combined effects of grief and alcohol.

"She walked out on me. Has a woman ever done that to you?"

"Yes. It happens all the time. As soon as she finds out that her man drinks liquor like a thirsty camel and uses cocaine and other stuff, she **vanishes** from his sight. He never sees her again. If he does, I **assure** you that he sees her **cuddling** in another man's arms."

"You **liar**! You're not telling me the truth. I don't believe a woman has ever walked out on you."

"I mean it, Professor Mark. Women think men who use drugs are losers. Nobody wants to be with a loser. So that's why you have to get your act together before your woman finds out you're using this stuff," advised Piccolo.

"She'll never return."

"Trust me, she will."

"When will she?"

"Sooner than you think," said Piccolo reassuringly.

Mark's eyes started to close as if they were in a desperate **quest** for restful sleep. Then his body began trembling uncontrollably. His forehead **gleamed** like a mirror with beads of sweat. As he **gnashed** his teeth, he **moaned** in pain like a wounded animal. Mark was not a **seasoned** alcoholic and could only **tolerate** three shots of hard liquor. Any more than that drowned him in unbearable physical pain.

Piccolo became **frantic** and frightened. He felt that Mark was going to have a heart attack. While his co-worker took over the bar and called for a replacement, Piccolo went for his car, which was parked three blocks away, and then returned to assist Mark. He **sprinkled** cold water on his head until he became fully conscious. With a customer's assistance, he hastily carried Mark outside and dropped him like luggage on the back seat of his car. He planned on bringing him to the emergency room at the hospital, but Mark insisted on going home no matter what Piccolo said. Piccolo eventually **succumbed** to his wish and **whisked** him away to his apartment.

Is Kathy a True Friend?

Mark woke around noon the next day. As he **sipped** his coffee, he reflected on what little he could remember of the incident in the bar and the conversation he had had with his former student. He could not believe that he had allowed himself to drink beyond what his body could **tolerate**. It was the first time in his life that he had drunk excessively, and he was embarrassed. He knew he had to call Piccolo to express his **gratitude** for the assistance he had **rendered** throughout his **infamous ordeal** in the bar. It was the most **despicable** thing he had ever done and the most **humiliating** experience of his life.

If it were not for Piccolo, the police would have been **summoned** and the incident would have been recorded by the police department. Although he probably would not have been charged with a crime, a statement from the police that he was drunk beyond control would have left an **indelible** mark on his character. In his judgment, this would have been **detrimental** and **injurious** to his career as a **budding** attorney. Mark had always been an **upright** and **law-abiding** man. He did not even have a minor **infraction**, such as a parking ticket, against his name. He was very proud of his **impeccable** record as a **model** citizen.

At the conclusion of a very long period of **reflection** and **introspection**, Mark called Kathy to come over to his apartment. He knew he had to deal with his feelings for Kamla in a more mature and positive way. Kathy was always the **pal** and **confidant** he could rely on during **crises**.

Kathy spent several hours with Mark in his apartment, talking about his relationship with Kamla. For Mark, it seemed more like a **marathon** therapy session from Kathy. She expressed surprise when Mark mentioned he had not heard from Kamla since the graduation dance. Classes had ended, so there was no need for Kamla to return to the university.

Kathy knew that Mark was insanely in love with Kamla and that he was having a difficult time coping with her sudden absence. She also knew that it was not in Kamla's personality to walk away from someone unless she was forced to, especially regarding someone like Mark, whom she adored, passionately loved, and respected. Kathy comforted Mark and assured him that Kamla probably had good reasons for what she had done. She encouraged him to be patient and understanding. Kathy said that she felt that Kamla would return to him very soon with a **plausible** explanation for her mysterious disappearance.

Later that evening, Mark and Kathy went to Central Park for a **leisurely stroll**. They talked while walking and agreed that Kamla's parents may have had something to do with her disappearance.

When Kathy returned home, her mother observed the **sullen** expression on her face. She too was alarmed to hear that none of Kamla's friends knew where she had gone after the dance. She hugged Kathy and **consoled** her.

Kamla was Kathy's best friend. She was wondering if someone had hurt her and if she would ever see her again. She wept bitterly for her only true friend, as if there were no tomorrow.

Dorothy: A Mother's Unconditional Love

For several days, Mark **contemplated** the idea of speaking with his mother, Dorothy, in the nursing home, but he did not have the courage to telephone her. He felt ashamed for **neglecting** her and wished he had spoken to her more frequently over the past few years. However, he knew that it was her motherly consolation and love that would prevent his life from becoming a nightmare.

Ashana Castro, the nurse who answered the telephone, told Mark that his mother had instructed her not to take calls from him. However, Mark successfully convinced Ashana that it was in his mother's best interest to speak with him immediately. Ashana knew from her professional experience that Dorothy's mental health would improve significantly if she **reunited** with her son, the only person she had ever mentioned to the staff at the nursing home. She encouraged Dorothy to take Mark's telephone call.

"Mother, it's me," he said in a **subdued** and depressed voice.

"Who are you?" she asked.

"Your son, Mark."

"I don't have a son. He died a long time ago. He died the day after he left me in this **despicable** nursing home."

"Mother, I'm truly sorry for neglecting you and leaving you in the nursing home."

"I know you're calling because there's nobody else for you to turn to."

"You're right, Mother. I'm ashamed of myself. I don't know how I could let the love for a woman blind me to the extent of ignoring the woman who **sacrificed** her entire life and happiness for my well-being. I promise this will never happen again."

"Who is this woman you're crazy about?" asked his mother.

"Her name is Kamla. She's a terrific person whom you'll **adore** once you get to know her."

"You sound as if you're serious about Kamla."

"I am. I'd like to marry her."

"I hope to meet her soon. Have you heard anything about your dad?"

"I have **surrendered** all hopes of knowing what happened to him. **Fate** has delivered a severe blow to us, Mother."

"Be **optimistic**, Mark. Don't give up so easily."

"I promise I'll come to visit you soon, Mother."

Mark's conversation with his mother **renewed** his spirit and **boosted** his morale and confidence. He eventually emerged **triumphant** from the bitter **bout** of depression caused by Kamla's sudden disappearance. He made a personal vow to **abstain** from alcohol consumption. After his bitter experience, Mark knew that **resorting** to alcohol to deal with his personal problems was the most **ridiculous** decision he had ever made.

EXERCISE 1

Applying the Words You Have Learned to Critical Thinking and Creative Writing

- Use the two questions in Section A below to discuss this chapter with your classmates. Be sure to apply your critical thinking skills.

- Write an essay about either question using the vocabulary words you know from real-life experiences and the new ones you have learned from this text.

Section A

Discussion Questions

1. How do you feel about the manner in which Mark dealt with Kamla's absence?

____

____

____

____

____

____

____

____

2. Was Kathy a true friend to Kamla and Mark?

____

____

____

____

____

____

____

EXERCISE 2

Synonyms: Multiple Choice

■ Circle the letter of the word or phrase that is most similar in meaning to the **boldfaced** word.

1. **trepidation**	**A.** apprehension	**B.** assumption	**C.** guess	**D.** danger
2. **tantalize**	**A.** arrest	**B.** tease	**C.** tolerate	**D.** surrender
3. **unique**	**A.** common	**B.** same	**C.** distinctive	**D.** similar
4. **universal**	**A.** worldwide	**B.** restricted	**C.** local	**D.** communal
5. **stationary**	**A.** mobile	**B.** moving	**C.** uneasy	**D.** unmoving
6. **stationery**	**A.** movement	**B.** paper materials	**C.** queries	**D.** space
7. **superb**	**A.** terrible	**B.** awful	**C.** splendid	**D.** miserable
8. **overwhelm**	**A.** surrender	**B.** overextend	**C.** assist	**D.** overcome
9. **originate**	**A.** end	**B.** begin	**C.** formalize	**D.** terminate
10. **obscure**	**A.** unclear	**B.** clear	**C.** insured	**D.** cured
11. **quandary**	**A.** puzzle	**B.** laundry	**C.** comedy	**D.** prediction
12. **quadruple**	**A.** fourfold	**B.** forty	**C.** square	**D.** triangular
13. **perplexed**	**A.** understood	**B.** confused	**C.** understated	**D.** clear
14. **purposeful**	**A.** wandering	**B.** lost	**C.** deviating	**D.** intentional
15. **transform**	**A.** internalize	**B.** cover	**C.** convert	**D.** form
16. **transparent**	**A.** dull	**B.** see through	**C.** dirty	**D.** opaque
17. **spendthrift**	**A.** stingy	**B.** extravagant	**C.** safe	**D.** hoarding
18. **stingy**	**A.** unwilling to spend	**B.** generous	**C.** tender	**D.** liberal
19. **turmoil**	**A.** normalcy	**B.** disturbance	**C.** peace	**D.** anger
20. **thrive**	**A.** die	**B.** waste	**C.** live	**D.** prosper

EXERCISE 3

Synonyms and Antonyms

■ Write the corresponding letter for the synonym and antonym of each **boldfaced** word.

	Synonym	Antonym			
1. **fail**	______	______	**A.** cancel	**B.** underachieve	**C.** succeed
2. **fake**	______	______	**A.** representative	**B.** false	**C.** real
3. **false**	______	______	**A.** broken	**B.** untrue	**C.** real
4. **familiar**	______	______	**A.** well-known	**B.** pressing	**C.** unknown
5. **famine**	______	______	**A.** starvation	**B.** partial	**C.** plenty
6. **fantastic**	______	______	**A.** terrific	**B.** awful	**C.** cheap
7. **farewell**	______	______	**A.** leaving	**B.** ready	**C.** arriving
8. **fascinate**	______	______	**A.** help	**B.** charm	**C.** bore
9. **fasten**	______	______	**A.** fall	**B.** join together	**C.** untie
10. **feasible**	______	______	**A.** possible	**B.** impossible	**C.** play
11. **feeble**	______	______	**A.** neutral	**B.** weak	**C.** strong
12. **ferocious**	______	______	**A.** fierce	**B.** friendly	**C.** gentle
13. **feud**	______	______	**A.** bitter quarrel	**B.** peace	**C.** strength
14. **fiction**	______	______	**A.** fantasy	**B.** essay	**C.** truth
15. **fidelity**	______	______	**A.** faithfulness	**B.** disloyalty	**C.** depth
16. **finish**	______	______	**A.** end	**B.** increase	**C.** begin
17. **fit**	______	______	**A.** suitable	**B.** hidden	**C.** inappropriate
18. **flaunt**	______	______	**A.** sell	**B.** display	**C.** conceal
19. **flaw**	______	______	**A.** price	**B.** defect	**C.** perfection
20. **flippant**	______	______	**A.** rude	**B.** smelly	**C.** polite
21. **foe**	______	______	**A.** enemy	**B.** soldier	**C.** friend
22. **fond**	______	______	**A.** loving	**B.** dislike	**C.** anger
23. **forfeit**	______	______	**A.** give up	**B.** overflow	**C.** gain
24. **forgive**	______	______	**A.** excuse	**B.** blame	**C.** frighten
25. **formal**	______	______	**A.** controlling	**B.** business-like	**C.** informal

	Synonym	Antonym			
26. **formidable**	_______	_______	**A.** powerful	**B.** absent	**C.** powerless
27. **fortitude**	_______	_______	**A.** courage	**B.** participation	**C.** weakness
28. **fragrant**	_______	_______	**A.** sweet-smelling	**B.** foul	**C.** joyful
29. **frail**	_______	_______	**A.** weak	**B.** hard	**C.** strong
30. **frank**	_______	_______	**A.** outspoken	**B.** obscure	**C.** deceitful
31. **frantic**	_______	_______	**A.** friendly	**B.** panicked	**C.** calm
32. **frigid**	_______	_______	**A.** ice-cold	**B.** wasted	**C.** hot
33. **gather**	_______	_______	**A.** collect	**B.** impress	**C.** scatter
34. **gigantic**	_______	_______	**A.** huge	**B.** sensitive	**C.** tiny
35. **glamorous**	_______	_______	**A.** extremely attractive	**B.** unappealing	**C.** mediated
36. **gradual**	_______	_______	**A.** exploratory	**B.** slow	**C.** sudden
37. **gratitude**	_______	_______	**A.** thankfulness	**B.** ungratefulness	**C.** award
38. **hamper**	_______	_______	**A.** fake	**B.** hinder	**C.** help
39. **handsome**	_______	_______	**A.** attractive	**B.** unappealing	**C.** fancy
40. **handy**	_______	_______	**A.** convenient	**B.** lenient	**C.** inconvenient
41. **haphazard**	_______	_______	**A.** lower	**B.** random	**C.** planned
42. **harm**	_______	_______	**A.** hurt	**B.** find	**C.** help
43. **harmonious**	_______	_______	**A.** agreeing	**B.** conflicting	**C.** reasonable
44. **harsh**	_______	_______	**A.** cruel	**B.** kind	**C.** fortunate
45. **havoc**	_______	_______	**A.** clarity	**B.** destruction	**C.** restoration
46. **hide**	_______	_______	**A.** move	**B.** conceal	**C.** reveal
47. **hinder**	_______	_______	**A.** impede	**B.** assist	**C.** respect
48. **hire**	_______	_______	**A.** employ	**B.** use	**C.** lay-off
49. **homage**	_______	_______	**A.** control	**B.** respect	**C.** disrespect
50. **horrible**	_______	_______	**A.** honest	**B.** terrible	**C.** splendid
51. **humble**	_______	_______	**A.** simple	**B.** petty	**C.** proud
52. **humiliate**	_______	_______	**A.** embarrass	**B.** harass	**C.** honor
53. **hurt**	_______	_______	**A.** harm	**B.** impede	**C.** help

	Synonym	Antonym			
54. **innocent**	______	______	**A.** blameless	**B.** guilty	**C.** safe
55. **insane**	______	______	**A.** concealed	**B.** mentally ill	**C.** sound
56. **insignificant**	______	______	**A.** unimportant	**B.** meaningful	**C.** attempted
57. **insolent**	______	______	**A.** rude	**B.** polite	**C.** favorite
58. **inspire**	______	______	**A.** encourage	**B.** tell	**C.** discourage
59. **invalid**	______	______	**A.** worthless	**B.** worthy	**C.** deliberate
60. **irrelevant**	______	______	**A.** unrelated	**B.** relevant	**C.** abhorrent
61. **irritate**	______	______	**A.** annoy	**B.** analyze	**C.** soothe
62. **ideal**	______	______	**A.** perfect	**B.** clear	**C.** imperfect
63. **identical**	______	______	**A.** alike	**B.** sad	**C.** different
64. **idle**	______	______	**A.** frustrate	**B.** inactive	**C.** busy
65. **ignoble**	______	______	**A.** disgraceful	**B.** deceased	**C.** honorable
66. **ignorant**	______	______	**A.** foolish	**B.** smart	**C.** terminal
67. **ignore**	______	______	**A.** avoid	**B.** withdraw	**C.** mind
68. **illegal**	______	______	**A.** unlawful	**B.** bright	**C.** legal
69. **illogical**	______	______	**A.** dirty	**B.** senseless	**C.** reasonable
70. **immaculate**	______	______	**A.** selected	**B.** very clean	**C.** dirty
71. **immature**	______	______	**A.** stupid	**B.** underdeveloped	**C.** grown-up
72. **immense**	______	______	**A.** inner	**B.** enormous	**C.** tiny
73. **immigrate**	______	______	**A.** keep	**B.** enter a place	**C.** leave
74. **immoral**	______	______	**A.** least	**B.** wrong	**C.** ethical
75. **impair**	______	______	**A.** weaken	**B.** improve	**C.** destroy

EXERCISE 4

Matching Meanings: Set 1

■ Match each word with its meaning.

_____	1. annihilate	**A.** disillusioned
_____	2. cognizant	**B.** go over a boundary; trespass
_____	3. disenchanted	**C.** clear of accusation
_____	4. equivocal	**D.** wipe out; destroy completely
_____	5. fatuous	**E.** easy-going; appearing casual
_____	6. transgress	**F.** prevent; hold back; slow-down
_____	7. ubiquitous	**G.** incapable of error; faultless
_____	8. vindicate	**H.** fully aware
_____	9. rapacious	**I.** seeming to be everywhere
_____	10. nonchalant	**J.** taking by force using violence; very greedy; selfish
_____	11. inhibit	**K.** silly or foolish
_____	12. infallible	**L.** vague; having two or more meanings

EXERCISE 5

Matching Meanings: Set 2

■ Match each word with its meaning.

_____	1. vivacious	**A.** full of scorn; arrogant
_____	2. supercilious	**B.** lively; full of spirit
_____	3. reprimand	**C.** extremely careful and precise
_____	4. nostalgia	**D.** an idea or a thought
_____	5. ingenious	**E.** enjoying pleasures of sensation; giving pleasure through the senses
_____	6. meticulous	**F.** insignificant
_____	7. sensuous	**G.** clever; having great mental ability; brilliant
_____	8. aggrandize	**H.** gain; win over
_____	9. concept	**I.** severely criticize; rebuke; express sharp disappointment
_____	10. conciliate	**J.** perfect example
_____	11. epitome	**K.** increase in intensity; make greater
_____	12. frivolous	**L.** longing to return to a time or place in the past

EXERCISE 6

Word Meaning in Context: Set 1

- Read each sentence and find the missing word in the box below. Fill in the blank with the correct *form* of that word.

cognizant	**annihilate**	**infallible**	**rapacious**
equivocal	**inhibit**	**disenchanted**	**vindicate**
fatuous	**ubiquitous**	**nonchalant**	**transgress**

1. Your attempt to ___________ the insects in this apartment is admirable, but it will prove useless in the end.
2. Before you attempt skydiving, you must be ___________ of the possible dangers.
3. She became ___________ with her job at the homeless shelter after seeing all the criminal activities that took place there.
4. Although he spoke passionately, his ___________ choice of words left the audience wondering what he really meant.
5. The idea that men are more intelligent than women is ___________.
6. The seeds of war were planted when soldiers began to ___________ the neighboring country's border.
7. Televisions are as ___________ in American homes now as radios were in the 1950s.
8. When the company was fined for not meeting pollution standards, the environmentalists felt ___________.
9. Greed was the main motive for the soldiers' ___________ looting of the town.
10. Although he was extremely nervous, Brian was able to appear ___________ during the job interview.
11. Morphine is given to dying patients to ___________ pain in their final hours.
12. Many Roman Catholics believe the Pope is ___________ on moral issues.

EXERCISE 7

Word Meaning in Context: Set 2

- Read each sentence and find the missing word in the box below. Fill in the blank with the correct *form* of that word.

frivolous	**nostalgia**	**supercilious**	**epitome**
conciliate	**vivacious**	**ingenious**	**aggrandize**
sensuous	**concept**	**reprimand**	**meticulous**

1. Most game shows on television want the contestants to be ___________.
2. His ___________ attitude toward his boss eventually caused him to be fired.
3. Steve was ___________ for leaving the cash register unattended while he went to the restroom.
4. Although he regularly suffered from ___________, he never returned to his hometown.
5. The company rewarded Mr. Johnson for his ___________ solution to the problem.

6. The tourists were able to find their way around every block in the city because their guide gave them __________ instructions.
7. Audrey loved the __________ feeling of sleeping on silk sheets.
8. The owner of the company __________ his wealth at the expense of his employees.
9. The __________ of a city without taxi services is impossible for most people to understand.
10. All attempts to __________ the two brothers were useless; they refused to speak to each other.
11. Because of his good manners, he was known at the club as the __________ of politeness.
12. Stephanie loved the gift, even though it was __________ and cost only a few dollars.

EXERCISE 8

Context Clues

■ Select the word or phrase that most closely matches the meaning of the **boldfaced** word. *Note that replacing the **boldfaced** word with the right answer might not produce a grammatically correct sentence.*

1. Today's computer science jobs require people who can **innovate** cutting-edge technology in software and design.
   A. borrow **B.** introduce **C.** analyze **D.** destroy

2. It is a good idea to ask for feedback and **input** from others when starting a new team project.
   A. desires **B.** advice **C.** fears **D.** objections

3. Magazine and newspaper **inserts** often fall out and become litter on the streets.
   A. sections **B.** copyrights **C.** covers **D.** ink

4. The history professor offered **insight** into the destructive effects of the American Civil War.
   A. a lecture **B.** biased ideas **C.** deep understanding **D.** a toast

5. In New York State, it is required that all cars be **inspected** each year to make sure they are in good running condition.
   A. painted **B.** examined **C.** detailed **D.** refurbished

6. Her employee evaluation listed every **instance** of her performing exceptionally well.
   A. belief **B.** résumé **C.** conference **D.** occasion

7. The charity **instituted** new health insurance policies for its employees and volunteers.
   A. bargained **B.** established **C.** denied **D.** abolished

8. To educate small children, one must **instruct** them with patience and understanding.
   A. teach **B.** employ **C.** discipline **D.** raise

9. Understanding how jet engines worked was **integral** to the airplane mechanic's ability to do her job.
   A. optional **B.** essential **C.** dangerous **D.** expensive

10. Doctors reported that patients became healthier when they **integrated** more fruits and vegetables into their diet.
    A. combined **B.** ate **C.** divided **D.** bought

11. The teacher was impressed by the student's **intelligence** when he quickly and correctly answered calculus problems.
    A. high mental capacity **B.** personality **C.** ability to cheat **D.** planning

12. The drama club students had to **interact** with the science students to put together a play about the famous physicist Albert Einstein.
    A. work together **B.** leave **C.** hide from each other **D.** think

13. After completing the introductory and **intermediate** classes in French, the student was well prepared to take the advanced course.
    A. optional **B.** extracurricular **C.** middle **D.** graduate

14. An **interval** between the two events provided a welcome rest for the audience.
    A. conference **B.** break **C.** venue **D.** decision

15. Jim became a millionaire in his thirties because he **invested** in companies that performed extraordinarily well on the stock market.
    A. designed products **B.** committed money **C.** analyzed **D.** sold

16. The governor **invoked** the Bible when asked to explain his position against the new law about abortion.
    A. referred to **B.** misquoted **C.** insulted **D.** read

17. The mayor was not re-elected because he had failed to deal with the **issues** that were important to the people of the city.
    A. job opportunities **B.** behaviors **C.** taxes **D.** unresolved matters

18. My mother forgot to buy an important **item** at the grocery store, so she was unable to bake the cake.
    A. an individual thing **B.** a bag of flour **C.** a recipe **D.** a mixing bowl

19. In order to get an extension on his research paper, he had to **justify** his request to his professor.
    A. explain **B.** beg **C.** deny **D.** infer

20. Consumers today demand that food **labels** on cans and packages list all ingredients and nutritional values.
    A. attached papers **B.** sharp blades **C.** boxes **D.** receipts

21. The chocolate cake had three **layers** covered in vanilla frosting.
    A. parts that lie over others **B.** lower grades of quality
    C. broken sheets of ice **D.** larger portions

22. The state senate had to **legislate** new rules that limited the amount of government aid their local districts could receive.
    A. deny responsibility **B.** clean up quickly **C.** make laws **D.** vote for

23. Local business owners were upset when the city wanted to **levy** an additional tax on their properties.
    A. eliminate **B.** decrease **C.** force upon **D.** accelerate

24. You need a **license** to carry a gun in certain countries.
    A. permit **B.** holster **C.** large coat **D.** position in the government

EXERCISE 9

Vocabulary Test

- Select the correct answer.
- Hint: Review the meanings of all the **boldfaced** words in this chapter before you take the test. This approach can help you to score 100 percent.
- Record the percentage of correct answers on the Master Self-Assessment table on page 397.

1 **Universal** company:

A. communal **B.** worldwide

C. local **D.** restricted

2 A **stationary** price is:

E. fixed **F.** variable

G. high **H.** low

3 A **superb** performance is:

A. terrible **B.** good

C. splendid **D.** awful

4 To **overwhelm** is to:

E. surrender **F.** assist

G. eliminate **H.** overpower or overcome

5 **Obscure** means:

A. unclear **B.** clear

C. cause **D.** cure

6 A **quandary** is:

E. a state of doubt

F. a bag of laundry

G. a prediction

H. an area where rocks are mined

7 **Quadruple** means:

A. forty

B. a number squared

C. having four parts

D. a number to the fourth power

8 **Perplexed** means:

E. confident

F. filled with uncertainty

G. upset

H. happy

9 **Transform** the laboratory into a classroom means:

A. invert

B. complete

C. return

D. change in structure

10 A **spendthrift**:

E. is stingy

F. saves money

G. spends money wastefully

H. hoards money

11 **Turmoil** in a city:

A. celebration

B. a state of great disturbance

C. peace

D. quiet

12 To **thrive** is to:

E. die

F. waste

G. live

H. succeed

13 A **feasible** project is:

A. possible

B. impossible

C. difficult

D. expensive

14 A **ferocious** dog is:

E. friendly
F. gentle
G. fierce
H. dirty

15 A **feud** between two friends is:

A. a companionship
B. a bitter fight
C. a partnership
D. an agreement

16 **Fidelity** means:

E. disloyalty
F. faithfulness
G. hope
H. cleanliness

17 To **flaunt** one's wealth is to:

A. conceal it
B. show it off
C. hide it
D. waste it

18 A personality **flaw** is:

E. a talent
F. a strength
G. a positive trait
H. an imperfection

19 **Flippant** comments are:

A. disrespectful
B. serious
C. without merit
D. polite

20 To **forfeit** a game is to:

E. win
F. lose
G. tie
H. play

21 A **formidable** boxer is:

A. weak
B. fearful
C. powerful
D. intelligent

22 To show **fortitude** is to:

E. show courage

F. be dishonest

G. show weakness

H. be truthful

23 **Fragrant** means:

A. bitter

B. sweet smelling

C. sour

D. foul odor

24 Someone **frail** is:

E. thin

F. muscular

G. physically strong

H. physically weak

25 **Frantic** means:

A. calm

B. emotionally out of control

C. peaceful

D. emotionally stable

26 **Frigid** water is:

E. extremely cold

F. tepid

G. warm

H. hot

27 **Gigantic** waves are:

A. tiny

B. average

C. huge

D. normal

28 A **glamorous** movie star is:

E. exceedingly attractive

F. unattractive

G. plain-looking

H. talented

29 To show **gratitude** is to show:

A. dissatisfaction

B. satisfaction

C. appreciation

D. concern

30 To **hamper** is to:

E. help
F. hold back
G. harm
H. hit

31 A **haphazard** manner is:

A. planned
B. predictable
C. well-organized
D. lacking order or planning

32 **Harmonious** relationships are:

E. agreeable
F. conflicting
G. melodious
H. hateful

33 To pay **homage** is to pay:

A. money
B. a reasonable price
C. respect or admiration
D. a contract

34 A **humble** person is:

E. showy
F. not proud
G. proud
H. petty

35 To **humiliate** someone is to:

A. put down
B. honor
C. praise
D. love

36 An **insolent** person is:

E. polite
F. disrespectful
G. kind
H. gentle

37 To **inspire** someone is to:

A. encourage
B. discourage
C. influence
D. control

38 An **invalid** identification card is:

E. ineffective

F. inexpensive

G. valuable

H. worthless

39 An antonym for **ideal** is:

A. perfect

B. satisfactory

C. imperfect

D. unsatisfactory

40 **Identical** cars are:

E. exactly the same

F. completely different

G. nearly the same

H. slightly different

41 **Ignoble** refers to:

A. low morale

B. high moral character

C. high morale

D. low moral character

42 **Immaculate** means:

E. dirty

F. holy

G. clean or spotless

H. unholy

43 **Immense** means:

A. medium-sized

B. normal-sized

C. very small

D. very large

44 An **impaired** judgment is:

E. weakened

F. strengthened

G. very wise

H. very harsh

45 To **annihilate** means to:

A. save

B. destroy completely

C. rebuild

D. build

46 To be **cognizant** of something is to be:

E. uninformed
F. unaware
G. fully aware
H. minimally informed

47 **Disenchanted** customers are:

A. dissatisfied
B. satisfied
C. cautious
D. disagreeable

48 **Equivocal** means:

E. being equal
F. having several different meanings
G. being complicated
H. speaking two languages

49 **Fatuous** remarks are:

A. critical
B. wise
C. silly or foolish
D. academic

50 **Vindicate** means to:

E. clear of an accusation
F. imprison
G. indict
H. falsely accuse

51 **Rapacious** behavior is:

A. suspicious
B. cunning
C. mentally unstable
D. very greedy or selfish

52 A **nonchalant** attitude is:

E. easy-going
F. uncommon
G. formal
H. free-spirited

53 To **inhibit** means to:

A. allow
B. slow down
C. encourage
D. assist

54 An **infallible** person is:

E. always wrong

F. never wrong

G. never right

H. always mean

55 A **vivacious** person is:

A. boring

B. tired and sleepy

C. lively and exciting

D. jumpy

56 A **supercilious** person is:

E. down-to-earth

F. aggressive

G. stuck-up or arrogant

H. kind-hearted

57 To **reprimand** someone is to:

A. praise

B. express sharp disappointment

C. punish

D. express approval

58 **Nostalgia** refers to:

E. nonsense

F. satisfaction with the present

G. longing for the future

H. affectionate feelings for the past

59 An **ingenious** person is

A. extremely stupid

B. clever with great mental ability

C. very studious

D. moderately intelligent

60 A **meticulous** person is:

E. fancy

F. precise about minute details

G. colorful

H. careless

61 **Aggrandize** means to:

A. decrease or make smaller

B. maintain the same size

C. make greater

D. rotate in large circles

62 To **conciliate** is to:

E. win over

F. conceal

G. offend

H. compromise

63 **Epitome** means:

A. a poor example

B. an adequate example

C. a perfect example

D. pattern of behavior

64 **Frivolous** activities are:

E. extremely important

F. of little importance

G. peaceful

H. hostile

65 An antonym for **irritate** is:

A. annoy

B. analyze

C. soothe

D. provoke

EXERCISE 10

Building a Stronger Vocabulary

- Review all the **boldfaced** words in this chapter before you proceed to the next exercise.
- Highlight the ones you are still having difficulty remembering.
- List them with their meanings on a table.
- Use them to compose your own sentences.
- Think of a synonym and an antonym for each word.
- Use checkmarks to indicate if each word you want to practice more has a prefix, suffix, and/or root.
- You may use the table below as a sample to write your answers in your notebook.

Word	Definition	Sentence	Synonym	Antonym	Prefix	Suffix	Root

EXERCISE 11

Creating My Own Powerful Word List

- Write the words and meanings from the above table on the **Creating My Own Powerful Word List** table on page 398. Review them often to build that super vocabulary you want to create for school, work, and everyday use.

Chapter 10 Kamla with Dr. Azeez in India

PRE-READING

About This Chapter from *Trial of Love*

- Read the names and descriptions of this chapter's main characters below.
  - Reshma Ram: Dr. Azeez's mother in India
  - Dr. Gopaul Ram: Dr. Azeez's father in India
  - Sosheila: Kamla's grandmother in India
  - Padma Singh: Kamla's close friend in India
  - Rajul Karan: Padma's boyfriend
  - Devi John: The village snitch
  - Rupa Roy: A medical school student in India
  - Dr. Azeez
  - Kamla Kumar

Story Vocabulary Exercise

- Before you begin reading this chapter, figure out the meanings of the unfamiliar **boldfaced** vocabulary words. You may use the Word List, Word Parts Chart, or your dictionary to assist you in finding their meanings.
- Look for the various types of context clues—synonyms, antonyms, general context, and examples—as you read.
- Write a word or phrase about the meaning of each **boldfaced** word in the margin.

Reading and Writing Exercise

- Skim the entire chapter and pay attention to the headings and the discussion questions that follow.
- Initial Response: Write a paragraph explaining, in your own words, what you think this chapter of the story will be about.
- Final Response: After you have read the entire chapter, compare your current understanding with your initial response above. If your initial response was accurate, you can simply write it again to fill in the blanks below. If it was not, then write a paragraph on what the chapter was really about instead.

Initial Response

This chapter **will** be about ______________________________

____

____

____

Final Response

This chapter **was** about ______________________________

____

____

____

KAMLA WITH DR. AZEEZ IN INDIA

Dr. Azeez and his parents were at the airport with Rita's mother, Sosheila, waiting to greet Kamla. When the flight did not arrive as scheduled, Sosheila left the waiting area to get a meal in the cafeteria. Dr. Azeez became **restless** and **uneasy** as they waited for the plane.

"Calm down, Son," encouraged his mother, Reshma Ram. "Flights from New York seldom arrive on time. Passengers are often **delayed** because they have to make several connections at airports in Europe before arriving in Mumbai."

"I have no **tolerance** for **tardiness**," complained Dr. Azeez.

"I'm **baffled** as to why you're so **anxious** to meet this girl, whatever her name is."

"Her name is Kamla, in case you conveniently forgot it, Mother. Don't embarrass me by referring to her as 'girl.' She's a young woman who **deserves respect**."

"Azeez, I'm terribly disappointed in you. How could an intelligent man like you be **misled** by an elderly village woman?"

"Kamla's grandmother didn't **mislead** me. I'm the one who expressed interest in Kamla."

"You're a doctor. You must find someone of your **status**. I'm positive you'll meet an **eloquent** and **articulate** doctor when you're at medical conferences if you look hard, Azeez."

"Kamla is a beautiful woman who would be the **ideal** wife for me."

"You're wrong, my son. A photograph could be misleading. You know nothing whatsoever about her, other than what her mother and grandmother told you. That isn't a good reason for wanting to marry Kamla."

"Mother, you fail to realize this is the only way I can go to America."

"Shame on you, Azeez! You shouldn't want to marry her for this reason. Our culture teaches us that marriage is a **sacred** and lifelong **commitment** to someone you love. Have you forgotten your **principles**?"

Dr. Azeez's father, Gopaul Ram, was listening **attentively** to their conversation. He was careful not to take sides, but was supportive of his wife's argument against Dr. Azeez, whose **sole** reason for wanting to marry Kamla was to have an opportunity to go to America. In his judgment, his son was making a serious **error** that could hurt his feelings and professional image.

Sosheila returned from the airport's cafeteria while Dr. Azeez and his mother were discussing Kamla. She had a strong feeling that Dr. Azeez's parents did not like her granddaughter, Kamla. Nevertheless, she remained friendly towards them.

Around 4:30 p.m., the flight arrived. Kamla recognized Dr. Azeez because she had his photograph in her possession.

After Sosheila introduced Kamla to Dr. Azeez and his parents, they left for Gangaram. Kamla went to stay with her grandma. Dr. Azeez's parents spent the night with him without his approval. It was the first time his family had visited him in the village. With the assistance of her husband, Reshma prepared dinner while Dr. Azeez was taking a shower.

"Reshma, I'm happy I came here tonight to see where our son is living," Gopaul said.

"Now that you've seen his **residence**, what do you think of it?"

"I wish I had visited him as soon as he **relocated** to this village. It's beyond my comprehension how he has been surviving under these **deplorable** conditions in this **filthy** place. I can't stand it here. There's no indoor plumbing or even electricity. The **offensive odor** from the garbage dump on the street is giving me an **excruciating** headache. Reshma, the **incessant buzzing** of these **vicious** mosquitoes is driving me **insane**. I'll lose my mind if I stay here another night."

After Dr. Azeez had a shower in a **portable** bathroom in his backyard, he entered the house from the back using the **rear** door. Reshma and Gopaul discontinued their conversation as he walked in with the bucket and cup that he had used for his shower.

"How do you like my place?" Dr. Azeez asked proudly.

His parents **stared** at each other and **pretended** they did not hear him. Dr. Azeez went to his bedroom to change his clothes before joining them in the kitchen to continue their conversation.

"I guess you aren't **comfortable** here," Dr. Azeez said.

"How have you managed to **survive** the past year in this village?" asked his mother, Reshma.

"At first, it was very challenging to **adjust** to this new place. I have to **admit** that **initially** it was very difficult to live here, but eventually I got **accustomed** to the living conditions."

"Azeez, what has gotten into you?"

"Let's not start another argument, Mother."

"My son, I can't believe you **surrendered** a comfortable life in Mumbai to live in this **dump**."

"Why can't you understand I'm tired of living the **glamorous** lifestyle of the only son of an **aristocrat**? My daddy is the Surgeon General of our country, and he's filthy rich. I don't want to follow in his footsteps. I want to make a contribution that will **enhance** the lives of the poor and needy, particularly the **economically disadvantaged** people of this village."

"Since when have you thought about the poor?" his mother asked curiously.

"Since I came to this village. Mother, throughout your entire life you've **scorned** and **shunned** them. But they're **genuine** people who have real needs and feelings like you do. I wish you could live among them for a while. Then you'd understand what I'm saying. Although they're poor, they're happy, loving, and caring. They're sincere in everything they say and do. Material things mean very little to them. They see them as **trivial** and **insignificant**. These villagers **derive** their joy and happiness from the small things in life that you and your rich friends take for granted. Is it their fault that they're born trapped in the **vicious** cycle of poverty, Mother?"

"Mother Theresa, that is, Kamla's grandmother, did a **superb** job at **brainwashing** you," said Reshma. She looked into the heavens through the kitchen window. "**Lord Krishna**, what sin have I committed to have a son like Azeez who talks like an educated **fool** and sounds like an **intellectual** moron?"

"Ma, why do you love to **infuriate** me?" asked Dr. Azeez angrily. "You make me angry every time you open your mouth to say something to me."

"I only tell the truth, Azeez."

"You know nothing about people other than your rich and **egotistical** friends who spit on your maids whenever they visit you. They **shun** them as if being of a lower **socio-economic** class makes them animals."

"Son, I love you dearly, and I don't want you to be hurt. Kamla and her family are **cognizant** of your wealth. Her family knows that she'll **inherit** everything we own if our family dies. Kamla has nothing to lose by marrying you. Azeez, she's an **assertive**, **sly**, and **cunning** woman who shouldn't be trusted. She's willing to trick people into giving her what she wants. Is a green card worth the heartache and **aggravation** you will experience when you marry her, if that's what you're seriously **contemplating**? Think clearly before you make a decision. Don't play with fire, Azeez. Kamla isn't your type. You need a **conservative** and **traditional** woman who will be **faithful** and **dutiful** and will do anything for you without any questions asked. Azeez, you need a woman who will be **loyal** and **obedient** to you."

"It's unfair of you to **degrade** someone whom you've met only once, Ma."

"Azeez, don't misunderstand me," said Reshma. "I'm not **bad-mouthing** Kamla or putting her down. I'm only speaking as a mother and from real-life experiences. Your dad shares my feelings about Kamla. We discussed this matter before coming to the airport." Gopaul nodded to show his support. Reshma continued angrily, "It's obvious that you don't care about my advice, though. We'll leave as soon as **dawn** arrives in the morning. **Dusk** will not find us in your house in the evening. This will give you **ample** time to spend with your newly arrived bride-to-be."

Kamla Visiting Dr. Azeez at His House

Very early the following morning, Gopaul and Reshma left for their home in Mumbai. Dr. Azeez was still sleeping when his mother kissed him good-bye on his forehead and left. Around 9:00 a.m., Kamla **confirmed** that his parents had left, then knocked on his door. He walked sleepily to open it.

"Oh my God!" he said, embarrassed. "I didn't expect to see you, Kamla."

"That's OK, Dr. Azeez. I've seen men in their pajamas before. It's nothing to be ashamed of. May I come in?"

"Sure. Make yourself comfortable while I get dressed."

While Dr. Azeez was changing, Kamla **browsed** through the living room. A few items caught her eyes as she was looking around. She picked one of them up, and then set it down when Dr. Azeez suddenly returned. He had a glass of freshly squeezed orange juice in his hand.

"May I offer you juice or tea?" he asked.

"You don't have to go through that trouble," she replied.

"How do you like living in America?" Dr. Azeez asked between **sips** of his juice.

"I love it!"

"What do you love best?"

"The freedom."

"Freedom? I thought there was plenty of that in India."

"I **beg to differ**, sir. I disagree **wholeheartedly**. People in India are too **narrow-minded**. They don't like to change their old ways of doing things. To be honest and **candid**, I came to **inquire** what your parents, particularly your mother, think about me."

"My parents are very **fond** of you, Kamla. They like you a lot," Dr. Azeez said, lying **boldly**.

"Really? Their attitude toward me at the airport and on our way to our village didn't **convey** that message."

"What do you mean, Kamla? Please **elaborate**. Explain what you mean."

"Your mother **detests** me. She has a **passionate** hatred for me. That was **obvious**. She hardly spoke and was somewhat **hostile** to me," said Kamla. She turned away and walked toward the door. "I'm sorry. I have to leave."

Dr. Azeez was speechless. He was disappointed that Kamla had observed his parents' **disapproval** of her as a **prospective** daughter-in-law. For the entire day, he **contemplated** ways to **persuade** her that his parents **adored** her.

Why Was Kamla Sent to India?

Later that day, Kamla's grandmother **interrogated** her about her mother's reason for suddenly sending her to India. At first, Kamla thought about **fabricating** some convincing lies, but she knew her grandmother was a **shrewd** woman who could not be **deceived** easily.

"Grandma, why have you hardly spoken with me since I returned from New York?"

"Kamla, I'm very sad to hear that you're having a relationship with Mark. Your mother called to tell me about it as soon as you left New York."

"Don't believe my mother's **overwhelming exaggeration** of my relationship, Grandma."

"Then tell me your **version** of it. Let me hear your side of the story. I want to know if Rita is **making**

a mountain out of a mole hill. Is your mother blowing everything out of proportion? Is she accusing my granddaughter of something she's innocent of? What do you have to say, Kamla?"

"Well, I went with Mark to our university's graduation dance without my parents' **consent**. Mark brought me to his apartment after the dance to spend some time with him. When I returned home at about 2:00 a.m., they were asleep." She hoped her grandmother wouldn't see through that one lie; she hadn't returned home until well after 5:00. Telling her the real hour would **insinuate** that she had slept with Mark. "The following day, they demanded I return to India because I was getting out of control. I left New York only to **appease** them. My departure probably made them very happy."

"Kamla, how dare you sleep with Mark before marriage?" demanded Sosheila, seeing straight through Kamla's deceit. "I'm ashamed you turned out to be a **cheap**, rather than a **dignified**, young woman. You've really disappointed me. I didn't expect a brilliant scientist to allow her emotions to **dictate** her actions."

"Grandma, a girl has needs too, needs that have to be **fulfilled**. Maybe according to Indian standards, I'm a **lewd** and **loose** woman without **scruples** or values, but dating is a normal practice in America."

"Needs, Kamla? As far as I am concerned, the only need you have is for a good old-fashioned **spanking** with a branch from the tamarind tree in the backyard. Going to America has certainly turned you into a **shameless**, **rebellious brat**. What an **audacious** and **pompous** rat I have for a granddaughter! You have some nerve telling me to my face that a girl has needs. No respect for your elders. Think twice if you think you are too old to be disciplined."

Kamla knew that her grandmother was a strict **disciplinarian** and listened attentively to her verbal abuse without uttering a word in her defense. She did not reply to her grandmother's accusation about her having intimate relations with Mark in his apartment after the dance.

Kamla Hosts a Party

That evening, Kamla hosted a party for her friends at her grandmother's house. They looked forward to it because they were anxious to hear about Kamla's experiences in New York. Padma Singh, one of her closest friends, was a **chatterbox** and the life of the party.

"Kamla, you haven't said much to us since you returned from New York," Padma complained.

"Things have been **hectic** around here for the past few days," Kamla replied.

"There has been no 'action' around here for a while, so I don't know what you're talking about, Kamla. Just tell us about your social life in New York," said Padma.

"Not much to say except that I have a boyfriend now."

"Really? Now it's getting juicy and delicious. I knew all along about the **suppressed** emotions and feelings that you were **stifling** before you left for America. Who's the **dude**? I hope he's a fine gentleman."

"Padma, I dislike hearing you speak like a classless **harlot**. Your words don't reflect that you're a person of substance. When will you change, my friend?"

"Just wait a minute, Kamla! I haven't said anything to **offend** you. Why are you so **tense**? What's bugging you? Don't think you're better than anyone here because you went to America," Padma said angrily.

Padma was upset that Kamla had **belittled** her. She left the group of friends who were sitting around the table with Kamla and requested that her date, Rajul Karan, dance with her. As the other guests arrived, the party gathered **momentum**. Everybody was dancing to the rhythm of Western music.

Devi John: The Village Snitch

When she was certain that nobody would miss her, Devi John, Kamla's high-school classmate, hurried home to telephone Dr. Azeez's mother.

"Hello, Reshma here. Who's calling?"

"Devi."

"Do you know what time it is?"

"I know it's late. But I think what I have to say is **urgent**. It cannot wait until tomorrow."

"Go ahead. I'm listening, Devi."

"As soon as you left yesterday, Kamla went to visit Dr. Azeez at his house."

"Devi, I'm afraid Kamla might trick him by becoming pregnant."

"You have a good reason to be nervous. Kamla isn't as innocent as she appears, Aunt Reshma."

"That was obvious the first time I met her. But Azeez can't accept it. He's too young and inexperienced when it comes to affairs with women. He has never had a girlfriend in his entire life. He was mostly a **bookworm**. Thank God nobody thinks of him as a **nerd** thinking only about his academic studies. Still, Kamla is experienced enough to get him to **eat out of the palm of her hand**," complained Dr. Azeez's mother. "My son is **naïve** and lacks **savviness** when it comes to dating women. Azeez will believe anything a woman tells him. His problem is that he believes every human being is honest."

"I've some information that'll convince him, Aunt Reshma. Kamla has a boyfriend in New York. At the party she's hosting tonight, I **overheard** her telling a friend that she's having relations with him."

"Good gracious! Azeez must be **apprised** of this. We have to inform him as soon as possible."

Reshma couldn't sleep the rest of the night. Her husband, Gopaul, tried to convince her that Devi was probably lying.

"Gopaul, don't you think there's a grain of truth in what Devi said?" asked Reshma.

"No, Reshma. Devi is lying because she doesn't want Azeez to marry Kamla. She's a **stranger** and not our **relative**. Why should we believe a **snitch**? This is an **informant** who cannot be trusted."

"Gopaul, I believe Devi. I must admit that I paid her to spy and to inform me about Kamla's activities with Azeez. She is a very poor villager who needs the money. Besides, these people have a good **reputation** for their honesty."

"Shame on you for not **disclosing** this earlier, Reshma. What should we do now?" asked Dr. Azeez's father.

"We have to be more **proactive** when it comes to our son's future, Gopaul. We shouldn't sit by and do nothing. How about introducing Azeez to Dr. Gupta's daughter, Rupa Roy, who will be graduating from medical school next year? Dr. Gupta is your best friend and Rupa is a **virtuous saint**. Maybe we should invite them over for dinner," suggested Reshma.

Dr. Azeez at Kamla's Party

Kamla greeted Dr. Azeez as soon as he walked into the house. She introduced him to her friends, most of whom had been her classmates at Noble University in New Delhi, India, where she had earned her PhD in Medical Science. Everybody enjoyed the party and expressed their appreciation to Kamla.

After the guests left, Kamla asked Dr. Azeez to sleep over at her house because her grandmother had gone to visit her friends two villages away. Dr. Azeez was surprised by her bold request. He felt that she wanted to be **intimate** with him and looked forward to an unforgettable night of romance.

After a fulfilling night, Dr. Azeez woke up very early and went home before anybody saw him leaving Kamla's home. He did not want anyone to **initiate** a **rumor** that he was starting an affair with Kamla. Nobody knew he had spent the night with her. He and Kamla **vowed** to keep it a secret for **eternity**.

Kamla worked with Dr. Azeez in his clinic for several weeks. It was a decision she and Dr. Azeez **mutually** agreed upon when he spent the night with her. She taught several health education workshops for the female villagers under his supervision.

It was nearing time for her to return to New York to **resume** her research and teaching at Rollins University. She was beginning to feel sad and happy at the same time. She did not miss the daily bickering and arguments she'd had with her parents in New York. Spending time with Dr. Azeez and working with the villagers was a breath of fresh air. Despite the good times she was having in the village, though, she felt as if something **indispensable** was still missing from her life. At that moment, nothing could fill the **void** in her heart.

"Kamla, I must admit that I've thoroughly enjoyed every minute I've spent working with you. I feel attached to you and will miss you very much."

"Dr. Azeez, I wish you knew how much I **admire** you."

"Do you really mean that, Kamla?"

"Of course, Dr. Azeez."

Dr. Azeez said excitedly, "Does that mean we can have a future together? Kamla, what I'm trying to say is that I'd like to marry you before you leave for New York."

Kamla had not expected Dr. Azeez to be as courageous and **forthright** as to **propose** to her. She was caught off-guard, surprised that he was willing to marry her even though he knew very little about her. A fleeting moment of fear and suspicion overcame her. She wondered why an educated professional like Dr. Azeez was ready to marry someone he had only known for weeks. Was it possible that he wanted to marry her for the opportunity to come to America, or did he genuinely want to be her husband? An **acute** case of **infatuation** on Dr. Azeez's part did not escape her mind as another possible reason.

Kamla was immensely confused because those conflicting thoughts were **invading** her mind. She knew that Indian couples married despite a **conspicuous** absence of love at the initial stage of their relationship. She reflected on her parents' marriage for a brief moment to make sense of the **dilemma** she was encountering. Rita and Sonny had been physically attracted to each other the moment they first met at an ice cream shop on their university campus. They convinced their parents they were in love and were ready for marriage three weeks after they met. As soon as their honeymoon period **elapsed**, the couple fought with bitter passion on a daily basis. There were marked differences in their personalities that created serious tension, conflict, and confrontation in their marriage. They **contemplated** divorce numerous times, but their grandparents, who served as their **mentors** and **therapists**, were **instrumental** in keeping their marriage intact for **decades**.

Kamla knew her parents' love had grown slowly over thirty-five years of marriage. It had taken a while to bloom and mature into the **perpetual** happiness and contentment they were now enjoying. She envied their **steadfast** love for each other and wished her marriage would eventually be as successful and **blissful** as her parents'.

Kamla's **ambivalence** was **dictating** her decisions and actions. She believed her feelings for Mark did not **stem** from **obsession** or infatuation. They felt real. A marriage to Dr. Azeez could only result in a **pseudo-affectionate** relationship, and they would have to try hard to fall in love. On the other hand, she would disappoint and hurt her immediate and extended family if she rejected Dr. Azeez's proposal. All the villagers would bury their heads in bitter shame because they would feel that their daughter had **humiliated** them by rejecting a proposal from a son of India.

Kamla was aware that Dr. Azeez was anxiously awaiting her reply to his proposal. She answered from a very practical and realistic perspective. "Well, Dr. Azeez. I don't know what to say. I'm **speechless**. Are you sure your parents will approve of my Western views of life and **embrace** me as their daughter-in-law, Dr. Azeez?" she asked with **firmness** in her voice.

"Kamla, I'm positive my parents will **adore** you. You're beautiful, charming, and intelligent. If you approve of my proposal, I'll phone my parents and ask them to make preparations for the wedding ceremony before you leave for New York."

As soon as Dr. Azeez finished speaking with Kamla, the telephone rang. He was expecting a call from one of his patients, but it was not from him.

"Hello, this is Dr. Azeez."

"Hi, Son. It's your mother."

"I was planning to telephone you a moment ago, Ma. You have been reading my mind. You must be a **psychic**," said Dr. Azeez happily.

"I'm surprised you were thinking of us, Azeez."

"Kamla and I are planning to marry before she leaves for New York."

Dr. Azeez's mother purposely ignored what he had just said and continued her conversation with him. "Son, could you join us for dinner this evening?" his mother asked.

"What's the special occasion, Mother?"

"Nothing special. But we'll be having a few guests."

"OK. I'll be there at 8:00 p.m."

As soon as he finished talking with his mother on the phone, Dr. Azeez, with great excitement, invited Kamla to have dinner with him at his parents' home that evening.

Promptly at 5:00 p.m., Dr. Azeez and Kamla left Gangaram for his parents' residence. The trip would take about three hours. He observed that Kamla was carrying a small suitcase and questioned her about it.

"What's in the suitcase, Kamla?" he asked.

"Clothes."

"Why do you need clothes?"

"In case we decide to spend the night at your parents'."

"Good idea!"

"Do you mind if we check into a hotel before going there?"

"You're full of surprises, Kamla. Is that necessary?"

"Of course. I'd like to freshen up before we get there."

"We'll have it your way," Dr. Azeez said.

Dr. Azeez exited onto Fantasy Boulevard and checked into the Sunside Hotel. He was very tired and fell **soundly** asleep because he had had a very **hectic** week seeing dozens of patients in the village. Before he fell asleep, Kamla mentioned she was going to the restaurant in the hotel to purchase sandwiches for them.

When Dr. Azeez woke up the next day after sleeping through the night without intent, Kamla was nowhere to be seen. He wept bitterly after reading the note she had left on the dresser in the room.

He **murmured** angrily to himself. "My mother was right to say that you're nothing but a cheap woman **devoid** of moral values. You smoke like a chimney and party like an untamed animal. You lack all the virtues of a good Indian wife."

Later that morning, he called his mother to say he was sorry for missing dinner with them and their guests. After his mother revealed Dr. Gupta's family had been their invited guests the night before, he suggested that she invite them again.

Reshma was happy to do so. It was her **earnest** desire for Dr. Azeez to marry Rupa, Dr. Gupta's only daughter.

EXERCISE 1

Applying the Words You Have Learned to Critical Thinking and Creative Writing

- Use the two questions in Section A below to discuss this chapter with your classmates. Be sure to apply your critical thinking skills.

- Write an essay about either question using the vocabulary words you know from real-life experiences and the new ones you have learned from this text.

Section A

Discussion Questions

1. Do you agree or disagree with Reshma Ram's opinions of Kamla?

2. How do you feel about Dr. Azeez's marriage proposal to Kamla?

EXERCISE 2

Matching Meanings: Science

■ Match each word with its meaning.

_____ 1. agronomy	**A.** physical nature and history of the earth
_____ 2. archaeology	**B.** physical features of a place
_____ 3. anthropology	**C.** study of weather
_____ 4. astronomy	**D.** the science of mental processes and behavior
_____ 5. botany	**E.** the study of drugs and medicines
_____ 6. biology	**F.** the science and economics of crop production
_____ 7. endocrinology	**G.** the science of human society
_____ 8. ecology	**H.** the study of poisons and their effects
_____ 9. geology	**I.** the study of animals and animal life
_____ 10. geography	**J.** the study of the nervous system and its diseases
_____ 11. histology	**K.** the study of past life and culture
_____ 12. meteorology	**L.** relationships between living organisms and their environment
_____ 13. toxicology	**M.** microscopic study of tissue structure
_____ 14. psychology	**N.** the study of humans
_____ 15. history	**O.** the study of the glands and their hormones in the body
_____ 16. pharmacology	**P.** recorded events of the past
_____ 17. zoology	**Q.** the science of the universe
_____ 18. sociology	**R.** the study of plants and animals
_____ 19. neurology	**S.** the study of plant life
_____ 20. oncology	**T.** deals with cancer and tumors

EXERCISE 3

Forming Synonyms

■ Fill in the blank(s) to complete the word that is similar in meaning to the **boldfaced** word.

1. **exemplify** s__ow
2. **endure** und__ __go
3. **errand** ta__k
4. **erupt** exp__ __de
5. **espionage** sp__ __ng
6. **formulate** pre__ __ __e
7. **fluent** well-ver__ __d
8. **concoct** cr__ __te
9. **fraud** tri__ __ery
10. **facade** pret__ __se
11. **fade** pal__
12. **falter** w__ __er
13. **fame** ren__ __n
14. **sabotage** under__ __ne
15. **famished** hun__ __y
16. **favorite** prefe__ __ed
17. **fee** ch__ __ge
18. **fetch** b__ing
19. **restrain** c__ __trol
20. **flame** f__ __e
21. **reside** l__ __e
22. **research** inv__ __ __ igate

EXERCISE 4

Matching Meanings: Set 1

■ Match each word with its meaning.

_____	1. assiduous	**A.**	frank; straightforward
_____	2. boisterous	**B.**	rising above pettiness; having or showing generosity
_____	3. candid	**C.**	calm; untroubled
_____	4. decipher	**D.**	showing care and effort; diligent
_____	5. exorbitant	**E.**	feeling of bitterness or spitefulness; hatred
_____	6. magnanimous	**F.**	noisy; rough; violent
_____	7. obstinate	**G.**	weaken
_____	8. placid	**H.**	find the meaning of
_____	9. rancor	**I.**	tiresome; wearisome
_____	10. tedious	**J.**	speed up
_____	11. debilitate	**K.**	stubborn; not easily overcome
_____	12. expedite	**L.**	overpriced

EXERCISE 5

Matching Meanings: Set 2

■ Match each word with its meaning.

_____ 1. agitate — **A.** changeable; unpredictable change; fickle

_____ 2. alleviate — **B.** disapprove of strongly

_____ 3. capricious — **C.** person living in a prison

_____ 4. controversy — **D.** example serving as a future rule

_____ 5. vicious — **E.** done openly

_____ 6. condemn — **F.** nervous disorder

_____ 7. gaudy — **G.** lessen; relieve

_____ 8. inmate — **H.** cruel; corrupt

_____ 9. neurosis — **I.** sorrowful repentance

_____ 10. remorse — **J.** clash of opinions

_____ 11. precedent — **K.** lacking in good taste

_____ 12. overt — **L.** disturb; rouse to action

EXERCISE 6

Word Meaning in Context: Set 1

■ Read each sentence and find the missing word in the box below. Fill in the blank with the correct *form* of that word.

expedite	**rancor**	**candid**	**assiduous**
tedious	**debilitate**	**decipher**	**exorbitant**
boisterous	**placid**	**obstinate**	**magnanimous**

1. __________ study let Frank complete his degree in two years instead of four.
2. The students became __________ when the teacher left the room to speak with a colleague.
3. The editor's __________ comments hurt the author's feelings at first, but they turned out to be very helpful.
4. The postman returned the letter because he could not __________ the handwriting on the envelope.
5. Charles expected to pay higher prices while on vacation, but he thought $10 for a cup of coffee was __________.
6. Mrs. Richards' gift of $100,000 to the university she had graduated from was considered __________.
7. Mules have a reputation for being __________ animals.
8. The bright sunshine and the __________ water of the lake made it a perfect day to go for a swim.
9. Although she claimed to have forgiven him, __________ filled her heart until her death.
10. The __________ hours he had to spend in the factory made him reluctant to go to work.
11. The stress of working two jobs and taking care of the house and children began to __________ her, making her look older than she actually was.
12. We need this project completed quickly, so please __________ it.

EXERCISE 7

Word Meaning in Context: Set 2

■ Read each sentence and find the missing word in the box below. Fill in the blank with the correct *form* of that word.

overt	**controversy**	**condemn**	**remorse**
agitate	**gaudy**	**neurosis**	**alleviate**
inmate	**vicious**	**precedent**	**capricious**

1. The citizens began to __________ for a revolution after years with no sign of recovery from the depression.
2. The witch doctor claims he can __________ headaches with medicinal herbs.
3. The __________ weather patterns made it difficult for the fishermen to plan the length of their work schedule.
4. The __________ over abortion has caused a division in the opinions of the American public.
5. The __________ dog was shot after it bit a young boy.
6. The serial killer was __________ to life in prison.

7. Wearing too much jewelry can make one look __________.
8. He spent five years as an __________ in the state prison.
9. The psychologist concluded that Tony's depression and irritability were the results of a __________ he had suffered from for several years.
10. Everyone in the courtroom was shocked by the murderer's lack of __________ over killing five innocent people.
11. Henry refused to lend money to his friend because he did not want to set a __________.
12. Although his hostility was not __________, everyone felt uncomfortable in his presence.

EXERCISE 8

Context Clues

- Select the word or phrase that most closely matches the meaning of the **boldfaced** word. *Note that replacing the* ***boldfaced*** *word with the right answer might not produce a grammatically correct sentence.*

1. He had once followed a strict diet that allowed him to lose thirty pounds, and he encouraged his wife to do **likewise**.
   A. something else **B.** better **C.** the same **D.** worse
2. Doctors agree that there is a **link** between eating fatty foods and having a high risk of heart disease.
   A. decision **B.** connection **C.** investigation **D.** study
3. The **logic** offered by the law students who argued for the rights of a homeless man impressed the judge.
   A. intimidation **B.** eviction **C.** thinking **D.** manipulation
4. The **margin** of error on the survey was large, making it difficult to conclude who would win the election.
   A. allowance **B.** scandal **C.** reporting **D.** victory
5. Gregory **maximized** his yearly income to impress his friends.
   A. borrowed **B.** increased **C.** lied about **D.** decreased
6. The gun manufacturer admitted that a **mechanism** on the gun's triggering device frequently malfunctioned.
   A. hollow bullet **B.** operational part **C.** handle **D.** gunpowder
7. Internet users have many different communications **media** at their disposal, such as email, Twitter, and Facebook.
   A. screen colors **B.** means of communication
   C. data **D.** magazines
8. The city's union leaders and the mayor could not agree on a pay-raise scale, and requested that the state provide someone to **mediate** their dispute.
   A. beg for money **B.** bring agreement to **C.** flip a coin **D.** create a conflict
9. The family was able to get the **medical** attention they needed because they had health insurance.
   A. relating to sports **B.** relating to money **C.** relating to medicine **D.** relating to hearing
10. At five feet and ten inches tall, he was a man of **medium** height.
    A. indescribable **B.** average **C.** measurable **D.** great

11. The death of her husband affected her **mental** state, resulting in a nervous breakdown.
    A. out of the hospital **B.** living in a residence **C.** of the mind **D.** of confusion

12. The high school principal created a new testing **method** to help prepare students for their college entrance examinations.
    A. a helping hand **B.** a way of doing something
    C. a strict rule **D.** a scientific finding

13. The Mexican farm workers **migrated** to the north of the country where there were more high-paying jobs.
    A. cycled **B.** drove
    C. moved to another place **D.** looked

14. Armed **military** guards are always present outside the president's home.
    A. relating to doctors **B.** relating to money **C.** relating to soldiers **D.** relating to trust

15. Students who do only **minimal** work often end up with poor grades.
    A. the least amount **B.** the most conceptual **C.** a large portion **D.** the least intimidating

16. The company **minimized** its expenses by hiring fewer people in order to make a higher profit.
    A. validated **B.** made small **C.** described **D.** exaggerated

17. He was appointed Head of the **Ministry** of Tourism because he had more than 35 years of experience in the industry.
    A. newspaper **B.** school **C.** government office **D.** promotion

18. The motor vehicle charges were **minor**, so the judge reduced the fine from $150 to $25.
    A. large **B.** dangerous **C.** small **D.** controversial

19. Large cities allow people to choose from several **modes** of transportation, making it easier to get to school or work.
    A. companies **B.** cars **C.** elevators **D.** forms

20. Doctors carefully **monitored** the vital signs, such as the temperature and pulse, of the patient who had undergone a heart transplant.
    A. watched carefully **B.** discussed **C.** wrote prescriptions **D.** charged

21. The firm's director hired an attorney to **negate** the accusations that his company had employed illegal workers.
    A. cause to be ineffective **B.** rely on justice
    C. seek forgiveness **D.** blame a colleague

22. He landed a job quickly because he had a **network** of professional friends from his college days.
    A. club **B.** small number **C.** connected group **D.** book

23. While it faced numerous budget problems, the college **nevertheless** had to consider the students' demands for lower tuition.
    A. barely **B.** in time **C.** still **D.** for profit

24. The child was warned that the flames would burn him, but he put his hand in the fire **nonetheless**.
    A. without cause **B.** without thinking **C.** anyway **D.** on a bet

EXERCISE 9

Vocabulary Test

- Select the correct answer.
- Hint: Review the meanings of all the **boldfaced** words in this chapter before you take the test. This approach can help you to score 100 percent.
- Record the percentage of correct answers on the Master Self-Assessment table on page 397.

1 **Botany** is:

A. commercial farming
B. a type of animal husbandry
C. the study of plant life
D. the science of planets and stars

2 **Archaeology** teaches about:

E. life
F. life after death
G. reincarnation
H. past life and cultures

3 **Astronomy** is the study of the science of:

A. chemistry
B. the universe
C. quantum physics
D. earth

4 **Anthropology** is the study of:

E. humans and their culture
F. living things
G. cities and towns
H. microscopic organisms

5 **Agronomy** is the study of :

A. animals
B. soil management and crop production
C. nature
D. marine life

6 **Biology** is the study of:

E. plants and animals
F. flowers
G. the natural world
H. plant husbandry

7 **Economical** means:

A. spending money
B. not wasting money
C. relating to the economy
D. buying very few goods

8 **Ecology** examines the relationship between:

E. people

F. plants and animals

G. humans and animals

H. living organisms and their environment

9 **Geology** refers to:

A. the excavation of rocks

B. the erosion of the earth's crust

C. the exploration of caves

D. the physical history of the earth

10 **Geography** explains:

E. wind energy

F. the physical features of a place

G. the shape of things

H. hydrodynamic energy

11 **Histology** refers to the:

A. study of history

B. study of blood

C. study of disease

D. study of tissue structure

12 **Meteorology** is the study of:

E. weather, climate, and atmospheric conditions

F. meters

G. hurricanes

H. meteors

13 **Metamorphosis** is:

A. a change of form

B. the creation of an insect

C. a new life

D. the molting of snake skin

14 **Psychology** is the:

E. science of depression

F. science of mental processes

G. study of language

H. study of dispensing antipsychotic drugs

15 A **historian**:

A. recalls recent events

B. predicts future events

C. studies the human body

D. records events of the past

16 A **pharmacist** prepares:

E. vaccines

F. drugs and medicine

G. diagnoses

H. patients for surgery

17 **Zoology** deals with:

A. plants
B. plant and animal life
C. animals
D. bacteria

18 **Sociology** is the science of:

E. human society
F. humans
G. plant interaction
H. animal psychology

19 A **hobby** is:

A. something dreary
B. something one does not like
C. household chores
D. something one does in spare time

20 **Hockey** is a:

E. board game
F. sport played on ice
G. card game
H. sport played by kicking the ball

21 **Assiduous** means:

A. lazy
B. inactive
C. diligent
D. inconsistent

22 A **boisterous** party is:

E. noisy
F. calm
G. orderly
H. casual

23 A **candid** person is:

A. reserved
B. frank
C. tricky
D. insincere

24 To **decipher** is to:

E. figure out
F. ignore
G. accept
H. confuse

25 An **exorbitant** item is:

A. underpriced
B. inexpensive
C. overpriced
D. on sale

26 A **magnanimous** person is:

E. selfish

F. greedy

G. stingy

H. kind and generous

27 **Obstinate** means:

A. stubborn

B. playful

C. obedient

D. reserved

28 A **placid** lake is:

E. turbulent

F. calm

G. deep

H. shallow

29 **Rancor** refers to:

A. happiness

B. satisfaction

C. bitterness

D. depression

30 A **tedious** journey is:

E. short

F. long

G. interesting

H. tiresome

31 **Debilitate** means to:

A. enhance

B. strengthen

C. weaken

D. shock the heart

32 To **expedite** is to:

E. speed up

F. delay

G. ignore

H. halt

33 To **agitate** someone is to:

A. calm

B. arouse to action

C. ignore

D. soothe

34 To **alleviate** pain is to:

E. increase it

F. aggravate it

G. relieve or lessen it

H. worsen it

35 **Capricious** means:

A. quiet

B. friendly

C. courteous

D. changeable

36 A **controversy** is an:

E. association with friends

F. expression of opposing views

G. argument over money

H. agreement of ideas

37 A **vicious** attack is:

A. violent

B. pleasant

C. mild

D. slight

38 A **gaudy** costume is:

E. plain

F. elaborate

G. classy

H. lacking in good taste

39 An **inmate** lives in a:

A. church

B. hotel

C. prison

D. house

40 **Neurosis** is a:

E. mental disorder

F. spinal disorder

G. physical disorder

H. emotional disorder

41 **Remorse** refers to:

A. hurtfulness

B. sorrow

C. delight

D. deep regret for wrongdoing

42 A **precedent** is:

E. an obstacle

F. an example for a future rule

G. a delay in court

H. an action to obtain property

43 **Overt** means:

A. concealed

B. confidential

C. secretive

D. open to view

44 A synonym for **nevertheless** is:

E. however

F. furthermore

G. moreover

H. additionally

45 Two people who have a **link** to each other have a:

A. piece of chain

B. lasting relationship

C. connection

D. professional relationship

46 A synonym for **margin** is:

E. paper

F. allowance

G. butter

H. ruler

47 Follow one's **logic**:

A. reasoning

B. research

C. feeling

D. reaction

48 To **mediate** is to:

E. concentrate

F. bring agreement to

G. convince to disagree

H. disagree

49 A **network** is:

A. a business meeting

B. the act of surfing the internet

C. a connected group

D. a television

50 To **migrate** means to:

E. make peace

F. move to a new place

G. settle a dispute

H. stay behind

EXERCISE 10

Building a Stronger Vocabulary

- Review all the **boldfaced** words in this chapter before you proceed to the next exercise.
- Highlight the ones you are still having difficulty remembering.
- List them with their meanings on a table.
- Use them to compose your own sentences.
- Think of a synonym and an antonym for each word.
- Use checkmarks to indicate if each word you want to practice more has a prefix, suffix, and/or root.
- You may use the table below as a sample to write your answers in your notebook.

Word	Definition	Sentence	Synonym	Antonym	Prefix	Suffix	Root

EXERCISE 11

Creating My Own Powerful Word List

- Write the words and meanings from the above table on the **Creating My Own Powerful Word List** table on page 398. Review them often to build that super vocabulary you want to create for school, work, and everyday use.

Chapter 11

PRE-READING

About This Chapter from *Trial of Love*

- Read the names and descriptions of this chapter's main characters below.
  - Dr. Varghese: Dr. Azeez's friend
  - Dr. Jerry Byrd: Sonny Kumar's doctor
  - Rita Kumar
  - Sheila

Story Vocabulary Exercise

- Before you begin reading this chapter, figure out the meanings of the unfamiliar **boldfaced** vocabulary words. You may use the Word List, Word Parts Chart, or your dictionary to assist you in finding their meanings.
- Look for the various types of context clues—synonyms, antonyms, general context, and examples—as you read.
- Write a word or phrase about the meaning of each **boldfaced** word in the margin.

Reading and Writing Exercise

- Skim the entire chapter and pay attention to the headings and the discussion questions that follow.
- Initial Response: Write a paragraph explaining, in your own words, what you think this chapter of the story will be about.
- Final Response: After you have read the entire chapter, compare your current understanding with your initial response above. If your initial response was accurate, you can simply write it again to fill in the blanks below. If it was not, then write a paragraph on what the chapter was really about instead.

Initial Response

This chapter **will** be about ____

____

____

____

Final Response

This chapter **was** about ____

____

____

____

DID KAMLA TRIGGER HER FATHER'S HEART ATTACK?

Dr. Azeez felt hurt and **rejected**. He had not expected Kamla to leave him **stranded** at the hotel. When he arrived at his parents' home, his mother observed the **sullen** expression on his face. She knew he was emotionally **distraught**.

"I was expecting you to bring Kamla," she said.

"I was, too, but she suddenly left last night."

"Where did she go?"

Dr. Azeez replied, "I don't know for sure. This probably happened for the best, though. Dr. Gupta and his family would have felt **awkward** in her presence." He knew his mother suspected Kamla had returned to New York to **reunite** with Mark.

Their guests arrived promptly at 6:00. Dr. Azeez's mother welcomed them to their home and showed them to the sitting room, where they chatted for a while. When Dr. Azeez met Rupa, he did not feel physically attracted to her. In his opinion, she could not match Kamla's beauty, **wit**, and **charm**. Rupa's **superior intellect** as a medical doctor in training did not matter to him.

In Rupa's eyes, Dr. Azeez was an **obnoxious** and **arrogant juvenile** struggling to **emerge** from his **cocoon** of **egotism** to become an honorable and sophisticated medical professional. She figured out his personal **flaws** from his attitude toward her. Although she felt hurt by his **blatant** rejection, she was **respectful**, **courteous**, and **civil** toward him throughout the evening. Her parents, who were physicians with numerous **accolades** for humanitarian work throughout India, had taught her those **priceless** values, and she was **uncompromising** about following them.

As soon as their guests left after dinner, Reshma **scolded** Dr. Azeez for not expressing personal interest in Rupa as a possible wife. His father, Gopaul, did not seem concerned with their conversation and went to bed. Dr. Azeez and Reshma continued chatting for a while before following suit by going to bed as well.

The next morning, Dr. Azeez was anxious to return to the village. Occasionally, he drove in excess of the speed limit, but he was lucky enough to avoid getting noticed by the highway patrol. In less than two hours after leaving his mother's residence, he arrived in Gangaram. Sosheila, Kamla's grandmother, was in her backyard tending to her vegetable garden. She breathed a sigh of relief as soon as she saw his car entering his driveway.

Reluctantly, Sosheila went to his house. She knocked on his door impatiently numerous times. He did not answer. It was only when she tried to enter forcefully that he responded.

"Go away, go away, you tricky old woman," Dr. Azeez said angrily and insensitively to her.

Sosheila was alarmed that he was yelling at her. She had never known him to be **disrespectful** and verbally **abusive** to anyone.

"Dr. Azeez, I'm sorry if I've disturbed you. I'm here to **escort** Kamla home."

"Old woman, don't pretend you don't know what Kamla did."

"Please tell me what happened. Let me in the house, Dr. Azeez. This is serious. Let's talk about it."

He **debated** for a while whether he should let her into his house. When he realized Sosheila could possibly be ignorant of what had **transpired**, he invited her in. Slowly, he was **regaining** his calm **composure** and **disposition**. He expressed his regret for being disrespectful to her. In his culture, he was expected to show the same love and respect to Sosheila as he would to his mother, because Sosheila and his mother were of the same age.

"Kamla left when I fell asleep in the hotel."

"Do you have any clue where she went, Dr. Azeez?"

He told her he did not. As Sosheila was leaving, Dr. Varghese, Dr. Azeez's friend, came to visit him. Although they were best friends, they had not seen each other for a year because of their **rigid** work schedules.

"Azeez, I was shocked to hear what Kamla had done when you telephoned earlier today. Do you have one of her photographs?"

"Sure," he answered as he gave him Kamla's photograph.

"I know you're **heartbroken**, but please, don't get depressed about Kamla. The right woman is out there for you, my friend. Be patient!"

"I can't wait to hear the good news you want to share with me, Varghese."

"A few days ago, I received a letter from New York Medical Hospital, an internationally **renowned** hospital, offering me a position as an **obstetrician**."

"Congratulations!"

"Guess why I got the position?"

"You're the best in your discipline."

"Partly correct. I was selected over a thousand applicants because of the technique I **pioneered** in pre-natal care."

"Do you mean the Sunshine technique that saves the lives of over ninety-eight percent of **premature** babies?"

"Precisely."

"Words are insufficient to express my happiness for you. I'll miss you, my friend."

"I'll try my best to arrange for you to work in New York as well, Azeez."

"I'd love that."

Before darkness fell, Dr. Varghese left for his home. Dr. Azeez had an **excruciating** headache and slept until the next day. He looked forward to **resuming** his work at the clinic and following his normal schedule again.

Sonny's Heart Attack

Sonny and Rita had just returned home from a late-night showing of a movie they had wanted to see for a long time. Sonny was not sleepy, so he urged Rita to stay up and play a few games of cards with him. The couple were having an enjoyable time and **cherished** the **privacy**. They were about to finish the last game when the telephone rang. Rita looked scared, while Sonny seemed unconcerned.

"Sonny, please answer the telephone," said Rita, whose voice was trembling with anxiety.

Sonny hesitated for a while and the ringing discontinued abruptly. The phone rang again and Sonny answered it without hesitation.

"Is this Sonny?" the caller inquired.

"Yes. Who's calling?"

"It's me, your mother-in-law," replied Sosheila.

"What a pleasant surprise! How're you doing?"

"I wish I could say I'm happy."

"What seems to be the problem, Ma?"

"Is Kamla with you?"

"No. Isn't she with you in India?"

"I don't know where she is, Sonny. She was here but suddenly disappeared."

"Oh my God! Kamla. . . ."

Sonny **collapsed** and cried out in pain. The telephone receiver fell from his hand and the call was disconnected.

"Please help me, Rita. I can't breathe," said Sonny in a **faint** and weak tone of voice.

"Tell me what to do!" she cried.

Sonny kept **groaning** with pain and was trying to massage his chest gently while lying on the floor. Rita was **hysterical** and ran out of the house and banged on their neighbor's door.

"Somebody please help me! My husband is dying!" she cried while banging.

When nobody responded, she rushed like a wild deer back into her house. Sonny's eyes were **semi-closed** and he was **semiconscious**. She grabbed the telephone and dialed 911. In less than three minutes, the ambulance was at her house. The paramedics rushed him into the ambulance, and Rita joined them in the back.

"Will my husband **recover** soon?" she asked one of the paramedics sitting next to her.

"It's difficult to say at this point. How long had he been collapsed before you called us?"

"About five to seven minutes."

"Ma'am, why didn't you telephone for help immediately?"

"I didn't know what to do, sir."

"You've done just fine, just fine," he reassured her.

"Please believe me. I didn't expect him to **collapse**. He was talking to my mother in India when he suddenly fell."

"Has this ever happened to him before?"

"Never. He was always a healthy man."

"When did he have his last physical examination?"

"He has never had one."

"Are you certain about this?"

"Yes, sir."

"Ma'am, please answer my questions to the best of your ability. Your answer will help the doctors in the emergency room make an accurate **diagnosis**."

"I understand."

"Does he smoke?"

"Yes."

"Is he a heavy smoker?"

"Sometimes two to three packs per day."

"Does he drink alcohol?"

"He **consumes** two to three drinks per day. He can't sleep unless he has his drinks."

"Has he always drunk and smoked heavily?"

"Sonny was **addicted** to nicotine and alcohol in India for most of his life. He stopped for a while, but recently he **resumed** drinking and smoking here in New York."

"Do you know what could've possibly caused him to start again?"

"I suspect the stress of life in America and family problems."

As soon as the ambulance arrived at the hospital, the medical team **wheeled** him to an examination room. With **infinite** care, the chief of the team examined him **meticulously** and **administered** an injection. Then he ordered a series of blood tests and instructed the laboratory technologists to report the results to him as soon as they were available. Approximately thirty minutes later, Sonny fully regained consciousness.

"Where's my wife?" he anxiously asked the nurse at his bedside.

Rita was standing in the hallway outside his room, sobbing.

"Doctor, will my husband feel well again?" Rita asked his physician eagerly as he was leaving Sonny's room.

"He has already made a **remarkable** recovery, Rita."

"Thank God!"

"We're just waiting for the results of the blood tests to determine a possible cause of his collapse."

"What would your guess be for the reason why Sonny fell down, doctor?"

"I suspect it was a heart attack."

"My goodness! Sonny has never complained of chest pain before."

"That doesn't mean his heart is in its best shape."

"Would you say it was a **minor** or a **major** attack?"

"I'm positive it was only a minor attack. We'll **apprise** you of his condition as soon as we can." The doctor's cellphone sounded impatiently, and he left in a rush. Rita went to visit Sonny and made a deliberate effort to **cheer** him.

"I'm delighted to see you," Sonny said. "For a minute, when the **penetrating** pain attacked me, I thought that was the end of my life. Accompanying the pain was a quick spell of dizziness and sweating. The chest pain extended to my left shoulder and down my back. Rita, I swear I had a close **encounter** with death. I'm scared."

"Sonny, the doctor said you're recovering **superbly** and there's nothing to **worry** about."

"Rita, they're saying that just to make me feel better."

"No, Sonny. There's nothing to worry about."

"Can you recall what **triggered** the pain?"

"It came suddenly when Sosheila mentioned Kamla couldn't be found in India. I'm afraid for Kamla. I hope she's safe wherever she—"

The equipment that was monitoring his heart rate had been beeping at the same rate **persistently**, but it suddenly **accelerated**. Several doctors raced down the hall to Sonny's room. On examining him, they determined that his blood pressure was **escalating** to a dangerous level. The doctors desperately tried to reduce it to the normal range. After Sonny received another injection, he felt fine again. The doctors advised Rita to return home to allow him to rest.

As soon as she entered the house, the telephone rang. Sosheila inquired as to why Sonny had hung up on her.

"Mother, Sonny didn't hang up on you. Sonny is asleep now," Rita lied to her mother. She feared that if she knew that Sonny was ill, she would feel guilty, believing that she was responsible for his **ailment**, and might become depressed.

Rita did not want Sosheila, her mother, to know that Sonny had suffered a heart attack. She **vowed** to **conceal** it until he returned home. Moments after Rita placed the telephone receiver down, Sheila arrived at her home looking **perplexed**.

"Rita, I've been trying to reach you for several hours without success. You look **uneasy**. What's the matter? Sonny isn't here. Where is he?"

Rita broke down in tears and hugged Sheila for comfort and **consolation**. "He's in the hospital," she answered, weeping **profusely**.

"What's the matter with him?"

"He had a minor heart attack."

"I don't believe this, Rita. He's too young to have a heart attack."

"Even young men are **prone** to it. It's a **myth** that only older men suffer from heart attacks."

"Is he **stable** now?"

"Yes. But the doctors want to **monitor** his condition for a few days before sending him home."

Sheila **assured** Rita that Sonny would recover soon and that he was not in **critical** condition. She asked Rita to come over to her home and stay there until Sonny was **discharged** from the hospital. Sheila was unable to convince Rita that it was a good idea.

"Sheila, I can't be away from home."

"Why not, Sister?"

"In case Kamla should telephone or return home. Kamla is missing."

"Missing? Impossible! Isn't she in India?"

"No. Mother telephoned to inform us that she was missing."

"Rita, this doesn't make sense. I was under the impression that she went to marry Dr. Azeez."

"That's what I expected. Obviously, she chose not to marry him."

"So the news that she's missing caused Sonny's heart attack, I **presume**."

"Sheila, I don't want anybody to know about this. Kamla will feel guilty for the rest of her life if she finds out that she was the cause of her father's heart attack."

"Frankly, I don't care about Kamla because she thinks very little of you and Sonny."

"She loves us dearly, Sheila."

"You're mistaken. She has no respect for you and Sonny. If she had, she would've honored your wishes."

"Times have changed. Young people these days are **disobedient** and **rebellious**. They don't listen to their parents."

"Correction, please! You're making a broad statement. You aren't tough enough with Kamla. That's why she's **manipulating** you and Sonny. She gets what she wants from both of you."

Sheila was **enraged** that Rita was defending Kamla. Although she was angry with Rita for allowing herself to be **bullied** by Kamla, she decided to sleep over that night because Rita was still weeping for her husband. Neither of them could close their eyes for a minute of sleep.

"Sheila, do you think I should inform Joshi about Sonny's condition?"

"How would that help Sonny?"

"Don't forget that our brother is a physician. I am sure that he would have some good advice."

"To think of it, you're right, Rita. Joshi is a **cardiologist**. Why didn't we think about this earlier?"

Joshi had just returned home from jogging. He was still breathing heavily when he spoke to Rita.

"I'm shocked to hear about Sonny, Rita. He looked healthy when I was in New York."

"Everybody else is surprised too."

"If you don't mind, I'll come to New York three days from today."

"No. I don't want to **impose** on you."

"Actually, if I hadn't scheduled patients for surgery for the next few days, I'd have taken the next flight from Dallas to New York."

"Joshi, his doctors feel he'll be **discharged** soon."

"OK. But in the meantime, I'll request that his cardiologist at the hospital give me a daily report on his condition. I promise to phone every day until he fully recovers. Don't worry, my sister. I'm here for you and your family."

"I feel better talking to you, Joshi. Please give my regards to my **sister-in-law**, Roxy, and my **adorable nephews** and **nieces**."

"Take care of yourself, Rita. I love you."

As soon as Joshi hung up the phone, Rita telephoned Kathy. She got her machine, so she left a message. Rita was very disappointed because she wanted to speak to Kathy. Fortunately, when they were about to leave for the hospital, Kathy returned her call.

"Rita, is everything OK? I'm very surprised to hear from you."

"Kamla's father is in the hospital, and I can't find her. Do you know where she is?"

"No."

"Please help me find her, Kathy, for her father's sake. Her presence will **hasten** his recovery."

"I'll do everything possible to help you, Rita."

"I appreciate it."

When Rita and Sheila arrived at the hospital the following morning, they did not see Sonny in his room. Although the doctors and nurses on duty desperately tried to explain what had happened during the night, the sisters cried until there were no more tears in their swollen eyes.

A few minutes later, after they regained their composure, one of the doctors, Jerry Byrd, sat them down and explained that Sonny was alive and had been taken to another room in the hospital for observation the **previous** night. Dr. Byrd assured Rita and Sheila that Sonny's life was not in danger. He indicated that Sonny had possibly had a very mild stroke, but could not **confirm** it at that moment because he had not gotten the results of several tests that had been done during the night.

Rita and Sheila breathed a sigh of relief after listening to Dr. Byrd's update on Sonny's condition. As soon as Dr. Byrd left, one of the nurses accompanied them to Sonny's room. Looking at their sorrowful and pitying eyes, Sonny knew they had been crying prior to entering his room. It pained him very much to see how distressed they looked. He tried very hard to assure them that he would **recuperate** from his illness and be ready to go home very soon. Both sisters concealed their **distress** to put him in an **upbeat** mood for the rest of the day. Sonny's condition improved greatly, and he was discharged from the hospital. He received specific instructions from Dr. Byrd to **adhere** to a very rigid physical therapy schedule to ensure a complete recovery.

EXERCISE 1

Applying the Words You Have Learned to Critical Thinking and Creative Writing

- Use the two questions in Section A below to discuss this chapter with your classmates. Be sure to apply your critical thinking skills.

- Write an essay about either question using the vocabulary words you know from real-life experiences and the new ones you have learned from this text.

Section A

Discussion Questions

1. Dr. Azeez was not physically attracted to Rupa Roy. What role does physical attraction play in a relationship?

2. Who should be blamed for Sonny's heart attack?

EXERCISE 2

Synonyms: Multiple Choice

■ Circle the letter of the word or phrase that is most similar in meaning to the **boldfaced** word.

1. **overt** **A.** closed **B.** open **C.** half-way **D.** harmful
2. **oblong** **A.** elongated **B.** triangular **C.** abnormal **D.** absent
3. **satisfied** **A.** unhappy **B.** content **C.** resistant **D.** sad
4. **terminate** **A.** travel **B.** initiate **C.** continue **D.** discontinue
5. **subversive** **A.** loyal **B.** lustful **C.** dedicated **D.** undermine
6. **succinct** **A.** clean **B.** long **C.** expressed in few words **D.** terminal
7. **recruit** **A.** newcomer **B.** counselor **C.** army **D.** friend
8. **condemn** **A.** criticize **B.** caution **C.** befriend **D.** endure
9. **transpire** **A.** occur **B.** expect **C.** give **D.** perspire
10. **reconciliate** **A.** restore to harmony **B.** distrust **C.** regret **D.** misery
11. **vanish** **A.** see **B.** disappear **C.** exclude **D.** erase
12. **serene** **A.** cheerful **B.** tender **C.** peaceful **D.** stormy
13. **tangible** **A.** invisible **B.** powerful **C.** legible **D.** touchable
14. **retaliate** **A.** accept **B.** deny **C.** fight back **D.** sin
15. **spontaneous** **A.** unprepared **B.** planned **C.** prepared **D.** ready
16. **vicinity** **A.** surroundings **B.** skyscraper **C.** town **D.** country
17. **subtle** **A.** indirect **B.** loud **C.** determined **D.** detected
18. **trait** **A.** brawl **B.** quality **C.** fighter **D.** traitor
19. **succumb** **A.** silence **B.** crumble **C.** give in **D.** sicken
20. **zeal** **A.** enthusiasm **B.** neglect **C.** pain **D.** sorrow

EXERCISE 3

Synonyms and Antonyms

■ Write the corresponding letter for the synonym and antonym of each **boldfaced** word.

	Synonym	Antonym			
1. **impatient**	______	______	**A.** restless	**B.** patient	**C.** slow
2. **imperfect**	______	______	**A.** faulty	**B.** unflawed	**C.** inept
3. **implement**	______	______	**A.** carry out	**B.** neglect	**C.** manufacture
4. **impolite**	______	______	**A.** rude	**B.** interpret	**C.** courteous
5. **import**	______	______	**A.** bring in	**B.** send	**C.** export
6. **important**	______	______	**A.** valuable	**B.** incredible	**C.** trivial
7. **impractical**	______	______	**A.** unworkable	**B.** reasonable	**C.** tiring
8. **improper**	______	______	**A.** ready	**B.** incorrect	**C.** appropriate
9. **improve**	______	______	**A.** develop	**B.** heat	**C.** worsen
10. **impure**	______	______	**A.** unclean	**B.** clean	**C.** intermittent
11. **inaccessible**	______	______	**A.** unreachable	**B.** available	**C.** useful
12. **inaccurate**	______	______	**A.** erased	**B.** incorrect	**C.** precise
13. **inactive**	______	______	**A.** sleepy	**B.** idle	**C.** busy
14. **inadequate**	______	______	**A.** insufficient	**B.** emotional	**C.** enough
15. **inappropriate**	______	______	**A.** unsuitable	**B.** proper	**C.** eliminated
16. **inclement**	______	______	**A.** stormy	**B.** excited	**C.** calm
17. **incompetent**	______	______	**A.** unfit	**B.** funny	**C.** efficient
18. **incomplete**	______	______	**A.** unfinished	**B.** gigantic	**C.** accomplished
19. **inconsiderate**	______	______	**A.** thoughtless	**B.** sensitive	**C.** frugal
20. **inconsistent**	______	______	**A.** disagreeing	**B.** agreeable	**C.** external
21. **indispensable**	______	______	**A.** essential	**B.** unnecessary	**C.** fervent
22. **inedible**	______	______	**A.** uneatable	**B.** fatal	**C.** delicious
23. **inert**	______	______	**A.** faulty	**B.** inactive	**C.** moving
24. **inexpensive**	______	______	**A.** cheap	**B.** costly	**C.** conclusive
25. **infamous**	______	______	**A.** bad reputation	**B.** respectable	**C.** biased

	Synonym	Antonym			
26. **inflate**	______	______	**A.** swell	**B.** deflate	**C.** conclude
27. **join**	______	______	**A.** help	**B.** connect	**C.** separate
28. **jovial**	______	______	**A.** misunderstood	**B.** joyful	**C.** sad
29. **jumble**	______	______	**A.** dispose	**B.** mix	**C.** organize
30. **junior**	______	______	**A.** younger	**B.** senior	**C.** reliable
31. **just**	______	______	**A.** fair	**B.** jovial	**C.** partial
32. **juvenile**	______	______	**A.** young	**B.** gloomy	**C.** old
33. **keen**	______	______	**A.** sharp	**B.** harmless	**C.** dull
34. **keep**	______	______	**A.** check	**B.** hold	**C.** discard
35. **kindle**	______	______	**A.** bore	**B.** light	**C.** extinguish
36. **languid**	______	______	**A.** cold	**B.** weak	**C.** energetic
37. **large**	______	______	**A.** big	**B.** constant	**C.** small
38. **last**	______	______	**A.** final	**B.** second	**C.** first
39. **lavish**	______	______	**A.** plentiful	**B.** scarce	**C.** internal
40. **lax**	______	______	**A.** calm	**B.** careless	**C.** strict
41. **lazy**	______	______	**A.** apathetic	**B.** inactive	**C.** busy
42. **leave**	______	______	**A.** depart	**B.** escape	**C.** arrive
43. **legal**	______	______	**A.** allowed	**B.** unlawful	**C.** superior
44. **lenient**	______	______	**A.** easy	**B.** hard	**C.** consistent
45. **liberal**	______	______	**A.** persistent	**B.** generous	**C.** conservative
46. **light**	______	______	**A.** short	**B.** weightless	**C.** heavy
47. **limp**	______	______	**A.** drooping	**B.** pacified	**C.** stiff
48. **literate**	______	______	**A.** can read and write	**B.** organized	**C.** uneducated
49. **load**	______	______	**A.** pack	**B.** unload	**C.** shake
50. **luxury**	______	______	**A.** prosperity	**B.** relaxation	**C.** poverty
51. **magnify**	______	______	**A.** enlarge	**B.** decrease	**C.** raise
52. **mad**	______	______	**A.** fearful	**B.** crazy	**C.** sane
53. **maternal**	______	______	**A.** motherly	**B.** brotherly	**C.** fatherly

	Synonym	Antonym			
54. **mature**	_____	_____	**A.** developed	**B.** cooked	**C.** immature
55. **melancholy**	_____	_____	**A.** sad	**B.** cheerful	**C.** excited
56. **merge**	_____	_____	**A.** combine	**B.** glue	**C.** separate
57. **misfortune**	_____	_____	**A.** episode	**B.** tragedy	**C.** luck
58. **misplace**	_____	_____	**A.** lose	**B.** habit	**C.** find
59. **mobile**	_____	_____	**A.** habitual	**B.** movable	**C.** stationary
60. **moral**	_____	_____	**A.** honest	**B.** unprincipled	**C.** consistent
61. **more**	_____	_____	**A.** adequate	**B.** extra	**C.** less
62. **mourn**	_____	_____	**A.** monster	**B.** grieve for the dead	**C.** rejoice
63. **murmur**	_____	_____	**A.** whisper	**B.** coax	**C.** shout
64. **naked**	_____	_____	**A.** undressed	**B.** covered	**C.** suspended
65. **neat**	_____	_____	**A.** organized	**B.** anxious	**C.** sloppy
66. **necessary**	_____	_____	**A.** required	**B.** courteous	**C.** unimportant
67. **neglect**	_____	_____	**A.** ignore	**B.** compare	**C.** care
68. **negligent**	_____	_____	**A.** careless	**B.** envious	**C.** careful
69. **nervous**	_____	_____	**A.** assertive	**B.** restless	**C.** calm
70. **neutral**	_____	_____	**A.** pale	**B.** impartial	**C.** involved
71. **normal**	_____	_____	**A.** usual	**B.** pertinent	**C.** different
72. **noxious**	_____	_____	**A.** harmful	**B.** harmless	**C.** transparent
73. **obey**	_____	_____	**A.** assist	**B.** follow instruction	**C.** refuse
74. **oblivious**	_____	_____	**A.** central	**B.** unaware	**C.** alert
75. **obtain**	_____	_____	**A.** acquire	**B.** lose	**C.** contain

EXERCISE 4

Matching Meanings: Set 1

■ Match each word with its meaning.

_____	1. vociferous	**A.** a strange trait or mannerism
_____	2. unanimous	**B.** clearly evident; apparent, but not necessarily true
_____	3. reprehend	**C.** loud; noisy
_____	4. regression	**D.** make less severe or painful
_____	5. quirk	**E.** sharing another person's feelings
_____	6. reticent	**F.** showing complete agreement
_____	7. ostensible	**G.** too showy
_____	8. oscillate	**H.** find fault; criticize
_____	9. mitigate	**I.** quiet; saying little; reserved
_____	10. fastidious	**J.** hard to please; quick to find fault
_____	11. flamboyant	**K.** going back
_____	12. empathy	**L.** swing to and fro

EXERCISE 5

Matching Meanings: Set 2

■ Match each word with its meaning.

_____ 1. hallucinate

_____ 2. hypocrite

_____ 3. interminable

_____ 4. insatiable

_____ 5. judicious

_____ 6. mishap

_____ 7. ludicrous

_____ 8. aggregate

_____ 9. ostentatious

_____ 10. perspicacious

_____ 11. surreptitious

_____ 12. empower

A. incapable of being satisfied

B. unfortunate accident

C. endless; lasting; forever

D. laughable; obvious absurdity

E. keen judgment or vision

F. put together

G. pretentious

H. give authority to

I. acting in a secret manner

J. having or showing sound judgment; wise

K. hear or see something that does not exist

L. one who pretends to be what he or she is not

EXERCISE 6

Word Meaning in Context: Set 1

■ Read each sentence and find the missing word in the box below. Fill in the blank with the correct *form* of that word.

flamboyant	**vociferous**	**reprehend**	**empathy**
mitigate	**reticent**	**quirk**	**unanimous**
fastidious	**ostensible**	**regression**	**oscillate**

1 .The students became ___________ when they were served tuna casserole for the third time in two weeks.

2. The vote to elect Mr. Chen as president of the building's co-op board was ___________.

3. My mother finds an opportunity to ___________ me no matter how hard I try to meet her expectations.

4. The elderly sometimes experience mental ___________, losing memories and becoming unable to perform simple tasks.

5. Anne's habit of drinking twenty glasses of water a day seemed rather strange to some people, but she excused it as just a ___________.

6. Simon's parents thought their son ___________, but when he was with his peers, he was quite talkative.

7. In many countries, the father is the ___________ head of the family, but the mother often makes the most important family decisions.

8. The pendulum in a grandfather clock ___________ when it is active.

9. No amount of money could ___________ the loss she experienced when the drunk driver killed her child.

10. Although he was ___________ in his dress, his apartment looked as if it had not been cleaned in a year.

11. It is advisable to dress in a conservative, rather than a ___________, manner when preparing for a job interview.

12. Because of her gift of ___________, Debbie was the first person her friends called when they had a problem.

EXERCISE 7

Word Meaning in Context: Set 2

■ Read each sentence and find the missing word in the box below. Fill in the blank with the correct *form* of that word.

mishap	**hypocrite**	**ostentatious**	**empower**
judicious	**insatiable**	**hallucinate**	**surreptitious**
ludicrous	**perspicacious**	**contemporary**	**interminable**

1. Severe sleep deprivation often causes people to ___________.

2. Pierre thinks his boss is a ___________ because he tells Pierre not to smoke, even though he smokes ten packs a day.

3. He said he would call back in an hour, but the wait seemed ___________.

4. No matter how much she fed him, her teenager's appetite seemed ___________.

5. Getting a degree in business seemed ___________ at the time, but he later regretted his decision not to follow his dream of becoming a musician.

6. The __________ would never have happened if he had checked the brakes on his car.
7. The veterinarian's proposal to train an army of cats to get rid of the rats in the subways was considered __________.
8. My grandmother does not appreciate __________ music, and prefers to listen to the music that was popular in the 1940s, when she was a teenager.
9. Their __________ displays of affection caused everyone to wonder if they were hiding problems with their relationship.
10. Although her patient's symptoms were vague, the __________ doctor made a surprising diagnosis and cured her.
11. The child made a __________ attempt to take an extra cookie, but his mother caught him anyway.
12. The CEO __________ the chief operating officer to take control of the company while he was away on overseas business.

EXERCISE 8

Context Clues

- Select the word or phrase that most closely matches the meaning of the **boldfaced** word. *Note that replacing the **boldfaced** word with the right answer might not produce a grammatically correct sentence.*

1. The standard day rate of the gardener was $150, which was the industry **norm**.
   A. statistic **B.** standard **C.** story **D.** ritual

2. The scientific report offers a different **notion** of whether daylight savings time is useful.
   A. idea **B.** situation **C.** concoction **D.** chart

3. **Notwithstanding** his arrogant attitude, he was still promoted to a managerial position.
   A. despite **B.** with care **C.** because of **D.** subsequent to

4. The bombings of Hiroshima and Nagasaki made **nuclear** war a reality.
   A. relating to vision **B.** relating to honor
   C. relating to atomic energy **D.** relating to guns

5. The family had so much trash in their garage that it **occupied** most of the space.
   A. smelled bad **B.** held down **C.** took up **D.** set aside

6. The city had to **offset** the cost of building the new school by reducing recreational costs.
   A. argue about **B.** make up for **C.** derail **D.** enlarge

7. The **ongoing** discussion of the disagreement has lasted for four hours and there is no sign that an agreement will be reached.
   A. fearsome **B.** continuing **C.** shameful **D.** ending

8. Fast-food restaurants offer many **options** other than burgers.
   A. packages **B.** meats **C.** prices **D.** choices

9. The college had to explain its services to the new students in order to **orient** them.
   A. familiarize **B.** employ **C.** scare **D.** inspect

10. In his annual report, the CEO of the company said this year's production **output** exceeded last year's.
    A. amount produced **B.** future vision **C.** life of service **D.** large containers

11. The teachers spent several months preparing their students for the state exams, so the school performed well **overall**.
    A. rarely **B.** in general **C.** unlucky **D.** uniformly

12. Despite the fact that the scientific investigations had much in common, there was no **overlap** in the results.
    A. having the same parts **B.** keeping good company
    C. fighting each other **D.** looking through a microscope

13. **Overseas** flights require travelers to be at the airport two hours before departure time.
    A. across the ocean **B.** under the water **C.** luxurious **D.** expensive

14. The construction workers installed a new **panel** of sheetrock in the house.
    A. section **B.** wood **C.** nail **D.** frame

15. The practice of buying bottled water led to the new **paradigm** that drinking tap water was unsafe.
    A. scam **B.** theory **C.** report **D.** news

16. The lawyer highlighted a **paragraph** in the legal brief that helped win his case.
    A. section of a piece of writing **B.** minor adjustment
    C. piece of paper **D.** sentence

17. Because the husband and wife had **parallel** work schedules, they had to hire a babysitter to take care of the kids while they were both at work.
    A. long **B.** similar **C.** inconvenient **D.** different

18. The engineers had to analyze the **parameters** of the municipal water system to make sure they complied with state environmental laws.
    A. boats **B.** workers **C.** rules **D.** contracts

19. It was easy to convince John to join the company softball team and **participate** in the games because he enjoyed playing sports.
    A. leave out **B.** be the best **C.** go first **D.** take part

20. The law **partner** was voted out of the firm and replaced with another member.
    A. station **B.** license **C.** associate **D.** follower

21. Experience and knowledge can help one **perceive** the reality of a situation.
    A. see **B.** adapt to **C.** surrender to **D.** imagine incorrectly

22. The two **percent** return on their stocks displeased the shareholders.
    A. double **B.** parts in one hundred **C.** money **D.** law

23. After waiting for a long **period** of time for his date to arrive, he returned home.
    A. length **B.** crisis **C.** proportion **D.** section

24. To ensure their study remained fair and balanced, the scientists made sure they had a team of people who had various **perspectives** on the subject.
    A. degrees **B.** views **C.** microscopes **D.** treatments

EXERCISE 9

Vocabulary Test

- Select the correct answer.
- Hint: Review the meanings of all the **boldfaced** words in this chapter before you take the test. This approach can help you to score 100 percent.
- Record the percentage of correct answers on the Master Self-Assessment table on page 397.

1 **Succinct** means:

A. clean
B. long
C. terminal
D. expressed in few words

2 **Tangible** things are:

E. invisible
F. powerful
G. legible
H. touchable

3 To **retaliate** is to:

A. accept
B. deny
C. sin
D. get even

4 A synonym for **spontaneous** is:

E. unplanned
F. planned
G. prepared
H. fabricated

5 **Vicinity** refers to:

A. city
B. an area near a place
C. town
D. country

6 A **subtle** remark is:

E. loud
F. direct
G. cheerful
H. not immediately noticeable

7 To **succumb** to something is to:

A. be silent
B. crumble
C. be sick
D. surrender or give in to

8 **Zeal** means:

E. neglect

F. eagerness or enthusiasm

G. pain

H. sorrow

9 To **implement** a new strategy is to:

A. carry out

B. wait

C. forget

D. ignore

10 A synonym for **impractical** is:

E. workable

F. unworkable

G. necessary

H. practiced

11 **Inaccessible** means:

A. reachable

B. workable

C. out of reach

D. easily accessed

12 To **obtain** something is to:

E. acquire it

F. break it

G. sell it

H. admire it

13 An **incompetent** person lacks the ability to do something.

A. True

B. False

14 **Inconsiderate** means insensitive to others.

E. True

F. False

15 An **inconsistent** person:

A. is regular

B. likes to have a routine

C. is uneasy

D. behavior does not stay the same

16 Something **indispensable** is:

E. easy

F. absolutely necessary

G. difficult

H. unnecessary

17 An **inedible** fruit is:

A. unfit to eat
B. tasty
C. fatal
D. fake

18 **Inert** means:

E. inept
F. alive
G. not moving
H. active

19 An **infamous** person:

A. is good
B. is outgoing
C. is a criminal
D. has a bad reputation

20 To **inflate** a balloon is to:

E. expand it
F. deflate it
G. puncture it
H. smash it

21 A **jovial** person is:

A. good-humored
B. sad
C. uncomfortable
D. athletic

22 **Keen** on doing something means:

E. uneasy
F. harmless
G. dull
H. enthusiastic or excited

23 To **kindle** a fire is to:

A. be bored with it
B. watch it
C. start it
D. extinguish it

24 A **languid** person is:

E. cold
F. strong
G. energetic
H. showing little energy or interest

25 To **lavish** gifts on someone means:

A. buy clothes

B. be stingy

C. offer help

D. give without limit

26 **Lax** means:

E. calm

F. not strict or severe

G. rigid

H. ill

27 Someone **lenient** is:

A. easy

B. hard

C. consistent

D. difficult

28 An antonym for **liberal** is:

E. persistent

F. generous

G. conservative

H. narrow-minded

29 **Limping** after an accident means:

A. jumping

B. walking unevenly

C. hiking

D. hurrying

30 **Literate** means able to:

E. add

F. read and write

G. multiply

H. teach

31 A life of **luxury** is a life of:

A. great comfort

B. poverty

C. sadness

D. value

32 To **magnify** something is to:

E. focus on it

F. decrease its size

G. record it on tape

H. make it appear larger than it is

33 **Melancholy** refers to:

A. anger
B. cheerfulness
C. excitement
D. sadness

34 To **merge** means to:

E. bring together
F. separate
G. lengthen
H. shorten

35 A **misfortune** is:

A. a missed opportunity
B. a favor
C. a mystery
D. an unlucky occurrence

36 **Mobile** means movable.

E. True
F. False

37 **Moral** refers to beliefs about what is right or wrong.

G. True
H. False

38 **Maternal** refers to having the qualities of a mother.

A. True
B. False

39 **Noxious** fumes are:

E. harmful to health
F. harmless
G. explosive
H. colorful

40 **Oblivious** to something means being:

A. respectful
B. unaware
C. aware
D. hidden

41 A synonym for **vociferous** is:

E. soft
F. soft-spoken
G. serious
H. loud-mouthed

42 The vote was **unanimous**, which suggested it was:

A. debatable

B. in total agreement

C. forged

D. inconclusive

43 **Reprehend** means to:

E. find fault

F. compliment

G. redirect

H. take into custody

44 **Regress** refers to:

A. living in the present

B. going to a previous state

C. being neutral

D. going forward

45 A **quirk** is a:

E. quack

F. weird feeling

G. sound ducks make

H. strange trait or mannerism

46 Someone who is **reticent** is:

A. very talkative

B. reluctant to speak freely

C. withdrawn

D. friendly

47 A synonym for **ostensible** is:

E. outrageous

F. supposed or alleged

G. simple

H. unaware

48 Something that **oscillates**:

A. is decisive

B. moves back and forth

C. stands firm

D. is idle

49 To **mitigate** a punishment is to:

E. increase it

F. avoid it

G. remember it

H. make it less severe

50 Someone **fastidious** is:

A. pleasant
B. hard to please
C. flexible
D. forgetful

51 Someone **flamboyant** is:

E. dull
F. boring
G. simple
H. showy and noticeable

52 When you show **empathy**, you:

A. criticize
B. are insensitive
C. are silent
D. share another person's feelings

53 Someone who **hallucinates**:

E. feels insecure
F. sees something that is not there
G. is excitable
H. often falls asleep

54 Someone with an **insatiable** desire for money is:

A. easily satisfied
B. incapable of being satisfied
C. always satisfied
D. not interested

55 **Judicious** means:

E. unintelligent
F. showing sound judgment
G. joking
H. joyful

56 Something **ludicrous** is:

A. intense
B. laughable because of foolishness
C. serious
D. easy

57 **Ostentatious** means:

E. ordinary
F. done pretentiously to impress others
G. unique
H. fluctuating

58 A **perspicacious** person:

A. is unperceptive

B. is serious

C. is sweaty

D. has keen judgment

59 **Surreptitious** visits are:

E. done secretly

F. done at noon

G. done rarely

H. done at night

60 To **empower** someone is to:

A. weaken

B. give authority

C. belittle

D. question

EXERCISE 10

Building a Stronger Vocabulary

- Review all the **boldfaced** words in this chapter before you proceed to the next exercise.
- Highlight the ones you are still having difficulty remembering.
- List them with their meanings on a table.
- Use them to compose your own sentences.
- Think of a synonym and an antonym for each word.
- Use checkmarks to indicate if each word you want to practice more has a prefix, suffix, and/or root.
- You may use the table below as a sample to write your answers in your notebook.

Word	Definition	Sentence	Synonym	Antonym	Prefix	Suffix	Root

EXERCISE 11

Creating My Own Powerful Word List

- Write the words and meanings from the above table on the **Creating My Own Powerful Word List** table on page 398. Review them often to build that super vocabulary you want to create for school, work, and everyday use.

Who Did Mark Marry?

Chapter 12

PRE-READING

About This Chapter from *Trial of Love*

- Read the names and descriptions of this chapter's main characters below.
  - Mark Edison Hubbard
  - Kamla Kumar
  - Kathy Precious Armstrong
  - Cindy Singh
  - Dr. Joshi

Story Vocabulary Exercise

- Before you begin reading this chapter, figure out the meanings of the unfamiliar **boldfaced** vocabulary words. You may use the Word List, Word Parts Chart, or your dictionary to assist you in finding their meanings.
- Look for the various types of context clues—synonyms, antonyms, general context, and examples—as you read.
- Write a word or phrase about the meaning of each **boldfaced** word in the margin.

Reading and Writing Exercise

- Skim the entire chapter and pay attention to the headings and the discussion questions that follow.
- Initial Response: Write a paragraph explaining, in your own words, what you think this chapter of the story will be about.
- Final Response: After you have read the entire chapter, compare your current understanding with your initial response above. If your initial response was accurate, you can simply write it again to fill in the blanks below. If it was not, then write a paragraph on what the chapter was really about instead.

Initial Response

This chapter **will** be about ______________________________

____

____

____

Final Response

This chapter **was** about ______________________________

____

____

____

WHO DID MARK MARRY?

"Good morning," a friendly telephone operator said to greet Kathy when she picked up the phone. "There's a collect call for Kathy."

"I'm Kathy. I'll accept it."

The operator connected Kathy with the caller. She was very eager to know who was calling.

"Kathy, is that you?" asked a soft, gentle voice.

"Kamla, where have you been? We're worried about you."

"It's a long story. I'll tell you about it later. How's Mark doing?"

"Mark suffered an **acute bout** of depression while you were away. He's feeling better now. Your presence will put him back to his old self."

"I can't wait to see him, Kathy."

"Where are you now?" Kathy asked.

"Kennedy Airport in New York City."

"Stay right there. I'll have Mark pick you up."

"I don't want him to know I've returned to New York. I want to surprise him."

"Aren't you going directly to your parents' home, Kamla?"

"I'm **confused**, Kathy. I don't know what to do. Please hurry and pick me up. I'm at the international terminal."

Kathy's mother prepared breakfast and invited Kamla to dine with them when she arrived from the airport. It was the first time Kamla had visited Kathy's family, and she was feeling **uneasy**.

"Please have a few slices of toast, Kamla. You've hardly eaten anything," said Kathy's mother.

"No thanks, ma'am. I'm not hungry," replied Kamla.

"Have some juice, at least."

"OK. I'll have some."

While they were eating, Kamla did not speak much. Kathy's mother was not pleased that Kamla had returned to New York. She had a secret desire for her daughter, Kathy, to fall in love with Mark and marry him. Upon Kamla's request, Kathy drove Kamla to Mark's apartment as soon as breakfast was over.

"Thanks for your moral support, Kathy. You're indeed a true and loyal friend."

"You're welcome, my friend," said Kathy as she pulled into the parking lot outside Mark's apartment. "I'll wait here while you give Mark a big hug and kiss."

"Why do you want to wait?"

"To drive you home."

"I'm not going home to my parents, Kathy. I mean it. I'm moving in with Mark."

"You can't do that."

"Why not?"

"Because **cohabitation** is not permitted by your Indian culture. Your culture does not allow a couple to live together before marriage. Furthermore, Mark may not approve of it."

"Let Mark tell me in his own words."

"Mark isn't a **candid** man. He won't come out and say it openly."

"He will. Mark isn't an **introvert**. He doesn't keep his feelings bottled up inside of him. He's an **extrovert**."

"Mark would never say you can't live with him in his apartment. He's too afraid of hurting your feelings."

"Kathy, only Mark and I know the intensity of our feelings. We were apart for a while, but that doesn't mean the flame of our passion is **extinguished**. It's still hot and will keep burning even after time **ceases** to exist."

"There you go again with your **juvenile** love talk. I'm disappointed in you, Kamla."

"I have the feeling that you don't want me to live with Mark. I wonder why."

Kathy was very upset by Kamla's insistence on living with Mark. It was against her Christian **beliefs**. By sleeping with Mark before marriage, Kamla was committing **fornication**, which was a **violation** of Kathy's principles. She could speak in street talk on occasion, but she never meant it. She certainly had never expected Kamla and Mark's relationship to turn out like this. She had always thought that Kamla's own beliefs would hold her back.

Kamla felt that Kathy was **meddling** in her relationship with Mark and **contemplated** telling her to mind her own business.

Mark was awakened by their loud conversation in the parking lot. When he looked through the window and saw Kamla, he ran outside and shouted, "Kamla, sweetheart, where have you been? I've missed you, honey."

Kathy left in a hurry while Mark **escorted** Kamla to his apartment.

"Why did you **abandon** me, my girl?" asked Mark as soon as they entered the apartment.

"Mark, please accept my **apology** for returning to India without telling you. I swear, it won't happen again," she assured him with confidence.

"I'm positive you have a good reason for what you did, Kamla."

"Grandma in India was ill. It was impossible for me to reach you before I left."

"Is Grandma completely **recovered** now?" Mark asked with genuine **sincerity**.

"Recovered from what?" Kamla asked **spontaneously**, without taking a moment to think about what she was saying.

"From her illness you just mentioned," Mark said.

"Oh! Of course."

"You don't seem to be certain," he said suspiciously.

Mark detected the **inconsistency** in her explanation for leaving New York, but he did not **dwell** much on the subject. He started talking about Sonny's heart condition, which he'd learned about earlier from Kathy. Kamla ignored Mark while he was talking about her father. She did not express any compassion for him and did not seem to be bothered by his health condition. Mark **persisted** in talking about Sonny.

"Kamla, I think your dad's condition is serious. Kathy says it is."

"I don't care. It's his life. Let him worry about his illness."

"I can't believe you're saying this about your father."

"Mark, if I visit him in the hospital, he'll insist that I don't move in with you. Sweetheart, I belong here with you, and I've no intention of leaving."

"As much as I want you to live with me, I still feel that you must visit your dad. It would be insensitive, cold, and **callous** on your part to ignore your father, who has **sacrificed** everything and risked his life to cross the border so that you could **pursue** your dream of becoming a Nobel Prize winner in America. Don't take your father for granted. You don't know what it's like not to have a father's love," said Mark angrily.

Kamla said calmly, "If you insist, we'll go to visit him at the hospital after our marriage."

A few days later, Mark and Kamla married at City Hall in New York City. They were accompanied by Kathy and Cindy, who had lunch with them at a restaurant after the ceremony. While they were dining, Kathy mentioned that she was taking a leave of absence from her job at Rollins University because her dad would be temporarily relocating to Guyana, South America. He had a new job assignment at the American Consulate. Kathy's three friends were very sad when she broke the news to them.

Mark and Kamla went to the airport to see them off. Kamla wept as she watched Kathy board the jet to Guyana. The departure of her only friend in New York made her feel lonely and sad.

Kamla and Mark's Honeymoon in Jamaica

A week after Kathy left for Guyana, Kamla and Mark went to Jamaica for their honeymoon. It was far from what Kamla had expected. She had looked forward to days and nights of endless romance, but instead she experienced bitter unhappiness that seemed as if it would reside **perpetually** in her heart. Mark hardly left the hotel for the entire week of their honeymoon. Kamla was baffled by his sudden mood swing from sheer joy and excitement in New York to what appeared to be some sort of **preoccupation** with something that Kamla could not figure out with certainty. However, she suspected it was related to Kathy's departure for Guyana.

On their return to New York, Kamla was wondering whether marrying Mark had been a wise decision. It seemed to her that her future with him would be a lifetime of **misery** and domestic **arguments**. Daily fights were beginning to be the norm. The day after they returned from their honeymoon was a perfect example.

"Kamla, I was under the impression you'd be visiting your father in the hospital after our wedding," Mark reminded her.

"Why have you suddenly developed a keen interest in my father, Mark?"

"He's ill. Maybe leaving your family has contributed to it."

"I've no reason to show compassion for him."

"Your **irrational** behavior toward your father is **mind-boggling**."

"You don't know the man as intimately as I do."

"During a **crisis**, one has to put aside one's differences and make an **intentional** effort to help the person in need."

"My father is a **bully**. He's a **mean** man."

"How could you make such insensitive statements about the man who has raised you to be the fine professional woman you are today?"

"Do you really want to know why I suddenly left for India?"

"Haven't you already explained the reason, Kamla?"

"I wasn't exactly honest."

"I'm anxious to hear the truth, Kamla."

"My father **masterminded** a plan for me to return home to marry Dr. Azeez, our village doctor."

"Why?"

"To **ensure** I wouldn't marry you."

"I can't understand how he could've arranged for you to marry a man you've never met."

"My mother met him when she visited recently. She practically **adores** him to the point of **worshipping** him."

"Kamla, why didn't you marry Dr. Azeez?"

"Because I love you, Mark. I couldn't marry someone I didn't love. I returned to New York without my grandma's knowledge to marry you."

"I can now make sense of why your dad became ill."

"Can you?"

"Yes. When he learned that you didn't marry the doctor, he became ill."

"Probably that's what happened."

"Kamla, although I **appreciate** your **loyalty** to me, you shouldn't have lied about your reason for returning to India after the graduation dance."

"I was afraid of losing you, honey."

"That explanation isn't good enough."

"Mark, every time you raise the subject of my family, we always end up arguing."

"I don't support your reasons for avoiding your father and mother. Little do you know how fortunate you are. I miss my parents and wish they were here with me. Only I know the sadness I **endure** when I feel I have nobody in this world."

As tears crowded Mark's eyes, Kamla drew closer to him in bed. He hugged her as if he were in a desperate **quest** for **solace** and comfort. She assured him that she was a **dutiful** wife who wanted to share her life selflessly with him. He was quick to express his appreciation for her warm affection.

Kamla Reunites With Her Father

For several months, Mark and Kamla did not discuss her family. But when she woke up early one morning after a horrifying nightmare about her father, she mentioned to Mark that she wanted to visit him at home, since he had been discharged from the hospital.

When the doorbell sounded, Joshi opened the door and let her in the house. Kamla was wondering if Joshi's presence meant her dad had passed away. Without speaking a word to him, she ran upstairs to her father's room. He was not there. She threw herself on his bed and cried out, "Daddy, I'm sorry for hurting your feelings, please forgive me!"

Joshi still had not spoken to her. He was in the living room watching television while Kamla was upstairs **sobbing** for her father.

When Kamla had no more tears left, she came downstairs to the living room to **initiate** a conversation with Joshi.

"Do you hate me as well?" Kamla asked her uncle, Joshi.

"No, Kamla. I don't hate you. It's just that I **despise** the way you've repeatedly and selfishly hurt your parents' feelings, particularly your dad's."

"But I couldn't marry Dr. Azeez. He wasn't the perfect man for me."

"Do you really believe there is such a thing as a perfect human being? Is Mark a perfect man?"

"How do you know about Mark?"

"Kathy telephoned your mother before leaving for Guyana. She said you and Mark were married."

During their conversation, Kamla heard a car entering the driveway. She looked through the window curiously. Suddenly, her face brightened. She ran to the door and opened it. Joshi's wife, Roxy, and Rita and Sonny were speechless when they saw her. As Kamla kissed her father on his forehead and tried to hug him passionately while he was still in his wheelchair, sweet tears of joy **trickled** down his cheeks. It was the first time in his entire life that his family had seen him weeping.

"I didn't expect to see you again," he said while wiping the tears away with his handkerchief.

"Will you forgive me, ***Pitaji***?"

"Of course. I am glad to hear you say 'pitaji' instead of 'father.' Your native language is still in your blood, my daughter."

"It was very childish of me to avoid you for the last seven months. I want you to know that I was thinking of you every day."

"I know you were, my child," said Sonny affectionately.

When Sonny unsuccessfully attempted to get out of the wheelchair, Kamla assisted him with **indubitable** daughterly love. He appreciated her **gesture** and kissed her on her cheek, as he had when he played with her on the beach in India when she was barely four years old. Both were left alone in the living room while the others went into the kitchen.

"How long will you be **confined** to your wheelchair, Daddy?"

"I don't know. But the **therapist** guesses that I should recover fully within the next few months."

"I'm **confused** as to why you're in a wheelchair."

"Didn't Joshi explain my condition?"

"No."

"After I recovered from the heart attack, I suffered a mild **stroke**. Fortunately, Joshi took time off his job to provide me with additional medical care. If it weren't for him, I wouldn't have made such a **spectacular** improvement in my condition. I pray that God blesses him and his family. He's an **everlasting gem** to be **cherished** forever."

"You look terrific, Daddy."

"So do you. You look. . . ."

"Pregnant?"

"Well, yes," said Sonny. "When are you expecting your son?"

"In about two months. Who says I'll have a boy?"

"I've always wanted a grandson."

"Mother prefers a granddaughter," countered Kamla.

"What's Mark's preference?"

"He doesn't care."

"Kamla, are you happy with Mark?"

"Well. . . ."

"Well . . . what's the matter?"

"Things could be better," said Kamla.

"In what respect?"

"We don't get along as well as I would like."

"What's the root of the problem?" asked Sonny.

"Mark seldom returns home on weekends."

"Where does he go?"

"He **resumed** his weekend classes in law school. When we were newly married, he came home after his classes. But during the last few months, he has **preferred** staying in the **dormitory** on campus on weekends."

"What's his explanation for staying on campus?"

"He claims that an atmosphere **conducive** to studying is nonexistent at home."

"Is he correct?"

"Of course not."

"I think the conflict in your marriage might stem from cultural differences."

"I'm beginning to agree with you, Daddy. I wish I had listened to you. I have become a **disobedient** daughter since I came to New York. And . . . and I'm very sorry for the trouble, the heartache, and the pain I've given you and mother. You didn't deserve it."

"Don't give up hope. Everything will be all right. You've got to keep working on your marriage. It's not easy these days."

"You and Mom . . . I mean, '***Mataji***,' have been married for more than thirty years. You've always made her happy. I wish Mark did the same for me."

"You know that our **faith** and **spirituality** are the **core** of our **blissful** marriage. You and Mark must always put God in the first place in your marriage. Then, and only then, will you enjoy a lifetime of **marital bliss**. The same goes for your children, too."

It was around dinnertime. Joshi interrupted Sonny and Kamla to invite them to dinner with the rest of the family at the neighborhood restaurant. It was an unforgettable evening for Rita and Sonny. They felt blessed that Kamla had **reunited** with them and their other family members. They wished Mark was there to **celebrate** the reunion.

EXERCISE 1

Applying the Words You Have Learned to Critical Thinking and Creative Writing

- Use the two questions in Section A below to discuss this chapter with your classmates. Be sure to apply your critical thinking skills.

- Write an essay about either question using the vocabulary words you know from real-life experiences and the new ones you have learned from this text.

Section A

Discussion Questions

1. How do you feel about the manner in which Kamla initially treated her father?

2. How do you feel about Kamla reuniting with her family?

EXERCISE 2

Matching Meanings: Science

■ Match each word with its meaning.

_____	1. amoeba	**A.** a single-celled microorganism
_____	2. fungi	**B.** an underground storage organ
_____	3. spirogyra	**C.** organisms with no true roots, stems and leaves; are parasites
_____	4. mammal	**D.** a structure that carries and distributes sugars in plants
_____	5. reptile	**E.** plants with a life cycle of more than two years
_____	6. pseudopodia	**F.** warm-blooded animals with mammary glands
_____	7. micronutrients	**G.** a relationship that benefits both parties
_____	8. macronutrients	**H.** a type of fish
_____	9. bulbs	**I.** green algae
_____	10. rhizome	**J.** the division of two nuclei
_____	11. symbiosis	**K.** cold-blooded animals with bony skeletons
_____	12. mistletoe	**L.** the smallest particle of an element
_____	13. xylem	**M.** relates to the back
_____	14. phloem	**N.** an element that is a gas
_____	15. perch	**O.** a creeping stem
_____	16. annuals	**P.** process by which green plants make food
_____	17. perennials	**Q.** the "feet" of an amoeba
_____	18. transpiration	**R.** plants that live only one year or season
_____	19. dorsal	**S.** nutrition required in tiny quantities
_____	20. oxygen	**T.** nutrition required in large quantities
_____	21. photosynthesis	**U.** the formation of two new nuclei
_____	22. meiosis	**V.** a structure that carries water and mineral salts in plants
_____	23. mitosis	**W.** a plant that grows on branches and trunks of trees
_____	24. molecule	**X.** the giving off of water vapor
_____	25. weed	**Y.** an uncultivated plant

EXERCISE 3

Forming Synonyms

■ Fill in the blank(s) to complete the word that is similar in meaning to the **boldfaced** word.

1. **flatter** comp__ __ment
2. **foolproof** as__ __red
3. **forecast** pred__ __ __ion
4. **spank** b__at
5. **founder** cr__ __tor
6. **guide** di__ect
7. **ghastly** drea__ful
8. **goal** a__m
9. **gossip** hear__ay
10. **hardship** dif__ __culty
11. **hit** st__ike
12. **hurry** r__sh
13. **illustrious** fam__ __s
14. **site** loca__ __ __n
15. **impact** eff__ __t
16. **sarcastic** mock__ __g
17. **indifferent** unconc__ __ __ed
18. **solitude** isol__ __ __on
19. **infer** conc__ __de
20. **impostor** pret__ __ __er

EXERCISE 4

Matching Meanings: Set 1

■ Match each word with its meaning.

______ 1. gullible	**A.** faultless; without flaw
______ 2. genesis	**B.** sweet and pleasant to taste
______ 3. hysterical	**C.** easily deceived
______ 4. impeccable	**D.** difficult to handle or deal with
______ 5. lethargy	**E.** declare blameless; free from guilt
______ 6. luscious	**F.** unreal; imaginary
______ 7. obnoxious	**G.** lively and happy
______ 8. cumbersome	**H.** beginning; origin
______ 9. dubious	**I.** undecided; uncertain
______ 10. exonerate	**J.** lack of energy
______ 11. elated	**K.** highly offensive; disagreeable
______ 12. fictitious	**L.** emotionally uncontrolled

EXERCISE 5

Matching Meanings: Set 2

■ Match each word with its meaning.

_____	1. luminous	**A.**	secret; concealed
_____	2. capitulate	**B.**	waver; sway to and fro
_____	3. condone	**C.**	costly; very expensive
_____	4. covert	**D.**	a contagious and deadly epidemic disease
_____	5. esoteric	**E.**	lack of emotion, feeling, or interest
_____	6. vacillate	**F.**	forgive; overlook; disregard
_____	7. unrest	**G.**	banish; exclude from social activities
_____	8. sumptuous	**H.**	give up or surrender
_____	9. subjugate	**I.**	intended for a small group with unique interests
_____	10. plague	**J.**	glows in the dark
_____	11. ostracize	**K.**	defeat or conquer; overpower
_____	12. apathy	**L.**	discontent; uneasiness

EXERCISE 6

Word Meaning in Context: Set 1

■ Read each sentence and find the missing word in the box below. Fill in the blank with the correct *form* of that word.

dubious	**obnoxious**	**gullible**	**exonerate**
elated	**genesis**	**luscious**	**acknowledge**
impeccable	**cumbersome**	**hysterical**	**lethargy**

1. Because she was so ___________, Amanda gave $100 to the stranger in the bus station who said she had lost her ticket.
2. The disease had its ___________ in a tropical country, but soon spread to other parts of the world.
3. Mrs. Roberts found the joke so funny that she broke down into ___________ laughter.
4. Although the candidate's opponents closely examined his past, they found nothing to use against him—his record was ___________.
5. ___________, a feeling of tiredness and weakness, is often a sign of depression.
6. A freshly picked peach tastes ___________.
7. While he thought his practical jokes were funny, his annoyed classmates found them ___________.
8. Although the mattress weighed little, it was ___________ because of its shape and size, and difficult to carry up the stairs.
9. The get-rich-quick guide's claim that you can invest $5 and make $5,000 within a week is ___________.
10. When the real murderer confessed his crime, the court ___________ the falsely imprisoned man and compensated him for the time he had spent in jail.
11. Susan was ___________ when it was announced that she was valedictorian of her class. She had worked very hard to earn that distinction.
12. When the governor's project cost the state thousands of jobs, she had no choice but to ___________ her mistake at the press conference.

EXERCISE 7

Word Meaning in Context: Set 2

■ Read each sentence and find the missing word in the box below. Fill in the blank with the correct *form* of that word.

condone	**luminous**	**unrest**	**apathy**
esoteric	**subjugate**	**vacillate**	**ostracize**
capitulate	**plague**	**sumptuous**	**covert**

1. John bought a clock with a ___________ dial that would help him see the time in the dark.
2. Because the discussion had gone on for two hours, Sidney decided to ___________ rather than continue arguing.
3. The army's ___________ operations in rural areas helped to overthrow the dictator.
4. Although the father understood the motives for his son's crimes, he could not ___________ them.

5. Despite the ____________ nature of the lecture, a large crowd showed up.
6. Because Chu always ____________ when pressed to make a decision, his wife usually made choices for him.
7. The government imposed a 10:00 p.m. curfew after several days of civilian ____________.
8. After spending an entire paycheck on a ____________ dinner, Svetlana could not afford to go out for three months.
9. Alice was tempted to buy the chocolate cake in the bakery window, but she ____________ the desire and walked away.
10. The Black ____________ of the 14th century wiped out about a quarter of the population of present-day Europe.
11. Billy was ____________ by his classmates because he always told his teachers when somebody broke the rules.
12. Many people choose not to vote because of their ____________ toward politics.

EXERCISE 8

Context Clues

- Select the word or phrase that most closely matches the meaning of the **boldfaced** word. *Note that replacing the **boldfaced** word with the right answer might not produce a grammatically correct sentence.*

1. The construction of the library was in its final **phase** when the inspectors arrived.
   A. reading **B.** part **C.** field **D.** adaptation

2. The students came to understand the **phenomenon** of space travel after a year of studying physics.
   A. something observed **B.** something fake
   C. something unimaginable **D.** something fast

3. His **philosophy** was that one should be kind and caring, even to those who are cruel.
   A. principles **B.** business **C.** religion **D.** favorite saying

4. His doctor encouraged him to plan a regular schedule of **physical** activity to maintain his good health.
   A. relating to the mind **B.** relating to the heart
   C. relating to the body **D.** relating to the earth

5. The company offered bonuses **plus** an additional personal day in order to attract skilled employees.
   A. beyond **B.** without **C.** along with **D.** minus

6. To be fair to students, our **policy** is to provide two warnings before punishing them.
   A. punishment **B.** procedure **C.** argument **D.** revenge

7. A **portion** of the school's budget was used to buy new computers for students.
   A. part **B.** schedule **C.** presentation **D.** meeting

8. Police often **pose** as street vendors to uncover drug activity on the streets.
   A. act **B.** beg **C.** steal **D.** harass

9. The student's exceptional performance in elementary school showed his **potential** as a talented mathematician.
   A. limits **B.** capability **C.** boundary **D.** authority

10. The hospital had very few general **practitioners**, so patients had to schedule routine appointments months in advance.

    A. critics **B.** doctors **C.** insurers **D.** engineers

11. The women who fought to receive the right to vote **preceded** the women today who serve in elected offices.

    A. did the work for **B.** gave loans **C.** came before **D.** arrived after

12. The architect was **precise** in his design so that the engineers could be exact in the building's construction.

    A. confused **B.** sketchy **C.** pricey **D.** accurate

13. He was selected as a contestant for the game show because he performed well in the **preliminary** interview.

    A. difficult **B.** first **C.** unimportant **D.** later

14. It is wrong to **presume** that John Lee's beliefs are incorrect until one has considered his point of view.

    A. believe **B.** say **C.** abstain **D.** hurt

15. The **primary** reason for changing the street-crossing rules was to keep children safe.

    A. most important **B.** unpopular **C.** least important **D.** intimidating

16. The computer was a **prime** seller because of its thin and lightweight design.

    A. last in rank **B.** getting old **C.** cheap **D.** first in rank

17. The idea that we can understand nature through observation is a key **principle** of science.

    A. poor argument **B.** basic truth **C.** unpopular belief **D.** outright lie

18. She had a history of working as a police officer **prior** to joining the military.

    A. later **B.** with honors **C.** earlier **D.** with care

19. The teacher's main **priority** was to improve the students' scores on the statewide examinations.

    A. something boring **B.** something important **C.** something sacred **D.** something harmful

20. The state **proceeded** with construction of the oil pipeline despite protests from residents.

    A. continued **B.** ceased **C.** collected **D.** concluded

21. The innovative construction **process** helped the contractor complete the park in one year instead of three.

    A. operation **B.** deforestation **C.** investigation **D.** introduction

22. She was hired as an engineering manager because of her **professional** experience.

    A. relating to space **B.** relating to history **C.** relating to career **D.** relating to fashion

23. His creative **project** earned him a full scholarship for four years of college.

    A. undertaking **B.** vehicle **C.** argument **D.** decision

24. **Prominent** people have to be very careful when they travel to certain countries.

    A. old **B.** poor **C.** well-known **D.** intelligent

EXERCISE 9

Vocabulary Test

- Select the correct answer.
- Hint: Review the meanings of all the **boldfaced** words in this chapter before you take the test. This approach can help you to score 100 percent.
- Record the percentage of correct answers on the Master Self-Assessment table on page 397.

1 An **amoeba** is an organism that:

A. walks on legs
B. uses pseudopodia to move about
C. uses wings to fly
D. crawls on dirt

2 **Fungi** are:

E. roadside plants
F. Japanese miniature trees
G. flowering plants
H. parasites with no true roots, stems. leaves

3 **Spirogyra** is a type of:

A. green algae
B. brown algae
C. animal
D. spinning organism

4 A **mammal** is a:

E. creature with fur
F. cold-blooded creature with scales
G. creature of the air
H. warm-blooded creature with mammary glands

5 A **reptile** is:

A. blood-sucking with wings
B. cold-blooded with a bony skeleton
C. cold-blooded with fur
D. warm-blooded with a bony skeleton

6 **Pseudopodia** are:

E. used as feet
F. used for balancing
G. used for flying
H. used as arms

7 **Micronutrients** are:

A. sometimes needed
B. rarely seen
C. required in small quantities
D. required in large quantities

8 **Macronutrients** are:

E. liquids

F. required in small quantities

G. small solid particles

H. required in large quantities

9 One example of a **bulb** is a(n):

A. onion

B. rose

C. carrot

D. tomato

10 **Rhizomes** are:

E. climbing plants

F. running vines

G. roots above ground

H. creeping stems

11 The **xylem** in a plant:

A. distributes sugars in the roots

B. carries water and mineral salts

C. stores plant nutrients

D. promotes photosynthesis

12 A **mistletoe** is a :

E. type of fruit

F. parasitic plant that grows on trees

G. rare flower

H. weed that grows on fences

13 The **phloem**:

A. absorbs plant sugars

B. provides oxygen for plants

C. is a type of leaf

D. carries and distributes sugars in plants

14 A **perch** is a:

E. fish

F. bird

G. mammal

H. snake

15 **Annuals** are plants that:

A. regenerate monthly

B. live only one year or season

C. lie dormant

D. bloom weekly

16 Plants that are **perennials**:

E. live only one year

F. have a life cycle of more than two years

G. are evergreens

H. have a life cycle of less than two years

17 When plants **transpire**, they:

A. give off water vapor
B. breathe oxygen
C. give off carbon dioxide
D. breathe carbon dioxide

18 **Oxygen** is:

E. a metal
F. an inorganic substance
G. a gas
H. a vapor

19 **Photosynthesis** refers to a green plant's:

A. respiratory process
B. absorption process
C. digestive process
D. food-making process

20 The process of **meiosis**:

E. eliminates dead cells
F. involves two nuclear divisions
G. creates cell addition
H. promotes cell multiplication

21 **Mitosis** is the process whereby:

A. nuclei are destroyed
B. complete cells are formed
C. two nuclei are formed
D. cells die

22 A **molecule** is:

E. an element
F. the smallest particle of an element
G. part of an atom
H. the largest particle of an element

23 A **weed** is:

A. an uncultivated plant
B. an illegal substance
C. an unusual plant
D. a rare plant

24 A **gullible** person is:

E. easily deceived
F. very clever
G. guilty
H. dim-witted

25 **Genesis** means:

A. a beginning
B. an ending
C. a holy book
D. a transition

26 **Impeccable** means:

E. not credible

F. extremely clean

G. without fault

H. not clean

27 **Lethargic** refers to:

A. being energetic

B. lacking energy

C. falling asleep

D. being hyperactive

28 **Luscious** means:

E. sour

F. bitter

G. sweet and pleasant to taste

H. salty

29 **Obnoxious** behavior is:

A. highly offensive

B. appropriate

C. acceptable

D. professional

30 **Cumbersome** means:

E. very large

F. difficult to handle or deal with

G. fragile

H. sturdy

31 **Dubious** means:

A. uncertain

B. careful

C. methodical

D. trusting

32 To **exonerate** is to:

E. declare blameless

F. assign guilt

G. withhold judgment

H. reveal terms of imprisonment

33 A **fictitious** story is:

A. real

B. unreal

C. interesting

D. frightening

34 A **luminous** object:

E. is very dark

F. is incapable of glowing

G. reflects light

H. glows in the dark

35 To **capitulate** means to:

A. give up or surrender
B. take by force
C. stand one's ground
D. compromise

36 To **condone** means to:

E. disagree
F. approve
G. forbid
H. prevent

37 A **covert** operation is:

A. widely known
B. open to the public
C. secret or concealed
D. a medical procedure

38 **Esoteric** refers to a:

E. congregation
F. small group with unique interests
G. rowdy crowd
H. large group with broad interests

39 To **vacillate** is to:

A. promote one theory
B. obtain immunization against disease
C. swing in circles
D. waver between opinions

40 **Unrest** is:

E. uneasiness
F. contentment
G. stability
H. drowsiness

41 A **sumptuous** preparation is:

A. absolutely delicious
B. costly or expensive
C. tasteless
D. cheap

42 To **subjugate** is to:

E. surrender
F. flee in fear
G. defeat or conquer
H. set free

43 A **plague** is a:

A. fever
B. deadly bacterial epidemic
C. mild virus
D. a substance that yellows teeth

44 Someone who is **ostracized** is:

E. banished or excluded

F. always welcomed

G. socially accepted

H. allergic to bird feathers

45 **Apathy** is:

A. an energetic mood

B. an intense emotional feeling

C. a lack of interest or feeling

D. extreme sadness

46 Feeling **elated** means feeling:

E. somber and depressed

F. bitter and angry

G. content and quiet

H. lively and happy

47 **Overt** means:

A. concealed

B. confidential

C. secretive

D. open to view

48 A **hysterical** person is:

E. sober

F. quiet

G. emotionally uncontrolled

H. slightly upset

49 Someone's **philosophy** refers to his or her:

A. principles

B. intelligence

C. physical activity

D. emotions

50 A synonym for **potential** is:

E. strength

F. capability

G. power

H. weakness

EXERCISE 10

Building a Stronger Vocabulary

- Review all the **boldfaced** words in this chapter before you proceed to the next exercise.
- Highlight the ones you are still having difficulty remembering.
- List them with their meanings on a table.
- Use them to compose your own sentences.
- Think of a synonym and an antonym for each word.
- Use checkmarks to indicate if each word you want to practice more has a prefix, suffix, and/or root.
- You may use the table below as a sample to write your answers in your notebook.

Word	Definition	Sentence	Synonym	Antonym	Prefix	Suffix	Root

EXERCISE 11

Creating My Own Powerful Word List

- Write the words and meanings from the above table on the **Creating My Own Powerful Word List** table on page 398. Review them often to build that super vocabulary you want to create for school, work, and everyday use.

Will Kamla Die?

Chapter 13

PRE-READING

About This Chapter from *Trial of Love*

- Read the names and descriptions of this chapter's main characters below.
  - Senator Rex: A politician in New York
  - Dorothy: Mark's mother
  - Maria: A nurse at the nursing home
  - Dr. Rachael Peterson: A physician in the emergency room
  - Dr. Varghese
  - Dr. Azeez

Story Vocabulary Exercise

- Before you begin reading this chapter, figure out the meanings of the unfamiliar **boldfaced** vocabulary words. You may use the Word List, Word Parts Chart, or your dictionary to assist you in finding their meanings.
- Look for the various types of context clues—synonyms, antonyms, general context, and examples—as you read.
- Write a word or phrase about the meaning of each **boldfaced** word in the margin.

Reading and Writing Exercise

- Skim the entire chapter and pay attention to the headings and the discussion questions that follow.
- Initial Response: Write a paragraph explaining, in your own words, what you think this chapter of the story will be about.
- Final Response: After you have read the entire chapter, compare your current understanding with your initial response above. If your initial response was accurate, you can simply write it again to fill in the blanks below. If it was not, then write a paragraph on what the chapter was really about instead.

Initial Response

This chapter **will** be about ____

____

____

____

Final Response

This chapter **was** about ____

____

____

____

WILL KAMLA DIE?

As soon as Mark left for work at Rollins University, Kamla packed a picnic basket with as much food as it could **accommodate**. She then rode the bus to the nursing home where Dorothy, Mark's mother, had been staying. Kamla had never met Dorothy, but the photograph she took from Mark's album **enabled** her to **identify** her.

"Could you please tell me where I can find Mrs. Dorothy Hubbard?" Kamla asked a nurse who was at the **receptionist**'s desk when she arrived at the nursing home.

"Oh! Dorothy. She's everybody's **favorite** here."

"Really?" Kamla said excitedly.

"We **adore** Dorothy," said the nurse. She shuffled through some papers in a folder and pulled one out. "Are you related to her?"

"I'm her daughter-in-law, Kamla."

"She never mentioned you."

"Actually, she doesn't know Mark and I are married."

"Who's Mark?"

"Her son."

"Strangely, Dorothy's admission form states she doesn't have any family," said Nurse Maria, looking at the paper in her hand.

"That's incorrect and **absurd**."

"Why would she sign to that statement on the form?"

"Nurse, is the signature on the form hers?"

"I don't think so."

"You sound positive."

"It's difficult for Dorothy to sign because of her **paralysis**," said the nurse. "Dorothy is right-handed and the entire right side of her body is **lifeless**."

"Who's the person who signed?"

"**Senator** Rex."

"Who's Senator Rex?"

"A politician. He always claims to be a friend of Dorothy."

Mark had never spoken of Senator Rex to Kamla. Kamla wondered why the senator was taking such keen interest in Dorothy. She felt something **fishy** was going on.

"Nurse, does Dorothy have visitors?"

"Nobody except the senator."

"But Nurse Maria, Mark told me that his mother has a very close friend. I'm positive she visits her frequently."

"Could you describe her, Kamla?" asked Nurse Maria.

"Mark says she's about five foot seven, medium built with blond hair."

"Is her name Eva?"

"Yes. Do you know her?"

"Of course. She attempted to visit Dorothy several times, but the senator's security guards always sent her away."

"Nurse, it seems as if the senator is **concealing** something that he fears Dorothy might **reveal**."

"He's **weird** but very powerful. Don't trust him, Kamla," cautioned Maria.

The nurse gave Kamla directions to Dorothy's room, then left to answer a resident's request for assistance. However, as Kamla was about to enter the room, two **baldheaded** men **approached** her. They were Senator Rex's security guards.

"Miss, you can't enter that room. It's **off-limits** to visitors," said one of them.

"Over my dead body!" Kamla said in a threatening manner. She walked up to them without **trepidation**. "Who do you think you are, **bozo**, to tell me I can't visit my mother-in-law?"

The men were upset by Kamla's fearless remarks and **menacing** attitude. As soon as they were about to grab her by her arms to **escort** her out the building, Dorothy shot out of her room in her electric wheelchair and struck both men in their groin with her cane, which she held **firmly** in her left hand. Both men cursed and doubled over. They were about to **retaliate**, but after realizing that she was physically **handicapped** and Kamla was pregnant, they limped to their security desk in the hallway not very far away from Dorothy's room. The risk of losing their jobs didn't seem nearly as bad as the risk of hurting the women in a struggle.

Kamla felt fortunate that Dorothy had saved her despite her physical limitation. Dorothy **manipulated** her electric wheelchair with ease with her left hand, thereby moving around without difficulty.

"Honey, you're a courageous woman. I'm glad you stood up to them," Dorothy said as a **compliment**.

"These men are shameless bullies. Who are they?" asked Kamla.

"I don't know. They have been keeping a watch over me since Mark left me in this **stinking** nursing home," replied Dorothy.

Kamla **adroitly** changed the subject from the security guards and the nursing home to Dorothy and her family. "You're as lovely as Mark said, Dorothy."

"Do you know Mark?" asked Dorothy **inquisitively**.

"Yes. Dorothy, we're family now."

Dorothy looked up at Kamla from her wheelchair. She stared at her briefly and nodded. Then she returned to her room. Kamla followed her after she observed the frown on her forehead.

"Mother," whispered Kamla as she placed her hands on her shoulder while standing behind her, "I'm your daughter-in-law. Sorry Mark didn't inform you."

Dorothy moved to the window in her room and gazed **momentarily** outside before turning back to Kamla. She was angry.

"What's your name?" Dorothy asked.

"Kamla."

"Oh, yes. Now I **recall**. Mark recently called, and during our conversation he mentioned he was in love with you. He mentioned he wanted to marry you, but he said nothing about planning a wedding. . . . I guess you're Indian."

"I'm Indian and **Hinduism** is my religion."

"Kamla, I shouldn't be **annoyed** with you. My son always disappoints me. I've always looked forward to the day of his wedding. Witnessing his marriage ceremony would have been the happiest day of my life. It would have been my only dream to come true. I guess all parents feel the same way about their children. Thank God your parents were blessed to do the **rituals** your culture expected of you. Kamla, I don't understand why my only son, my only child, **concealed** his marriage from me, his darling mother."

Dorothy wept as she expressed her **profound** and sincere feelings about her expectations of her son, Mark. Kamla **consoled** her as she tried desperately to **suppress** her emotions while discussing Mark. After Dorothy **regained** her **composure**, Kamla continued chatting with her.

"Mother, don't feel bad. I'm his wife and yet Mark **seldom** listens to me. I **implored** him to bring you to City Hall, where we were married, but he refused. I regret that I didn't come to visit you earlier and have you and my family plan a beautiful wedding ceremony for us together."

"My dear Kamla, I feel Mark doesn't care about me."

"What makes you feel so, Dorothy?"

"I'm not positive. But I guess he's **ashamed** of my physical handicap. Thank God I am **regaining** some strength in my right arm."

"Mother, I disagree with you. He is not **embarrassed** about your handicap. Mark loves you dearly."

"What reason would he have to stay away from me, Kamla? I needed him desperately for moral support when I initially came here. Unfortunately, he never returned the hundreds of phone calls I made to him."

"I promise I'll find out why he was behaving strangely toward you, Mother."

Their conversation was briefly interrupted by Dorothy's nurse. She brought her medication and inquired as to what she wanted for lunch. Kamla told her that she had prepared a home-cooked meal for Dorothy. The nurse was happy to hear that. It was the first time Dorothy had enjoyed food from home since she had entered the nursing home.

"That's very thoughtful of you to prepare lunch for me," said Dorothy.

"I wasn't certain whether you would give me a warm reception and **embrace** me as your daughter-in-law."

"Why were you uncertain? Do you think I won't accept you because you're Indian?

"I don't know."

"Listen to me, my daughter. We're all God's children regardless of how we look or where we're from. My psychology and sociology professors in college always said that cultural differences have their own **unique** strengths that we often fail to **acknowledge** and respect. Nowadays, our failure to accept people for who they are seems to be the **catalyst** for **conflict**, **confrontation**, and **upheaval** in our 'global village,' as they call it. I don't even want to talk about our world, which is **replete** with misery, greed, poverty, and **bigotry**. Children rebel against parents if they are around to perform their parental duties. Nations fight against nations. And the list of **maladies** may be **infinite**. I love the **technology**, the devices, and scientific advancement, that I read about in the newspaper and on the Internet. But is there a price we're paying for it, Kamla?"

Kamla was caught off-guard by Dorothy's **candor**. At one point, she thought she was listening to a preacher or possibly a professor. Kamla knew she was an educated woman and had great respect for her **intellect** and knowledge of world affairs. Her visit to Dorothy was meant to help her **bond** with her as her daughter-in-law. It seemed she had succeeded. Dorothy was already very comfortable with her, and it was difficult to get her to **quit** talking as if there were no tomorrow. They ate together, and after enjoying the food, Dorothy eagerly continued her conversation with Kamla.

"Tell me when my grandchild is expected, Kamla."

"Two more months of sleepless nights."

"I hope Mark is assisting you with the household **chores**. The cleaning, cooking, and other **tasks**."

"He's **seldom** at home. I'm **extremely** unhappy, Mother. I didn't expect marriage would have brought so much **immeasurable** pain, such **unbearable agony**. It seems as if my **destiny** has **imprisoned** me in **unspeakable** sorrow."

On hearing those words, Dorothy bent forward from her wheelchair and tried to hug her with her left arm. Kamla wept in **solemn** silence.

"My daughter, you can always count on my affection."

"I'm positive of that. But Mark has **betrayed** me."

"What has he done?"

"I suspect he's having an **extramarital** affair."

"No doubt you have reasons for suspecting that he is having an **intimate** relationship with someone."

"I do. Mark hasn't slept with me for several months."

"Kamla, recently my anger towards him has been growing in **magnitude**."

"I fear what might happen after the child I'm carrying is born."

"Be positive and **valiant**. You must be brave and strong. You must face the future with courage and **confidence**."

"Mother Dorothy, I **admire** you for your spirit to carry on **boldly** despite your physical limitation."

"Honey, this is only a temporary inconvenience, a **setback** that I'll eventually **surmount**."

"Mother, how long will you be here?"

"Only time can tell."

"I want to bring you home with me."

Instantaneously, a broad smile appeared on Dorothy's face at Kamla's expression of genuine care and compassion. The smile **lingered** as she thoughtfully said, "This is the most generous offer I've had. But I'd rather not be a **burden** on you."

"Please, I **insist** you live with me."

"No, my dear. All I want is for you to be there if I need help," said Dorothy.

"You can **rely** on me. I'll always be there for you."

It was a beautiful, sunny summer day. The sky was clear and the breeze was **soothing**. People were enjoying themselves in the park nearby. Dorothy looked forward to spending the rest of the day with Kamla.

Slowly, Kamla wheeled Dorothy outside the nursing home to have dessert under a tree in the park. They **conversed** on a variety of subjects, but only one in particular caught Kamla's attention.

"Dorothy, I observe you're very sensitive when it comes to discussing your physical handicap," Kamla said with **tact**.

"Don't misunderstand me. I can **cope** with it. It would be silly of me not to deal with it in a positive manner."

"I'm glad you feel so."

"Specifically, what do you want to ask about my handicap?"

"Who's paying your medical expenses?"

"I don't know. Isn't this a government-supported nursing home?"

"No. It's the most expensive private institution in New York City."

"This doesn't make sense, Kamla. Nobody asked me about payment or insurance coverage."

"Senator Rex is probably arranging payment."

Dorothy suddenly dropped her glass of iced tea. It was obvious that she was upset and **irate**.

"What do you know about Senator Rex?" Dorothy asked.

"Nothing much."

"I **presume** you were told about my husband as well."

"Mark mentioned his working relationship with Senator Rex."

"Do you think my husband was murdered or **kidnapped**?"

"It's difficult to say if it's a case of **homicide**. But I have the feeling that Mark will determine this soon."

"I hope so."

"Dorothy, did your doctor say what the chance of your complete recovery is?"

"**Slim**. He said highly unlikely."

"I don't agree with him. There's a medical center in Mumbai, a major city in India, that is **famous** for successfully treating this sort of paralysis. Its director is the world's **authority** on it. I'm positive there'll be no need for a wheelchair after he treats you."

"I'd imagine this sort of surgery and follow-up therapy can cost **approximately** one million dollars."

"That's a close **estimate**. Post-surgery therapy can last for about a year or more."

"My child, where will I get this **astronomical** amount of money?"

"Don't worry. I'll **devise** a plan. I'll figure out a way to get it."

"You're **incredible**, Kamla. You're unbelievable. My **steadfast** love for you is forever."

"I'll always love you too, Dorothy."

"Can you keep a promise, Kamla?"

"Certainly."

What Did Dorothy Give Kamla to Keep?

Dorothy reached under her blouse and **meticulously** removed a small object, about three by three inches in size, from her bra. It was **wrapped** with gift paper and sealed with Scotch tape. She gave it to Kamla.

"What's this?" Kamla asked while examining the package curiously.

"It's a gift. I want you to have it. But you cannot open it until the most **propitious** time. You must not tell anybody about it, including your husband."

"How will I know when the appropriate time is?"

"You'll know. Your **intuition** will **compel** you to open it when the time is right."

"May I ask why you were concealing it in your bra?"

"I think it's invaluable. It's **priceless**. And that was the safest place to hide it."

"You remind me of my grandma in India. She is the only one I know who would hide something in her bra. By the way, what is it that you are hiding?" asked Kamla.

"You're not supposed to know as yet," insisted Dorothy.

"I promise I won't ask again. But how do you know it's priceless?"

"I caught those two **hoodlums**, the men who were **harassing** you before I **intervened**, **rummaging** through my room the day I was brought here."

"It's difficult to believe they were as **bold** and **presumptuous** as to **commit** such a **despicable** act in your presence."

"They didn't do it in my presence."

"Where were you?"

"In my bathroom. They thought I was elsewhere with the nurse."

"How do you know this package is what they were searching **frantically** for?"

"My **intuition**, my daughter. My gut feeling. After that day, I kept it in my bra. Even my nurse isn't aware of it."

"Then I guess Senator Rex is after it if these **scoundrels** are working for him."

"Absolutely. But I **vow** to beat him at his own **devious** tricks. Just **ensure** he doesn't find out you have it."

Dorothy suddenly saw Senator Rex's security guards coming in their direction. The looks on their faces said that something had changed their minds about hurting her and Kamla. She commanded Kamla to leave immediately, before they saw her. Kamla **protested vehemently**.

"Don't be foolish, my dear. I beg you to leave before those two devils get here," said Dorothy, pointing to the security guards.

"No. I can't **abandon** you. I can't leave you alone out here. I'll take you back to your room," Kamla insisted.

"My nurse will assist me. Please go away for your own sake. I love you, my child."

Kamla sensed that Dorothy must have **detected** danger was **lurking**, so she left hurriedly on her insistence. When she was less than fifteen yards from the exit of the nursing home's **compound**, the two men yelled at her to wait for them. She began running but did not get too far. Kamla **stumbled** and fell. As she screamed with agonizing pain **emanating** from her stomach, she lost consciousness. The men became afraid and walked away, pretending they had never seen her before.

Were Kamla and Her Unborn Baby Saved?

The doctor on duty in the emergency room, Rachael Peterson, knew Kamla's condition was **complicated** and **critical**. She did not have much experience dealing with her medical condition and immediately **summoned** the chief of **obstetrics** to the emergency room. He was trained to deal with pregnancy problems and would know what to do. When he entered the room, he stared at Kamla for a minute as if he were studying her.

"Dr. Varghese, would you stop staring at her and do something?" Dr. Peterson asked **vociferously** while the other staff members were anxiously waiting for instructions.

"Sorry, Rachael," Dr. Varghese said. "No need to be so loud."

Dr. Varghese proceeded to examine Kamla. The medical staff had always looked forward to working with him because of his **expertise** and international **reputation** in saving the lives of premature babies They were eager to see him at work.

"What's the matter, Dr. Varghese?" asked Dr. Peterson when he took off his gloves.

"I don't think there's much we can do for her, Rachael."

"We just can't leave her bleeding to death."

"The injection you saw me **administering** will minimize the bleeding shortly."

Dr. Peterson inquired, "Can't we save the baby? The baby is about seven months old."

"Are you aware that if we operate to save the mother, the baby will possibly die? If we attempt to save the baby, the mother will likely die," replied Dr. Varghese.

"But it's this hospital's policy to save the mother first. I don't understand why we're wasting precious time that could mean the difference between her life and her death," Dr. Peterson reminded him.

"Please be patient, Doctor . . . Rachael," said Dr. Varghese.

"Dr. Varghese, are you feeling well?" asked Dr. Peterson after observing Dr. Varghese's unusual facial expression.

"Of course."

"It seems as if you know this patient."

"She is dear to me. I have her photograph at home. It was given to me," remarked Dr. Varghese.

"Then do something. Help the poor woman."

"We must save the mother and the unborn child," said Dr. Varghese.

"That's impossible, Doctor. Nobody has done this before with a woman in her state of health."

"But we must take the **risk**."

"Will you do the procedure?"

"I dare not."

"Then who will?"

Dr. Varghese did not reply, but he rushed to the nearest telephone to make a call. It was Saturday night, and he was not certain whether his friend and classmate from medical school was at home.

The telephone rang more than a dozen times. Then, for a moment, there was silence. He worried that he might have been **disconnected**. Luckily, as he was about to hang up, his friend's answering service responded. Dr. Varghese felt relieved and walked **briskly** to the operating room to make preparations for an emergency operation.

"You haven't answered my question, Dr. Varghese," Dr. Peterson reminded him.

"What question?"

"Who's doing the procedure?"

"Be patient, Rachael. I have everything under control now."

The staff of the operating room was ready to assist the surgeon, but he had not arrived as yet. Dr. Varghese's nervousness was becoming **evident**. More than thirty minutes had **elapsed** and he felt his friend should have already arrived. As he was about to dial his number again, he saw him rushing down the hallway in his direction.

"Thanks for coming. We have a young woman who fell an hour ago," said Dr. Varghese to **apprise** his friend of the situation. They entered the scrub room and began preparing for surgery. "The child is probably seriously hurt. The mother is seven months pregnant."

"Help me with the gown while I put these gloves on. Was the staff briefed on the procedure?" his friend asked.

"Yes. We've even made arrangements in case complications should arise."

Both doctors **proceeded** to the operating room. Dr. Varghese was prepared to take a few **abusive** remarks from his friend that night.

"You **idiot**, Varghese, how could you've done this to me?" asked his friend with **fierce** anger.

"What are you **alluding** to, Azeez?" asked Dr. Varghese **presumptuously**.

"You **moron**, Varghese, do you expect me to deliver this **tramp's** baby? Do you think I forgot how she **humiliated** me in India?" asked Dr. Azeez.

Dr. Azeez extracted his hands from his gloves and threw them on the floor angrily. He rushed out of the operating room. Dr. Varghese ran after him and **scolded** him vigorously.

"My friend, I agree that Kamla hurt your feelings. But you can't **permit** your emotions to **interfere** with your judgment, professional **obligation**, and commitment to your patient. You've taken an oath to **preserve** and save lives. Have you forgotten the significance of the **Hippocratic Oath** you have taken as a medical doctor?"

"She's your patient and not mine, Varghese," replied Dr. Azeez.

"A woman and her unborn baby are desperately **clinging** to their final **shred** of life," Dr. Varghese **lectured** him. "You're their last hope, Azeez. Don't deprive them of **precious** life. Beneath that **dense** cloud of anger you have been **nurturing**, there's still a **comforting** pillow of love for Kamla. **Refrain** from making **derogatory** remarks about her. She is not the loose woman you always **portray** her to be. Having **multiple** relationships with men does not make her a **lascivious**, **lewd**, or **lustful** woman. She isn't a woman of loose morals. She was just being **assertive** in her **quest** for the right guy to marry. Times have **radically** changed. And you must change with them too, especially if you are going to live in America. You are now **residing** in a **cosmopolitan** area, not a **rural** one. New York isn't like the tiny village of Gangaram from where you came. So get back in the operating room and do what you do best."

"Varghese, you're a **master manipulator**. You're **adept** at **inflicting** guilty feelings on my clear **conscience**," Dr. Azeez complained to his **pal**, Dr. Varghese.

The operation lasted for at least eight hours. A **cardiologist** and a **pulmonologist** were on **standby** to **render** assistance if something went wrong with either patient's heart or lungs. Occasionally, during the surgery, Dr. Azeez felt helpless to save Kamla and her child because of serious complications, but his **confidant**, Dr. Varghese, was at his side to advise him and **urge** him on. Neither regretted the risk they took because a healthy, male baby was born.

Kamla was slowly **regaining** consciousness. Dr. Peterson and the staff cheered Dr. Azeez's **superb** success. He had just performed a **miracle**. Never before had an **intricate** surgery like the one he had just performed been done in America. The United States Citizenship and Immigration Service had not **erred** in its judgment when it **awarded** Dr. Azeez a green card because of his **exceptional expertise** in the field of obstetrics.

"Varghese, why did you let me perform the operation?" asked Dr. Azeez when they were back in the scrub room.

"Because of the power of love."

"Stop talking like a teenager, Varghese."

"You and I know that the chance of saving the baby was very **slim**. Somehow, I felt that because of your love for Kamla, you'd **exhaust** your **mental faculties** to save the child. I didn't have the **expertise** to perform that historical operation. I'm proud of your **remarkable**, **spectacular**, and **stellar** performance, Azeez. You made India proud!"

Dr. Azeez was a very simple and **humble** doctor. He was not good at accepting **compliments**. He felt it was his moral obligation as a doctor and a human being to save lives. He was sorry for the temper **tantrum** he had **displayed** when he saw Kamla prior to operating on her. Still, Dr. Azeez did not have any love for Kamla now. He felt relieved now that he had **vented** the anger that had been **residing** in his heart since the day Kamla had left him at the hotel in India. It had given him a great feeling of relief. He felt as if a ton of rocks had been lifted off his shoulders.

"Can you do something for me, Varghese?"

"Depends—"

"I'd appreciate if you didn't tell Kamla I'm working here," interrupted Dr. Azeez. "Please don't mention I performed the surgery."

"I can't **conceal** the truth, Azeez."

"Why are you indirectly insisting that I stay in touch with Kamla?"

"Try to **forgive** her. Put the past behind you. Kamla is more **mature** now than she was a year or two ago. Everybody makes mistakes. Nobody is **infallible**."

"I can't forgive her for putting me through the emotional **turmoil** I experienced after she left me in India without an explanation."

Dr. Peterson entered Dr. Varghese's office to inform him that Kamla had completely regained consciousness and wanted to speak to her doctor. Dr. Azeez suspected Dr. Varghese would ask him to visit Kamla, so he left the hospital without informing him.

"Hi Kamla, I'm Dr. Varghese. How are you feeling?"

"**Enervated**. Very weak. Will my baby grow up to be a healthy child?"

"Of course. Almost all premature babies eventually grow as healthy as other kids. Don't you worry, dear!"

"Thanks for saving my baby's life."

"I didn't perform the operation."

"Who was it?"

Later that day, Dr. Varghese was laughing endlessly as Dr. Azeez **stormed** up to him. Dr. Azeez was **furious** because Dr. Varghese had tricked him into visiting Kamla.

"That's not funny, Varghese," Dr. Azeez **growled**.

"It was meant to be a **prank**, Azeez. Don't be so **uptight** and **stiff**. You don't have to be so firm and inflexible."

Confession of Love

Dr. Varghese had purposely hidden Dr. Azeez's apartment keys in his pocket so that he could lead him to Kamla's bedside, where he was standing. Kamla immediately recognized Dr. Azeez and was **startled** by his presence. She initiated a conversation with him and tried very hard to be **civil** and **cordial** to him. "Dr. Azeez, are my eyes **deceiving** me?" Kamla asked.

"No. But I'm surprised you remember my name," he replied as Dr. Varghese left them alone in the room.

"I'll understand if you never speak to me again. What I did to you in India was **cruel**, insensitive, inhuman and—"

"Please, there's no need to **recall** that incident. My primary **motive** is to ensure that you and your baby are healthy," interrupted Dr. Azeez.

"But I want to explain why I ran away from you, Dr. Azeez."

"It doesn't matter now."

"It does, Dr. Azeez. I was in love with Mark at that time. I found myself slowly starting to love you as well. So I became frightened. I didn't know how to deal with my feelings, so I returned to New York and married Mark."

"Kamla, I appreciate your honesty and sincerity. Things happen for the best sometimes. I'm glad that you have a family. Your life is complete now, and you seem to be happy."

"Things aren't always as rosy as they seem. **All that glitters is not gold**!"

"What do you mean, Kamla?" Dr. Azeez inquired.

"Things are not what they look like on the surface. Marrying Mark was the most **deleterious** decision I have made in my life. I'm angry, bitter, and frustrated."

"Why do you say that?"

"**Numerous** reasons. Do you see him here?"

"I don't know him."

"Dr. Peterson and her staff requested that he visit me in the emergency room several times, but he never showed up."

"Why?"

"He doesn't care about me. I have the feeling that he wants a **divorce**."

"I hope both of you can work things out and save the marriage."

"That's very kind of you to wish us well in spite of the way I treated you in the hotel in India. When did you come to New York?"

"A few months ago. Varghese **persuaded** his boss that I was the best applicant for this job. I'm **indebted** to him. I owe him a lot. He is a true friend."

"Dr. Azeez, I'm feeling a bit tired. I must rest a few hours. Thanks for saving my baby and my life."

"It was my duty. Get some rest—you've lost a substantial amount of blood. Either Dr. Varghese or I will drop by to examine you and the baby tomorrow."

EXERCISE 1

Applying the Words You Have Learned to Critical Thinking and Creative Writing

- Use the two questions in Section A below to discuss this chapter with your classmates. Be sure to apply your critical thinking skills.

- Write an essay about either question using the vocabulary words you know from real-life experiences and the new ones you have learned from this text.

Section A

Discussion Questions

1. Can you guess what Dorothy gave Kamla to keep?

2. As a medical doctor, did Dr. Azeez behave professionally toward Kamla?

EXERCISE 2

Synonyms: Multiple Choice

■ Circle the letter of the word or phrase that is most similar in meaning to the **boldfaced** word.

1. **yearn**	**A.** irritate	**B.** satisfy	**C.** suffice	**D.** crave
2. **zest**	**A.** silence	**B.** danger	**C.** simplicity	**D.** passion
3. **yell**	**A.** whisper	**B.** murmur	**C.** scream	**D.** chatter
4. **seduce**	**A.** tempt	**B.** leave	**C.** minimize	**D.** like
5. **vulgar**	**A.** respectable	**B.** vicious	**C.** obscene	**D.** known
6. **vigilant**	**A.** careless	**B.** alert	**C.** carefree	**D.** sleepy
7. **vent**	**A.** closet	**B.** door	**C.** opening	**D.** valve
8. **whine**	**A.** complain	**B.** agree	**C.** support	**D.** bark
9. **wrinkle**	**A.** crease	**B.** iron	**C.** bend	**D.** scratch
10. **synchronize**	**A.** elicit	**B.** cause to happen at same time	**C.** resist	**D.** mark
11. **surrender**	**A.** reject	**B.** run	**C.** speed	**D.** give up
12. **sullen**	**A.** satisfied	**B.** joyful	**C.** unhappy	**D.** jubilant
13. **transient**	**A.** stable	**B.** passing	**C.** permanent	**D.** stubborn
14. **trespass**	**A.** intrude	**B.** invite	**C.** stay	**D.** implore
15. **salient**	**A.** significant	**B.** unimportant	**C.** shocking	**D.** salty
16. **vehement**	**A.** passive	**B.** blunt	**C.** secure	**D.** forceful
17. **vulnerable**	**A.** protective	**B.** strong	**C.** unprotected	**D.** secure
18. **valiant**	**A.** cowardly	**B.** brave	**C.** valuable	**D.** awkward
19. **warp**	**A.** deform	**B.** normalize	**C.** conform	**D.** decide
20. **whisper**	**A.** shout	**B.** murmur	**C.** yell	**D.** snore

EXERCISE 3

Synonyms and Antonyms

■ Write the corresponding letter for the synonym and antonym of each **boldfaced** word.

	Synonym	Antonym			
1. **moderate**	_____	_____	**A.** average	**B.** considerable	**C.** liberal
2. **morbid**	_____	_____	**A.** controlling	**B.** ghastly	**C.** pleasant
3. **minute**	_____	_____	**A.** tiny	**B.** short	**C.** enormous
4. **magnificent**	_____	_____	**A.** splendid	**B.** fearful	**C.** plain
5. **mandate**	_____	_____	**A.** command to act	**B.** request	**C.** purpose
6. **miniature**	_____	_____	**A.** small	**B.** huge	**C.** thrilling
7. **miscellaneous**	_____	_____	**A.** tasty	**B.** diversified	**C.** homogeneous
8. **mischievous**	_____	_____	**A.** naughty	**B.** exciting	**C.** obedient
9. **mistreat**	_____	_____	**A.** abuse	**B.** protect	**C.** propose
10. **mutual**	_____	_____	**A.** shared	**B.** useful	**C.** separate
11. **negligent**	_____	_____	**A.** careless	**B.** careful	**C.** irregular
12. **nuisance**	_____	_____	**A.** annoyance	**B.** criminality	**C.** delight
13. **need**	_____	_____	**A.** buy	**B.** want	**C.** have
14. **nominal**	_____	_____	**A.** small	**B.** dastardly	**C.** large
15. **nullify**	_____	_____	**A.** void	**B.** enact	**C.** arrest
16. **nebulous**	_____	_____	**A.** unclear	**B.** shiny	**C.** apparent
17. **nonchalant**	_____	_____	**A.** easygoing	**B.** tense	**C.** expensive
18. **notify**	_____	_____	**A.** inform	**B.** withhold	**C.** distrust
19. **objective**	_____	_____	**A.** unbiased	**B.** subjective	**C.** similar
20. **oblivious**	_____	_____	**A.** ingenious	**B.** unaware	**C.** knowledgeable
21. **obligate**	_____	_____	**A.** require	**B.** fear	**C.** release
22. **optimum**	_____	_____	**A.** eager	**B.** best	**C.** worst
23. **optimistic**	_____	_____	**A.** hopeful	**B.** discouraging	**C.** tolerable
24. **organize**	_____	_____	**A.** orate	**B.** arrange	**C.** disorder
25. **pathetic**	_____	_____	**A.** pitiful	**B.** frightful	**C.** cheerful

	Synonym	Antonym			
26. **parallel**	______	______	**A.** similar	**B.** different	**C.** pleasant
27. **passive**	______	______	**A.** desperate	**B.** inactive	**C.** busy
28. **patron**	______	______	**A.** customer	**B.** brilliance	**C.** owner
29. **pain**	______	______	**A.** ache	**B.** pleasure	**C.** fear
30. **patience**	______	______	**A.** tolerance	**B.** anxiety	**C.** hospital
31. **ponder**	______	______	**A.** think about deeply	**B.** ignore	**C.** liberate
32. **predominant**	______	______	**A.** principal	**B.** terse	**C.** minor
33. **prerequisite**	______	______	**A.** frozen	**B.** required	**C.** non-essential
34. **prevalent**	______	______	**A.** widespread	**B.** fiery	**C.** limited
35. **prompt**	______	______	**A.** punctual	**B.** late	**C.** fussy
36. **plausible**	______	______	**A.** likely to be true	**B.** unbelievable	**C.** hateful
37. **prudent**	______	______	**A.** pleased	**B.** wise	**C.** foolish
38. **proficient**	______	______	**A.** capable	**B.** dangerous	**C.** inept
39. **panic**	______	______	**A.** scare	**B.** comfort	**C.** deceive
40. **paralyze**	______	______	**A.** disable	**B.** heal	**C.** justify
41. **pardon**	______	______	**A.** charge	**B.** forgive	**C.** punish
42. **partial**	______	______	**A.** incomplete	**B.** restricted	**C.** whole
43. **pensive**	______	______	**A.** thoughtful	**B.** uninterested	**C.** showy
44. **perturb**	______	______	**A.** disturb	**B.** calm	**C.** damage
45. **postpone**	______	______	**A.** carry	**B.** delay	**C.** expedite
46. **positive**	______	______	**A.** certain	**B.** doubtful	**C.** sick
47. **resign**	______	______	**A.** quit	**B.** remain	**C.** fight
48. **rescue**	______	______	**A.** organize	**B.** save	**C.** abandon
49. **retain**	______	______	**A.** retail	**B.** maintain	**C.** discard
50. **revoke**	______	______	**A.** cancel	**B.** defend	**C.** restore
51. **rupture**	______	______	**A.** break	**B.** mend	**C.** aggravate
52. **respond**	______	______	**A.** touch	**B.** reply	**C.** question
53. **scandal**	______	______	**A.** disgrace	**B.** humor	**C.** honor

	Synonym	Antonym			
54. **severe**	______	______	**A.** serious	**B.** talkative	**C.** mild
55. **sane**	______	______	**A.** sensible	**B.** irrational	**C.** honorable
56. **satisfy**	______	______	**A.** please	**B.** toughen	**C.** displease
57. **stimulate**	______	______	**A.** arouse	**B.** stifle	**C.** complicate
58. **submit**	______	______	**A.** present	**B.** import	**C.** withdraw
59. **solace**	______	______	**A.** comfort	**B.** distress	**C.** dictation
60. **sporadic**	______	______	**A.** irregular	**B.** frequent	**C.** jumpy
61. **seduce**	______	______	**A.** energize	**B.** tempt	**C.** repel
62. **select**	______	______	**A.** offer	**B.** choose	**C.** reject
63. **sentimental**	______	______	**A.** emotional	**B.** subsidize	**C.** unfeeling
64. **significant**	______	______	**A.** important	**B.** trivial	**C.** phobia
65. **steal**	______	______	**A.** pilfer	**B.** earn	**C.** grant
66. **sterilized**	______	______	**A.** abnormal	**B.** disinfected	**C.** contaminated
67. **substitute**	______	______	**A.** replace	**B.** sustain	**C.** develop
68. **succulent**	______	______	**A.** juicy	**B.** dry	**C.** fresh
69. **surpass**	______	______	**A.** exceed	**B.** weep	**C.** fail
70. **suspicious**	______	______	**A.** distrustful	**B.** awkward	**C.** trusting
71. **render**	______	______	**A.** give	**B.** withdraw	**C.** omit
72. **replenish**	______	______	**A.** renew	**B.** use	**C.** torture
73. **request**	______	______	**A.** ask	**B.** respond	**C.** invert

EXERCISE 4

Matching Meanings: Set 1

■ Match each word with its meaning.

_____	1. vehement	**A.** shining through
_____	2. tenuous	**B.** full of intense feeling; violent
_____	3. urgency	**C.** too willing to serve or obey
_____	4. superfluous	**D.** unclear; vague; indefinite
_____	5. translucent	**E.** having little substance; weak
_____	6. quagmire	**F.** overwhelm with a great amount
_____	7. panorama	**G.** immediate action
_____	8. obsequious	**H.** not planned; unintentional
_____	9. malicious	**I.** spiteful; intentionally mischievous
_____	10. nebulous	**J.** excessive; unnecessary
_____	11. inadvertent	**K.** a wide view in all directions
_____	12. inundate	**L.** a difficult situation that is not easy to avoid

EXERCISE 5

Matching Meanings: Set 2

■ Match each word with its meaning.

_____	1. corroborate	**A.** not respectable; having a bad reputation
_____	2. dexterous	**B.** make more intense; aggravate
_____	3. disreputable	**C.** hint or suggest
_____	4. dissent	**D.** give support; confirm
_____	5. exacerbate	**E.** noise; disorder; confusion
_____	6. fallacy	**F.** that which cannot be corrected; not curable
_____	7. garrulous	**G.** a record of daily happenings
_____	8. imply	**H.** clever or skillful with hands or body
_____	9. inculcate	**I.** a false opinion or idea; misleading
_____	10. pandemonium	**J.** differ in opinion or belief
_____	11. incurable	**K.** impress upon by persistent urging
_____	12. journal	**L.** talking too much about unimportant things

EXERCISE 6

Word Meaning in Context: Set 1

■ Read each sentence and find the missing word in the box below. Fill in the blank with the correct *form* of that word.

quagmire	**superfluous**	**inadvertent**	**vehemence**
nebulous	**urgent**	**inundate**	**panorama**
obsequious	**malicious**	**tenuous**	**translucent**

1. Despite the ___________ of his doctor's warnings, Oliver continued to smoke.
2. The prosecutor destroyed their ___________ defense with a single question.
3. The teacher received an ___________ message to call home while he was in the middle of class.
4. Taking large doses of vitamins is thought to be ___________ by many doctors.
5. You cannot see through stained glass windows, but they allow light to enter the room because they are ___________.
6. Having too many credit cards often puts one in a ___________ of debt from which it is difficult to escape.
7. The ___________ of the Painted Desert is breathtaking.
8. His ___________ behavior toward the boss angered his fellow workers, but he got the raise he wanted.
9. Her friend's ___________ comment hurt her and brought tears to her eyes.
10. The young girl's ___________ idea of God was of an old man who sat on clouds and had a long, white beard.
11. Although the senator's remark was ___________, it caused an uproar the following day when the newspapers reported it as a deliberate attack.
12. After winning the lottery, she was ___________ with calls from friends and relatives.

EXERCISE 7

Word Meaning in Context: Set 2

■ Read each sentence and find the missing word in the box below. Fill in the blank with the correct *form* of that word.

fallacy	**pandemonium**	**incurable**	**corroborate**
dexterous	**garrulous**	**imply**	**disreputable**
journal	**dissent**	**inculcate**	**exacerbate**

1. The evidence ___________ the witness's testimony that Latif was not at the scene of the crime.
2. One has to be somewhat ___________ to master origami, the Japanese art of paper folding.
3. Do not buy a used car from that man; he is ___________.
4. A murmur of ___________ arose from the crowd when the president announced yet another tax increase.
5. Arguing with her will only ___________ an already uncomfortable situation and could result in a fight.
6. Since bulls are colorblind, it is a ___________ that they charge the bullfighter because of the red cape.
7. A ___________ nature is a good quality in a salesperson.

8. Although he did not directly say that he was unhappy, his frequent absences from home __________ a dissatisfaction with his marriage.

9. Parents can __________ a love of literature by reading to their children at an early age.

10. __________ broke out when they announced that the concert was sold out, and the police were called in to restore order.

11. Many forms of cancer are __________.

12. Keeping a __________ is a good way to improve writing skills.

EXERCISE 8

Context Clues

■ Select the word or phrase that most closely matches the meaning of the **boldfaced** word. *Note that replacing the **boldfaced** word with the right answer might not produce a grammatically correct sentence.*

1. She was a genius at **promoting** new fashion ideas, and the clothing she marketed was often worn by movie stars.
   A. delaying publication **B.** making popular **C.** stealing from others **D.** buying at low cost

2. Eating meals with a higher **proportion** of animal products than plant products may result in weight gain.
   A. cost **B.** fattiness **C.** oil **D.** amount

3. The job **prospect** had a promising outlook because she had experience.
   A. candidate **B.** application **C.** recruiter **D.** employer

4. The factory has a **protocol** of strict safety rules to prevent accidents.
   A. bias **B.** code **C.** journal **D.** lack

5. Doctors of **psychology** can counsel people who face emotional challenges, but only psychiatrists can prescribe drugs.
   A. the study of wildlife **B.** the study of the ocean
   C. the study of the mind **D.** the study of society

6. According to an article in a scientific **publication**, several psychiatrists have determined that the new drug does not treat depression effectively.
   A. periodical **B.** something erased **C.** something found **D.** something praised

7. Janet was thrilled to learn her poem would be **published** in the university's literary magazine.
   A. read **B.** printed **C.** paid **D.** reviewed

8. Mayor Ronald Jones told a reporter that she had not accurately **quoted** the words he had used at a press conference.
   A. investigated **B.** mocked **C.** repeated **D.** slandered

9. He made a **radical** change in his career by leaving his position as a medical doctor to become a skydiving instructor.
   A. extreme **B.** scary **C.** planned **D.** traditional

10. He was surprised when he was **randomly** selected from the audience to sing in the national talent show.
    A. done with too much planning **B.** done without plan
    C. done professionally **D.** done in a timely manner

11. The children were amazed at the **range** of games they could play at the amusement park.
    A. cost **B.** height **C.** variety **D.** joy

12. Because it is such a popular idea, the **ratio** of the number of people who want a new school built to those who do not is ten to one.
    A. relationship **B.** argument **C.** enthusiasm **D.** money

13. Commuters **reacted** with anger when an increase in bus fares was announced.
    A. cheered **B.** responded **C.** steamed **D.** laughed

14. Many nutritionists discourage people from eating **refined** foods because of their poor nutritional value.
    A. tainted **B.** flavored **C.** processed **D.** bubbly

15. People cheered when younger, more progressive elected leaders replaced the old military **regime**.
    A. form of government **B.** form of prayer **C.** form of praise **D.** form of discussion

16. Gangaram was the only town in the **region** that was experiencing job growth.
    A. agenda **B.** government **C.** area **D.** decision

17. After several years of dispute, the homeowners were able to **resolve** their argument about whether to keep the trees that bordered their homes.
    A. wrestle **B.** waste **C.** settle **D.** confess

18. The African continent has always been rich in natural **resources** and now has a recently discovered oilfield.
    A. fields of corn **B.** wisdom
    C. natural wealth **D.** jewels

19. He **responded** by threatening violence when his boss told him he was losing his job.
    A. lied **B.** reacted **C.** yelled **D.** thought

20. He was relieved when the computer technician **restored** his Internet service, allowing him to return to work.
    A. gave away **B.** held up **C.** brought back **D.** discontinued

21. The **revenue** that the non-profit organization reported to the board was lower than expected.
    A. faith **B.** clarity **C.** income **D.** bridge

22. The state government refused to **reverse** its decision to increase tolls despite protests against it.
    A. go back on **B.** agree with **C.** explain **D.** ignore

23. A **revolution** began when the dictator refused to step down after thirty-five years in office.
    A. victory **B.** sentiment **C.** uprising **D.** violence

24. The promotion put Sandra in a new **role** with more responsibilities and higher pay.
    A. ceremony **B.** office **C.** plan **D.** position

EXERCISE 9

Vocabulary Test

- Select the correct answer.
- Hint: Review the meanings of all the **boldfaced** words in this chapter before you take the test. This approach can help you to score 100 percent.
- Record the percentage of correct answers on the Master Self-Assessment table on page 397.

1 **Vulgar** remarks are:

A. respectable
B. clear
C. unknown
D. obscene; offensive

2 A **vigilant** guard is:

E. careless
F. watchful
G. carefree
H. sleepy

3 To **vent** your feelings is to:

A. let them out forcefully
B. close them
C. suppress them
D. hold them

4 To **whine** is to:

E. support
F. agree
G. see
H. complain

5 To **synchronize** things is to:

A. resist them
B. mark them with labels
C. pack them in a box
D. make them happen at the same time

6 **Transient** rain showers:

E. are stable
F. are permanent
G. last only a short time
H. follow a particular path

7 To **trespass** on someone's land is to:

A. stay
B. enter without permission
C. implore to be admitted
D. be invited

8 **Salient** facts are:

E. most important or significant
F. alarming
G. unimportant
H. shocking

9 Someone who is **vulnerable** is:

A. protected
B. strong
C. secured
D. open to attack

10 A **valiant** person is:

E. cowardly
F. brave
G. quiet
H. articulate

11 Something **warped**:

A. is normal
B. becomes damaged by bending
C. is decisive
D. has been confirmed

12 A **magnificent** palace is usually:

E. exceptionally beautiful
F. plain and simple
G. dull and dirty
H. crowded with people

13 A **mandate** is:

A. an authoritative command
B. a request
C. a release
D. an article

14 **Mischievous** means:

E. playfully annoying
F. being a bully
G. leading a group
H. fighting an enemy

15 A **mutual** interest in sports is:

A. shared
B. selfish
C. obsessive
D. long-lasting

16 Someone who is a **nuisance** is:

E. annoying
F. fearful
G. happy
H. peaceful

17 **Nominal** means:

A. very small

B. very large

C. tall

D. short

18 To **nullify** means to:

E. ignore

F. reinstate

G. cancel

H. embrace

19 Someone who has a **nonchalant** attitude:

A. is tense

B. is serious

C. is frustrating

D. appears not to worry or care

20 To **notify** someone is to:

E. distrust

F. inform

G. scold

H. punish

21 If you are **oblivious** to something, you are:

A. aware

B. educated

C. unaware

D. supportive

22 To **obligate** means to:

E. make indebted

F. fear

G. release

H. ignore

23 A **pathetic** person is:

A. fearful

B. cheerful

C. sad and helpless

D. desperate

24 To **ponder** something is to:

E. consider thoughtfully

F. forget

G. ignore

H. punch

25 Something **predominant** is:

A. minor

B. unimportant

C. unnoticeable

D. most important

26 A **prerequisite** is a:

E. story
F. necessity
G. course
H. class

27 Something **prevalent** is:

A. fiery
B. uncommon
C. widespread
D. scarce

28 A **plausible** explanation is:

E. believable
F. unreal
G. unclear
H. detailed

29 A **prudent** person is:

A. fearless
B. careless
C. wise and careful
D. harmless

30 A **proficient** mechanic is:

E. incapable
F. dangerous
G. neglectful
H. skillful

31 **Panic** is a:

A. dream
B. pain
C. fantasy
D. sudden, overpowering fear

32 To **revoke** a license is to:

E. maintain it
F. restore it
G. cancel it
H. destroy it

33 To **rupture** something is to:

A. burst it open
B. mend it
C. join it
D. connect it

34 To **stimulate** an interest in something is to:

E. provide
F. rouse to action
G. ignore
H. discuss

35 **Solace** refers to:

A. distress

B. advice

C. comfort in trouble

D. peace

36 **Sporadic** visits happen:

E. regularly

F. at irregular intervals

G. never

H. frequently

37 To **seduce** someone is to:

A. respect

B. ignore

C. be silent

D. lead astray by false promises

38 Another word for **sentimental** is:

E. emotional

F. rigid

G. unemotional

H. sensible

39 Something **significant** is:

A. trivial

B. casual

C. meaningless

D. meaningful

40 To **sterilize** a room is to:

E. contaminate it

F. make it free from germs

G. search it

H. decorate it

41 To **surpass** is to:

A. fail

B. signal

C. surprise

D. outdo or go beyond in achievement

42 To **render** assistance is to:

E. provide

F. withdraw

G. conceal

H. withhold

43 When you **replenish** something, you:

A. utilize it

B. repeat it

C. fill it again

D. drink it

44 To **corroborate** is to:

E. disagree

F. contest

G. ignore

H. confirm

45 A **dexterous** person is:

A. left-handed

B. right-handed

C. disabled

D. clever and skillful with hands

46 **Exacerbate** means to:

E. calm

F. improve

G. worsen

H. please

47 A **fallacy** is a:

A. truth

B. false or mistaken idea

C. fact

D. faraway place

48 A **garrulous** person is:

E. quiet

F. calm

G. hated

H. talkative about unimportant things

49 To **inculcate** means to:

A. calculate

B. impress repeatedly

C. graduate

D. counsel

50 **Pandemonium** at the parade means:

E. excitement

F. noisy and uncontrolled behavior

G. fear

H. boredom

51 **Vehement** opinions are:

A. respectable

B. mild

C. polite

D. strong feelings expressed forcefully

52 A **tenuous** argument is:

E. weak or has little substance

F. supported by fact

G. strong

H. opposed by most

53 **Superfluous** means:

A. insufficient

B. surprising

C. excessive or unnecessary

D. enough

54 Being in a **quagmire** means being in a:

E. nightmare

F. peaceful place

G. depression

H. difficult situation not easy to avoid

55 **Panorama** refers to a:

A. tour

B. wide view of an area in all directions

C. trip

D. limited view

56 An **obsequious** person is:

E. disobedient

F. obedient and very willing to serve

G. unwilling

H. secretive about unimportant things

57 A synonym for **malicious** is:

A. hateful

B. affectionate

C. happy

D. intelligent

58 Something **nebulous** is:

E. very clear

F. visible

G. not clear

H. nasty

59 An **inadvertent** mistake is:

A. unintentional

B. intentional

C. deliberate

D. silly

60 **Inundated** with something is to feel:

E. uncomfortable

F. comfortable

G. overwhelmed

H. uneasy

EXERCISE 10

Building a Stronger Vocabulary

- Review all the **boldfaced** words in this chapter before you proceed to the next exercise.
- Highlight the ones you are still having difficulty remembering.
- List them with their meanings on a table.
- Use them to compose your own sentences.
- Think of a synonym and an antonym for each word.
- Use checkmarks to indicate if each word you want to practice more has a prefix, suffix, and/or root.
- You may use the table below as a sample to write your answers in your notebook.

Word	Definition	Sentence	Synonym	Antonym	Prefix	Suffix	Root

EXERCISE 11

Creating My Own Powerful Word List

- Write the words and meanings from the above table on the **Creating My Own Powerful Word List** table on page 398. Review them often to build that super vocabulary you want to create for school, work, and everyday use.

Who is the Father of Kamla's Child? Chapter 14

PRE-READING

About This Chapter from *Trial of Love*

- Read the names and descriptions of this chapter's main characters below.
  - Julia: Mark's classmate in law school
  - General Geraldo: A general in the Cuban military
  - Senator Rex: United States Senator
  - Maxwell Edison: Mark's father
  - Dorothy Hubbard
  - Captain Turney: An employee of the Federal Bureau of Investigation
  - Erwin: Kamla's newborn baby
  - Perdita: General Geraldo's daughter
  - Debono: An employee of Senator Rex
  - Rev. Peter James: General Geraldo's cousin
  - Mark Edison Hubbard

Story Vocabulary Exercise

- Before you begin reading this chapter, figure out the meanings of the unfamiliar **boldfaced** vocabulary words. You may use the Word List, Word Parts Chart, or your dictionary to assist you in finding their meanings.
- Look for the various types of context clues—synonyms, antonyms, general context, and examples—as you read.
- Write a word or phrase about the meaning of each **boldfaced** word in the margin.

Reading and Writing Exercise

- Skim the entire chapter and pay attention to the headings and the discussion questions that follow.
- Initial Response: Write a paragraph explaining, in your own words, what you think this chapter of the story will be about.
- Final Response: After you have read the entire chapter, compare your current understanding with your initial response above. If your initial response was accurate, you can simply write it again to fill in the blanks below. If it was not, then write a paragraph on what the chapter was really about instead.

Initial Response

This chapter **will** be about ______________________________

____

____

____

Final Response

This chapter **was** about ______________________________

____

____

____

WHO IS THE FATHER OF KAMLA'S CHILD?

As soon as they heard, Kamla's family rushed to the hospital. The visit made her forget the **excruciating** pain of childbirth and its aftereffects. Nothing made her feel better than watching her father standing at her bedside wearing a broad, happy smile. He had fully recovered from his recent **stroke**. While Kamla and her father were chatting, Rita and Sheila went to the nursery to visit the baby.

"Isn't he **adorable**, Rita?" remarked Sheila as she lifted him cautiously.

"I love his large, innocent brown eyes," Rita said while kissing his cheeks. "He's such a **cute** baby."

A little while later, Sonny entered the nursery. Immediately, he took the baby from Sheila and hugged him affectionately.

"I hope you turn out to be just like me," whispered Sonny to the baby.

"Don't be foolish, Sonny," said Sheila. "Why would you want the kid to be **awkward** like you?" she joked.

"Don't pay attention to your aunt, Son. She's insanely jealous of the attention you'll be getting from me," Sonny said playfully.

At that moment, Dr. Azeez entered the room. He examined Kamla and then the baby.

"The baby is in good health," he said to Kamla. "There is no evidence of the infection suspected by Dr. Varghese."

"Dr. Azeez, I'm **obliged** to you for the **miracle** you performed," Kamla said.

On hearing Kamla's expression of her appreciation, Sonny introduced himself to Dr. Azeez. Rita listened attentively to their conversation. When they paused for a moment, Rita told Dr. Azeez that she was sorry about the outcome of the friendship between him and Kamla. Dr. Azeez did not reply and excused himself to examine his other patients down the hall.

"What a fool you were to run away from Dr. Azeez," Sonny **scolded** Kamla as soon as Dr. Azeez left her room.

"Please don't remind me of past mistakes, Papa," Kamla implored.

"The guy has everything a woman needs."

"Sonny, don't blame her for not marrying Dr. Azeez. I support her because she wasn't in love with him," interjected Rita.

"Mom and Dad, why can't we put the past behind us? Let's not argue in the hospital. Save it for home," Kamla said in a weak voice.

At approximately 8:00 p.m., the nurse reminded them that visiting hours were over and they had to leave. Sheila requested an additional fifteen minutes to talk with Kamla while her parents waited in the lobby.

"Aunty Sheila, you seem to be in the mood for a serious conversation," Kamla said.

"It would make me happy if you'd **clarify** something that has been on my mind since Dr. Azeez left the nursery," said Sheila. "Kamla, did you sleep with Dr. Azeez when you were in India?"

Kamla did not reply.

"Were you using contraceptives, Kamla?"

"No. What's your point, Aunt Sheila?"

"Kamla, this baby could possibly be Dr. Azeez's."

"Please go away. Go away now," Kamla said to Sheila as her **weary** eyes closed.

Mark Visits Kamla at the Hospital

Mark eventually went to visit Kamla at the hospital. The receptionist at the nursing station told him

Kamla was in Room 101 of the hospital's south wing. However, when he went there, he found the room **vacant**. Nobody was there. Anxiously, he hurried to the nursing station to inquire about Kamla.

"Ma'am, where's the patient who was in Room 101?" Mark asked the nurse.

"She was **discharged** an hour ago."

With the flame of anger burning within him, Mark took a cab to the residence of Kamla's parents. His anger immediately cooled when he saw their house. He was worried about facing Kamla's parents. When he knocked on the door, Sonny answered.

"Is Kamla here?" he asked **nervously** and **reluctantly**.

"Yes. Please come in," Sonny said politely.

"Where are they?" asked Mark as he entered the house.

"Upstairs in her room. You can visit them. Go on. It's OK, Mark," Sonny said encouragingly.

Mark ran up the stairs and pushed the door open. Kamla was breast-feeding the baby when he entered.

"Why did you bother to come now, Mark?" Kamla said in an angry tone of voice.

"Don't be angry with me. I couldn't visit you at the hospital."

"Because you were engaged in something more important than us, right," she stated flatly.

"Is our baby a boy or a girl?"

"A boy. Does it really matter?"

"No," he answered. "Have you given him a name as of yet?"

"Erwin."

"Erwin? What sort of name is that?"

Erwin slowly drifted to sleep. Mark laid him in the crib and kissed his chubby cheeks. Then he hugged Kamla.

"I sincerely apologize for hurting your feelings. I promise it won't happen again when you return home."

"What makes you think I'm returning home, Mark?"

"That's where you belong."

"You're wrong. I belong there only if I'm loved and cared for."

"Kamla, I've been **preoccupied** with my mother's illness and my dad's **mysterious** disappearance. Lately, I've been doing poorly in my studies. So one of my classmates, Julia, volunteered to tutor me on campus."

"I'm suspicious of your **clandestine** meetings on campus on weekends, Mark."

"Don't you trust me, Kamla?"

"Mark, get out of here and don't you dare return. I hate you."

Who Was Perdita and What Was She Doing in New York?

Perdita's flight from Cuba arrived at JFK airport in New York City at approximately 2:45 p.m. She cleared the immigration checkpoint without being **hassled** by the officers.

A man was standing outside the exit door of the airport, waiting for her. After he saw that she appeared to look like the person in the photograph he had in his hand, he approached her and introduced himself.

"Madam, are you Perdita?" he asked confidently.

She hesitated before replying to him.

"Who are you?"

"I'm Debono. And welcome to New York," he said. "Your dad asked my boss to pick you up from the airport and assist you with your living arrangements in New York. My boss is a very busy man. He asked me to drive you from the airport to your apartment in Manhattan because he has a very **hectic** work schedule today and is unable to be here at the airport to welcome you personally."

Perdita said, "Thank you, sir."

Debono assisted Perdita with her luggage, which he loaded in the trunk of his car. He asked her for the briefcase she was holding with a very **firm grip**. Debono mentioned that her dad was going to send the briefcase to his boss, Senator Rex. Perdita knew that Debono was telling the truth and willingly handed it over to him.

Debono knew that Senator Rex had been communicating with General Geraldo, Perdita's father, for several years. He had always wanted to find out the nature of their relationship and how it started. Debono figured that this was the **opportune** time. It was the appropriate occasion to **pry** information from Perdita. He initiated a brief conversation with her while driving from the airport to Manhattan.

"Perdita, how did your father meet Senator Rex?" asked Debono cautiously.

Perdita paused a moment before replying. "I've never met Senator Rex. But I heard my parents mention that he was born in our village in Cuba and came with his parents to America when he was about ten years old."

"So he's not a real American," said Debono. "I wonder how he became a senator if he was born in Cuba."

"You should know that. According to American law, you don't have to be born in America to become a candidate for a United States senator position. But I know for a fact that you can't be a candidate for president unless you are born here. You should know the laws of this country. You speak as if you were born in America."

Debono replied, "So Senator Rex knew your dad when he was in Cuba."

"I'm positive about that, Debono."

"I'm curious as to how they managed to stay in touch with each other over the years."

"They didn't. They started their personal friendship at my cousin's graduation ceremony in New York."

"Very interesting. Tell me more about it."

"My cousin, Peter James, came from Cuba to a **seminary** in New York to study to become a priest. He returned home and became the pastor of his village. Peter invited my dad to his graduation ceremony, where Senator Rex was the commencement speaker. My dad, who has a **superb** memory, remembered Senator Rex from his childhood days in Cuba. Their friendship started at this occasion in New York and grew over the years."

Perdita at Rollins University

Early the following morning, Perdita arrived at Rollins University. She **encountered** a teacher who was on his way to the gymnasium on campus.

"Good morning," he said, greeting her with a friendly smile.

Perdita was **semi-fluent** in English, and after a brief pause, she replied, "A very good morning to you too, sir."

"I've never seen you on campus before. Are you new here?"

"Yes, today is my first day."

"Are you from Spain? I **detect** an **accent**."

"No. I'm from Cuba. I'm here to study only English. I'm Perdita. What's your name, sir?"

"Mark. Where did you learn English, Perdita?"

"I took a few English classes at a boarding school. Many Cubans learn English from the Americans who are living there. Our driver is an American. You **resemble** him, Mark. To think about it, you are a **duplicate** of him. A **replica**."

Perdita was **perplexed** by the **barrage** of questions that suddenly **ensued** about her driver in Cuba, but concealed it cleverly.

Mark left for his office instead of going to the gym as he had originally planned. His conversation with Perdita had left him feeling **restless**.

What Did Senator Rex Want to Get From the Briefcase?

It was very late Friday night when Senator Rex returned from Washington, D.C. Instead of going home, he went directly to his office. Debono had been very tired and was **dozing** on the sofa in the senator's office. Senator Rex entered and locked the door, and then gently tapped Debono on his shoulder.

Debono woke immediately. He sat up. "Senator, I felt uneasy leaving the briefcase in your office, so I decided to stay until your return."

"There is nothing of value in the briefcase. Perdita's father simply asked me to deliver it to one of his friends in Washington. His friend is the Consul General of Spain."

Debono was exhausted and hungry. He went to purchase food at a restaurant a few blocks away. Senator Rex bolted the main door again and hurried to his study as soon as Debono left the office. Anxiously, he broke the briefcase's lock and emptied its contents on his desk. Stacks of money poured out. He randomly selected a bundle of bills and extracted a few notes, which he examined under the light of his desk lamp. Then he curiously felt their texture. Senator Rex was convinced that General Geraldo in Cuba had sent him **counterfeit** money. Before Debono returned, he put the bundles of bills in the briefcase and hid it in the safe in his office. When he could no longer hold his composure, he banged his fists on his desk and screamed, "Cheater! Cheater! You'll pay for this!"

Somebody knocked on the door. Senator Rex took a moment to calm down, then answered it. Debono came in with a bag of sandwiches and passed one to the senator.

"How's the general's daughter, Perdita, **adjusting** to New York?" Senator Rex inquired as they ate.

"Fine. Senator, I think you should know that I saw her talking with a professor on campus earlier today. You asked me to follow her around while she's in New York. I've begun to do so, Senator."

"Do you know the professor's name?"

"Mark."

To Senator Rex's knowledge, there was only one professor named Mark at Rollins University. He knew Mark and his family intimately.

"Debono, I smell trouble in the air! Get back out there and don't let Perdita out of your sight."

"I won't disappoint you, Senator."

"I appreciate your **loyalty**. I'll ensure you get a **substantial** increase in your salary this year."

Will Mark Find His Father?

Mark could not sleep that night. He tossed and turned in bed. He could not wait to rush to the nursing home to tell his mother about his conversation with Perdita about her family's driver.

It was around 9:00 a.m. when he arrived at the nursing home. Dorothy hugged her son tightly as tears **trickled** down her cheeks. She was anxious to speak with him because her **intuition** signaled that Mark wanted to have a serious discussion about something. Luckily, the senator's men were nowhere to be seen. It seemed as if they had something more important to do that day.

"Son, I'm **elated** that you've come to visit me," said Dorothy.

"Today is a very special day for both of us, Mother," Mark replied.

"Then I guess you have news about your dad."

"How did you know, Mother?"

"God is great!"

"Perdita, a Cuban student at Rollins, suspects that my father is her family's driver. Does that make sense, Mother?"

"No. But we have to **pursue** every lead we have."

"Are you suggesting that I go to Cuba?"

"No, you silly boy. Call her home now. We have nothing to lose."

Mark stuck his head out of Dorothy's room and **peered** cautiously down the hallway to ensure nobody was listening to their conversation. Perdita had said that their driver always ate breakfast at their home at about 9:30 every morning. He glanced nervously at his watch and waited for three minutes. Then he dialed Perdita's home phone number in Cuba, which he had found on the Internet.

"Hello, this is General Geraldo's residence. May I help you?" answered someone speaking in Spanish.

"Daddy, is that you?" Mark asked in a disguised voice.

"Wrong number, wrong number," repeated the person nervously.

"No. Please listen to me, Maxwell. Aren't you Maxwell?"

"Yes. How do you know my name?" asked Maxwell in a serious tone of voice.

"I'm your son, Mark, from New York."

"Mark, my Mark?"

"Yes, Daddy," cried Mark. "Why did you leave us?"

"I didn't. I was thrown into this situation by Senator Rex."

"We're not surprised. We suspected that **scoundrel** was involved in your **mysterious** disappearance," said Mark with confidence. "How did you end up in Cuba?"

"Because of Senator Rex. He's responsible for my **predicament** and the deaths of his wives."

"I don't understand the connection between his wives' deaths and your sudden disappearance."

"I overheard an argument the senator had with a very dangerous man. A few days later, I questioned him in his office about the argument, but he denied it had taken place."

"That was stupid of you to **confront** him, Dad. I guess that's when he decided to **eliminate** you."

"Yes. He convinced me that Cuba was **establishing** a naval base close to Miami but within its own territorial waters. When I agreed to gather intelligence about Cuba's intentions, he **assigned** me to a pilot whom he said knew the art of staying undetected while flying in Cuban airspace. It was supposedly a government operation, but something seemed off about it. Now I know he was trying to get rid of me.

"I took aerial photographs of Cuba's principal military base while flying outside the borders of Cuba during the first two days of the mission," Maxwell continued. "On the third day, our jet **exploded** in a ball of flame less than a mile south of Cuba. The pilot probably died, but fortunately, I managed to swim to a small village in Cuba, where I was rescued by two fishermen. I was semi-conscious and very ill with **pneumonia**. One of the fishermen, Peter James, was the pastor of the village and a cousin of General Geraldo. Thank God for him. He and his family **nurtured** me back to good health."

Pastor Peter did not like General Geraldo very much. During Maxwell's stay, he **confided** in Maxwell that the general was very corrupt and was engaged in illegal activities with a United States senator representing New York. The pastor also told Maxwell how Senator Rex had met General Geraldo. Upon hearing this, Maxwell became very curious. He found out from Pastor Peter that Senator Rex was the general's **accomplice** in New York, and both were **culprits** in the same crimes.

Maxwell then became determined to nail his boss, Senator Rex, for trying to kill him, murdering his wives and the fighter pilot, and working with the general. He knew that he had to get closer to General Geraldo to learn about his activities with the senator. He ascertained from Pastor Peter that the general needed a driver, preferably someone who could speak **fluent** English.

The following day, Maxwell was introduced by Pastor Peter to General Geraldo. The general had an instant **disdain** for Maxwell for no reason. However, Pastor Peter convinced him that there were not too many English-speaking people in Cuba and he had no alternative but to hire Maxwell. Maxwell was excited to work for the general. He did not regret becoming his driver, a position he would never have considered in New York because he was a **status-conscious** man.

Maxwell was very excited to tell Mark what he had learned about General Geraldo and Senator Rex. They continued their conversation as if they had a whole world of time.

"Son, I discovered something else about Senator Rex," boasted Maxwell.

"Another murder?"

"No. He's engaged in drug trafficking with General Geraldo, a top-ranking officer in the Cuban military. That's not all. A while ago, I learned that the senator had plans to sell a blueprint of a modern American missile to General Geraldo."

"The senator is a **traitor**, Dad! You should leave Cuba immediately. Why did you risk your life working for the general as his driver? What if he finds out what you're doing? What if the Cubans arrest you as a spy?"

"It was the only way to get the evidence I need to prove that Senator Rex is guilty of engaging in **illicit** activities."

"What are you planning on doing with the evidence, Dad?"

"We'll discuss that when I return to New York. I want you to go immediately to the FBI headquarters and speak with Captain Turney. He's the assistant chief of the bureau and a personal friend of mine. At exactly 5:30 p.m. today, tell him to have the Coast Guard rescue me at Margarita Island, about ten miles outside the southern tip of Cuba. Don't worry, Son. The United States Coast Guard is **acquainted** with this island."

"Dad, have you carefully thought about this plan?"

"Yes. Where's your mother, Mark?"

"Right here."

"Is she fine?"

"No. She was hurt in an accident."

"How did it happen, Mark? No, wait, don't tell me now—I need to hurry. We've been talking too long. Tell her not to worry. I'll take care of everything when I come home. Tell her to keep my diary in a safe place, because it contains all the information I gathered on the illegal activities the senator was engaged in over the years. This is the evidence we will use to **convict** him of crimes that will get him sentenced to at least seventy years in prison."

"Be careful, Dad."

"Take care of your mother until I return, Son. I love you and your mom dearly. I really miss both of you. Ask Turney to provide security for her in case the senator plans to hurt her."

As Mark was about to place the telephone on the receiver, he heard footsteps slowly fading away outside his mother's room at the nursing home. He rushed to see who it was, but nobody was in sight. For fear that his mother might be harmed, Mark did not go to the FBI headquarters as requested by his father. Instead, he telephoned Captain Turney and asked him to rush to the nursing home. In less than ten minutes, he arrived with several agents. Mark explained the circumstances that had led to his father's **dilemma**. Immediately, the captain assigned two agents to **trail** Senator Rex and an additional two to guard Dorothy at the nursing home. Mark flew to Miami with him and his team an hour later.

EXERCISE 1

Applying the Words You Have Learned to Critical Thinking and Creative Writing

- Use the two questions in Section A below to discuss this chapter with your classmates. Be sure to apply your critical thinking skills.

- Write an essay about either question using the vocabulary words you know from real-life experiences and the new ones you have learned from this text.

Section A

Discussion Questions

1. Who do you believe is the father of Kamla's child?

____

____

____

____

____

____

____

____

2. What type of person is Senator Rex?

____

____

____

____

____

____

____

EXERCISE 2

Matching Meanings: Science

■ Match each word with its meaning.

_____ 1. artery — **A.** inflammation of the liver

_____ 2. arteriosclerosis — **B.** high blood pressure

_____ 3. hemoglobin — **C.** higher than normal body temperature

_____ 4. hepatitis — **D.** an antibiotic

_____ 5. pneumonia — **E.** pumps blood; contracts and expands

_____ 6. leukemia — **F.** a swelling

_____ 7. cancer — **G.** carries blood away from the heart

_____ 8. lump — **H.** calcium deficiency

_____ 9. glucose — **I.** red-colored matter of red blood corpuscles

_____ 10. plasma — **J.** excessive activity of thyroid gland

_____ 11. pupil — **K.** abnormally low blood sugar

_____ 12. dermis — **L.** infection associated with the lungs

_____ 13. epidermis — **M.** a malignant tumor

_____ 14. anesthesia — **N.** layer of skin below the epidermis

_____ 15. acupuncture — **O.** outermost layer of the skin

_____ 16. kidney — **P.** abnormal thickening of the walls of arteries

_____ 17. liver — **Q.** a disease; excessive production of white blood cells

_____ 18. heart — **R.** opening in the iris of the eye

_____ 19. lung — **S.** a sugar found in fruits and the blood

_____ 20. hypoglycemia — **T.** loss of consciousness

_____ 21. hyperthermia — **U.** organ associated with excretion

_____ 22. hypertension — **V.** a respiratory organ

_____ 23. hyperthyroidism — **W.** secretes bile; detoxifies poisonous substances

_____ 24. hypocalcemia — **X.** fluid part of the blood

_____ 25. penicillin — **Y.** use of needles to relieve body pain

EXERCISE 3

Forming Synonyms

■ Fill in the blank(s) to complete the word that is similar in meaning to the **boldfaced** word.

1. **idea** tho__ __ht
2. **imbecile** f__ol
3. **imitate** co__y
4. **immerse** sub__ __ __ge
5. **impeach** ch__ __ge
6. **impede** hind__ __
7. **implement** st__ __t
8. **symbolize** repr__ __ent
9. **interrogate** que__t__on
10. **intuition** instin__ __
11. **irreparable** ru__ __ed
12. **inspect** ex__ __ __ne
13. **integrity** h__nor
14. **invalid** disa__ __ed
15. **jerk** p__ll
16. **jest** __oke
17. **job** du__y
18. **journey** tr__p
19. **judge** med__ __te
20. **stereotype** cate__ __ __ize

EXERCISE 4

Matching Meanings: Set 1

■ Match each word with its meaning.

______	1. gush	**A.** a sudden flow
______	2. gallant	**B.** continuous; never-ending
______	3. infidelity	**C.** widely known in an unfavorable manner
______	4. innuendo	**D.** keep out or prevent
______	5. incessant	**E.** surrender or give up
______	6. monotonous	**F.** brave and noble
______	7. notorious	**G.** hypnotize or fascinate
______	8. mesmerize	**H.** substitute; taking the place of another person or thing
______	9. preclude	**I.** unfaithfulness or disloyalty
______	10. retrospective	**J.** having no variety
______	11. relinquish	**K.** thinking of the past
______	12. vicarious	**L.** a hint or sly remark

EXERCISE 5

Matching Meanings: Set 2

■ Match each word with its meaning.

_____	1. arsonist	**A.**	something added to complete a whole
_____	2. compliment	**B.**	an odd person
_____	3. charismatic	**C.**	involving confidence or trust
_____	4. complement	**D.**	done or provided without charge; free
_____	5. eloquent	**E.**	popular; arousing; having leadership quality
_____	6. extricate	**F.**	skillful with words
_____	7. eccentric	**G.**	delicate; easily broken
_____	8. fragile	**H.**	express courtesy or respect
_____	9. fiduciary	**I.**	conspicuously bad; outrageous; notorious
_____	10. flagrant	**J.**	come together; assemble
_____	11. gratuitous	**K.**	set free from difficulty
_____	12. gather	**L.**	someone who maliciously sets fires

EXERCISE 6

Word Meaning in Context: Set 1

■ Read each sentence and find the missing word in the box below. Fill in the blank with the correct *form* of that word.

gallant	**monotonous**	**innuendo**	**notorious**
gush	**mesmerize**	**preclude**	
incessant	**retrospect**	**relinquish**	

1. The poor villagers cheered when the first ___________ of oil spouted from the ground.
2. Opening a door for a woman was considered ___________ twenty years ago; now, many women consider it sexist.
3. The crime boss spoke in ___________ to avoid attracting the attention of the nearby police officer. While he only mentioned fruits and vegetables, the other criminals knew he was really talking about drugs.
4. Her ___________ chatter made her seem friendly at first, but after listening to her talk for two hours, everyone just wanted her to stop.
5. Many people hate elevator music because it is so ___________ and dull.
6. Seattle is ___________ for its rainy weather.
7. The prosecutor ___________ the jury with his detailed account of the crime.
8. The insufficient evidence presented by the prosecutor ___________ a conviction.
9. In ___________, Jenny saw that marrying at such a young age had been a serious mistake.
10. The kidnapper said he would ___________ the hostage upon the receipt of $100,000.

EXERCISE 7

Word Meaning in Context: Set 2

■ Read each sentence and find the missing word in the box below. Fill in the blank with the correct *form* of that word.

fragile	**gratuitous**	**gather**	**eccentric**
arsonist	**fiduciary**	**eloquent**	**predominant**
extricate	**compliment**	**flagrant**	**complement**

1. At first, the fire department thought the fire was an accident; later, they discovered that an ___________ had set it.
2. Franklin ___________ his date on her beautiful dress.
3. A Bengal tiger has black stripes and white markings, but its ___________ color is orange.
4. Could you tell me which wine would best ___________ Mexican food?
5. After an ___________ plea by their pastor, the parishioners gave generously to help the victims of the tsunami.
6. Despite his best efforts, Chang was unable to ___________ himself from the web of lies he had woven.
7. Mr. Ortiz was known as an ___________ because, in spite of owning several limousines, he chose to travel about town by bicycle.
8. Please handle this box with care as the contents are very ___________ and can be broken easily.

9. A banker must be careful and honest when carrying out his or her __________ responsibilities.
10. Sam was arrested for driving at seventy miles per hour, a __________ violation of the local speed limit of fifty.
11. Although nobody ever asked for her opinion, Maria was always ready to offer __________ advice.
12. Each year, the family __________ from every corner of the country for a reunion.

EXERCISE 8

Context Clues

■ Select the word or phrase that most closely matches the meaning of the **boldfaced** word. *Note that replacing the **boldfaced** word with the right answer might not produce a grammatically correct sentence.*

1. The tour guide took the visitors on a scenic **route**, driving along a mountain road rather than taking the highway.
   A. a grassy field **B.** a dangerous cliff **C.** a shadowy park **D.** a traveled way

2. When traveling in the wilderness, it is always best to be prepared for worst-case **scenarios**, such as being attacked by wild animals or getting lost.
   A. weather **B.** pain **C.** situations **D.** tents

3. Every morning the supervisor posted a **schedule** of duties she expected her employees to complete by the end of the day.
   A. list **B.** poorly written note **C.** experience **D.** growth

4. As the woman listened to the man's method for deceiving people into giving him money, she sensed a **scheme** developing.
   A. business **B.** plan **C.** gamble **D.** attack

5. The **scope** of the investigation widened as more evidence was gathered.
   A. safety **B.** extent **C.** profit **D.** faith

6. Mike bought tickets for seats in the lower **section** of the football stadium so he would have a better view of the game.
   A. score **B.** staircase **C.** game **D.** part

7. One **sector** of the housing development was set aside for renting by low-income families.
   A. conference room **B.** area **C.** office **D.** contract

8. The owners **secured** their house by locking all the doors and windows before leaving for vacation.
   A. abandoned **B.** protected **C.** aligned **D.** deducted

9. They tried to **seek** more information on their missing friend.
   A. buy **B.** read **C.** search for **D.** guess

10. Moviegoers loved the thrilling action **sequence** at the end of the film.
    A. surprise **B.** explosion **C.** chain of events **D.** actor

11. A high incidence of robberies in the neighborhood led to a **series** of meetings between residents and police.
    A. performance **B.** number **C.** minute **D.** decrease

12. There are two **sexes**: male and female.
    A. reproductive characteristics **B.** psychological motivations **C.** workplace complaints **D.** family traits

13. The economic **shift** from strong recovery to sudden slowdown confused consumers about the future of the stock market.
    A. lift **B.** gears **C.** unpopularity **D.** movement

14. The twins were not only identical in looks, but also **similar** in personality.
    A. unlike **B.** aggressive **C.** alike **D.** happy

15. The movie about the lunar landing **simulated** the real event.
    A. lied about **B.** imitated **C.** paid for **D.** preceded

16. The **so-called** graffiti artist turned out to be a fake whose work was not original.
    A. falsely named **B.** heavily clothed **C.** criminal **D.** brilliant

17. He was the **sole** survivor of the plane crash, leaving him as the only witness to the accident.
    A. single **B.** careful **C.** smart **D.** weak

18. Rather than being excited about living in an upper-class neighborhood, he was **somewhat** nervous.
    A. extremely **B.** cautiously **C.** serenely **D.** slightly

19. The labor department is an excellent **source** of employment information.
    A. thing that gives **B.** thing that defines **C.** thing that measures **D.** thing that takes

20. I know you want ice cream, but I need to know which **specific** flavor you want.
    A. good **B.** particular **C.** expensive **D.** silly

21. The advertisement did not **specify** the requirements for the job, so many unqualified people called to apply.
    A. consider **B.** state in detail **C.** criticize **D.** ignore

22. The famous World Trade Center **sphere** sculpture, made in the image of a bronze ball, is still located in lower Manhattan.
    A. a blunt object **B.** a round object **C.** a rectangular object **D.** a divisive object

23. His bosses like him because he is **stable** and consistent in his work habits.
    A. greedy **B.** indebted **C.** steady **D.** grateful

24. The economic report lacked fact-based information, such as the latest **statistics** on unemployment.
    A. numbers **B.** money **C.** participants **D.** curves

EXERCISE 9

Vocabulary Test

- Select the correct answer.
- Hint: Review the meanings of all the **boldfaced** words in this chapter before you take the test. This approach can help you to score 100 percent.
- Record the percentage of correct answers on the Master Self-Assessment table on page 397.

1 The **epidermis** is the inner layer of skin.

A. True　　**B.** False

2 **Anesthesia** is associated with loss of consciousness.

E. True　　**F.** False

3 **Acupuncture** is inserting needles into the body to relieve pain.

A. True　　**B.** False

4 The **kidney** is an organ associated with digestion.

E. True　　**F.** False

5 The **liver** is associated with circulation.

A. True　　**B.** False

6 The **heart** pumps blood.

E. True　　**F.** False

7 The **lung** is an organ of secretion.

A. True　　**B.** False

8 An **artery** is a vessel that carries blood away from the heart.

E. True　　**F.** False

9 **Arteriosclerosis** is associated with an abnormal thickening of the walls of the arteries.

A. True　　**B.** False

10 **Hemoglobin** refers to the red-colored matter of red blood corpuscles.

E. True　　**F.** False

11 **Hepatitis** is a disease that causes inflammation of the heart.

A. True

B. False

12 **Pneumonia** is an infection associated with the kidneys.

E. True

F. False

13 **Leukemia** is a disease associated with the lack of production of white blood cells.

A. True

B. False

14 A **lump** is a swelling.

E. True

F. False

15 **Plasma** is the fluid part of blood.

A. True

B. False

16 The **pupil** is located at the side of the eye.

E. True

F. False

17 The **dermis** is the outermost layer of skin under the epidermis.

A. True

B. False

18 A patient with **hypoglycemia** is likely suffering from:

E. excessive blood sugar

F. abnormally low blood sugar

G. fits of anger

H. high blood pressure

19 **Hyperthermia** refers to:

A. low blood pressure

B. higher than normal body temperature

C. mild fever

D. indigestion

20 **Hypertension** refers to:

E. low blood sugar

F. high blood pressure

G. inflammation

H. sleep

21 **Hyperthyroidism** relates to:

A. low thyroid activity

B. low blood sugar

C. no thyroid activity

D. excessive activity of the thyroid gland

22 **Hypocalcemia** is:

E. calcium deficiency

F. excessive sodium

G. excessive blood cells

H. fever

23 **Penicillin** is:

A. an injection

B. a probiotic

C. an antibiotic

D. a disease

24 **Gush** refers to:

E. running water

F. a sudden flow

G. a steady flow

H. dripping water

25 A **gallant** person is:

A. brave and noble

B. scared

C. fearful

D. gullible

26 **Internal** refers to:

E. under

F. above

G. below

H. inside

27 **Infidelity** refers to:

A. goodness

B. helpfulness

C. trust

D. unfaithfulness

28 An **innuendo** is a:

E. compliment

F. hint or suggestion

G. rebuke

H. few

29 Something **incessant** is:

A. sporadic

B. rare

C. educational

D. continuous

30 **Monotonous** means:

E. lacking in variety

F. full of life

G. exciting

H. windy

31 A **notorious** person is:

A. unknown
B. widely known in an unfavorable manner
C. honorable
D. inactive

32 To **mesmerize** is to:

E. mislead
F. fascinate
G. overcome
H. estimate

33 **Preclude** means to:

A. exclude
B. represent
C. permit
D. unlock

34 When you **replenish**, you:

E. renew
F. use up
G. throw out
H. absorb

35 **Retrospective** refers to:

A. thinking of the present
B. thinking of the past
C. thinking of the future
D. thinking of dreams

36 To **relinquish** a position is to :

E. surrender or give up
F. claim
G. keep
H. accept

37 **Vicarious** means:

A. unconcerned
B. selfish
C. unimportant
D. taking the place of another person

38 An **arsonist** is someone who:

E. steals
F. cleans buildings
G. sets fires illegally
H. paints graffiti

39 To pay a **compliment** is to:

A. give money
B. add something to complete a whole
C. disrespect someone
D. express courtesy and respect

40 A **charismatic** person has:

E. personal charm
F. tolerance
G. patience
H. breathing problems

41 To **complement** is to:

A. express gratitude
B. express courtesy and respect
C. insult someone
D. add something to complete a whole

42 An **eloquent** speaker is:

E. skillful with words
F. unclear
G. dull and boring
H. tongue-tied

43 To **extricate** is to:

A. entangle
B. set free from difficulty
C. involve in a crime
D. send to prison

44 An **eccentric** person is:

E. odd or strange
F. normal
G. uneasy
H. stable

45 **Fragile** means:

A. very strong
B. delicate or easily broken
C. transparent
D. sturdy

46 **Gratuitous** services are:

E. essential
F. very expensive
G. provided free
H. paid weekly

47 **Fiduciary** refers to:

A. distrust
B. involvement of confidence or trust
C. free services
D. lack of confidence

48 **Flagrant** behavior is:

E. unimportant

F. conspicuously bad

G. secretive

H. polite and well-mannered

49 To **gather** is to:

A. separate

B. let go

C. bring together

D. scatter

50 To **convince** means to:

E. defend

F. discourage

G. persuade

H. accept

EXERCISE 10

Building a Stronger Vocabulary

- Review all the **boldfaced** words in this chapter before you proceed to the next exercise.
- Highlight the ones you are still having difficulty remembering.
- List them with their meanings on a table.
- Use them to compose your own sentences.
- Think of a synonym and an antonym for each word.
- Use checkmarks to indicate if each word you want to practice more has a prefix, suffix, and/or root.
- You may use the table below as a sample to write your answers in your notebook.

Word	Definition	Sentence	Synonym	Antonym	Prefix	Suffix	Root

EXERCISE 11

Creating My Own Powerful Word List

- Write the words and meanings from the above table on the **Creating My Own Powerful Word List** table on page 398. Review them often to build that super vocabulary you want to create for school, work, and everyday use.

Chapter 15

PRE-READING

About This Chapter from *Trial of Love*

- Read the names and descriptions of this chapter's main characters below.
  - Maribella: General Geraldo's wife in Cuba
  - Maxwell Edison
  - Mark Edison Hubbard
  - Dorothy Hubbard

Story Vocabulary Exercise

- Before you begin reading this chapter, figure out the meanings of the unfamiliar **boldfaced** vocabulary words. You may use the Word List, Word Parts Chart, or your dictionary to assist you in finding their meanings.
- Look for the various types of context clues—synonyms, antonyms, general context, and examples—as you read.
- Write a word or phrase about the meaning of each **boldfaced** word in the margin.

Reading and Writing Exercise

- Skim the entire chapter and pay attention to the headings and the discussion questions that follow.
- Initial Response: Write a paragraph explaining, in your own words, what you think this chapter of the story will be about.
- Final Response: After you have read the entire chapter, compare your current understanding with your initial response above. If your initial response was accurate, you can simply write it again to fill in the blanks below. If it was not, then write a paragraph on what the chapter was really about instead.

Initial Response

This chapter **will** be about ______________________________

____

____

____

Final Response

This chapter **was** about ______________________________

____

____

____

WHO BROKE THE HEART OF THE GENERAL'S WIFE?

General Geraldo was at work. Maribella, his wife, enjoyed **flirting** with Maxwell and wanted a deeper relationship with him. She was taking a shower while Maxwell was talking with Mark in the nursing home. Just as Maxwell was about to leave the general's study, the telephone rang impatiently. He was suddenly **numb** with fear, unable to feel any part of his body. He wondered if General Geraldo had planted a listening device in his study and heard his conversation. As he was **debating** whether he should answer the call, the caller left a message for General Geraldo on the answering machine.

"General, the bug on Dorothy Hubbard's phone finally paid off. We have trouble on our hands. Your driver, Maxwell, is a dangerous enemy. He knows of our secrets and is determined to put us away in jail. Maxwell was my aide. I tried to kill him, but he **miraculously** survived the explosion from the bomb I had planted on the fighter jet he was on. You must make sure that he does not leave Cuba. Get rid of him immediately.

"General, do you know where your daughter, Perdita, is?" the voice continued. "Apparently, she has left New York in **haste**. My security **aide** reported that her **belongings** are not in her apartment. Please take this matter seriously."

Moments after the message was recorded, Maribella stepped out of the bathroom **clad** in a pink robe.

"Darling, where are you?" asked Maribella as she entered the living room.

"I'm here, dear," replied Maxwell, leaving the general's study.

"What are you doing in the study?"

"Nothing in particular. Just **browsing**. My boss has an **impressive** collection of history books."

"He's a **fanatic** when it comes to historical events," said Maribella.

Maxwell was not hungry, yet he asked Maribella to prepare something for him to eat. "Can you prepare breakfast? I'm hungry, sweetheart."

"Breakfast? Isn't it too late for breakfast, Maxwell?"

"You're correct. I lost track of time. A sandwich may **suffice**."

"Would you like to help me in the kitchen? I promise I won't ask you to assist with the dishes today."

"I'd love to help, but can I finish the story I began reading in the study, Maribella?"

"I guess that would be fine, but I must warn you that my husband would be upset if he knew you were in his study."

"This will be another one of our secrets."

"Then you must hurry."

Maxwell went to the study as soon as Maribella entered the kitchen. He took a book from the bookshelf and placed it on the desk. Then he removed the cassette that contained Senator Rex's message to General Geraldo from the answering machine and hid it in his pocket. After he took a deep breath of relief, he sat at the desk and pretended to read the book. Shortly after, Maribella entered the study to inform him that lunch was ready.

"Maxwell, did my husband tell you that he'll be leaving for an overseas **conference**?" asked Maribella.

"Yes. As a matter of fact, I have to leave in a few minutes to bring him to the airport from his office downtown," replied Maxwell, who was talking with his mouth half-full with his sandwich. "We can go sailing when General Geraldo is away."

"That's a great idea! Do you want me to make the arrangements, Maxwell?"

"If you don't mind."

"What day should I **reserve** the boat for?"

"Today. We'll leave as soon as I return from the airport."

"I don't think I'll be able to rent a boat in such a short time."

"Use your influence, Maribella. Tell the owner of the company that your husband needs a boat for official business. Or think of another excuse."

"Consider it done, Maxwell," said Maribella with excitement.

"I also want you to purchase fifty gallons of fuel."

"Fifty gallons! We don't need that much."

"We do because we'll be sailing in the Caribbean Sea around the southern tip of Cuba. This is where couples go for a romantic evening."

"You're such a romantic man, Maxwell," she said flirtatiously. "I wish my husband were as loving as you are. Your wife is blessed to have a husband like you."

As Maxwell got up from behind the table, his elbow struck the book he was pretending to read. It fell on the floor. As he bent down to pick it up, the cassette fell from his shirt pocket. Maribella watched him grab it and nervously put it in his pants pocket.

"Where did you get that cassette?" she inquired with a serious expression on her face.

"I bought it from the music store yesterday."

"I wasn't aware you were **fond** of Latin music."

"Every night I listen to music before going to bed. I've slowly developed an appreciation for Latin music since I started living in Cuba."

"May I listen to the cassette while you go to the airport?"

"Um . . . um . . . no. I'd like to listen to it on my way to the airport. The general will find it relaxing."

"There isn't a cassette player in the limousine."

"I promise to lend you it as soon as I return," Maxwell said, pretending he hadn't heard her.

Maribella sat at the table **pondering** the cassette Maxwell was reluctant to lend her. She knew he was lying about purchasing it from the music store. The handwriting on the label that was stuck on the cassette was her husband's. Immediately after Maxwell left, she went to the study and examined the answering machine. She was convinced that Maxwell had removed the cassette. At that moment, she could not think of an explanation for why he had stolen the cassette other than he could not afford one. After slipping into a red pair of shorts and a low-cut white T-shirt, Maribella went downtown to rent a sailing boat for her evening cruise with Maxwell.

General Geraldo on an Overseas Assignment

General Geraldo was **elated** about his trip overseas. It was one of the few challenging assignments he had ever been eager to **embark** on. When they were less than ten minutes from the departure terminal, Maxwell reminded him to review his checklist to ensure he did not forget any of his essentials before boarding the plane.

Maxwell assisted General Geraldo in getting his luggage to the terminal and waited until his flight departed. Without delay, he sped to the general's residence to pick up Maribella. However, when he was nearing it, he observed several cars surrounding the house. Instantly, he figured the general's security agents were in **pursuit** of him. The guards **despised** Maxwell because he was an American, and they felt he was spying in Cuba. When General Geraldo was away on overseas assignments, they repeatedly harassed him, hoping he would **quit** his job and return to America. Everybody in the military knew about the secret affair Maxwell was having with the general's wife. This enraged them greatly, especially because they knew the general would never believe his wife had **betrayed** him even if they disclosed the relationship to him.

Maxwell turned around abruptly and drove to a nearby abandoned building, where he observed their movements. The agents spent at least fifteen minutes in the house before they left hurriedly.

Maxwell pulled the general's shotgun out of the trunk of the limo and approached the house with **caution**. Carefully, he tip-toed up the stairs and slowly pushed the door **ajar** with the barrel of the gun. He stepped into the house and searched every corner. Nobody was there. He glanced at his watch. It was 3:30 p.m., just two hours away from his targeted time to escape from Cuba.

Maribella's Bitter Regret

Maribella had gone to her hairdresser. Before leaving, she had left a note on the dining table at home informing Maxwell that the sailing boat was ready at the wharf at Dowling Street, and she would return in less than an hour for their cruise.

Maxwell kissed the note and hurried to Dowling Street. He drove the boat to Margarita Island, just outside Cuban territory, where he had instructed Mark to have the United States Coast Guard rescue him. The Coast Guardsmen welcomed him home to the United States like a long-lost hero.

When she returned home from her hairdresser, Maribella found a very brief note from Maxwell stating that he had to return to New York. She **wept** bitterly after reading it. She felt pained that Maxwell had **deserted** her and left for the United States. It had never crossed her mind for a moment that the only man she had truly loved in her entire life would **exploit** her trust and generosity to satisfy his selfish and animalistic needs.

Several months later, Maribella's broken heart slowly started to heal. Maribella knew that Maxwell had been missing his wife and son in New York. She had great satisfaction knowing that he had **reunited** with them. This **aided** her in her battle to overcome her grief over losing Maxwell forever.

In the end, her broken heart was mended by her love for her daughter, Perdita, who returned from New York without completing her short course in English at Rollins University. After being in New York only a week, Perdita had been overcome by homesickness.

Maribella made a **solemn pledge** to herself that she would never have eyes for another man. "Never again. Never again," she said to herself regretfully. She prayed for Geraldo's safe return and waited, determined to be a more loyal and loving wife than ever before.

EXERCISE 1

Applying the Words You Have Learned to Critical Thinking and Creative Writing

- Use the two questions in Section A below to discuss this chapter with your classmates. Be sure to apply your critical thinking skills.

- Write an essay about either question using the vocabulary words you know from real-life experiences and the new ones you have learned from this text.

Section A

Discussion Questions

1. How do you feel about the manner in which Maxwell treated Maribella?

2. Do you feel Maribella was sincere about her feelings for Maxwell?

EXERCISE 2

Synonyms: Multiple Choice

■ Circle the letter of the word or phrase that is most similar in meaning to the **boldfaced** word.

1. **weep**	**A.** sing	**B.** cry	**C.** laugh	**D.** mock
2. **withdraw**	**A.** jeer	**B.** take back	**C.** reside	**D.** resign
3. **transfer**	**A.** take	**B.** move from one place to another	**C.** covet	**D.** settle
4. **temporary**	**A.** short-lived	**B.** permanent	**C.** stable	**D.** stylish
5. **quit**	**A.** start	**B.** begin	**C.** slow	**D.** discontinue
6. **omit**	**A.** include	**B.** instill	**C.** exclude	**D.** replace
7. **misery**	**A.** happiness	**B.** danger	**C.** sorrow	**D.** laughter
8. **lethal**	**A.** safe	**B.** secure	**C.** warm	**D.** can kill
9. **invert**	**A.** overturn	**B.** repeat	**C.** spin	**D.** slant
10. **hasty**	**A.** swift	**B.** silent	**C.** slow	**D.** sluggish
11. **decision**	**A.** verdict	**B.** delay	**C.** speech	**D.** report
12. **easy**	**A.** difficult	**B.** simple	**C.** hard	**D.** smooth
13. **collaborate**	**A.** oppose	**B.** work together	**C.** advocate	**D.** sharpen
14. **astonish**	**A.** disappoint	**B.** detest	**C.** amaze	**D.** deplorable
15. **brawl**	**A.** match	**B.** game	**C.** season	**D.** fight
16. **chaos**	**A.** quality	**B.** organization	**C.** confusion	**D.** dance
17. **complicate**	**A.** confuse	**B.** challenge	**C.** distance	**D.** frighten
18. **abandon**	**A.** obey	**B.** forsake	**C.** accept	**D.** assist
19. **convert**	**A.** change	**B.** keep	**C.** offer	**D.** carry
20. **enemy**	**A.** friend	**B.** counselor	**C.** pal	**D.** foe

EXERCISE 3

Synonyms and Antonyms

■ Write the corresponding letter for the synonym and antonym of each **boldfaced** word.

	Synonym	Antonym			
1. **spacious**	______	______	**A.** excited	**B.** roomy	**C.** confining
2. **strenuous**	______	______	**A.** deliberate	**B.** hard	**C.** easy
3. **sturdy**	______	______	**A.** strong	**B.** weak	**C.** funny
4. **successful**	______	______	**A.** prosperous	**B.** failing	**C.** fluctuating
5. **suitable**	______	______	**A.** fitting	**B.** inappropriate	**C.** erratic
6. **summarize**	______	______	**A.** condense	**B.** externalize	**C.** expand
7. **surplus**	______	______	**A.** guilt	**B.** excess	**C.** lack
8. **suspend**	______	______	**A.** postpone	**B.** threaten	**C.** resume
9. **thorough**	______	______	**A.** complete	**B.** incomplete	**C.** faulty
10. **tolerate**	______	______	**A.** honor	**B.** permit	**C.** prohibit
11. **timid**	______	______	**A.** shy	**B.** small	**C.** bold
12. **tremendous**	______	______	**A.** vast	**B.** small	**C.** furious
13. **trouble**	______	______	**A.** disturb	**B.** calm	**C.** frequent
14. **tumult**	______	______	**A.** great confusion	**B.** hostility	**C.** quiet
15. **turbulent**	______	______	**A.** fictitious	**B.** violent	**C.** peaceful
16. **unable**	______	______	**A.** culpable	**B.** incapable	**C.** capable
17. **uncertain**	______	______	**A.** unsure	**B.** confident	**C.** perplexed
18. **under**	______	______	**A.** below	**B.** above	**C.** beside
19. **underrate**	______	______	**A.** portray	**B.** belittle	**C.** overestimate
20. **unfair**	______	______	**A.** prejudiced	**B.** selfish	**C.** just
21. **unfit**	______	______	**A.** unsuitable	**B.** appropriate	**C.** fragile
22. **unreal**	______	______	**A.** imaginary	**B.** shocking	**C.** existing
23. **unskilled**	______	______	**A.** inexperienced	**B.** rough	**C.** skilled
24. **vacant**	______	______	**A.** empty	**B.** gloomy	**C.** occupied
25. **vague**	______	______	**A.** unclear	**B.** messy	**C.** understood

	Synonym	Antonym			
26. **weak**	______	______	**A.** feeble	**B.** playful	**C.** strong
27. **deficit**	______	______	**A.** shortage	**B.** harm	**C.** abundance
28. **degenerate**	______	______	**A.** deteriorate	**B.** improve	**C.** stabilize
29. **deplete**	______	______	**A.** sadden	**B.** drain	**C.** replace
30. **distant**	______	______	**A.** outer	**B.** far away	**C.** close
31. **diligent**	______	______	**A.** disturbed	**B.** hard-working	**C.** lazy
32. **deceive**	______	______	**A.** betray	**B.** contain	**C.** enlighten
33. **defy**	______	______	**A.** oppose	**B.** harm	**C.** support
34. **denounce**	______	______	**A.** criticize severely	**B.** praise	**C.** sell
35. **detain**	______	______	**A.** delay	**B.** perfect	**C.** release
36. **deter**	______	______	**A.** discourage	**B.** encourage	**C.** appreciate
37. **deteriorate**	______	______	**A.** diminish	**B.** decay	**C.** improve
38. **deplore**	______	______	**A.** disapprove of	**B.** approve	**C.** disgust
39. **detest**	______	______	**A.** hate	**B.** tease	**C.** love
40. **despondent**	______	______	**A.** depressed	**B.** ashamed	**C.** cheerful
41. **detrimental**	______	______	**A.** intermittent	**B.** harmful	**C.** beneficial
42. **dexterous**	______	______	**A.** real	**B.** skillful	**C.** inept
43. **discreet**	______	______	**A.** careful	**B.** fearful	**C.** careless
44. **despair**	______	______	**A.** hopelessness	**B.** disturbance	**C.** optimism
45. **disparity**	______	______	**A.** dissimilarity	**B.** resemblance	**C.** certainty
46. **dissipate**	______	______	**A.** scatter	**B.** gather	**C.** fabricate
47. **deprive**	______	______	**A.** hold back	**B.** bestow	**C.** negate
48. **disgrace**	______	______	**A.** carelessness	**B.** shame	**C.** honor
49. **disturb**	______	______	**A.** remove	**B.** irritate	**C.** calm
50. **debate**	______	______	**A.** demonstration	**B.** argument	**C.** agreement
51. **deduct**	______	______	**A.** reduce	**B.** retain	**C.** add
52. **delicate**	______	______	**A.** fragile	**B.** delicious	**C.** healthy
53. **deliver**	______	______	**A.** hand over	**B.** keep	**C.** excite

	Synonym	Antonym			
54. **donor**	______	______	**A.** destiny	**B.** giver	**C.** recipient
55. **drastic**	______	______	**A.** limited	**B.** extremely severe	**C.** mild
56. **egocentric**	______	______	**A.** self-centered	**B.** religious	**C.** humble
57. **entertain**	______	______	**A.** amuse	**B.** bore	**C.** plentiful
58. **emerge**	______	______	**A.** appear	**B.** vanish	**C.** poke
59. **endorse**	______	______	**A.** support	**B.** disapprove	**C.** protrude
60. **encounter**	______	______	**A.** foretell	**B.** meet with	**C.** avoid
61. **endowment**	______	______	**A.** valuable gift to college	**B.** blessing	**C.** loss
62. **esteem**	______	______	**A.** respect	**B.** scorn	**C.** gamut
63. **extensive**	______	______	**A.** broad	**B.** narrow	**C.** bored
64. **elaborate**	______	______	**A.** detailed	**B.** disastrous	**C.** simple
65. **embarrass**	______	______	**A.** disgrace	**B.** honor	**C.** delegate
66. **exhaust**	______	______	**A.** taste	**B.** deplete	**C.** conserve
67. **explicit**	______	______	**A.** clear	**B.** famous	**C.** ambiguous
68. **expel**	______	______	**A.** dismiss	**B.** frighten	**C.** welcome
69. **excel**	______	______	**A.** surpass	**B.** fail	**C.** shorten
70. **estrange**	______	______	**A.** separate	**B.** reconcile	**C.** accept
71. **exhilarate**	______	______	**A.** enliven	**B.** puzzle	**C.** discourage
72. **escalate**	______	______	**A.** climb	**B.** increase	**C.** decrease
73. **earn**	______	______	**A.** obtain	**B.** spend	**C.** store
74. **emphasize**	______	______	**A.** stress	**B.** downplay	**C.** debate
75. **employ**	______	______	**A.** accept	**B.** hire	**C.** dismiss

EXERCISE 4

Matching Meanings: Set 1

■ Match each word with its meaning.

_____ 1. voracious	**A.** weird; strange and difficult to explain; mysterious
_____ 2. viable	**B.** greedy in eating or desire
_____ 3. transform	**C.** combine or bring together in a whole
_____ 4. unscrupulous	**D.** state of uncertainty; dilemma
_____ 5. uncanny	**E.** take an idea and pass it off as one's own
_____ 6. ratify	**F.** foolish; laughable
_____ 7. synthesize	**G.** able to live or survive
_____ 8. scrutinize	**H.** well-filled; plentifully supplied
_____ 9. quandary	**I.** change or alter
_____ 10. replete	**J.** without principles; not honorable
_____ 11. preposterous	**K.** confirm or approve
_____ 12. plagiarize	**L.** examine or look at closely and carefully

EXERCISE 5

Matching Meanings: Set 2

■ Match each word with its meaning.

_____ 1. acute — **A.** easily seen or noticed

_____ 2. adroit — **B.** lessen the value or price

_____ 3. bigot — **C.** a baffling person or situation that is difficult to understand; mysterious

_____ 4. bias — **D.** frivolously amusing; not serious

_____ 5. conspicuous — **E.** intolerant of a race that is not one's own

_____ 6. condescend — **F.** showing great intensity of feeling

_____ 7. depreciate — **G.** extremely joyful

_____ 8. dissuade — **H.** cleverly skillful; resourceful

_____ 9. enigmatic — **I.** go beneath one's dignity

_____ 10. exuberant — **J.** advise against

_____ 11. facetious — **K.** sharp; severe

_____ 12. fervent — **L.** prejudice; predisposed point of view

EXERCISE 6

Word Meaning in Context: Set 1

■ Read each sentence and find the missing word in the box below. Fill in the blank with the correct *form* of that word.

scrutinize	**unscrupulous**	**plagiarize**	**viable**
preposterous	**voracious**	**replete**	**synthesize**
transform	**quandary**	**ratify**	**uncanny**

1. Her __________ appetite for knowledge is amazing. She read more than one thousand books last year.
2. Adopting a vegetarian diet may be a __________ solution for people with high cholesterol.
3. Caterpillars enter cocoons to __________ into butterflies.
4. Throughout the town, he was known as being __________, so no one wanted to do business with him.
5. The girl's __________ resemblance to her dead mother made John think he was seeing a ghost.
6. As soon as Congress __________ the bill, it will become law.
7. Many drugs formerly obtained from plants are now __________ in laboratories.
8. It is always a good idea to __________ a contract before signing it to avoid agreeing to something you will regret.
9. Being presented with two excellent job offers put her in a __________.
10. The bar was __________ with every variety of liquor one could imagine.
11. The idea that there could be life on other planets is no longer considered __________.
12. His degree was revoked by the university's board of trustees when it was discovered that he had __________ his doctoral dissertation.

EXERCISE 7

Word Meaning in Context: Set 2

■ Read each sentence and find the missing word in the box below. Fill in the blank with the correct *form* of that word.

fervent	**dissuade**	**conspicuous**	**bigot**
facetious	**depreciate**	**enigmatic**	**adroit**
exuberant	**acute**		

1. Dogs have a more __________ sense of smell than humans do.
2. When it comes to fixing cars, no one is more __________ than my brother, who has a degree in mechanical engineering and is very good with his hands.
3. The __________ of the neighborhood united to prevent Mr. Sullivan from selling his house to foreign investors.
4. When walking in the woods during hunting season, it is wise to wear blazing orange to be __________ to hunters so they will not mistake you for a deer.
5. Mobile homes are not considered good buys because their value generally __________ over the years.

6. Despite their pleas, her parents were unable to ___________ her from marrying her alcoholic boyfriend.
7. The Mona Lisa is famous for the subject's ___________ smile.
8. The children were ___________ when they heard school had been canceled because of snow.
9. Although said with a straight face, everyone knew Tim's comment was meant to be ___________.
10. ___________ golfers will play even in the rain.

EXERCISE 8

Context Clues

- Select the word or phrase that most closely matches the meaning of the **boldfaced** word. *Note that replacing the **boldfaced** word with the right answer might not produce a grammatically correct sentence.*

1. He lost his **status** as a leader in the community when charges of rape were brought against him.
   A. house **B.** position **C.** friends **D.** dowry

2. It was a clear-cut decision that offered a **straightforward** solution.
   A. easy to understand **B.** old-fashioned
   C. sharp and cutting **D.** hard to understand

3 The diplomatic **strategy** offered a good approach to ending the war.
   A. sense **B.** call **C.** plan **D.** trick

4. The organization changed the **structure** of its management team to become more efficient.
   A. the way something is maintained **B.** the way something is organized
   C. the way something is destroyed **D.** the way something is averted

5. Pedro's management **style** was admired by everyone, and he was recognized as the best executive in his company.
   A. the way something is created **B.** the way something is ended
   C. the way something is done **D.** the way something is consumed

6. Shawn's co-workers complained that he made them feel **subordinate** and inferior.
   A. cost-effective **B.** less important **C.** underdressed **D.** more important

7. The government **subsidy** to farmers kept food prices low across the country.
   A. place of business **B.** granted money **C.** call to duty **D.** high taxes

8. As the last living member of her family, she would be the only **successor** to her parents' fortune and business.
   A. end of tradition **B.** top wage-earner **C.** one who follows **D.** written contract

9. He lost a large **sum** of money after investing in high-risk ventures.
   A. amount **B.** parcel **C.** sketch **D.** suitcase

10. An environmental group **surveyed** the swampland to make sure it had returned to its natural state.
   A. destroyed **B.** restored **C.** examined **D.** wrote about

11. The passengers on the cruise ship became anxious to return home after they **survived** a dangerous storm.
    A. easily escaped **B.** lived through **C.** became lost **D.** perished

12. The Cross is a **symbol** that can be seen in many Christian churches.
    A. an inexpensive decoration **B.** an item that stands for something else
    C. a list of charitable donors **D.** a window made of colored glass

13. Several types of **tape** can be used to seal packages for mailing.
    A. a thin sticky strip of material **B.** a place of business
    C. a plan of action **D.** a set of records

14. The archery team was excited that it hit all its **targets** and won the regional championship.
    A. marks to shoot at **B.** new people **C.** moving objects **D.** judges

15. The college basketball **team** won several tournaments because its members were skilled and athletic.
    A. people in charge **B.** star player **C.** group of people **D.** professor

16. One must have a **technical** computer background to be a car mechanic today.
    A. limited **B.** dazzling **C.** scientific knowledge **D.** adaptable nature

17. The more she practiced, the more her dancing **technique** improved.
    A. interaction with others **B.** expression of emotions
    C. identification of rhythm **D.** way of doing something

18. Computer **technology** enables doctors to make more accurate diagnoses than were possible fifty years ago.
    A. quick calculations **B.** applied scientific knowledge
    C. personnel **D.** remote control

19. While the book's **text** was not especially interesting, the photographs were fantastic.
    A. correct answer **B.** written matter **C.** fancy border **D.** hidden channel

20. The magazine article introduced a new idea on the age-old **theme** of finding the perfect soul-mate.
    A. main subject **B.** special presentation **C.** dramatic monologue **D.** deep emotion

21. In the early 1940s, nuclear energy was only a **theory**, but scientists were eager to investigate whether it was possible.
    A. idea **B.** experiment **C.** weapon **D.** battle

22. Nobody liked Dr. Henry because he was always **condescending** about being wealthier and better educated than everyone else.
    A. uptight **B.** talk down to **C.** selfish **D.** sad

23. His doctoral **thesis** explaining his idea for a new vaccine was widely read in the medical community.
    A. guide **B.** research project to earn a degree
    C. distribution of a publication **D.** experience

24. The detectives **traced** the robber's footprints to the house next door, where they found him and placed him under arrest.
    A. covered up **B.** followed **C.** guessed about **D.** scoured

EXERCISE 9

Vocabulary Test

- Select the correct answer.
- Hint: Review the meanings of all the **boldfaced** words in this chapter before you take the test. This approach can help you to score 100 percent.
- Record the percentage of correct answers on the Master Self-Assessment table on page 397.

1 To **weep** is to:

A. unite
B. cry
C. mock
D. wipe

2 To **withdraw** means to:

E. take back
F. advance
G. jeer
H. resign

3 To **transfer** is to:

A. settle
B. go from one place to another
C. cease
D. hold

4 A **temporary** assignment is:

E. long-lasting
F. short-lived
G. stable
H. stylish

5 To **quit** a job is to:

A. start
B. begin
C. leave
D. find

6 To **omit** details from a report is to:

E. include
F. insert
G. provide
H. leave out or exclude

7 A **lethal** shot is:

A. safe
B. secure
C. a warning
D. deadly

8 **Invert** means:

E. secure

F. top

G. change

H. turn upside down

9 A **hasty** action is:

A. silent

B. slow

C. stable

D. speedy or done without much thought

10 When you **collaborate** with someone, you:

E. think

F. work together

G. party

H. disagree

11 A **brawl** is a:

A. match

B. game

C. fight

D. bat

12 **Chaos** refers to:

E. order

F. confusion

G. choirs

H. organization

13 Something **complicated** is:

A. simple

B. distant

C. forsaken

D. hard to understand

14 To **abandon** something is to:

E. obey it

F. accept it

G. assist it

H. leave it completely

15 A synonym for **enemy** is:

A. foe

B. fan

C. friend

D. pal

16 A **spacious** room is:

E. small

F. large in size and area

G. confining

H. beautiful

17 A **strenuous** activity:

A. is easy

B. is challenging

C. requires hard work

D. causes chaos

18 Something **sturdy** is:

E. weak

F. strongly built

G. expensive

H. of poor quality

19 A synonym for **surplus** is:

A. extra

B. less

C. substitute

D. deficient

20 To **tolerate** means to:

E. punish

F. threaten

G. insult

H. put up with

21 To **underrate** means to:

A. praise

B. fail to recognize one's intelligence and importance

C. ignore

D. congratulate

22 A synonym for **deficit** is:

E. shortage

F. surplus

G. quantity

H. defeat

23 Something **detrimental** to one's health is:

A. harmful

B. harmless

C. good

D. useful

24 To **denounce** means to:

E. praise

F. liberate

G. criticize severely

H. decide

25 To **deter** someone from doing something is to:

A. discourage

B. encourage

C. motivate

D. insist

26 His health **deteriorated**, meaning that it:

E. improved

F. became worse

G. stabilized

H. was ignored

27 **Deplore** means to:

A. disapprove of

B. encourage

C. approve

D. report

28 To **detest** someone is to:

E. love

F. admire

G. tolerate

H. hate or dislike

29 Feeling **despondent** means feeling:

A. happy

B. encouraged

C. hopeless

D. bored

30 A **disparity** is a:

E. noticeable difference

F. similarity

G. likeness

H. fault or flaw

31 To **deduct** is to:

A. add on

B. subtract

C. divide

D. attach

32 **Drastic** measures are:

E. limited

F. normal

G. small

H. extreme

33 An **egocentric** person:

A. is depressed

B. is self-centered or thinks highly of one's self

C. has low self-esteem

D. lacks confidence

34 To **endorse** a candidate for an election is to:

E. approve or support

F. reject

G. ban

H. discourage

35 **Exhausting** one's savings means:

A. increasing

B. multiplying

C. using up completely

D. sharing

36 Something that is **explicit** is:

E. unclear

F. restricted

G. clear

H. hidden

37 **Estrange** means:

A. unite

B. together

C. make up

D. break a bond of loyalty or affection

38 Prices of goods **escalate**:

E. decrease

F. increase

G. stabilize

H. decline

39 A **viable** organism is:

A. struggling

B. fragile

C. able to survive

D. inferior

40 To **transform** is to:

E. change completely

F. stay the same

G. move on

H. leave out

41 An **unscrupulous** person is:

A. respectable

B. wealthy

C. honorable

D. lacking principles

42 Something that is **uncanny** is:

E. comforting

F. rewarding

G. strange and difficult to explain

H. enjoyable

43 To **ratify** is to:

A. decline

B. question

C. confirm by expressing approval

D. reject

44 To **synthesize** means to:

E. combine
F. extract
G. separate
H. keep apart

45 To **scrutinize** something is to:

A. browse
B. ignore
C. examine carefully
D. recognize briefly

46 **Quandary** refers to a:

E. happy mood
F. negative feeling
G. state of uncertainty
H. quarter of something

47 **Replete** means:

A. lacking
B. insufficient
C. repeated
D. full of

48 A **preposterous** plan is:

E. very foolish and unreasonable
F. sensible
G. serious
H. enjoyable

49 To **plagiarize** an article is to:

A. borrow it
B. use it as one's own
C. be tested on it
D. summarize it

50 An **acute** pain is:

E. sharp or severe
F. painless
G. fatal
H. imaginary

51 An **adroit** fisherman is:

A. very clever and skillful
B. careless
C. carefree
D. ignorant

52 A **bigot** is someone who:

E. loves books
F. is intolerant of different beliefs or creed
G. is generous and considerate
H. feels passionate about the world

53 A **conspicuous** object is:

A. easily seen or noticeable

B. hidden

C. unavailable

D. concealed

54 **Condescending** people:

E. assume an air of superiority

F. are humble

G. are always friendly

H. enjoy activities with others

55 **Depreciating** means:

A. being valuable

B. being very expensive

C. lessening in value

D. being undervalued

56 An **enigmatic** person is:

E. simple

F. mysterious and difficult to understand

G. pleasant

H. energetic

57 To **dissuade** someone is to:

A. advise against

B. educate

C. encourage

D. threaten

58 An **exuberant** person is:

E. peaceful

F. talkative

G. weak

H. full of energy and excitement

59 A **facetious** remark is:

A. meant to be funny

B. serious

C. sincere

D. vulgar

60 A synonym for **fervent** is:

E. boredom

F. funny

G. passionate or enthusiastic

H. famous

EXERCISE 10

Building a Stronger Vocabulary

- Review all the **boldfaced** words in this chapter before you proceed to the next exercise.
- Highlight the ones you are still having difficulty remembering.
- List them with their meanings on a table.
- Use them to compose your own sentences.
- Think of a synonym and an antonym for each word.
- Use checkmarks to indicate if each word you want to practice more has a prefix, suffix, and/or root.
- You may use the table below as a sample to write your answers in your notebook.

Word	Definition	Sentence	Synonym	Antonym	Prefix	Suffix	Root

EXERCISE 11

Creating My Own Powerful Word List

- Write the words and meanings from the above table on the **Creating My Own Powerful Word List** table on page 398. Review them often to build that super vocabulary you want to create for school, work, and everyday use.

PRE-READING

About This Chapter from *Trial of Love*

- Read the names and descriptions of this chapter's main characters below.
  - Senator Rex
  - Ronald Spinster: A detective
  - Andrew Stevenson: DA (District Attorney) of Manhattan
  - Dibagio Alexander: Senator Rex's attorney
  - Pamela Tate and Diana Katori: Senator Rex's deceased wives
  - Harley Davidson: A hit man
  - Dorothy
  - Maxwell
  - Mark
  - Kamla
  - Dr. Azeez
  - Berry: Kamla's former student

Story Vocabulary Exercise

- Before you begin reading this chapter, figure out the meanings of the unfamiliar **boldfaced** vocabulary words. You may use the Word List, Word Parts Chart, or your dictionary to assist you in finding their meanings.
- Look for the various types of context clues—synonyms, antonyms, general context, and examples—as you read.
- Write a word or phrase about the meaning of each **boldfaced** word in the margin.

Reading and Writing Exercise

- Skim the entire chapter and pay attention to the headings and the discussion questions that follow.
- Initial Response: Write a paragraph explaining, in your own words, what you think this chapter of the story will be about.
- Final Response: After you have read the entire chapter, compare your current understanding with your initial response above. If your initial response was accurate, you can simply write it again to fill in the blanks below. If it was not, then write a paragraph on what the chapter was really about instead.

Initial Response

This chapter **will** be about ______________________________

____

____

____

Final Response

This chapter **was** about ______________________________

____

____

____

IS SENATOR REX GUILTY OR INNOCENT?

For several weeks, Detective Ronald Spinster had been studying the evidence he had accumulated on Senator Rex that could link him to the murder of his ex-wives. Twice he had planned to arrest him. However, he stopped both times because he feared the senator would be **acquitted** because of his political influence. That had changed now that Maxwell Edison had provided him with solid evidence. After much encouragement and persuasion from his boss, Detective Spinster presented all his findings on Senator Rex to Andrew Stevenson, District Attorney of Manhattan. To Spinster's intense delight, Senator Rex was summoned by the DA for questioning. **Excerpts** from a week of **interrogation** indicated the DA's **fervent** desire to **prosecute** Senator Rex. Dibagio Alexander, Senator Rex's attorney, had been present during questioning.

"Senator Rex, evidence was submitted to me that could possibly **warrant** charges against you for **conspiracy** to murder your ex-wives, Pamela Tate and Diana Katori. During the course of the week, witnesses may be presented to **testify**. If you haven't done so, please consult with your attorney, who will **apprise** you of your legal rights. May I **proceed** with my questions?"

"Certainly."

"Senator, I'll begin by asking questions about Pamela."

"That's fine with me."

"How did Pamela die?"

"Pamela and I went skiing last January in Maine. Unfortunately, she suddenly fell from a slope while skiing. As a consequence, her neck was broken and she died on **impact**."

"To your knowledge, had anyone ever died at that resort before that incident?"

"No."

"Why do you think that is?"

"I don't know."

"Her death has **baffled** investigators. Records indicate that the slope was gentle and not steep enough to cause someone's death. Nobody has ever died at that resort since it was established in 1849."

"Pamela was an **amateur** and was speeding despite my warning her against it."

"Were you skiing with her at the time of the incident?"

"No."

"Then how do you know she was speeding?"

"I am guessing."

"That means she could've been skiing cautiously when she fell."

"Possibly."

"Where were you while she was skiing?" Andrew Stevenson asked.

"In the **lodge**, having coffee."

"Can you **confirm** that?"

"Well, yes. There were several people in the lodge at that time."

"Can you name one person who saw you there?"

"I can't think of a name. I didn't know anybody there."

"Did you love Pamela, Senator?"

"What sort of question is that?"

"Did you?"

"She was the woman of my dreams."

"Is that a 'yes' or a 'no'?"

"I loved Pamela dearly," Senator Rex said.

"Have you ever inquired about the progress of the investigation of her death?"

"It wasn't necessary because it was an accident. Besides, it was Spinster's job to investigate how she died."

Dibagio was taking notes while the DA was questioning Senator Rex. He was convinced that the questions asked were **routine** and the DA did not have a case against his client. After a brief **recess**, the DA questioned the senator about Diana's death.

"Senator, how long after Pamela's death did you marry Diana, your second wife?"

"Six weeks."

"Were you having an affair with Diana while you were married to Pamela?"

"Objection!" interrupted Dibagio. "Your question is **irrelevant**. This isn't a case about the senator's love life."

"Senator, how did Diana die?" continued the DA.

"She went to a **yoga retreat** in Bangladesh. On the final day, she attended a **banquet**. Regrettably, someone pushed her from the balcony of the banquet hall."

"Do you know who the **culprit** is?"

"I would have had the person arrested if I knew him."

"Him? How do you know it was a male?"

"I didn't mean to say it was a male."

"Where were you when the incident occurred?"

"At home, in America."

"Why didn't you go with her to Bangladesh?"

"People considered her strange because she was an **ardent** follower of Vishnu Biswas, a **yogi**. Diana was in a **relentless pursuit** of inner peace and desperately seeking a channel to connect with the **Supreme** Being. Meditation through faithful practice of yoga was a **medium** for connecting with the Supreme Being, according to her. I have no interest in yoga."

"Sir, how much money did you receive from her life insurance policy?"

"What insurance policy?"

The DA read a letter from the insurance company to Senator Rex concerning Diana's policy. Then he confronted him.

"Senator, you're the beneficiary of five million dollars, aren't you?"

"Correct. For a minute I had a mental block."

"How convenient," the DA said with bitter **sarcasm**.

"Honestly, I had forgotten that I received that sum of money."

"No more questions. If you and your counsel agree, that'll be all for today."

When the hearing **resumed** the following day, Dorothy was brought in for questioning. The senator did not feel **intimidated** by this. She was in her wheelchair across from him and appeared to ignore his presence.

"Senator, do you know that woman?" said the DA, pointing to Dorothy Hubbard.

"Certainly, she's Dorothy."

"What was your relationship with her?"

"She worked for me."

"In what capacity?"

"Dorothy was my secretary."

"Why did you hire her?"

"Her husband, Maxwell Hubbard, was my loyal political **aide**," said the senator.

"Is that why you hired her?"

"I sent Maxwell on a dangerous mission overseas. Since he didn't return when expected, I concluded he was killed. So I hired Dorothy because she was unemployed and desperately needed money to take care of herself and her son, Mark."

"Can you elaborate on the mission, Senator?"

"In the interest of national security, I can't."

"Who else was working for you?"

"Jasmine Furlough."

"How would you describe the relationship between Dorothy and Jasmine?"

"They were good friends."

"Did Jasmine ever visit Dorothy at her house?"

"I don't know."

"Are you certain?"

As soon as the DA asked the question, Senator Rex poured a glass of water and **gulped** it nervously. "Is that all?" he asked the DA.

A confident smile lingered on the DA's face as he continued with his thoughtful questions. "Senator, did you murder Pamela and Diana?"

Dibagio, who was tapping his pen on his notepad and seeming to pay no attention to the DA, suddenly stamped his feet and pounded the table with his fists. Then he yelled, "Stop this nonsense, stop harassing my client! He knows nothing about their deaths! He's innocent!"

The DA ignored him and proceeded with more **provocative** questions.

"Senator, did you murder your wives?"

"Don't answer, Senator," advised Dibagio.

"Dibagio, I have nothing to conceal because I'm not **guilty**. I'm innocent," said Senator Rex.

"Senator, you didn't murder Pamela and Diana," the DA said, "but you paid someone to commit the crimes. About ten minutes prior to Pamela's death, you were seen with someone wearing a purple ski mask. He fits the description of a **notorious hit man** who occasionally worked for the mob, according to Detective Spinster. This **scoundrel** was also seen at the **retreat** in Bangladesh."

"That is **mere speculation**," said Senator Rex. "I don't know any hit man."

"A patrolman at the ski lodge saw you talking to him. The yogi confirmed his presence at the banquet."

"I insist that I don't know any hit man," replied Senator Rex confidently.

The DA stared at Detective Spinster and nodded. Spinster left the room but returned within a minute with a man in handcuffs.

"Sir, what's your name?" questioned the DA.

"Harley Davidson. And yeah, before you ask, my dad liked his motorcycles."

"Have you seen that gentleman before?" he asked, pointing at Senator Rex.

"Yes."

"What's his name?"

"Senator Rex."

"Were you ever associated with him?"

"Definitely."

"Can you elaborate?

"He paid me to murder his first wife, Pamela, while she was skiing in Maine."

"Did he also pay you to murder his second wife in Bangladesh?"

"Yes. I was paid a total of two hundred and fifty thousand dollars for both murders."

"Liar! Who set you up to frame me?" shouted Senator Rex.

"Sir, the senator is a cheap man," Harley continued, paying no attention to Senator Rex's outburst. "When I called him for my fee, he initially refused to pay the sum we agreed on. Without hesitation, I stormed into his office the following day and aimed my pistol at his forehead. He trembled uncontrollably. But slowly, he loaded stacks of bills into my duffle bag. Then I left for Brazil because that was part of our agreement. Unfortunately, Spinster tracked me down in Brazil and brought me back to New York."

"Thank you, Mr. Davidson," the DA said.

Although Senator Rex was angry, he didn't **refute** this last part of Davidson's testimony. Dibagio was visibly perplexed and **racking** his brain for a convincing and credible **defense**. As soon as Davidson was **escorted** to the holding cell, the DA read his conclusion to the hearing.

"Maxwell Hubbard learned of your criminal acts and threatened to report the incidents to Detective Spinster. Before he took action, you **assigned** him to that life-threatening mission that you say you cannot disclose, hoping he'd die. When Dorothy casually mentioned at work that he wrote detailed notes in his diary, you suspected she also knew of the murders. You hired her hoping either you or Jasmine would gain access to her house and have a chance to steal the diary.

"Dorothy read the diary," the DA continued. "She figured out your plan from the numerous questions Jasmine had been asking her every day at work. Dorothy bought a **blank** diary and skillfully **forged** Maxwell's handwriting, but omitted the sections pertaining to your wives. In other words, she created a **fake** diary, which she placed in their safe.

"Senator, you stole the fake diary from the safe when you visited her house on the night you had planned for her death. Detective Spinster found your **fingerprints** on the safe. Stealing the diary was a simple task for you. You had studied the layout of the entire house from photographs Jasmine had secretly taken a week earlier, when she had visited Dorothy for dinner. Although the fake diary didn't contain information about the murders, you were not certain of how much information her husband had disclosed to her about your illegal dealings. You were therefore determined to have her crushed to death in a parking garage.

"A waiter at Tavern Inn, where you frequently dined, overheard you instructing someone on the telephone to kill Dorothy by running over her. You said to do it in the parking garage **adjoining** Best Steak, her favorite restaurant, where she ate every Saturday evening.

"Fortunately, that person you hired was highly **intoxicated** when he tried to run over her. He only hit her right side. You were alarmed that she had miraculously survived. Although Dorothy was paralyzed, you were determined to have her killed as you had initially set out to do. To **accomplish** your evil objective, you placed her in the nursing home owned by your friend, Harry Ruthless. Ruthless agreed to **waive** Dorothy's fee for her care in the nursing home because you had helped him obtain federal **grants** in the amount of ten million dollars during the past three years. Additionally, Ruthless was the top **donor** to your re-election campaign.

"Senator, you placed Dorothy in Ruthless's nursing home because you knew you had easy access to it and could finish your plot to kill Dorothy. Although Ruthless **facilitated** your request to have security guards stationed at the nursing home, watching over Dorothy around the clock to ensure she posed no threat while you figured out how best to finish her off, you were unsuccessful again. Luck was on Dorothy's side. Her son, Mark, **intervened** in time to save her from you, an evil and cruel man.

"Earlier, you were **dumbfounded** when Dorothy's daughter-in-law, Kamla, became determined to **blackmail** you. Dorothy had given her the original diary with the records of the murders. Willingly, you paid Kamla a million dollars for the diary. Kamla signed an affidavit stating that she had given you the **original** diary. This was true. However, she **submitted** a **photocopy** of the journal to me. Senator, what do you have to say in your **defense**?"

"Nothing, except that you can't prove these **accusations**. Is Detective Spinster ready to read my rights?" asked Senator Rex with a sullen expression on his face.

"No. I'm not done with you, Senator," replied the DA.

"Why are you determined to send me to jail?"

"That's where **monsters** like you belong. Now, there are a few more people who have agreed to **participate** in this hearing. Are you prepared to listen to other charges Captain Turney has brought against you?"

"Who?" asked Senator Rex and Dibagio in **unison**.

"Captain Turney works for the FBI," replied the DA mockingly.

"This is **ludicrous**! What charges did he **fabricate**? I warn you to **quit harassing** the senator," said Dibagio to the DA in a threatening voice.

Maxwell was proud as a peacock. As he entered the room with Mark and Turney, Senator Rex stared at him like a **moon-gazer**. Maxwell sat opposite him at the table.

For the first time since the hearing had begun that day, Dorothy smiled. She watched her husband and son and continued to **ignore** the senator.

"Senator, I have been able to present **substantial** evidence so far only because these gentlemen cooperated with me," the DA said. "Captain Turney requested that I **investigate** the charges that you're engaged in drug trafficking with a Cuban military officer. Furthermore, there's also evidence that you planned to sell our American secrets to him. As you're aware, this is a serious charge."

Dibagio angrily threw his notepad into his briefcase and got out of the chair. "Senator, let's go. We've wasted enough time listening to this **wiseacre**. He thinks he has a case but he doesn't. He thinks he has all the wisdom of the world."

The DA giggled like a playful child and said, "Senator, your life is on trial. Not Dibagio's. If I were you, I wouldn't make **hasty** decisions."

Senator Rex knew he would be **convicted** without a doubt if he were brought to trial. He turned to Dibagio and said, "I'll tell you when it's time to leave this room."

The DA smiled and continued speaking with the senator.

"Sir, do you know a Cuban general whose name is Geraldo?"

"I don't think so."

"Could you please **cooperate** with me, Senator?"

"As a matter of fact, I recall someone by that name. I met him at a conference in New York. We had dinner before he returned to Cuba. "

"Were you engaged in drug trafficking with him?"

"Of course not."

"Sir, did you promise to sell American military secrets, including the blueprint of a missile, to him?"

"No. No. I'm **loyal** to my country. I'm a **patriot** and not a **traitor**. That's why New Yorkers elected me to be their senator."

Maxwell's cheeks **flushed** with intense hatred the moment Senator Rex **denied** his association with General Geraldo. The DA inserted a cassette in a tape recorder and urged Senator Rex to listen attentively to it.

"Ungrateful good-for-nothing! You traitor! Why have you **betrayed** me, Maxwell?" yelled Senator Rex when the first part of the tape finished playing.

"Sir, I urge you to take a minute to regain your composure," the DA said.

"Sorry. I'm OK. But you can't believe that **hypocrite**, Maxwell. He **distorted** another person's voice to sound like mine on the tape."

"That was you speaking to General Geraldo," Maxwell insisted. "I was at his home when you telephoned him. General Geraldo always taped his conversations and incoming calls from everybody. I stole that cassette from his study to present it as evidence of your crime. Do you want to listen to another section of the tape? The part with the message you left for him about Mark's conversation with me from the nursing home where you placed my wife, Dorothy, under tight security?"

"No. I **underestimated** your abilities."

"Rex, I hope you rot in jail for the pain you've caused me and my family," Maxwell said angrily. "My wife is **confined** to a wheelchair because of you. Mark's emotional **turmoil** has **strained** his marriage. Despite my years of **unfaltering** loyalty, you attempted to murder me. You're nothing but a wild **beast** and a **disgrace** to the United States Senate."

A month later, Senator Rex was tried and sentenced to fifteen years in prison. In addition, the judge **revoked** his United States citizenship. He was deported to Cuba the same day he finished his prison term in New York. The judge was **lenient** with Senator Rex because he **cooperated** with the DA during the hearing and admitted his **guilt**.

The news of Senator Rex's case spread across the Internet through Twitter, Facebook, and other forms of **social media**. The entire world learned what he had been doing with General Geraldo on the day he was tried.

General Geraldo's attempt to steal American military secrets was an embarrassment to the Cuban government that had been working long and hard to improve its relationship with the United States. The government had never **authorized** General Geraldo to engage in illegal activities with Senator Rex. The Attorney General of Cuba decided to make an example of General Geraldo who was eventually sentenced to seventy-five years in prison.

Jasmine was not charged with any criminal activities. She visited Senator Rex regularly in prison for about a year. Eventually, she joined the Peace Corps and was **stationed** in Nepal. Jasmine did not regret her decision to refuse Senator Rex's marriage proposal when she had first started to work for him.

Maxwell's testimony of Senator Rex's criminal offenses earned him immense international **eminence**. He used that popularity and fame to run for Senator Rex's position in the United States Senate. Although the polls revealed that he would undoubtedly **replace** Senator Rex, he spent several months **campaigning** with Mark.

Throughout his time on the campaign trail, Mark thought constantly of Kamla. Part of him was angry that she had sold his father's diary to Senator Rex, even if she had handed another copy to the police. The other part hoped that their time apart would help her to forgive him. Whatever happened between him and Kamla, he knew he had to return and be a father to Erwin. He would not put his son through the same things he had suffered when his own father had disappeared.

Why Did Kamla Sell the Diary to Senator Rex?

At long last, Dorothy was discharged from the nursing home and allowed to move back in with her husband, Maxwell. The nightmare of living under Senator Rex's thumb had ended. Although Maxwell had to leave to campaign elsewhere in the state, he took the time to have the house made wheelchair accessible first, and arranged to have a nurse check in on Dorothy once a day.

Dorothy suspected Kamla had a compelling reason for selling the diary that she had given her, wrapped with gift paper, when she visited the nursing home. After **mustering** sufficient courage, she telephoned Kamla to invite her to her home. Excitedly, Kamla accepted her invitation and brought her son, Erwin, to visit his grandmother for the first time. Dorothy was overjoyed to see and play with Erwin. Despite the excitement expressed by Dorothy, Kamla sensed that something was bothering her. Kamla **diplomatically** asked her about it.

"Kamla, I was excited to see you when you initially came to visit me in the nursing home. But I nearly **collapsed** in disbelief when the DA said you sold the diary to Senator Rex. I thought I would fall right out of my wheelchair."

Kamla felt hurt after listening to Dorothy. She was speechless for a few minutes. Tears were in her eyes. She felt as if Dorothy distrusted her.

Dorothy asked, "Kamla, why are you quiet? What do you have to say?"

Kamla replied, "To be truthful, I **anticipated** that you'd **confront** me about selling the diary."

"Why did you sell it, dear?" asked Dorothy **eagerly**.

Kamla replied, "I have a surprise for you, Dorothy."

"What is it?"

"Someone will be visiting you later this evening."

"Who? Can't you be **forthright**?"

"Be patient, Dorothy!"

"Is it someone I know?"

"No. Do you recall when I mentioned the world's leading **neurosurgeon**, who lives in India?"

"I think of him every day, even though I haven't met him. Kamla, the only wish I have is to **regain** the partial memory I lost and be able to walk again. The accident that Senator Rex **masterminded** did a number on me."

"The neurosurgeon is a personal friend of Dr. Azeez's dad."

"Who's Dr. Azeez?"

"The doctor who delivered your grandson. He's now a close friend of our family—I promise, you'll meet him soon. The surgeon will be arriving tonight. Dr. Azeez has already made arrangements for your surgery at the hospital where he's working."

"I'm not having that surgery."

"Why not?

"I can't afford it."

"I paid the bill a few weeks ago."

"Where did you get the money?"

"The only reason I sold the diary was to have money for the surgery."

"Kamla, you should've consulted with me. I don't feel comfortable that you used blood money to pay for my surgery."

"Can we argue about this after the surgery, Dorothy?"

When Dorothy regained consciousness after her operation, she called for Kamla to come to her bedside. Kamla stayed with her throughout her recovery. In less than one week, Dorothy's memory loss was **reversed** and she slowly began to walk.

When Mark and Maxwell returned home from campaigning in upstate New York that weekend, they were astonished to see her walking around the house. Neither was aware that she had gone in for surgery. Dorothy wanted to keep it a secret.

"Mother, how did you manage to make arrangements for the surgery? You could have hardly done it yourself."

"Well. . . ." she said, searching for words.

"Who assisted you?" he asked anxiously.

"An angel who cares deeply about you and me."

"Stop speaking in **riddles**, Mother. Who helped you?"

"It was Kamla, Mark."

"I don't believe you! I was under the impression you **despised** her for selling the diary to Senator Rex. Didn't she **betray** you?"

"At first, I hated her for what she had done. But she had a good reason."

"I'm curious to hear her explanation."

"She sold the diary only to pay for the surgery and related expenses. However, the doctor returned the money after the surgery. He is a very generous **philanthropist**. Kamla donated every penny of it to the medical clinic serving the **underprivileged** in her village in India.

"Really! Kamla did that for you?"

"Yes. We've **misjudged** her. Mark, Kamla is the perfect wife you've been looking for all your life. You're lucky to have found her."

"I thought a great deal about her and the baby while we were campaigning, Mother. I neglected her for several months because I was preoccupied with law school and Dad's disappearance. I don't blame her for leaving me. But I wish she'd return so that we could start over again."

"Kamla is upstairs with the baby in your bedroom. I'm happy that you love her as much as I do, Mark."

Maxwell left the bedroom with Erwin as soon as Mark entered. Kamla knew Mark still loved her. They had a long conversation and made up. Kamla understood that Mark had spent so much time away because he had been hot on the trail of his father, and had often been too caught up in critical parts of the investigation to return home. She only wished he had shared his problems and asked for her help rather than shutting her out. He vowed to do so from then on.

Later that day, Maxwell spent several hours getting to know Kamla. He embraced her as the daughter he had wished for his entire life.

Who Is the Father of Kamla's Child?

Three weeks later, they **celebrated** Maxwell's **victory** at his campaign headquarters in Manhattan. It was a **memorable** night for Kamla. As she was about to sip her drink, she felt a gentle tap on her shoulder.

"I haven't seen you for ages, Professor Kamla. I went to campus a few times but couldn't find you. Where have you been?" Berry asked curiously.

"I am currently on **maternity** leave, Berry. I'm surprised you remember me," said Kamla.

"How could I forget my favorite professor at Rollins University? Your words of inspiration **motivated** me to graduate with my degree in criminology," Berry said appreciatively.

"Are you working for the police department as you **aspired** to when you were in school?" asked Kamla.

"Professor Kamla, I'm now the **deputy** commissioner of my police department. Also, I **arrested** those criminals who shot my dad during the bank robbery I talked to you about. Thank God he survived. I'm in charge of security for this event tonight."

"Congratulations, Berry! I'm really proud of you. I hope you continue your studies to earn an advanced degree. You certainly have the intellectual capability and **perseverance**," said Kamla encouragingly.

"Thank you, Professor, for your confidence in me. I won't disappoint you. Guess who else is here tonight, Professor Kamla?"

"Who?"

"Your **pals**, Kathy and Cindy."

"Where are they?"

"I saw them in the lobby of the hotel a while ago. Wait a minute! They've just entered the room." Berry clapped his hands to get their attention. When they saw Kamla, they ran and hugged her, and the three of them chattered ceaselessly like in the good old days.

"What brings you ladies here?" asked Kamla.

"We wanted to visit you," replied Kathy.

"Your mother told us you'd be here," added Cindy.

"Kathy, when did you return from Guyana?" asked Kamla.

"Last night. My dad has completed his assignment at the consulate," replied Kathy.

Kamla and her friends spent the night talking about the wonderful times they had spent together at Rollins University. Before they left the political event that night, Kamla expressed her appreciation to Cindy for introducing her to Swami Venkat. She was excited to tell her and Kathy that all his predictions had been one hundred percent accurate. Kamla also explained to them that the life-threatening situation he had mentioned was related to her pregnancy.

Kathy remarked that what happened to Kamla was nothing more than a **coincidence**. She said to Cindy and Kamla, "I still don't believe in that stuff. God is above man. Only He knows the future."

Both Cindy and Kamla ignored her. They felt that their beliefs had been **vindicated**.

The three good friends said good-bye to each other and went home. Their friendship only grew stronger when they returned to work together, and it continued even after they **retired** from Rollins University.

Kathy and Cindy married two brothers from Guyana. Kathy had met them when she lived there briefly with her parents. Both women frequently went on vacation with their spouses and children.

Mark went on to graduate from law school and worked as an assistant district attorney in New York City. Kamla continued teaching at Rollins University and was a devoted mother to Erwin.

A few weeks after the celebration of Maxwell's successful campaign, Mark and Kamla finally returned to their apartment with their baby. They immediately invited their friends and family to a dinner party. They did not plan the party earlier because they had been waiting for Rita, Sonny, and Joshi and his family to return from India after a long vacation. Kamla's grandma came with them to New York for a brief stay. Unexpectedly, they ran into Dr. Azeez and his wife at the airport in New York. The couple were on their way to a medical conference in California. They greeted each other with mutual respect.

Kamla's parents met Mark's family for the first time at the dinner party. They got along very well despite the distinct cultural differences of the two families.

Rita and Sonny's only regret was that Kamla had lost her **keen** interest in pursuing medical science research. Their hope for their daughter to win a Nobel Prize, their only reason for coming to America, was **shattered** temporarily, if not permanently.

In **retrospect**, Kamla saw the day of the party as a day of **reconciliation**. Everybody had hurt the people they loved, but at that party, everything was forgiven. All of their wounds had healed.

Kamla was confident that Mark, and not Dr. Azeez, was the father of her son, because she had never had an **intimate** relationship with Dr. Azeez. They had spent that night together in India talking and had gone no farther. Yet over the years, she kept Sheila's suspicious mind **wandering** like a restless river.

EXERCISE 1

Applying the Words You Have Learned to Critical Thinking and Creative Writing

- Use the two questions in Section A below to discuss this chapter with your classmates. Be sure to apply your critical thinking skills.

- Write an essay about either question using the vocabulary words you know from real-life experiences and the new ones you have learned from this text.

Section A

Discussion Questions

1. What is *Trial of Love* about?

2. What did you learn from it?

EXERCISE 2

Matching Meanings

■ Match each word with its meaning.

_____	1. cardiologist	**A.** a cancerous growth
_____	2. dermatologist	**B.** specializes in the nervous system and its diseases
_____	3. podiatrist	**C.** prediction of the course of a disease
_____	4. ophthalmologist	**D.** microorganism that causes infectious diseases; has an RNA or DNA core
_____	5. gynecologist	**E.** a substance that speeds up chemical reactions without being changed itself
_____	6. urologist	**F.** weariness or exhaustion
_____	7. neurologist	**G.** one-celled microorganisms; spherical, spiral or rod-shaped
_____	8. orthopedics	**H.** protected against a certain disease
_____	9. bacteria	**I.** reduction in the number of red blood corpuscles
_____	10. virus	**J.** removal of body tissue for examination
_____	11. cardiovascular	**K.** specializes in the care of the feet
_____	12. cholesterol	**L.** increased body temperature
_____	13. prognosis	**M.** studies the heart and its functions
_____	14. catalyst	**N.** specializes in the skin and its diseases
_____	15. fatigue	**O.** specializes in the urinary system and its diseases
_____	16. allergy	**P.** part of the body that performs specific functions; has specialized tissues
_____	17. cell	**Q.** relating to the heart and blood vessels
_____	18. serum	**R.** studies the anatomy, function and diseases of the eyes
_____	19. insulin	**S.** a structural unit of plant and animal life
_____	20. immune	**T.** a clear yellowish fluid of the blood
_____	21. fever	**U.** hypersensitivity to certain substances or conditions
_____	22. carcinoma	**V.** the correction or prevention of skeletal deformities
_____	23. anemia	**W.** chemical substance that can cause heart disease
_____	24. biopsy	**X.** assists the body in using carbohydrates
_____	25. organ	**Y.** specializes in diseases of the female reproductive system

EXERCISE 3

Forming Synonyms

■ Fill in the blank(s) to complete the word that is similar in meaning to the **boldfaced** word.

1. **knock** h__t
2. **lead** gui__ __
3. **motive** pur__ __se
4. **liable** accou__ __able
5. **label** ma__k
6. **magnitude** grea__ __ess
7. **vertical** er__ct
8. **mania** fix__ __ion
9. **menace** thr__ __t
10. **morale** confi__ __ __ce
11. **massage** str__ke
12. **matrimony** wed__ __ng
13. **malady** sic__ness
14. **massacre** slaug__ __er
15. **meander** __wist
16. **merchandise** go__ds
17. **mistake** er__or
18. **modify** ch__ __ge

EXERCISE 4

Synonyms and Antonyms

■ Write the corresponding letter for the synonym and antonym of each **boldfaced** word.

	Synonym	Antonym			
1. **prefer**	______	______	**A.** favor	**B.** dislike	**C.** repose
2. **prevent**	______	______	**A.** stop from doing	**B.** allow	**C.** pretend
3. **prohibit**	______	______	**A.** prevent	**B.** permit	**C.** fight
4. **purchase**	______	______	**A.** buy	**B.** fill	**C.** sell
5. **puzzle**	______	______	**A.** deplore	**B.** confuse	**C.** aware
6. **quite**	______	______	**A.** although	**B.** totally	**C.** incompletely
7. **resist**	______	______	**A.** toughen	**B.** oppose	**C.** comply
8. **render**	______	______	**A.** give	**B.** receive	**C.** take
9. **rational**	______	______	**A.** logical	**B.** unreasonable	**C.** slanted
10. **refute**	______	______	**A.** prove false	**B.** debate	**C.** support
11. **rebuke**	______	______	**A.** jest	**B.** scold	**C.** praise
12. **resilient**	______	______	**A.** bend easily	**B.** stiff	**C.** internal
13. **repugnant**	______	______	**A.** disgusting	**B.** stylish	**C.** attractive
14. **resist**	______	______	**A.** settle	**B.** oppose	**C.** succumb
15. **reply**	______	______	**A.** answer	**B.** ask	**C.** resign
16. **regret**	______	______	**A.** displeasure	**B.** sense of loss	**C.** satisfaction
17. **recognize**	______	______	**A.** identify	**B.** miss	**C.** perform
18. **recollect**	______	______	**A.** accept	**B.** remember	**C.** forget
19. **recommend**	______	______	**A.** suggest	**B.** distance	**C.** disapprove
20. **record**	______	______	**A.** put down in writing	**B.** delete	**C.** confuse
21. **rectify**	______	______	**A.** correct	**B.** support	**C.** damage
22. **relax**	______	______	**A.** amaze	**B.** rest	**C.** labor
23. **relentless**	______	______	**A.** continuous	**B.** ending	**C.** cunning
24. **require**	______	______	**A.** devote	**B.** need	**C.** have
25. **sufficient**	______	______	**A.** multiple	**B.** enough	**C.** deficient

	Synonym	Antonym			
26. **superficial**	______	______	**A.** without depth	**B.** slow	**C.** thorough
27. **supplement**	______	______	**A.** add to	**B.** reduce	**C.** divide
28. **taste**	______	______	**A.** experience	**B.** disregard	**C.** abstain
29. **talent**	______	______	**A.** sorrow	**B.** ability	**C.** weakness
30. **tear**	______	______	**A.** rip	**B.** exchange	**C.** mend
31. **tell**	______	______	**A.** notify	**B.** debate	**C.** conceal
32. **tense**	______	______	**A.** anxious	**B.** calm	**C.** tepid
33. **threaten**	______	______	**A.** intimidate	**B.** comfort	**C.** yearn
34. **turbulent**	______	______	**A.** stormy	**B.** rigid	**C.** quiet
35. **ultimate**	______	______	**A.** final	**B.** initial	**C.** multiple
36. **unforgettable**	______	______	**A.** lasting	**B.** unchanged	**C.** unmemorable
37. **uproar**	______	______	**A.** chaos	**B.** order	**C.** upright
38. **usual**	______	______	**A.** common	**B.** easy	**C.** atypical
39. **unique**	______	______	**A.** organized	**B.** distinctive	**C.** common
40. **uncomfortable**	______	______	**A.** uneasy	**B.** flexible	**C.** relaxed
41. **unconscious**	______	______	**A.** deformed	**B.** not awake	**C.** aware
42. **undercover**	______	______	**A.** secret	**B.** cooperative	**C.** known
43. **understand**	______	______	**A.** simplify	**B.** grasp	**C.** misinterpret
44. **urge**	______	______	**A.** delay	**B.** encourage	**C.** dissuade
45. **unrest**	______	______	**A.** dissension	**B.** silence	**C.** harmony
46. **unstable**	______	______	**A.** erratic	**B.** stable	**C.** secure
47. **unanimous**	______	______	**A.** united	**B.** disagreeable	**C.** jeering
48. **void**	______	______	**A.** tired	**B.** empty	**C.** full
49. **vile**	______	______	**A.** overt	**B.** impure	**C.** clean
50. **vindictive**	______	______	**A.** permanent	**B.** revengeful	**C.** forgiving
51. **valid**	______	______	**A.** genuine	**B.** unhealthy	**C.** false
52. **validate**	______	______	**A.** give approval to	**B.** reject	**C.** retreat
53. **versatile**	______	______	**A.** flexible	**B.** opaque	**C.** limited

	Synonym	Antonym			
54. **vigorous**	_____	_____	**A.** energetic	**B.** frail	**C.** changed
55. **vital**	_____	_____	**A.** important	**B.** unnecessary	**C.** confused
56. **vacation**	_____	_____	**A.** tribute	**B.** holiday	**C.** work
57. **virtue**	_____	_____	**A.** tension	**B.** goodness	**C.** wickedness
58. **various**	_____	_____	**A.** many	**B.** frequent	**C.** few
59. **vary**	_____	_____	**A.** change	**B.** disappoint	**C.** maintain
60. **vast**	_____	_____	**A.** immense	**B.** sly	**C.** limited
61. **vengeance**	_____	_____	**A.** retaliation	**B.** difficulty	**C.** forgiveness
62. **verbal**	_____	_____	**A.** spoken	**B.** written	**C.** tasty
63. **veto**	_____	_____	**A.** reject	**B.** hire	**C.** approve
64. **visible**	_____	_____	**A.** outdoor	**B.** noticeable	**C.** unseen
65. **variety**	_____	_____	**A.** assortment	**B.** chaos	**C.** similarity
66. **warn**	_____	_____	**A.** caution	**B.** initiate	**C.** encourage
67. **wash**	_____	_____	**A.** clean	**B.** soil	**C.** jeer

EXERCISE 5

Matching Meanings: Set 1

■ Match each word with its meaning.

_____ 1. belligerent

_____ 2. benevolent

_____ 3. bereft

_____ 4. blatant

_____ 5. cantankerous

_____ 6. clandestine

_____ 7. complacent

_____ 8. capacitate

_____ 9. promiscuous

_____ 10. perpetual

_____ 11. potpourri

_____ 12. pompous

A. obvious; conspicuous

B. self-satisfied; unconcerned

C. having sex with many people on a casual basis

D. mixture of petals and spices used as a fragrance

E. ready to fight or quarrel

F. ill-tempered; quarrelsome

G. lasting forever

H. self-important; feeling more important than others

I. done secretly

J. good; kindly

K. prepare; enable

L. deprived of; lacking

EXERCISE 6

Matching Meanings: Set 2

- Match each word with its meaning.

_____ 1. ambivalent

_____ 2. antihistamine

_____ 3. aesthetic

_____ 4. arbitrary

_____ 5. proponent

_____ 6. profound

_____ 7. poignant

_____ 8. pacify

_____ 9. impeach

_____ 10. intoxicated

_____ 11. insidious

_____ 12. inexorable

A. left to one's judgment or choice

B. deeply felt

C. calm down

D. discredit a person's reputation; accuse of misconduct

E. more dangerous than seems evident

F. drunk; inebriated

G. cannot be influenced

H. a synthetic drug

I. doubtful; having conflicting feelings

J. emotionally touching or moving; feeling of sadness

K. one who supports a proposal

L. appreciation of beauty

EXERCISE 7

Word Meaning in Context: Set 1

■ Read each sentence and find the missing word in the box below. Fill in the blank with the correct *form* of that word.

pompous	**complacent**	**cantankerous**	**bereft**
perpetual	**belligerent**	**promiscuous**	**clandestine**
potpourri	**blatant**	**capacitate**	**benevolent**

1. His ___________ attitude made many see him as a bully looking for a fight.
2. Robert could never pass a beggar without giving something; he was known as the most ___________ man in the neighborhood.
3. When in love, many people are ___________ of their senses—they cannot think straight.
4. Even though the teacher's error was ___________, none of the students dared to point it out for fear of upsetting her.
5. Because he was so ___________, most of us avoided Uncle Jim at family gatherings. Every conversation with him turned into an argument.
6. Since their parents disapproved of their relationship, all meetings between the lovers had to be ___________ and take place where people would not see them.
7. Because she partied frequently and was ___________ in her studies, she did not graduate from college.
8. Increasing the memory on your computer will ___________ it to run faster.
9. Neighbors gossiped that the new tenant was ___________ because she had male visitors at all hours of the day and night.
10. Buffalo, New York, is known for its ___________ snow showers in the wintertime.
11. The refreshing aroma of ___________ filled the living room.
12. His overly correct English made everyone regard him as ___________.

EXERCISE 8

Word Meaning in Context: Set 2

■ Read each sentence and find the missing word in the box below. Fill in the blank with the correct *form* of that word.

profound	**antihistamine**	**inexorable**	**pacify**
arbitrary	**insidious**	**impeach**	**proponent**
intoxicated	**aesthetic**	**poignant**	**ambivalent**

1. Cynthia was ___________ about her feelings toward Frank and could not decide whether she loved him enough to marry him.
2. People with hay fever can take an ___________ in the spring and summer to control their symptoms.
3. The two painters were part of the same artistic movement, but their unique ___________ made it easy to tell their work apart.
4. The manager offered no reason for canceling the meeting. As far as everyone else in the office knew, the decision was entirely ___________.

5. Do not wear your fur coat to Sally's party—she is a ___________ of animal rights.

6. Helen felt a ___________ sense of loss when her mother died.

7. The scene of the child learning he had cancer was so ___________ that half the audience burst into tears.

8. Nothing would ___________ the child when he found out that his favorite blanket had been lost.

9. The president was ___________ by Congress for participating in criminal activities.

10. Someone added liquor to the punch, and soon many guests were ___________ and unable to drive home.

11. His drinking habit was ___________: he drank one or two beers a night at first, but that eventually turned into seven or eight, and soon his liver was failing.

12. Nobody could ever change his mind, as he was ___________ in his opinions.

EXERCISE 9

Context Clues

■ Select the word or phrase that most closely matches the meaning of the **boldfaced** word. *Note that replacing the **boldfaced** word with the right answer might not produce a grammatically correct sentence.*

1. It is easy to break ancient **traditions** when living in the modern world.
   A. figures of speech **B.** practices handed down
   C. contractual agreements **D.** relics one inherits

2. She could not contact her family because she was in **transit** to her next destination.
   A. the act of moving **B.** a place of business **C.** a debt **D.** a conversation

3. Before the invention of the telephone, people used the telegraph to **transmit** messages.
   A. assemble **B.** pay for **C.** send **D.** delay

4. Cargo ships **transport** commercial goods to harbors around the world.
   A. guarantee **B.** sink **C.** carry **D.** possess

5. Some people believe that fashion **trends** should not be taken seriously because they change every year and can be costly.
   A. current styles **B.** acts of persuasion **C.** price points **D.** the next level

6. Her friend's sudden negative remark **triggered** her mood to change from happiness to anger.
   A. detained **B.** caused **C.** pulled back **D.** misguided

7. They had already climbed 20,000 feet up Mt. Everest, but they still had a long way to go—their **ultimate** goal was to reach the final peak.
   A. very dangerous **B.** happening at the end
   C. coming first **D.** at a premium cost

8. The new military recruits had to **undergo** several months of vigorous training to prepare for the war.
   A. bypass **B.** go through **C.** redefine **D.** innovate

9. He said he was motivated by his desire to help the poor, but his **underlying** reason for founding the charity was to become rich.
   A. friendly **B.** historical **C.** brave **D.** basic

10. When he became a firefighter, he also **undertook** additional responsibilities to train medical technicians.
    A. argued against **B.** thought about **C.** agreed to **D.** forbid

11. Tomatoes sold in the supermarket are **uniform** in size because people distrust variety.
    A. big **B.** always the same **C.** small **D.** ripe

12. The teacher **unified** her students so they could work together.
    A. sent away **B.** brought together **C.** tricked **D.** rewarded

13. After eighteen years on the road, the truck was no longer a useful **vehicle**.
    A. thing made of metal **B.** example of success
    C. thing that provides transportation **D.** example of cleanliness

14. Paul's **version** of the story contradicted what Jonas had told her earlier.
    A. exchange **B.** download **C.** lies **D.** account

15. She was happy to receive a letter **via** airmail instead of getting a text message.
    A. in addition to **B.** by **C.** besides **D.** in time

16. The underage driver **violated** the traffic law when he drove without a license.
    A. questioned **B.** broke **C.** went through **D.** talked about

17. Watching 3D movies at home provides a **virtual** experience that older generations could only get at a movie theater.
    A. almost real **B.** historical **C.** better **D.** cartoonish

18. After seven years of hard work, she fulfilled her **vision** of becoming a medical doctor.
    A. guidance from a mentor **B.** time for confession
    C. imagined future **D.** financial agreement

19. **Visual** aids, such as drawings, charts, and photographs, are helpful when explaining theoretical concepts.
    A. attained by sight **B.** borrowed **C.** changed over time **D.** quiet

20. His mother insisted that he reduce the **volume** on his video game so she could go to sleep.
    A. size **B.** brightness **C.** loudness of a sound **D.** data

21. The main responsibility of parents is to maintain the **welfare** of their children.
    A. place of living **B.** time of growth
    C. inner thoughts **D.** happiness, health, and success

22. She always thought several moves ahead when playing chess, **whereas** he never used a strategy.
    A. while **B.** with luck **C.** without standards **D.** overall

23. Small businesses must create an action plan **whereby** they can compete with the new mall.
    A. geographically **B.** in time **C.** by which **D.** for profit

24. The typhoon caused **widespread** damage. It was impossible for vehicles to deliver emergency aid because all of the roads were destroyed.
    A. spread out **B.** in the past **C.** only a little **D.** costing money

EXERCISE 10

Vocabulary Test

- Select the correct answer.
- Hint: Review the meanings of all the **boldfaced** words in this chapter before you take the test. This approach can help you to score 100 percent.
- Record the percentage of correct answers on the Master Self-Assessment table on page 397.

1 A **cardiologist** studies the heart and its functions.

A. True **B.** False

2 An **ophthalmologist** studies the feet.

E. True **F.** False

3 A **neurologist** studies the nervous system.

A. True **B.** False

4 A **gynecologist** studies the diseases of the male reproductive system.

E. True **F.** False

5 **Prognosis** is a prediction of the course of a disease.

A. True **B.** False

6 **Allergy** refers to hypersensitivity to certain substances or functions.

E. True **F.** False

7 **Insulin** assists the body in using carbohydrates.

A. True **B.** False

8 A **carcinoma** is a cancerous outgrowth.

E. True **F.** False

9 **Anemia** refers to the reduction in the number of white blood cells.

A. True **B.** False

10 A **biopsy** involves the removal of body tissue for examination.

E. True **F.** False

11 **Motive** means purpose.

A. True **B.** False

12 **Magnitude** means greatness.

E. True

F. False

13 Another word for **mania** is fixation.

A. True

B. False

14 **Menace** means nonthreatening.

E. True

F. False

15 Another word for **morale** is confidence.

A. True

B. False

16 **Malady** does not refer to sickness.

E. True

F. False

17 Another word for **massacre** is slaughter.

A. True

B. False

18 **Meandering** does not mean twisting.

E. True

F. False

19 **Modify** means to change.

A. True

B. False

20 To be **liable** for something is to be accountable.

E. True

F. False

21 To **prohibit** is to:

A. allow

B. accept

C. prevent

D. hide

22 **Resistance** is:

E. opposition

F. difficulty

G. approval

H. compliance

23 **Render** means to:

A. keep

B. give

C. refuse

D. show

24 To **refute** is to:

E. prove false
F. agree
G. be silent
H. accept

25 To **rebuke** is to:

A. praise
B. scold
C. worship
D. hate

26 A synonym for **repugnant** is:

E. happy
F. sorry
G. disgusting
H. pleasant

27 To **recollect** is to:

A. neglect
B. remember
C. forget
D. gather

28 An antonym for **rectify** is:

E. enlighten
F. correct
G. damage or ruin
H. resolve

29 Someone **relentless** is:

A. cunning
B. persistent
C. swift
D. flexible

30 A synonym for **superficial** is:

E. not thorough
F. deep
G. thorough
H. superb

31 To **supplement** is to:

A. subtract
B. divide
C. add to
D. undermine

32 **Tense** means:

E. calm
F. anxious
G. patient
H. jealous

33 Another word for **turbulent** is:

A. peaceful
B. neglectful
C. calm
D. stormy

34 If there is an **uproar**, there is:

E. chaos
F. silence
G. assistance
H. an angry jungle cat

35 An antonym for **unique** is:

A. distinctive
B. common
C. organized
D. rare

36 If you are **urging** someone, you are:

E. discouraging
F. delaying
G. encouraging
H. rushing

37 If there is **unrest** in the city, there is:

A. peace
B. disturbance
C. silence
D. celebration

38 **Unanimous** means:

E. majority vote
F. dissenting vote
G. tie vote
H. total agreement

39 Another word for **void** is:

A. empty
B. full
C. overflowing
D. dark

40 A **vindictive** person is:

E. forgiving
F. accepting
G. revengeful
H. one who avoids conflict

41 If something is **valid**, it is:

A. false
B. genuine
C. unique
D. unreal

42 To **validate** is to:

E. extend

F. limit

G. authorize

H. deny

43 **Versatile** means:

A. limited

B. rigid

C. various

D. flexible

44 **Vigorous** means:

E. dull

F. sleepy

G. energetic

H. rough

45 **Virtue** refers to:

A. wickedness

B. goodness

C. immorality

D. evil

46 Another word for **vengeance** is:

E. wrath

F. forgiveness

G. kindness

H. retaliation

47 **Veto** means to:

A. reject

B. approve

C. consider

D. vote for something

48 **Pompous** refers to:

E. humbleness

F. pushiness

G. self-importance

H. meekness

49 **Perpetual** means:

A. lasting

B. temporary

C. annually

D. weekly

50 **Promiscuous** means:

E. dating a person

F. having sex with several partners on a casual basis

G. exercising vigorously

H. refraining from sex

51 A synonym for **complacent** is:

A. responsible
B. upright
C. self-satisfied
D. irresponsible

52 **Clandestine** means to do something:

E. openly
F. secretly
G. willfully
H. carefully

53 A synonym for **cantankerous** is:

A. generous
B. silent
C. quarrelsome
D. agreeable

54 A mistake that is **blatant** is:

E. unseen
F. not noticeable
G. incorrect
H. obvious

55 **Bereft** means:

A. deprived of
B. plentiful
C. abundant
D. excessive

56 A **benevolent** person does acts that are:

E. demonic
F. good
G. supernatural
H. vicious

57 **Belligerent** means:

A. forgiving
B. ready to fight or quarrel
C. peaceful
D. accepting

58 To be **ambivalent** is to be:

E. astute
F. reliable
G. doubtful
H. decided

59 A **proponent** is:

A. a politician
B. a priest
C. an attorney
D. someone who supports a proposal

60 To **impeach** is to:

E. praise
F. imprison
G. remove from office
H. discredit someone's reputation

61 Someone who is **intoxicated** is:

A. sober
B. drunk
C. unconscious
D. gluttonous

62 **Arbitrary** means:

E. dictatorial
F. powerful
G. appointed
H. left to one's choice

63 Something **profound** is:

A. deeply felt
B. unimportant
C. serious
D. failing

64 **Poignant** means:

E. mean
F. making someone sad
G. unkind
H. soft

65 **Aesthetic** refers to:

A. appreciation of beauty
B. intake of oxygen
C. pleasant aromas
D. going to a beauty salon

66 To be paid **biweekly** means to be paid:

E. quarterly
F. once every three weeks
G. once every two weeks
H. monthly

67 A **bizarre** object is:

A. pretty
B. strikingly odd
C. willful
D. common

68 A **house guest** is:

E. a short-time visitor
F. a salesman
G. a family member
H. a servant

69 A **hotheaded** person is someone who is:

A. happy

B. anxious

C. even-tempered

D. unthinking; easily angered

70 **Hostility** refers to:

E. happy feelings

F. invisibility

G. unfriendliness

H. lack of conflict

71 **Lawless** means:

A. a disregard for the law

B. abiding by the law

C. abundant

D. becoming angry

72 **Orthodox** refers to:

E. conforming to an approved form of doctrine

F. having a mix of beliefs

G. having no values

H. untraditional

73 An **ostentatious** person is someone who is:

A. rude

B. showing off

C. unattractive

D. critical of others

74 **Plausible** means:

E. truthful

F. reasonable and proven

G. faulty

H. believable

EXERCISE 11

Building a Stronger Vocabulary

- Review all the **boldfaced** words in this chapter before you proceed to the next exercise.
- Highlight the ones you are still having difficulty remembering.
- List them with their meanings on a table.
- Use them to compose your own sentences.
- Think of a synonym and an antonym for each word.
- Use checkmarks to indicate if each word you want to practice more has a prefix, suffix, and/or root.
- You may use the table below as a sample to write your answers in your notebook.

Word	Definition	Sentence	Synonym	Antonym	Prefix	Suffix	Root

EXERCISE 12

Creating My Own Powerful Word List

- Write the words and meanings from the above table on the **Creating My Own Powerful Word List** table on page 398. Review them often to build that super vocabulary you want to create for school, work, and everyday use.

Appendix 1

Chapter	Percentage of Correct Answers
1	
2	
3	
4	
5	
6	
7	
8	
9	
10	
11	
12	
13	
14	
15	
16	

Word	Meaning

Word	Meaning

TEXT CREDITS

Atkinson, Rhonda Holt, and Debbie Guice Longman. *Vocabulary for College and Beyond.* St. Paul, MN: West Publishing Company, 1990.

Bolander, Donald O., Dolores D. Varner, and Elliot Pine. *Instant Synonyms and Antonyms.* New York: Dell Publishing, 1970.

Coxhead, Averil. "A New Academic Word List." *TESOL Quarterly* 34 (2000): 213–38.

Dunn-Rankin, Patricia. *Vocabulary.* New York: McGraw-Hill, Inc., 1990.

Fitzpatrick, Carolyn H., and Marybeth B. Ruscica. *The Complete Sentence Workout Book.* Second ed. Lexington: D.C. Heath and Company, 1988.

Gibaldi, Joseph, and Walter S. Achtert. *MLA Handbook for Writers of Research Papers.* Third ed. New York: Modern Language Association of America, 1988. Print.

Henry, D. J. *The Effective Reader.* Third ed. Upper Saddle River, New Jersey: Pearson Education Inc., 2014.

Huntley, Helen. *Essential Academic Vocabulary: Mastering the Complete Academic Word List.* Boston: National Geographic Learning, a part of Cengage Learning, 2006.

Huntley, Helen. *Essential Academic Vocabulary: Mastering the Complete Academic Word List.* USA: Heinle/ELT, a part of Cengage Learning, Inc., 2006.

Krane, Louis. *Phonics is Fun.* Book 3. Cleveland: Modern Curriculum Press, 1985.

Longman Advanced American Dictionary. Essex, England: Pearson Education Limited, 2007.

The Merriam-Webster Dictionary of Synonyms and Antonyms. Springfield: Merriam-Webster, Inc., 1992.

Raimes, Ann. *Grammar Troublespots: An Editing Guide for Students.* Second ed. New York: St. Martin's Press, Inc., 1992.

Raimes, Ann. *How English Works: A Grammar Handbook with Readings.* New York: St. Martin's Press, Inc., 1990.

The Random House Dictionary. New York: Random House, Inc., 1980.

Smith, R. Kent, and Janet M. Goldstein. *English Brushup.* Marlton: Townsend Press, Inc., 1993.

Warriner, John E., and Francis J. Griffith. *English Grammar and Composition.* New York: Harcourt Brace Jovanovich, Inc., 1977.

Webster's Intermediate Dictionary. Springfield, MA: Merriam-Webster, Inc., 1986.

Webster's New World College Dictionary. Third ed. New York: Simon & Schuster, Inc., 1988.

Webster's Ninth New Collegiate Dictionary. Springfield, MA: Merriam-Webster, Inc., 1987.

Wittels, Harriet, and Joan Greisman. *The Clear and Simple Thesaurus Dictionary.* New York: Grosset & Dunlap, Inc., 1971.

Young, A. Robert, and Ann O. Strauch. *Nitty Gritty Grammar.* New York: St. Martin's Press, Inc., 1994.

Websites

Dictionary.com. Dictionary.com, LLC, 2014. Web. 30 Nov. 2014.

Google Dictionary Tool. Google, 2011. Web. 30 Nov. 2014.

Merriam-Webster.com. Merriam-Webster, 2011. Web. 30 Nov. 2014.

OxfordDictionaries.com. Oxford University Press, 2014. Web. 30 Nov. 2014.

TheFreeDictionary.com. Farlex, Inc, 2014. Web. 30 Nov. 2014.

Thesaurus.com. Dictionary.com, LLC, 2014. Web. 30 Nov. 2014.

Software

Microsoft Word 2013 Thesaurus. Microsoft, 2013. Computer software. 30 Nov. 2014.